Evacuee Cinema

This new history of partition and South Asian cinema is narrated through the careers of émigré film personnel, as well as through the distinctive genres and ancillary ventures that accompanied the aftershocks of partition. Moving beyond arguments about social contingency and political intent, *Evacuee Cinema* suggests that the creative energies, production and subsequent circulation of popular cinema can offer fresh insights into partition.

Pointing to regional connections across national boundaries, the book asserts that the cinemas of India and Pakistan must be explored in tandem to uncover the legacy of partition for the culture industries of the region, one that is not hewn out of national erasures. The leitmotifs of émigré personnel, gossip and satire in film print culture, the partisan repertoire of a theatre company, the film genres of the Muslim social, romantic comedies and *charba*s (remakes), and the unruly film archives of post-colonial nation states, when accessed through the lens of a divisive decolonisation, reveal the parallaxes and confabulations of the 'national' on both sides.

Salma Siddique is a media historian and filmmaker by training. Born in Maiduguri, Nigeria, she grew up in Aligarh and New Delhi in India. She completed her PhD at the University of Westminster, London, in Media, Art and Design in 2015. Since 2016, she has been teaching and researching in Germany. Currently, she is research faculty at Humboldt-Universität zu Berlin, Germany.

METAMORPHOSES OF THE POLITICAL: MULTIDISCIPLINARY APPROACHES

The Series is a publishing collaboration of Cambridge University Press with The M. S. Merian–R. Tagore International Centre of Advanced Studies 'Metamorphoses of the Political' (ICAS:MP). It seeks to publish new books that both expand and de-centre current perspectives on politics and the 'political' in the contemporary world. It examines, from a wide array of disciplinary and methodological approaches, how the 'political' has been conceptualized, articulated and transformed in specific arenas of contestation during the 'long twentieth century'. Though primarily located in India and the Global South, the Series seeks to interrogate and contribute to wider debates about global processes and politics. It is in this sense that the Series is imagined as one that is regionally focused but globally engaged, providing a context for interrogations of universalized theories of self, society and politics.

Series Editors:
- Niraja Gopal Jayal, King's College, London
- Shail Mayaram, formerly at Centre for the Study of Developing Societies, Delhi
- Samita Sen, University of Cambridge, Cambridge
- Awadhendra Sharan, Centre for the Study of Developing Societies, Delhi
- Sanjay Srivastava, SOAS, University of London, UK
- Ravi Vasudevan, Centre for the Study of Developing Societies, Delhi
- Sebastian Vollmer, University of Göttingen, Germany

ICAS:MP is an Indo-German research collaboration of six Indian and German institutions funded by the German Federal Ministry of Education and Research (BMBF). It combines the benefits of an open, interdisciplinary forum for intellectual exchange with the advantages of a cutting-edge research centre. Located in New Delhi, ICAS:MP critically intervenes in global debates in the social sciences and humanities.

Other Titles in the Series:
- *The Secret Life of AnOther Indian Nationalism: Transitions from the Pax Britannica to the Pax Americana* • Shail Mayaram
- *Properties of Rent: Community, Capital and Politics in Globalising Delhi* • Sushmita Pati
- *Saffron Republic: Hindu Nationalism and State Power in India* • Edited by Thomas Blom Hansen and Srirupa Roy
- *Rule of the Commoner: DMK and Formations of the Political in Tamil Nadu, 1949–1967* • Rajan Krishna, Ravindran Sriramachandran, and V. M. S. Subagunarajan
- *Streets in Motion: The Making of Infrastructure, Property, and Political Culture in Twentieth-century Calcutta* • Ritajyoti Bandyopadhyay
- *Women, Gender and Religious Nationalism* • Edited by Amrita Basu and Tanika Sarkar

Evacuee Cinema

Bombay and Lahore in
Partition Transit (1940–1960)

Salma Siddique

Metamorphoses of the Political
Merian Tagore International Centre of Advanced Studies

CAMBRIDGE
UNIVERSITY PRESS

CAMBRIDGE
UNIVERSITY PRESS

University Printing House, Cambridge CB2 8BS, United Kingdom

One Liberty Plaza, 20th Floor, New York, NY 10006, USA

477 Williamstown Road, Port Melbourne, vic 3207, Australia

314 to 321, 3rd Floor, Plot No.3, Splendor Forum, Jasola District Centre, New Delhi 110025, India

103 Penang Road, #05–06/07, Visioncrest Commercial, Singapore 238467

Cambridge University Press is part of the University of Cambridge.

It furthers the University's mission by disseminating knowledge in the pursuit of
education, learning and research at the highest international levels of excellence.

www.cambridge.org
Information on this title: www.cambridge.org/9781009151207

First published 2022

Printed in India by Avantika Printers Pvt. Ltd.

A catalogue record for this publication is available from the British Library

ISBN 978-1-009-15120-7 Hardback

For my father, Ahmad Siddique

Also for Phuphijaan, Atti and Eki Chacha

Contents

Figures

Acknowledgements

I would like to thank my PhD supervisor, Rosie Thomas, for her intellectual guidance, sturdy patience and generous friendship through the course of writing this book. The doctoral scholarship received at the University of Westminster allowed me to study in London for three years and conduct ambitious fieldwork across several cities in South Asia. Senior colleagues at Westminster, especially May Ingawanij, Anthony Nichols and Margherita Sprio, shared valuable insights which have shaped this work. The Dahlem Research School postdoctoral fellowship, between 2016–2018, helped me expand this work in different directions and revisit some of the key concerns in a new light. The Berlin Graduate School of Muslim Cultures and Societies, Freie University, Berlin, not only gave this project the much-needed space and resources, but also placed me within a larger community of scholars who were pursuing the answers to similar research questions in different regions of the globe. I am particularly grateful to Nadja Christina-Schneider at Humboldt University, Berlin, and Lars Ostermeier at Freie University for supporting a six-month Berlin-based fellowship in early 2018, which allowed me to focus on shaping this book. Vazira Zamindar kindly facilitated my month-long research visit at Brown University, Rhode Island, in 2016 and helped in moving forward on publishing the manuscript.

There are many archives, libraries and individuals without whose support and resources, this book would have been impossible. The National Film Archive (Pune), the Nehru Museum Memorial and Library (New Delhi), the Maharashtra State Archives (Mumbai), the British Library and the British Film Institute (London) were spaces of enchanting discoveries and obliging staff members. Aslam Ilyas of

Nigar Weekly was extremely generous in giving access to their archival collection and records in Karachi. Guddu Khan has been a treasure trove of film trivia, cinephilic energies and memorabilia, some of which have been reproduced in this book. I am very grateful to Ali Fazli and Sohail Fazli for welcoming me in their Lahore office without prior notice on a hot July afternoon. My fieldwork in Pakistan would not have been possible without the help and hospitality of Syeda Rizvi, Bahzad Alam Khan, Sultan Arshad, Ajay Darshan Behera and Nukhbah Langah. Hana Haq and S. Hassan rescued me when I got stuck with city-visa regulations in Lahore and magnanimously hosted me in their lovely household. I am grateful to all the respondents who took out time at short notice and were generous in sharing their insights – these include Ibn Abdur Rahman, Pervez Rahi, Ahmad Salim, Asif Noorani, Omar Adil, Saeed Shiraz and Zulfiqar Ramzi. Bhavna Dave introduced me to Dalsukh Pancholi's extended family in Mumbai. I am indebted to Hersh Pencholi, Sunil Shanbagh and Kunal Kapoor of Prithvi Theatre for providing me access to important photographs and family records. Cherished friends, Danish Siddiqui, Rike Harrant, Aditya Basu and Asad Hussein, helped me navigate fieldwork in Mumbai. I am lucky to have friends in Nidhi Khurana, Namita Walia, Meera Viswanathan, Pavithra Ralapalli, Rebecca Kahn and Rhoda Francisco, who have sustained me with their care and banter in Delhi, London and Berlin.

Many friends and colleagues have listened to and commented on the manuscript in parts. Endless thanks are due to Rakesh Ankit and Layli Uddin, fellow squatters of 1940s–1960s South Asia, who have been brilliant and bighearted interlocuters at different stages. The drafts of the chapters have benefitted from the scholarly attentions of Kartik Nair, Isabel Huaceja, Tupur Chatterjee and Richard Williams. Faisal Devji's erudite support has been enormously reassuring in carrying this work beyond the discipline of media studies. Responses from mentors and participants, especially Iftikhar Dadi and Daniel Elam, at a dissertation-to-book workshop at the Madison South Asia Conference, Wisconsin, proved to be extremely helpful. Arguments presented in the book have gained from valuable questions and conversations in different conferences and settings with Lotte Hoek, Ira Bhaskar, Neepa Majumdar, Ranjani Mazumdar, Priya Jaikumar, Anupama Prabhala, Aswin Punathambekar, Debashree Mukherjee, Usha Iyer, Priyanjali Sen, Kuhu Tanvir, Pallavi Raghavan and Chris Moffat. I am also grateful for the analytical comments received from the two anonymous peer reviewers of the manuscript.

The institutional and intellectual milieu of Delhi has had a decisive influence on this work. Media teachers and feminist gurus at AJK Mass Communication Research Centre, Jamia Millia Islamia, Shohini Ghosh and Sabeena Gadihoke have been a formidable and fun presence in my life. My teachers at the History Department at St Stephen's College, University of Delhi, taught me to think resourcefully about the craft of history and the proximate stakes involved in writing about the past. Aditya Pratap Deo and Tasneem Suhrawardy, amongst others, have been supportive all along. Ravi Vasudevan at the Centre for the Study of Developing Societies (CSDS) has been inspiring, intuitive and exacting in our conversations, in ways that only he can be.

Finally, this book is unimaginable without the extensive support of my immediate and extended, *filmzada* family separated by the border. Ahsan Siddique, Quratulain Nauman and Monis Siddique accompanied me protectively on fieldwork in Karachi and unhesitatingly provided endless DVDs and witticisms. Sohail Akbar, Saba Siddiqui and Khalil Siddiqui have been engaged listeners and indulgent kin. My sister, Soofia Siddique, has been an invaluable interlocuter and a happy reader of all words drafted and undrafted. I have unabashedly leaned on her perceptive understanding and affectionate wisdom for as long as I can remember. Ishan Bhat has been a caring husband who could patiently spot the light at the end of the writing tunnel. I am immensely thankful to my mother, Zarina Siddique, for cheerily teaching me, among other things, Urdu and the subtle art of being willful.

Introduction

A Moving Picture

The cinema is a *double-edged weapon*.[1]
Why did Khurshid and Nurjehan migrate to Pakistan?
They thought it would be better to observe purdah.[2]

With the recent decision to ban the import of Indian films into Pakistan, I shall miss Dilip's acting, Mehboob's direction and above all, Naushad's music.[3]

Between Bombay and Lahore, a national fault line was drawn so darkly that it intercepted and rendered faint, existing markings of pre-national film cultures. The aforementioned fragments of disquiet in film magazines are caused by the fault line and its spectres, better known as partition. The cautionary imaging of cinema as a weapon signals a battleground of modernity. Despite its cleverness, the repartee about Khurshid and Noorjahan betrays malice at the actresses' departure. And overarchingly, the state proscription of a public pleasure fosters a personal loss and nostalgia. Opening out South Asian film history to partition, this study recovers film narratives, film personnel and film publics coursing through the historic passage to nation states. Through the case studies of émigré personnel, this work brings forth hitherto lost or unremarked films and genres into the academic domain of Hindi–Urdu cinema.

The 1951 *Report of the Film Enquiry Committee of India* devotes but a short paragraph to the impact of partition on the Indian film industry:

Then came the partition and like other spheres of economic activity, the cinema industry was affected considerably. There was at first a temporary loss of a portion of the market. Disturbances in this country affected cinema earnings to some extent. Finally, the shortage of certain building materials, which were required in large quantities for housing displaced persons, led to the imposition of a ban on the construction of new cinemas in many States of the Union. In spite of these adverse factors, however, there was no drop in the production of new films.[4]

Appearing four years after the division, the report describes loss in exclusively economic terms, an account that oscillates between emphasising the enormity of the partition and claiming its minimal impact. To a certain extent, this is symptomatic of a Janus-like approach in India to partition, which 'as a wreckage of colonialism' is unable to subdue the onward national march.[5] If the Indian account is only too keen to emphasise continuity and progress, its Pakistani counterpart is equally invested in a break and an impasse. The earliest available appraisal from Pakistan is the *Film Industry in Pakistan* report published by the *Board of Economic* Enquiry, Punjab, in 1957, in which, as the founding moment of the nation, partition has utmost centrality and gets extensive attention, right from its opening lines.

Film industry is one of the youngest industries in Pakistan.... After August 1947, Lahore became the only centre in Pakistan for film production. As in the case of other fields, this industry in pre-independence days was controlled mainly by non-Muslim organizers, financiers and technicians who migrated to India, paralyzing the industry here. The communal disturbances at the time of the partition did great damage to the property on both sides of the border including studios and cinemas, some of which were completely burnt down. As a result, the film industry in Pakistan had to be started from scratch.[6]

As in the Indian account, partition is also assessed here in purely economic terms: while involving a 'temporary loss' for India, it is a 'start from scratch' for Pakistan. Both official accounts treat cinema as more of a commodity and property and less as a cultural form central to the project of defining national culture. Making room for its political and cultural implications for cinema in South Asia, this book brings forth partition as a productive force in cinema. Influencing film genres, star personas, publicity machinery and production strategies, partition led cinema to perform emotive functions to reckon with political transitions. In other words, I identify in the following chapters a vernacularisation of intellectual currents, bureaucratic violence and nation-state dissonances. In the process, partition also transformed the dynamic and transcultural cinema of undivided India, referred to in the contemporary sources as all-India film. Here, my specific concern is the Hindi–Urdu cinema, which in the 1930s–1940s was largely generated across a triangle of productive relations struck between three film cities – with Bombay at the commercial apex[7] and Calcutta and Lahore constituting the base.[8]

While these years have been associated with studio control, which only waned in the mid-1940s, there are intimations of film itinerancy at the lower levels. The rise of the 'freelance' producer and director during the war years was also accelerated by this pre-existing itinerancy at the lower echelons in the studio, whereby ambitious technicians and assistants often moved cities in order to work at an advanced level. Instances of film-makers, writers and aspiring artistes moving first to Calcutta from Lahore and then further to Bombay are encountered in several life histories. After experimenting with the Bhatti Gate group in Lahore, film-makers A. R. Kardar and S. Nazir Khan migrated to Calcutta in the early 1930s and later finally moved to Bombay at the end of the decade. Kasur-born singing star Noorjahan found her first job with a performing company in Calcutta and debuted in Dalsukh Pancholi's *Yamla Jatt* (1939) in Lahore, before moving to Bombay in the early 1940s. Film-maker Shaukat Hussain Rizvi started out as a lab technician in a Calcutta studio, worked briefly in Lahore as the editor of *Khazanchi* (1941) and the director of *Khandaan* (1942) and migrated to Bombay a little later. With partition, the years of carefree social and professional mobility along these film axes came to an end. Situated in the divided provinces, both Lahore and Calcutta were severely affected by the violence and large-scale migration. The demographic shift within the film centres involved the exodus of non-Muslim personnel from Lahore to Bombay and Calcutta, and a number of Muslims from Bombay and Calcutta to Lahore. Focused on the transregional axis and the productive relationship constituted between Bombay and Lahore, this study follows the axial reorganisation of the two cities into national equivalence by partition – an equivalence that was symbolic and remained plagued by an acrimonious division.

Partition as Impending Pakistan

Words like 'cataclysmic', 'traumatic' and 'horrific' are often used to convey the enormity of partition in the life of the Indian subcontinent. Staggering numbers constitute the dead, the displaced and the violated. The division of British India on the basis of religion at the time of decolonisation has been a subject of intense historiographical and ideological debate, often invested in ascertaining its inevitability and apportioning responsibility between the colonial interests of Britain, the All-India Muslim League–led movement for Pakistan and the Indian National Congress's claims to an all-India representation. The discursive space of film magazines such as *Filmindia* also echoes these debates as they unfolded. What is undeniable, however, is that before the civil war of 1947,[9] partition was mostly understood as the impending, albeit perplexing, Pakistan.[10] The demand for Pakistan loomed large in Bombay certainly, where Mohammad Ali Jinnah, the charismatic leader of the Muslim League, lived and often received political dignitaries. In addition to the restive energies of political manoeuvres of the 1940s,[11] the mobilisation for communal representation also had a strong ideological dimension.[12] Existing scholarship that takes into account a longer history of 'values that influenced Muslim political action from the late nineteenth century', as well as the 'persistent discourse on the political community as an extension of Muslim religious fellowship', cautions against reading Muslim nationalism as a mere manipulation of cultural symbols by politically interested elites.[13]

This act of picturing Pakistan – one not restricted to a 'bargaining counter' of elite politics but with an identifiable idiom and wielding a wider purchase to marshal the economic logic of films – also emerges in a new genre of the all-India film in the 1940s. The Muslim social film arrives as a distinct and popular genre in the lead up to the division. In this context, this book proposes that the cinematic rendition of Pakistan preceded its territorial realisation, without of course suggesting that an impending Pakistan is explicit in the Muslim social film as either a separate nation state or a loose autonomous confederation. Such a realm of abstraction is tenable, especially if we recognise that the idea at the heart of Muslim nationalism involved rejecting the principle of territorially based community.[14] Comparing Pakistani nationalism with Indian nationalism, Faisal Devji argues that

> ... ways of thinking about sovereignty are deeply embedded in each country's respective nationalism, one relying on the language of historical continuity and its betrayal by Pakistan, while the other depends upon rejecting the past, and in so doing acknowledging both states as coeval in their utter novelty.[15]

These radically different ways of being and belonging would be central to the way cinematic address and audience identification would work in the all-India film enterprise heading towards decolonisation and national divide. As an interface between speculative ideas and their images, films produce new ways of thinking. The publicness of cinema, and the popular space it occupied in the late colonial period along with other visual–aural practices in a deeply stratified society, made it an important site for the unfolding of differently preoccupied nationalist impulses.

Indeed, I propose to stretch the understanding of partition backwards, beginning with the Lahore Resolution of 1940, which signalled what Gyanendra Pandey calls 'the first partition'.[16] Thus, the 'long partition' that Vazira Zamindar identifies in her meticulous work on mass displacement, controlled movement and the making of citizenship is at play in cultural production even before 1947. The popular Indian theatre group Prithvi Theatre begins performing 'partition' in 1945 and imagines the territorial divide as a wall between a joint patriarchal household. Of course, no one escapes the bureaucratic violence of 1947 involving shadow boundaries and nationalising identities in the face of mass displacement and refugee rehabilitation. Prithvi Theatre too gets involved with refugee relief, rehabilitation and citizen-making both on and off the stage in the long partition.

A key intellectual debt of this research is to feminist interventions of Urvashi Butalia, Ritu Menon and Kamla Bhasin that have brought to the fore partition's gendered experience.[17] Relying methodologically on oral testimonies of survivors and relief workers, these studies retrieved the history of partition that consisted of sexual violence, honour killings, abductions, religious conversions and procedures of recovery by patriarchal nation states. Attentive to multiple voices, the feminist project complicated the notion of *choice* by pointing to women's asymmetrical relationship to nationality and citizenship.[18] They identified partition as posing 'the question of "belonging" in a way that polarized choice and allegiance, aggravating old and new antagonisms'.[19] Choice becomes important in the way star comedienne Meena Shorey exercises it through rites of passage involving religious and national conversions in order to continue working in films. It also surfaces again in the fact of an Indian child star Rattan Kumar's migration to Pakistan under the tutelage of his film-producing family.

Ascertaining choice in terms of cultural production by migrant and minority personnel is also a way to question the inevitability of the historical outcome of partition as two separate nation states with distinct religious majorities. Aamir Mufti's intervention in examining writer Saadat Hassan Manto's oeuvre for its minoritisation and Faiz Ahmed Faiz's oeuvre for adjournment of belonging is instructive in this regard.[20] Pondering over the limited choices available to Muslims of the subcontinent, Mufti points out that becoming a citizen of an Islamic nation state or else a national minority were both equally new-fangled identities. *Evacuee Cinema* examines the fate of minority film-makers on both sides. For the non-Muslim film migrants from western Punjab such as Roop K. Shorey, I. S. Johar and Dalsukh Pancholi, making films in Bombay, where they were now part of the national majority, and for a changed demographic was a new challenge. Displacement involved an unlearning, reorientation and rescaling for the celebrated entrepreneurs of erstwhile Lahori film who could not replicate their success in Bombay. The material losses that studio evacuees Shorey and Pancholi incurred in partition also involved the loss of a film-making context – undivided Punjab – for both India and Pakistan.

Listening to the Movement

This book unsettles the consensus that exists in most scholarly works that a 'silence on partition' was maintained by the film production community in Bombay in the early years of nationhood. Part of this belief originates from Gyanendra Pandey's identification of a collective amnesia around partition, which establishes partition as India's 'limit case of history'.[21] Film scholarship has worked through this silence by identifying allegories, oblique references and thematic detours.[22] There were almost no book-length studies on Indian cinema and partition until about a decade ago,[23] when Bhaskar Sarkar's influential work *Mourning the Nation* appeared.[24] Responding to the 'silence' on partition maintained by films in the early years, Sarkar locates a strong allegorical impulse in the cinema of the 1950s and 1960s and identifies popular Indian cinema (Hindi and Bengali) as a repository of collective consciousness. He identifies certain themes in the popular films of the 1950s and 1960s that obliquely articulate the trauma of partition. Instances of self-mutilation, amnesia, accidents, natural disasters, doubling and women's experiences are understood as being allegorical of the partition experience. His work responds to an earlier article by Ravi Vasudevan which proposed that 'traces of epochal events such as partition must be sought far beyond direct reflections' and unearthed through themes that are highly allegorical.[25]

There are key ways in which this book departs from the assumptions and methods of Sarkar's work. First, my concern is with the effects of partition on the pre-existing film axis between Bombay and Lahore rather than simply apropos representation of partition in film. Retrieving the oeuvre of active film-makers and actors from the cross-hairs of national histories, this book takes on board the experience of dislocation and trajectories of movement of these personalities and engages with this complex as its analytical entry point. There is a need to listen closely to the commotion caused by movement and uprooting.[26] Second, the moment we move away from an all-encompassing investment in the film object to consider its processes of production, as well as the institutional and ancillary-like film publicity, journalism, censorship and theatre performances, there emerges a cacophony around partition. Partition, or a looming Pakistan, is present in these immediate contexts of film. Instead of silence, I argue that partition has a discursive and performative power. A significant product of this performative force is the secular stance of Bombay cinema, discussed at length in Part 1 of the book. Finally, this book brings forth the complex allegiances and competing nationalisms of the partition years and argues that national allegiances were never so rigidly categorical and instead subject to fluctuations, especially as partition acquired a more violent form. For instance, film-maker Mehboob along with collaborator and brother-in-law A. R. Kardar left Bombay for Karachi for a few months in late 1947 and, by some Pakistani accounts, considered staying on before returning to Bombay. These production networks of Muslim producers in colonial Bombay, identified in Chapter 4, could neither continue unchanged in post-colonial Bombay nor be relocated to Pakistan in their entirety. While rising to prominence in the decade leading to the formation of separate nation states, these networks weakened rapidly in the face of movement controls and new laws on citizen property in the following years.

An attentive following of the movement of active personnel reveals two different timelines (1947–1948 and 1956–1957) of departures and arrivals, which are otherwise unavailable in cursory summaries of the migration of film personnel, such as that presented here:

> [Partition] affected the Indian film industry by destabilizing two major film centres of undivided India – Bombay (now Mumbai) and Lahore. Legendary film personalities like Noor Jahan, Zia Sarhady and Ghulam Mohammad [sic] left for Pakistan. Similarly, prominent Indian filmmakers such as Gulzar and Govind Nihalani, B.R. Chopra and Yash Chopra migrated from what became Pakistan.[27]

The problem with this statement, representative of several such obligatory statements in literature pertaining to cinema and partition, are the flawed comparisons. Noor Jahan, Zia Sarhadi and Ghulam Haider were indeed prominent film artistes by this time. On the other hand, Gulzar (thirteen years old in 1947), Govind Nihalani (seven years old in 1947) and Yash Chopra (fifteen years old in 1947) were not even involved with film-making. Such a comparison omits Dalsukh Pancholi, Roop K. Shorey and actor Pran, the real counterparts of Noorjahan, Sarhadi and Ghulam Haider, who were actively making films in Lahore. An additional problem with the list is the placement of Sarhadi in the same bracket as Noorjahan and Ghulam Mohammad, thereby glossing over the fact that Sarhadi left for Pakistan a decade after his other two colleagues. By opting for schematic clarity, such comparisons leave little room for the examination of ideological complexities and the not-so-neatly aligned individual–national trajectories. Sarhadi's case is illustrative: having 'opted' for India in 1947, the writer-director left for Pakistan in 1956.

A timeline of migration between the two cities listing personnel featured in this study is provided in Table I.1, which shows exits and returns during an interval of time. I argue that discrete and often, discreet migration from Bombay (India) to Lahore (Pakistan) occurred, which is important to underline not merely as a long partition but also as individualised trajectories of nationality that 'fracture the totality of [national] history by interrupting it with a record of difference'.[28] Despite the reciprocal nature of migration between Bombay and Lahore, the historic experience of partition between the two cities was drastically different. While the 'refugee personnel' from Punjab were driven out by the violence, some Muslim personnel left Bombay for reasons that have been ignored and left unidentified in the limited work on the subject, perhaps because those were questions considered 'best left unasked'. I am interested in the decisions to migrate made by certain Muslim personnel of the Bombay film industry as constituting a political and cultural choice, active or enforced, which, for instance, was not available in the same manner to Hindu personnel in Lahore. And while this 'choice' may have been exercised in a highly individualistic fashion, it nonetheless also constitutes, I suggest, a comment on Bombay and its film enterprise.

Table I.1   Notable migrations

Year of migration		Occupation(s)
From Lahore (Pakistan) to Bombay (India)		
1947	Dalsukh Pancholi	Producer, director, studio owner
1947	I. S. Johar	Writer, director
1947	Kuldeep Kaur	Actress
1947	Majnu	Actor
1947	Meena Shorey	Actress
1947	Pran	Actor
1947	Roop K. Shorey	Producer, director, studio owner
1947	Roshan Lal Shorey	Producer, director, studio owner
From Bombay to Lahore		
1947	Ghulam Haider	Music director
1947	M. Luqman	Director
1947	Nazir Ahmed Khan	Producer, director
1947	Neena	Actress
1947	Noorjahan	Actress
1947	Sibtain Fazli	Producer, director
1947	Swarnlata	Actress
1947	W. Z. Ahmad	Producer, director
1947	Shaukat Hussain Rizvi	Producer, director
1948	Saadat Hassan Manto	Writer
1955	Hasnain Fazli	Producer, director
1956	Rattan Kumar	Child actor
1956	Meena Shorey	Actress
1956–1957	S. M. Yusuf	Producer, director
1956–1957	Zia Sarhadi	Writer, director
Bombay–Karachi–Bombay		
1947–1948	A. R. Kardar	Producer, director, studio owner
1947–1948	Mehboob Khan	Producer, director

Source: Compiled by the author.

Whither All-India Film?

During the war years, 'all-India film' was frequently used to signal a national taxonomy for films produced in colonial India. This category was made coherent through the cartographic representations of undivided India, claiming connection between the on-screen narratives and off-screen demography and linking film themes, often tenuously, to matters of 'national importance'. The cartographic representation of undivided India as a film-making resource and a circulation territory involves a limiting – in Benedict Anderson's terms – as well as a distending of the geographical space of consumption. Both Bombay and Lahore films laid claim to this circulatory context until the late 1940s. Chapter 1 examines the representational claims of a Lahori film on this territory and reflects on the possibilities that pre-partition Lahore offered, including experiments with the 'hybrid' and *masala* form.

The category of all-India film exceeds the geo-temporal frame of the nation state in South Asia and therefore signals a 'cine-ecology' different from the Hindi–Urdu cinema produced in India after independence.[29] In his introduction to the monumental *Encyclopaedia of Indian Cinema*, Paul Willemen warns against restricting the account of Indian cinema to the geo-temporal frame constituted by the Indian nation state since partition, as this would require us to ignore some of the most admirable cinematic achievements realised in colonial India.[30] More damagingly, he points out, it would also rule out any engagement with the long-term dynamics that have shaped post-partition Indian cinema. Here, Priya Jaikumar's nuanced post-colonial foray into *Cinema at the End of Empire* works within a period of transition, recognising the 'multiple modernisms' of colonial Indian cinema, and gestures towards a divided nation.[31] Alert to the centripetal and centrifugal forces that constituted the colonial all-India film category, this book draws attention to the *competitive* anti-colonial impulses – Hindu nationalism, Muslim nationalism and secular nationalism – that undergirded national transitions in India and Pakistan.

While the Hindi film industry at Bombay has been understood as involving a regionally, culturally and religiously differentiated set of practices, the ideological persuasions of the pre-independence film conglomerate have been perceived as cohesive and benign. Erik Barnouw and S. Krishnaswamy's appraisal of the war years in film production finds most film producers supporting the Congress position and adopting a casual introduction of Congress symbols into the films – 'the spinning wheel, Gandhi's portrait in stores and Nehru's portrait at home, soundtrack of a favourite Congress song etc'.[32] Producer Chandulal Shah's address to the First Indian Motion Picture Congress in 1939 suggests the investment of the industry in a national government:

Whatever the academic theories of profit, not labour, not capital not skill, alone or in concert, can make profits for an Industry, if there is no National Government to help it. In this struggle of yours, therefore, you have a handicap, for India has no National Government of her own. And *therefore whether you wish it or not*, the place of this Industry will always be with those who are struggling to achieve such Government for this country.[33]

A year later in 1940, the Lahore Resolution would complicate the very shape of the country(-ies) and its (their) 'National Government[s]'. Are we then to understand that the colonial film enterprise at Bombay was politically and ideologically a cohesive formation, which, while collaborating in a singular national struggle and actively imagining 'self-governance', politely receded into inaction and remained aloof as far as the thorny question of partition was concerned? What was the version of national struggle for the supporters of Pakistan in the Bombay film enterprise, and which casual symbols did they insert in their films? What happened to these symbols and their memory in independent India and Pakistan? What about the political place of film-making in colonial Lahore? This book raises and answers these questions.

The Indian left's presence, though not quite extraneous to the Congress, has been noted in the Bombay film industry in the Progressive Writers' Association (PWA) and Indian People's Theatre Association (IPTA) faction, which included, among others, K. A. Abbas, Ismat Chughtai and Krishan Chandar. The situation of some of these within the industry has been described as 'ambivalent',[34] as the film-industry jobs discounted 'their experimental and radical writerly personas' reserved for their own fictions, while for others like K. A. Abbas, who made a bold experiment with *Dharti ke Lal*, 'the need to engage cinema on its own terms' became evident after the film's economic loss.[35] We must ask what the terms of such a cinema were, where certain symbols and themes could make their way into films without risking business, while others could not. Indeed, the collaborative and profit-oriented impulse of film production cannot reduce it to a depoliticised institution. All-India film operated as much through networks of patronage, interests and the community as through creative affiliations. Given the singularity of partition in the history of South Asia, it is imperative to highlight how the outside world constantly entered film-making and the cinematic frame itself.

Writing Two Histories Together

Indian cinema, and Hindi cinema at Bombay in particular, has invited far more forays into history writing than cinema in Pakistan.[36] And while there are many ways of writing these film histories, tracing the beginnings of an 'Indian cinema' in the early efforts of Dadasaheb Phalke, through the viscerality of *Alam Ara* (1931) – the first talkie – and arriving at the golden age of the 1950s with an emphasis on institutional and artistic innovation is an approach that fuses the twin zeniths of the national and cinematic.[37] This rather neat schema of evolutionary history, moving linearly, and one may add retrospectively, to assume the status of 'national cinema', is guilty of many omissions. The breaks, dead ends and diversions are glossed over in order to achieve the orderliness that any national film history routinely requires.

Even when partition appears in these accounts, it is treated more as an issue of Hindu–Muslim relations and less as an event that had implications for the kind of nations that were being imagined and that emerged.[38] For instance, a partition-sensitive history of the iconic film *Mughal-e-Azam* (1960) would foreground how the crew and cast kept changing in the tumultuous years of 1945–1960. The production of *Mughal-e-Azam* began in 1945,[39] before partition, and the film was another in the line of the many Mughal historicals of the 1940s such as *Pukar* (1939), *Humayun* (1945) and *Shahjahan* (1945). The first financier of the film, Shiraz Ali Hakim, migrated to Pakistan in 1947, after having invested a considerable sum in the project. His son Saeed Shiraz, settled in Karachi as a film distributer, in a personal interview spoke of the long-protracted and ultimately unsuccessful negotiations that Hakim conducted with the Pakistani state to import the film into the country as his 'property'.[40] The Pakistani side of the making of *Mughal-e-Azam* needs to be written together with the Indian side.

Instructive for this call to writing bilateral histories is Mushtaq Gazdar's cinephilic *Pakistan Cinema*.[41] A longer time sweep (1947–1997) enables him to observe trends, and, though progressing within the national trajectory, he writes the history of Pakistan's cinema through the 'voice and career of the individual'.[42] He acknowledges that Pakistan's 'performing arts and culture have a common background with what was known as the subcontinent of India'[43] – no less than a political gesture, considering the politics of writing separate and laterally inverted histories in India and Pakistan. Dictated by the national geography, Gazdar keeps his eyes focused on film production in Lahore, recuperating the pre-national period of the 1940s of this region. If Gazdar's first chapter is underscored by the common roots of the two nations, the second chapter details the immigration of film artistes in the wake of partition only after conveying the dominant mood of the period, where mainstream film-makers did not expect the partition to 'disrupt the common heritage of culture, art, literature, music and films', and most thought 'that once the riots and social upheavals subsided, the flow of people, trade, commerce and cultural activities would resume as before'.[44] Similarly, his discussion of the famous '*Jaal* agitation' of 1954 against the import of Indian films in Pakistan lays bare the antagonistic interests of distributors and producers in Pakistan, dismantling the assumption of a cohesive national film industry.[45] The distributors in Pakistan and the Indian producers were conjoined across political boundaries through their common interest in harnessing the markets of Pakistan. Due to their technical finesse and well-established stars, Bombay films did better business than the Pakistani films produced by migrants or new film-makers. The agitation also alerts us to the fraught emotions and disappointment of the Pakistani producers at the non-mutuality of film exchange with India.

However, even nationally confined approaches from both India and Pakistan can and do accommodate difference. The claim that the Hindi–Urdu cinema of India has 'an undeniable national character'[46] is one sustained through attention to its transnational, transregional and intercultural influences. Rosie Thomas's work on the oriental fantasy genre maintains that stories from the transnational *Arabian Nights* were present at the birth of cinema in India, borrowing from the local traditions of oriental tales, already made popular by the Urdu–Parsi theatre.[47] The *Arabian Nights* fantasies prove to be extremely popular in post-partition Pakistan, giving rise to a very different reality of A, B and C circuits of circulation, as discussed in Chapter 6 on remakes and fantasy. With regard to cultural differentiation, Rachel Dwyer points out that religion has long been present in Indian cinema, not only in literal representations of religious beliefs and communities but also through 'wider concerns with custom and society that can be said to be religious however loosely'.[48] Not only Hindu mythologicals, *bhakti* devotionals and the Islamicate film, but also the omnibus social are some categories through which Dwyer examines the cultural and religious pan-Indianism produced at Bombay. To this list of 'Indian cinema', I would also add the Islamic warrior films, which were occasionally present in the all-India market and made a resurgence in independent Pakistan in the 1950s and the early 1960s.

Within the religious registers, the Islamicate roots of Hindustani cinema were first delineated at some length by Mukul Kesavan in the mid-1990s.[49] A full-length study by Ira Bhaskar and Richard Allen further located distinctive generic forms of the Islamicate idiom.[50] They note that over the 1940s–1960s, these Islamicate genres performed significant imaginative, emotional and political tasks. These constructed forms evoked an Islamicate imagery that, according to the authors, was both constituted by and constitutive of a 'Muslimness' that became charged with a significance and value that may vary historically, depending on the ideological investment in these identities.[51] In the Muslim social, the authors detect a self-conscious discourse aimed directly at the community. They obliquely suggest that partition might have played a role in distilling narratives around *nawabi* (princely) lives, since the film-makers associated with the middle- and working-class genres like Fazli Brothers and Shaukat Hussain Rizvi migrated to Pakistan in 1947. My research finds that while the class dimension stated by Bhaskar and Allen is certainly an important observation, the elite register was earliest evident in Sohrab Modi's *Khan Bahadur* (1937), while Fazli Brothers' films like *Chowranghee* (1942) and *Dil* (1946) played on the contrast between rich and poor and were not exclusively narratives of the working class. More strikingly, what we observe in the pre-partition Muslim social cycle is the projection of idealised images of the North Indian middle class as a template for Muslim independence and self-realisation.

Taking off from Gazdar's work, an article by Iftikhar Dadi focuses on Urdu films belonging to the 'transitional period' in Pakistani cinema of the 1960s.[52] He suggests that the 'social film' in Pakistan needs to be contextualised in relation to the creation of the Muslim social genre in India and argues that it 'continues the project of secularised reform in Pakistan'. While secularised reform might be the desired vision in Muslim socials emerging in post-partition Bombay, this was not always the case with the genre. As Chapter 4 shows in detail, the pre-partition Muslim social has a deeply religious mode. Therefore, surely, what is more interesting is the mutation of a deeply religious genre of the 'all-India film' into a secularised one in Pakistan and a romanticised one in India after partition.

This book deals with collectivities such as nations, genres and communities while recognising their inherent instabilities. The popular Hindi cinema has been recognised as 'a central arena for the definition and celebration of the modern Indian identity'.[53] While it has been recognised that the Hindi cinema does not have a trouble-free relationship with the nation state,[54] the recourse to internal tensions also forecloses an engagement with pressures beyond the temporal and territorial limits of the nation state, which have shaped both the nation and the film industry in it. Ravi Vasudevan, while stressing on the need to think of film publics beyond the territorial and ideological parameters of the nation in South Asia, reminds us that the only way to do this is by remaining alert to the significance of the 'nation in defining crucial parameters of historical possibility'.[55] Identifying the pre-nation-state era as a significant way to think about cinematic forms, where the peculiar fluidity of empire mobilised people and culture, in sharp contrast with the rigidities enforced by the formation of nation states, he asks: '… in the perception of people, what had been lost in the division of the subcontinent and what, conversely could have been gained by the formation of distinct national-ethnic states?' I have already mentioned the loss of a film-making context (undivided Punjab), the circulatory horizon of high nationalism (all-India film) and a production network (Muslim film-makers networked in colonial Bombay). Pertinent to the cinematic processes, any answer will also have to engage with the severe dislocation that partition entailed – of personnel as well as spectators. While signifying a territorial divide, partition also involved a temporal dislocation, where in their new independent selves both India and Pakistan were in states of exile from the past. Is it possible, then, that partition also set into cinematic motion an exilic process, where 'the frustrating elusiveness of return makes it magically potent'?[56]

Indicative parallels are available in the context of post-colonial émigrés to the West since the 1960s, which Hamid Naficy identifies as 'an accented cinema' of exile and diaspora that concerns de-territorialisation and is produced in the interstices of cultures and cinematic production practices. Naficy states that 'although there is nothing in common about exile and diaspora, de-territorialised people and their films share certain features'.[57] In the displaced film-makers' relationship to their films and to the authoring agency within them, Naficy discerns not solely parentage but performance as well. Tracing extended film migration and star personas until the late 1950s, my study finds bureaucratic categories and the partition figures of the 'refugee', 'evacuee', 'recovered woman' and 'muhajir', being applied to film migrants and imbuing star personas while also encoding film meaning.

My proposed term 'evacuee cinema' as a reflection of exilic cinema is based on the historic specificity of partition involving the two-way migration and impasses of ownership. Central to the conception of this book are the trajectories of departing and arriving film personnel in Bombay and Lahore. In the process, the book also encapsulates the continuities and disruptions in terms of the pre-nation-state 'all-India film', which bequeathed post-colonial, nationally distinct cinemas in South Asia. Yet the term is not merely descriptive; it also declares a method whereby I have sought to extend a bureaucratic category used to manage land and property proprietorship by both nation states into a conceptual frame to characterise cultural production. *Evacuee Cinema* seeks to convey the discordant, chaotic and transformative force of partition by identifying the evacuation, rehabilitation and voiding that went into the making of nationally separate cinemas. *Evacuee Cinema* is thus neither solely Indian nor solely Pakistani but delves into interstitial and transitionary film-making during the long partition which was anticipating and accommodating new national orders. Similar to the bureaucratic category of evacuee property,[58] *Evacuee Cinema* is a story of dislodgement involving two sides.

An Archival Disposition

The pitfalls of an official state archive with its selective versions and preservations are an all too familiar hazard of an archive-based method. But in the context of Pakistan, where official and elite antipathy to indigenous cinema has translated into a lack of any dedicated repository of film cultures, this has profound implications. First, cinema history then escapes the careful orchestration and ideological organisation that characterises official historical narratives in any nation state. Second, it gives rise to private collections shaped by different preservation impulses. The building of collections as cinephiles, family members, journalists and proprietors together produces a complex archive. Of course, this conglomerate exists as such only in the mind of the researcher, and individual collectors protect their separate turfs emphatically. My personal experience of archival work was most heavily inflected by being an Indian researcher in Pakistan, thus constituting in Carolyn Steedman's sense 'an important rite of passage'.[59] The possibilities offered by the individual collections were far greater than they could have been in the case of an official state archive where one would have required government permissions and a research approval for accessing collections, which is a near impossible task given the visa regimes between the two countries. Additionally, in the absence of an institutional archive and the proliferation of scattered collections, the observations and histories of the people I interviewed were also rich sources for this book. Asif Noorani, the editor of the *Eastern Film* magazine who magnanimously shared his collection with me, liked to introduce himself as one who hailed from a town in Uttar Pradesh, called Karachi. While many would find this nostalgia of the Urdu-speaking literary elite of Pakistan familiar, a recognition of this phenomenon of translocated nostalgia also enabled my project methodologically in approaching historical sources and reconstructing film biographies. It established above everything else the ambivalence of film provenance and dislocated geographies in South Asia, where film-making predated the appearance of national boundaries in the region. In India my approach was more conservative and largely confined to the institutional collections in the National Film Archive in Pune and the Nehru Memorial Museum and Library and the National Archives in Delhi. Several surprising discoveries were also made in the British Library and British Film Institute in London, as well as within an increasing database of films on the internet.

The study is methodologically designed to shift its vantage points between the film cities of Bombay and Lahore to comment on visualisations of freedom, cultural rivalries and two-way movement that were constitutive of partition. I have followed found material, often through serendipitous connections and leads. A chance conversation with a housemate in London revealed her to be a distant relation of the pre-partition Lahore producer Dalsukh Pancholi, and she connected me to the nearest kin, now living in Mumbai. Browsing around old Urdu bookshops in Lahore, I found myself outside the office of the deceased film-maker Sibtain Fazli's two sons (Figure I.1). Here, I met the second-generation Fazli Brothers, who spoke extensively about their father's career and his choices and shared their collection. One of them felt strongly about the absence of his father and uncle from popular Indian film histories.[60] It was as if, he said, they never existed. The chapter on Fazli Brothers in this book recuperates their Indian past. In the earliest surviving issues of Pakistan's oldest Urdu film magazine, *The Nigar Weekly*, still in publication from a two-room office in Karachi (Figure I.2), I found the sauciest of film headlines and cartoons, many of which announced the return of the 'Lara Lappa Girl'[61] to the national fold. The significance of Meena Shorey's Indian stardom and Pakistani reinvention became evident here. In several interviews, especially with film journalists, the word *charba* appeared. This genre of film remakes or duplicates looms large in film discussions in Pakistan, remaining an object of derision and dismissed all too easily. This is the pivot for the last chapter, for its association with a migrant child star Rattan Kumar.

Figure 1.1   The Fazli Associates office in Lahore
Source: Photograph by the author, 2012.

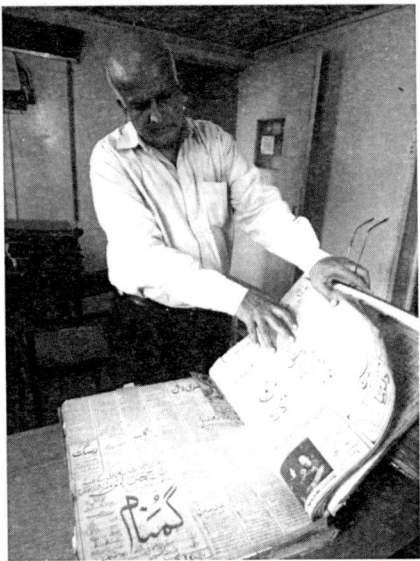

Figure 1.2   Aslam Ilyas, the editor-proprietor of *Nigar Weekly*, in his Karachi office
Source: Photograph by the author, 2012.

Unstructured interviews occasionally cited in the book have shaped it in important ways. In the absence of literature on the period, the selection of certain themes and certain films over others required familiarising myself with nodes of popular curiosity and the corpus of remembered films in Pakistan. Through this I have tried to avoid reinforcing the hegemony of nationally canonised texts and to bring into discussion previously unexamined sets of films. This study makes use of source materials and cultural products that emanate from different historical and national contexts: British India (1940–1947), India (1947–1960) and Pakistan (1947–1960). The research sources include films, film transcripts, periodicals, compendiums, life-writings, biographies, play-scripts, publicity ephemera like song booklets and photographs, and newspapers from all three contexts. Government reports, legislative records and home department files contain the official life of films. This history is developed in the face of a patchy film archive where many pre-partition and, in the case of Lahore, several post-partition films and their production details are lost forever.

The work is restricted to the cinematic complex constituted by Lahore and Bombay between 1940 and 1960, and focuses on production dynamics vis-à-vis West Pakistan. The case of East Pakistan is not included in this study. The work of Lotte Hoek in mapping cross-wing film-making between East and West Pakistan between the 1950s and 1960s[62] awaits a pre-history that examines the partition of Bengali cinema. While important for a comprehensive understanding of partition and film production in the subcontinent, the distinctiveness of the Bengali case makes it a separate part of the larger story. Language is an important dimension of this study, and with my fluency restricted to Urdu, Hindi and to some extent Punjabi, this research remains limited to the western region. Most projects on partition have followed similar regional exclusivity, focusing on either the Punjab or Bengal province. I also made a pragmatic choice of selecting those personnel whose cinematic careers preceded their decisions to migrate in either direction and thus offer a possible template for the study of inflections. In the face of national, linguistic and geographical shifts, individuals, film themes and the materiality of cinematic cities provide continuities.

An Itinerant Anatomy

In order to unsettle the hold of national borders on film histories in South Asia, this book approaches the all-India film category of the pre-nation-state era through film-making in Lahore. The opening chapter examines the entrepreneurial and experimental spirit of Lahore led by two family-run studios, Pancholi and Shorey, which benefitted from the freelance film workers in the years preceding partition. The next part, Part 1, consists of two chapters on the complex historical milieu of 1940s Bombay and complicates the 'silence on partition' through three forms of creative expressions: the *Filmindia* magazine, Prithvi Theatre's performances and memoirs of two migrant Muslim film-makers. The title of Chapter 2, 'Hindu Camera, Muslim Microphone', is extracted from the pages of *Filmindia*, which became a profitably vituperative publication in the late 1940s by covering film news through the lens of religious politics. Juxtaposed with *Filmindia*'s anti-Pakistan prose are the memoirs of two directors who left Bombay for Pakistan that describe the prejudicial as well as cooperative transactions and networks in the film business. Chapter 3 analyses in detail the partition repertory of Prithvi Theatre, which was performed on the proscenium stage and toured Indian cities until the mid-1950s.

In transit from the colonial to the post-colonial, 'Between Bombay and Pakistan' (Part 2) comprises three chapters on émigré personnel and genre innovations. The self-conscious producers and 'pioneers' of the Muslim socials, Fazli Brothers (active years 1940–1960), are the case study in Chapter 4. Appearing at the height of the movement for Pakistan, their Muslim socials are marked by devotional iconography, the motif of two women and allusions to poet-philosopher Muhammad Iqbal. Here the claims of the community appear paramount and involve a sacrifice of individual romantic desires. In sharp contrast, Chapter 5 focuses on the national and religious boundaries actively crossed in the alliance between actress Meena Shorey (active years 1940–1965) and a refugee producer from Lahore, Roop K. Shorey (active years 1935–1970), in post-partition Bombay. The professional and conjugal relationship between a Muslim Meena and a Hindu Roop resisted the parochial pressures of this decade and privileged a cosmopolitan stance. Most strikingly, their collaborative films filter a historical trauma by innovating on the form of the Hollywood screwball comedy. Finally, the migration of the child star Rattan Kumar (active years 1950–1969) from Indian to Pakistani screens is the subject of the last chapter. Owing his popularity to the neorealist aesthetics of Bombay films in the early 1950s, Rattan embodied the image of the 'national orphan' of newly independent India. Migrating to Pakistan in 1957, his image was set forth into a complicated orbit of disavowal and appropriation, intensely realised in his double roles, swashbuckling acts in *Arabian Nights* fantasies and retaliatory remakes of Bombay films known as *charbas*. Focused on the national splitting of personnel and publics of the all-India film enterprise following the partition of British India in 1947, this book discovers in genre iconography, personas and industrial strategies an active negotiation of partition. I end with a reappraisal of this productive force of partition, which has hitherto largely been understood as destructive and debilitative, and offer a lens to understand South Asian film history and partition studies.[63]

Translations

The study has extensive translations from Urdu and Hindi sources, including the films. While at most places I have provided the original text and its translation together, in certain instances where extracts are important for their content and broad sense, and not the form, only the English translations have been given. Except for verses from Muhammad Iqbal's works, the translations are mine, often in consultation with learned family and friends.

Notes

1   K. A. Abbas, 'Communalists Keep Out!' *Filmindia*, February 1940, 33.

2   'Question Box', *Filmfare*, 11 July 1952, 39.

3   'Our Readers Say', *Filmfare*, 12 December 1952.

4   *Report of the Film Enquiry Committee* (New Delhi: Government of India Press, 1951), 13.

5   Indivar Kamtekar writes of the elisions and emphases that have gone in producing the moment of freedom and the story of 1947. Indivar Kamtekar, 'The Fables of Nationalism', *India International Quarterly* 26, no. 3 (Monsoon 1999): 44–54, 50.

6   *Film Industry in Pakistan* (Lahore: Board of Economic Enquiry, Punjab, 1957), 2.

7   Kaushik Bhaumik calls it the 'productive relationship between the Bombay industry and other regional centres'. Kaushik Bhaumik, 'The Emergence of the Bombay Film Industry, 1913–1936', PhD diss., University of Oxford, 2001, 109.

8   Madras, the other important film production centre from the late 1930s onwards, produced only two Hindi-language films in its first decade of sound production. Its big Hindi success came in 1948, with Srinivasan's *Chandralekha*. Erik Barnouw and S. Krishnaswamy, *Indian Film* (New York: Oxford University Press, 1980), 173.

9   I borrow this understanding of civil war (instead of partition violence) from Shruti Kapila's work on the fratricidal nature of partition mass killings. Shruti Kapila, 'Armitage on Civil Wars', *Global Intellectual History* 4, no. 3 (2019): 318–321, 318.

10   I base this understanding on B. R. Ambedkar's tract 'Pakistan or the Partition of India', available as an online book, with a foreword by Francis Pritchett, http://www.columbia. edu/itc/mealac/pritchett/00ambedkar/ambedkar_partition/index.html (accessed on 11 June 2021).

11   Ayesha Jalal, *The Sole Spokesman* (Lahore: Sang-i-Meel Publications, 1999), 4.

12   Francis Robinson, *Separatism among Indian Muslims: The Politics of the United Provinces' Muslims 1860–1923* (Cambridge: Cambridge University Press, 1974).

13   Farzana Shaikh, *Community and Consensus in Islam* (Cambridge: Cambridge University Press, 1989), 200.

14   Faisal Devji points out that Pakistan was not only a precedent to Israel but its closest relation too, involving a rejection of Benedict Anderson's modular nationalism. Established both in the name of minorities and as a result of vast migrations, these religious states have had to reject the principle of territorially based community that gives meaning to majority nations. Faisal Devji, *Muslim Zion: Pakistan as a Political Idea* (Cambridge, MA: Harvard University Press, 2013), 16.

15   Ibid., 90.

16   In March 1940, the All-India Muslim League first voiced its demand for independent Muslim states in the north-west and the north-east of India. Arguing for different conceptions of partition, Pandey identifies three partitions that went into the making of the partition of 1947. Gyanendra Pandey, 'Remembering Partition: Violence Nationalism and History in India', in *The Gyanendra Pandey Omnibus* (New Delhi: Oxford University Press, 2008), 25.

17   Ritu Menon and Kamla Bhasin, *Borders and Boundaries: Women in India's Partition* (New Delhi: Kali for Women, 1998); Urvashi Butalia, *The Other Side of Silence* (New Delhi: Penguin, 1998).

18   While the two works are independent and separate, their methodological approach, intellectual vein as well as the timing of their appearance make it possible to see these as constituting a common project.

19   Menon and Bhasin, *Borders and Boundaries*, 21.

20   Aamir Mufti, *Enlightenment in the Colony: The Jewish Question and the Crisis of Postcolonial Culture* (Princeton: Princeton University Press, 2007).

21   Pandey, 'Remembering Partition', 45.

22   For three phases of partition representations, see Gita Vishwanath and Salma Malik, 'Revisiting 1947 through Popular Cinema: A Comparative Study of India and Pakistan', *Economic and Political Weekly* 44, no. 36 (September 2009): 61–69. For thematic detours such as Punjabiyat and Kashmiriyat, see Srijana Das, 'Partition and Punjabiyat in Bombay Cinema', *Contemporary South Asia* 15, no. 4 (December 2006): 453–471; and Nirmal Kumar, 'Kaisi Sarhaden Kaisi Majbooriyan', in *Filming the Line of Control: The Indo-Pak Relationship through the Cinematic Lens*, ed. Meenakshi Bharat and Nirmal Kumar, 128–139 (New Delhi: Routledge, 2008).

23   This was particularly the case of Hindi cinema, whereas the Bengali cinema of Ritwik Ghatak and its deep evocation of partition displacement have been an area of enquiry. See Souvik Raychaudhuri, *Partition Trauma, the Oedipal Rupture, Dreaming: The Cinematic Will of Ritwik Ghatak* (Calcutta: Papyrus, 2000).

24   Bhaskar Sarkar, *Mourning the Nation: Indian Cinema in the Wake of Partition* (Durham, NC: Duke University Press, 2009).

25   Ravi Vasudevan, 'Dislocations: The Cinematic Imagining of a New Society in 1950s India', *Oxford Literary Review on India: Writing History, Culture, Post-coloniality* 16, nos. 1–2 (1994): 93–124, 109. Also, in a much earlier intervention, Rosie Thomas identifies the evocation of partition in the images of streams of refugees leaving their homeland in a song sequence in *Mother India* (1957). Rosie Thomas, 'Sanctity and Scandal: The Mythologization of Mother India', *Quarterly Review of Film and Video* 11, no. 3 (1989): 11–30, 19.

26   Such listening and documentation of movement are evident in the 1947 archive project which records testimonies from partition survivors and their families. See the website 1947 Partition Archive, https://www.1947partitionarchive.org/mission (accessed on 11 June 2021).

27   Vishwanath and Malik, 'Revisiting 1947', 62.

28   Faisal Devji, 'Hindu/Muslim/Indian', *Public Culture* 5, no. 1 (Fall 1992): 1–18, 3.

29   Debashree Mukherjee, *Bombay Hustle: Making Movies in a Colonial City* (New York: Columbia University Press, 2020).

30   Ashish Rajyadhaksha and Paul Willemen, *Encyclopaedia of Indian Cinema* (New Delhi: British Film Institute–Oxford University Press, 1994), 8–9.

31   Priya Jaikumar, *Cinema at the End of Empire: A Politics of Transition* (Durham, NC: Duke University Press, 2006).

32   Barnouw and Krishnaswamy, *Indian Film*, 124.

33   Jaikumar, *Cinema at the End of Empire*, 195 (emphasis mine).

34 Sumita Chakravarty, *National Identity in Indian Popular Cinema* (Austin: University of Texas Press, 1993), 61.

35 Priyamvada Gopal, *Literary Radicalism in India: Gender, Nation and the Transition to Independence* (London: Routledge, 2005), 125–127.

36 New work on cinema in Pakistan includes anthologies such as Ali Khan and Ali Nobil Ahmed (eds.), *Film and Social Change in Pakistan* (Karachi: Oxford University Press, 2016) and Vazira Zamindar and Asad Ali, *Love, Longing and War: Essays on Cinema in Pakistan* (Karachi: Oxford University Press, 2020).

37 Two representative instances are Chakravarty, *National Identity in Indian Popular Cinema*, and Barnouw and Krishnaswamy, *Indian Film*.

38 In Sumita Chakravarty's book, the discussion of partition arises in her reading of the magnum opus of *Mughal-e-Azam* (1960), which is read as resolving the contradictions of the present and opening out to the 'conditions of social life in India for Hindus and Muslims in relation to each other and to history and its reversals'. Chakravarty, *National Identity in Popular Indian Cinema*, 165.

39 Chakravarty acknowledges the trauma faced by the film-makers. 'Because the film took fifteen years to make, *Mughal-e-Azam*'s makers no doubt experienced the trauma, although it is not known to what degree they were directly affected by the events of the time.' Ibid., 166.

40 Saeed Shiraz (son of Shiraz Ali Hakim), interview with author, Karachi, Pakistan, July 2012.

41 Mushtaq Gazdar, *Pakistan Cinema 1947–1997* (Karachi: Oxford University Press, 1998).

42 Rehan Ansari, 'On Mushtaq Gazdar's History of Pakistani Cinema', in *Sarai Reader: The Public Domain*, 69–70 (New Delhi: Centre for the Study of Developing Societies, 2001), 69.

43 Gazdar, *Pakistan Cinema*, 2.

44 Ibid., 21.

45 The '*Jaal* agitation' refers to the protests held by actors, producers and directors of the Lahore film industry in 1954 demanding the ban of Indian films in Pakistan. The agitation was so named because the protestors were seeking an immediate withdrawal of the Indian film *Jaal* (1952) from local theatres.

46 Madhava Prasad, *Ideology of the Hindi Film: A Historical Construction* (Delhi: Oxford University Press, 1998), 4.

47 Rosie Thomas, *Bombay before Bollywood: Film City Fantasies* (New Delhi: Orient Blackswan, 2014).

48 Rachel Dwyer, *Filming the Gods: Religion and Indian Cinema* (Oxon: Routledge, 2006), 3.

49 Mukul Kesavan, 'Urdu, Awadh and the Tawaif: The Islamicate Roots of Hindi Cinema', in *Forging Identities: Gender, Communities and the State*, ed. Zoya Hasan, 244–257 (New Delhi: Kali for Women, 1994).

50 Ira Bhaskar and Richard Allen, *Islamicate Cultures of Bombay Cinema* (New Delhi: Tulika Books, 2009).

51 For the period covered by this book, the Muslim historicals and Muslim socials are the two relevant subgenres of the 'Islamicate'. Their signifying work changes in the transition from the colonial to the independent nation. In the colonial context, the celebration of Mughal achievements in the Muslim historicals, while being a significant anti-colonial gesture, was also a reaffirmation of the value of Muslim culture against

the majoritarian Hindu political mobilisation. In the post-independence Nehruvian period, this rhetoric marked the secular credentials of the new nation state and became critically important in countering negative discourses about Muslims in the country. Bhaskar and Allen, *Islamicate Cultures of Bombay Cinema*, 6.

52   Iftikhar Dadi, 'Registering Crisis: Ethnicity in Pakistani Cinema of the 1960s and 1970s', in *Beyond Crisis*, ed. Naveeda Khan, 145–176 (New Delhi: Routledge, 2010).

53   Rosie Thomas, 'Melodrama and the Negotiation of Morality in Mainstream Hindi Film', in *Consuming Modernity: Public Culture in a South Asian World*, ed. Carol Breckenridge, 157–182 (Minneapolis: University of Minnesota Press, 1995), 158.

54   Referring to a deepening popular disillusionment with the Congress-led government in the 1970s and the early 1980s, Ranjani Mazumdar reads anger and crisis in the cinematic portrayal of urban life. See Ranjani Mazumdar, *Bombay Cinema: An Archive of the City* (Minneapolis: University of Minnesota Press, 2007).

55   Ravi Vasudevan, 'Geographies of the Cinematic Public: Notes on Regional, National and Global Histories of Indian Cinema', *Journal of the Moving Image* 9 (2010): 94–117, http://www.jmionline.org/film_journal/jmi_09/article_06.php (accessed on 10 July 2011).

56   Hamid Naficy, *Home Exile and Homeland* (New York: Routledge, 1999), 3.

57   Hamid Naficy, *An Accented Cinema: Exilic and Diasporic Filmmaking* (Princeton: Princeton University Press, 2001), 3.

58   For a contemporary commentary on the evacuee property ordinances in the two dominions in the 1950s, see Joseph B. Schechtman's 'Evacuee Property in India and Pakistan', *Pacific Affairs* 24, no. 4 (December 1951): 406–413.

59   As Carolyn Steedman puts it eloquently, 'As might be expected of an experience that is an important rite of passage, no one historian's *archive* is ever like another's'. Carolyn Steedman, *Dust* (Manchester: Manchester University Press, 2001), 9.

60   References to Fazli Brothers appear in Bhaskar and Allen's *Islamicate Cultures* and in Ravi Vasudevan's 'Geographies of the Cinematic Public'.

61   Meena Shorey acquired the moniker of 'Lara Lappa Girl', after the success of the film *Ek Thi Ladki*, referring in particular to the limb-tapping office song in the film: 'Lara lappa, lara lappa, lai rakhda'.

62   Lotte Hoek, 'Cross-wing Filmmaking: East Pakistani Urdu Films and Their Traces in the Bangladesh Film Archive', *BioScope: South Asian Screen Studies* 5, no. 2 (2014): 99–118.

63   The exhibition curated by Iftikhar Dadi and Hammad Nassar, 'Lines of Control: Partition as a Productive Space', approached partition as a productive act that generated new regimes of control, maps and borders. See Hammad Nasar, 'Lines of Control: Partition as a Productive Space', *Tanqeed*, December 2015, http://www.tanqeed.org/2015/12/lines-of-control-partition-as-a-productive-space/ (accessed on 18 June 2021).

1 The All-India Ambitions of Lahore

In early 1947, Swaran Singh, a coalition minister from undivided Punjab, performed the *mahurat*[1] of the film *Roop Rekha*[2] at Pancholi Studios in Lahore.[3] It was rare for a political notable to inaugurate a film shoot, and this was hailed as a sign of film production having confidently taken root in the region. Sporadic and flippant attempts at film-making, the speeches reveal, were to give way to an era of planned and well-directed films with a message. Such optimism five months before the partition plan was hardly misplaced, given that the beginning of the 1940s had seen increased and commercially viable film production in the city of Lahore, despite the restrictions of the war. As was the case with the city's printing presses and banks,[4] the studios and film companies in Lahore were owned by non-Muslims. This ownership pattern of the film companies and studios made these targets of sectarian violence in 1947 despite employing a sizeable number of Muslims.

Existing research on colonial film centres in India approaches the 'partnership' between the two cities from the vantage point of Bombay's sponge-like emergence of a transregional film centre. Kaushik Bhaumik claims that by the mid-1930s, Bombay had not only absorbed Lahore's personnel but also dictated how Punjabi themes were presented.[5] In his work, Lahore is identified as imbued by an experimental sensibility, one that provided Bombay with musical talent in the 1930s. While Bhaumik concedes a brief revival in the early 1940s, the blow dealt by partition has in most part tossed Lahore into teleological insignificance for most authoritative studies of Indian cinema. A brief footnote besides Lahore's nominal presence in Erik Barnow and S. Krishnaswamy's *Indian Film* reminds readers that 'Lahore later became part of Pakistan'[6] and is a typical example of pre-independence film histories written from the territorial limits of later-day nation states. The following section will detail the 'brief revival of the 1940s', according to a readjusted view from Lahore, and appraise the significance of its creative energies.

Enquiry committee reports and newspaper advertisements of this period mention several film-producing companies that quickly changed hands or went bust.[7] While these instances suggest the instability of film enterprise at this time, in no way limited to Lahore,[8] they also confirm a gentle throb of film production and its ancillary activities in the city. New film journals were being launched in the city until late 1946, while the editor of Lahore's well-established film magazine *Cine Herald*, B. R. Chopra, was planning to make his first film *Lala Rukh* in the city. The same year two studios, Leela Mandir and Shorey, both within the city limits, caught fire and caused deliberation in the local press over the increasing presence of studios in Lahore's residential areas. Lahore's transformation from an experimental film centre in the late 1930s to a profit-oriented one in the mid-1940s was in particular overseen by two family-based film companies, the Pancholis and the Shoreys, who had survived the war years and benefitted from the weakening of the studio system in the Indian industry. The entrepreneurial men who became synonymous with the success of their respective production companies were brothers Rewashankar and Dalsukh Pancholi, and father–son Roshan Lal and Roop Kishore Shorey.

Punjab on the Film Map of India

Rewashankar Pancholi entered the business of film exhibition in the late 1920s and acquired the earliest cinema halls in Karachi, the Imperial Cinema and the Picture House. A letter written in the early 1980s by a business associate of the brothers to Rewashankar's son refers to the Pancholis as the 'Cinema Kings' of Karachi who at the time of independence had monetary stakes in film exhibition extending as far as Rangoon.[9] In 1933, the brothers moved into film distribution, setting up a company office, the Empire Talkies distributors in Calcutta, which had exclusive rights in British India for RKO (Radio-Keith-Orpheum) Pictures, Walt Disney Pictures and RCA (Radio Corporation of America) talkie equipment. Later, Hindi and Bengali films were also included in the Empire Talkies' distribution net. The Pancholis' territorially expansive commercial interests demanded a highly mobile life, with a traveling case of essential items always kept ready at home for Dalsukh for urgent travels.[10]

With feet firmly planted in film exhibition and distribution, Dalsukh Pancholi ventured into production in the late 1930s. The premises of an optical factory in Lahore were converted into a film studio, and, by 1934, the Pancholi Art Pictures was born. Their earliest forays were in Punjabi, starting off with *Dassi* (Handmaiden, Punjabi, 1938), *Gul Bakavali* (The Flower of Bakavli, Punjabi, 1939) and *Yamla Jatt* (Punjabi, 1940). *Yamla Jatt* was the debut film of actor Pran Sikand, 'the arch baddie' of Hindi cinema. In his biography, Pran recollects the time when he was spotted by writer Wali Mohammad at a *paan* shop in the red-light district of Heera Mandi in Lahore, a usual scouting ground for producers and directors, and later taken to the Pancholi Studio.[11]

> The moment we reached there, they began work on my screen test. First, Moti B. Gidwani did my make-up. I came to know later that he was the director of this film.[12]

Yamla Jatt was followed by *Choudhry* (Punjabi, 1941), also starring Pran. The biographer's contention that 'there was no better springboard for being catapulted to stardom than to be groomed and presented by Pancholi Art Pictures and Studios ... a colossus in the film producing fraternity'[13] requires a more tempered appraisal: the significance of the Pancholis stems from their vertically integrated approach to film business as exhibitors, distributors and now producers. The Pancholi film company successfully carved its space in the all-India film enterprise by their iconic association with Punjab, starting off with Punjabi films and from this location proceeding into the 'all-India circuit' with Hindi–Urdu productions.

The advancement of the Second World War in Southeast Asia brought unprecedented business and employment opportunities to willing men and entrepreneurs in the colonial cities, especially Lahore. Pran Neville calls this a trade boom, which was also reflected in the cinema business in Lahore.[14] Wartime boom meant that films found financiers in Lahore more easily than before. The first Hindi film of Pancholi Art Pictures was *Khazanchi* (The Treasurer, 1941), an adaptation of Paramount Pictures' *The Way of All Flesh* (1940). Starring Ramola, S. D. Narang, M. Ismail and the cyclist Jankidas, *Khazanchi* became hugely popular for its songs. In their descriptions of the film's production and success, the life narratives of Jankidas and Balraj Sahni offer fascinating glimpses into a regenerated relationship between cinema and Lahore. The leisurely yet zestful sensibility of the city infused the locally produced films, while film activity became an added attraction of the city. Once during his daily practice on Lahore's Mall Road for the forthcoming cycling championship at the Olympics, Jankidas discovered Dalsukh Pancholi's car following him down the road.[15] With a finger on the profit pulse, Dalsukh coaxed Janki into acting and signed him for a sum of 11,000 rupees, making the 'World Champion Cyclist' the 'initial draw' of *Khazanchi*.[16] The cyclist dramatically recounts his adventure on the first day of a fairly elaborate shoot set-up, as he pedalled at the speed of 40 miles an hour down the Lahore–Amritsar Road.

> The first day of my shoot was so well advertised and publicised that more than ten thousand citizens of Lahore, Kasur, Amritsar and Ferozepur came all the way to see me in action on the Lahore-Amritsar road. Cameras were fixed on both sides of the deserted part of the road. Another car with a camera was following me.... While I was in this 'Olympic Reverie,' I suddenly heard

cries, wails and horn blowings ... my gosh! I saw in front of me a speeding
truck overtaking two giant juggernauts and dashing towards me.... I hurled
my bicycle through the narrow space in the twinkling of an eye. The road
was dusty and a big cloud of dust enveloped me. All the members of the film
unit along with the bewildered truck drivers gave a unanimous shriek as if I
were dead and had rolled on to the road, devoured by the dust.... There was
pindrop silence, hushed moments as if witnessing a tragic death. The sharp
eyes of director Moti B. Gidwani, director of *Khazanchi*, however seemed to
pierce through the clouds of dust, and to the amazement of one and all, he
pointed out a disappearing racing-cyclist on the horizon. He yelled: 'there goes
Jankidas, a ghost of himself!'[17]

An enduring highlight of the film, the sequence is cross-cut with a courtroom drama
in which the cyclist's timely arrival and testimony save an innocent man from the
gallows. However, it was not merely a celebrity spectacle that made Bombay sit up and
take notice of a film from Lahore. Sahni's autobiography reproduces a conversation
with his film-maker friend Chetan Anand that suggests that *Khazanchi* was noticed
as an innovation. According to Anand, the all-India films by Prabhat in Pune and
New Theatres in Calcutta, sharing the leitmotif of tragedy, had become monotonous
for viewers. The person who infused a fresh style was Dalsukh Pancholi, 'the Lahore
producer who took advantage of the state of things'.[18]

He made a film, which was an *amalgam* of all the ingredients which were sure
to transplant the viewers to dream world, where happiness reigned supreme.
These were catchy tunes based on popular folk songs, beautiful girls, titillating
dances, romances, playful banter, and a dash of vulgarity and nudity. It was
Pancholi Sahab's *Khazanchi*, which was the first *amalgam*, and this *amalgam*
proved to be very heady! *Khazanchi* went on to become a super hit, and became
a model for several other films, which followed in its wake. Prabhat and New
Theatres films became *passé*.

As the 'first amalgam', *Khazanchi* could well be the prototype of the hybrid or *masala*
form characterising Bombay films. As Punjabis waiting to make their mark in the
Bombay film industry during the mid-1940s, Anand and Sahni could have equally
exaggerated Lahore's moment, even though the latter was far from uncritically
identifying with the film's popularity. Sahni was a BBC radio presenter in London
when *Khazanchi* was released, and he recounts that the film's hybrid 'Indian and
Western music' in the context of Indian nationalism's anti-Western modality had
caused him embarrassment at work.

On listening to them, every one of our employees had made fun of their tunes,
a hybrid of Indian and Western music. I remember we had just stacked those
records in an obscure corner. Indeed, we hadn't the courage to play them when
our English colleagues were around.[19]

However, the listeners of the radio broadcasts, especially the target audience of Indian army soldiers deployed in British forces during the Second World War, thought otherwise. In hindsight, Sahni was of the opinion that *Khazanchi*'s music was a trendsetter.

> We began receiving from India an unending procession of records whose tunes had unmistakable echoes of [*Khazanchi*'s music]. And it was these records, which the *jawans* now wanted played in the request programmes! Being far away from India, we had looked upon this change in public taste as a passing phase, little realizing that before long it was going to revolutionise film music.[20]

Music was key to *Khazanchi*'s popularity, as evident in a print advertisement saturated with the song sensation 'Sawan ke Nazaare Hain' (The Splendid Sights of Monsoon) to promote the Lahore film running in its fifth month in Bombay.[21] The song also finds its way into Shaukat Hussain Rizvi's memoir, where he recalls having innovatively found a solution to edit a moving background for a song filmed on the cycling crooners.[22] The music composer of *Khazanchi* and other Pancholi films was Ghulam Haider, also credited with introducing iconic singers like Noorjahan and Lata Mangeshkar. Composing music for both Lahore and Bombay films until 1948, he chose to stay and work in Lahore after partition.

After *Khazanchi*, Pancholi Art Pictures produced seven more Hindustani films before partition.[23] While none of the films made after *Khandaan* survived, which may also suggest their average returns and poor circulation, the plot details are available in film reviews and publicity columns. These were *Zamindar* (Feudal Lord, 1942, dir. Moti Gidwani), *Shirin Farhad* (1945, dir. Prahlad Dutt), *Kaise Kahoon* (How Do I Say, 1945, dir. Moti Gidwani), *Poonji* (Lifesavings, 1946, dir. Ram Dave), *Dhamki* (A Threat, 1945, dir. Ravindra Dave) and *Shehar se Dur* (Far from the City, 1947, dir. Barkat Mehra). The studio regulars included actors M. Ismail, S. D. Narang, Noorjahan, Pran, Ragini, 'Miss' Manorama, 'Baby' Akhtari; composer Ghulam Haider; writer Imtiaz Ali Taj; directors Modi B. Gidwani, Ravindra and Ram Narayan Dave; and cameraperson Ishaan Ghosh. Imtiaz Ali Taj, Lahore-based Urdu writer who penned the famous play *Anarkali* in 1922, wrote the screenplay for *Khandaan, Zamindar, Dhamki* and *Shehar se Dur* and stayed on in Lahore after 1947. Dalsukh Pancholi's nephews Ravindra Dave and Ram Narayan Dave, who directed *Dhamki* and *Poonji* respectively, migrated to India.

The news stories on Pancholi Art Pictures reported punctilious studio schedules with a nine-to-six working shift, akin to a 'well-regulated factory routine'.[24] The tantalising highlights of each of the films were publicised in the weekly film columns of city newspapers, such as the *lathi* fight scene in *Zamindar* in which 800 people took part: 'the attack was very furious and director has picturised it in true colour and atmosphere'.[25] A new technique of storytelling was the focus in *Poonji*, where 'something is happening all the time. Every gag, every punch and every purple patch is woven in the term of the tale!' The rise of the freelance system in the early 1940s allowed Lahore studios to bring in stars from Bombay and provided occasions to build up anticipation around the film. Bombay-based actress Shanta Apte's arrival in Lahore in January 1942 for the shoot of the film *Zamindar* was widely publicised,[26] including the massive payment she received for it.[27] These production dalliances with Bombay were also susceptible to running into rough waters, as is evident in the Apte–Pancholi collaboration saga, with Dalsukh suing the 'Shanta Apte Concern' for 100,000 rupees by mid-1942 for an alleged breach of contract.[28] Similarly, when Dalsukh cast Meena (Shorey) in *Shehar se Dur*, the studio owner Sohrab Modi, her employer in Bombay, slapped damages on Pancholi.

> *Shehar se Dur*, featuring Meena Shorey in the lead role, was the final release of Pancholi Art Pictures before partition and released in February 1947.[29] A review in the Motion Picture Film Magazine, apart from commenting on the 'mesmerizing beauty of fresh-faced Meena', also pointed out the unusual 'girl meets girl story'.
>
> … where a girl meets another girl and falls in love with her. There is the usual romance between a youth and a girl in the film, but it is only in the background, the hero appearing only in the beginning and the end of the story. *Shehr se Dur* besides these interesting points is a tragedy and a justifiable tragedy at that.[30]

The homoerotic tenor of the film while radical for those years was hardly a flash in the pan. It came close on the heels of the *Lihaaf* controversy during the years 1942–1945, where a Lahore court tried the writer Ismat Chughtai on charges of obscenity for her short story about a lesbian relationship between the neglected wife of a *nawab* and her woman attendant. Released in 1946, Pancholi's *Shehar se Dur* was located in these intellectual and creative undercurrents that had enveloped the city in the preceding years.

In March 1947 unprecedented violence paralysed Lahore, with all commercial activities, including film production and exhibition, shutting down. While the cinema houses opened again by the end of the month, the choice at hand for cinemagoers of Lahore between an RKO Radio musical and a 20th Century Fox thriller was indicative of the production standstill that the city faced over the next few months.[31] The shooting of the Pancholi film *Patjhad* with Meena Shorey was paused and ultimately completed in Bombay in 1948, an instance of evacuee filming practices during this time. The Pancholis had good reasons to wait for the storm to blow over. They now controlled two active studios in the city, having acquired the second unit, Pradhan Pictures, in 1942. Credited with putting Punjab on the film map of India, it was a matter of months before Dalsukh would ultimately be forced to leave Lahore in late 1947. Among the relocation options briefly considered by the family were Kabul and London, but they ultimately settled for Bombay. Dalsukh produced four films in independent India before his demise in 1959.[32] These were

Patjhad (Autumn, 1948, dir. Ravindra Dave), *Meena Bazaar* (1950, dir. Ravindra Dave), *Nagina* (Female Mystical Serpent, 1951, dir. Ravindra Dave) and *Aasmaan* (Sky, 1952, dir. Dalsukh Pancholi). The Pancholis also partnered with K. K. Modi in film distribution, where Rewashankar's sons travelled to Libya and Egypt with a film projector, screening Hindi films like *Jhanak Jhanak Payal Baje* (Chimes of an Anklet, 1955, V. Shantaram) in Beirut and Alexandria.

The Jocular Vein of Lahore

The Shoreys were the other prominent film-producing family of Lahore before partition. Starting his career in 1921 as a representative cameraperson for the Department of News Film Corporation, Roshan Lal Shorey had received training in New York and held a diploma of merit in motion picture production. Apart from a number of documentary and instructional films, Shorey also filmed several Indian National Congress (hereafter, Congress) sessions as well as Gandhi's campaigns in the late 1920s. His first feature film was *Kismet ke Here Phere* (The Mischiefs of Destiny, 1931), a silent 'comedy with suspense, stunts and thrills',[33] which was followed by one of the earliest talkies of India, called *Zulm-i-Kans* (The Oppression of King Kans) or *Radhe–Shyam* (1932), and shot in Bombay. By then the Shoreys had joined Kamla Movietone at Lahore whose distributors in the eastern as well as the southern circuits were the Calcutta-based Aurora Film Corporation. By the end of the decade, the father–son team had moved their company to the New Theatres Studio Hall on the Canal Bank in Lahore.

Roop K. Shorey, who had assisted his father, made his first film *Majnu* in 1935, a parody of the love epic *Laila Majnu*, which had been adapted four years earlier by the film company Madan and its rival Krishna, in Calcutta and Bombay, respectively. Roop's friend Harold Lewis played the lead role and thereafter took 'Majnu' as his screen name. This was followed by *Tarzan ki Beti* (Tarzan's Daughter, Hindi, 1938), which was a commercial success and was distributed overseas, including Australia.[34] Like the Pancholis, the Shoreys made both Punjabi and Hindi films in Lahore. These included *Khooni Khanjar* (Bloody Knife, Hindi, 1935), *Sohni Mahiwal* (Punjabi, 1940), *Dulla Bhatti* (Punjabi, 1940), *Himmat* (Courage, Hindi, 1941), *Mangti* (The Beggar Girl, Punjabi, 1942) *Koyal* (Nightingale, Punjabi, 1944) and *Shalimar* (Hindi, 1946). *Dulla Bhatti* and *Sohni Mahiwal* were adaptations of Punjabi folklores. Actress Ragini recalls being discovered by Roshal Lal Shorey, her friend's father who came to her house to recruit for *Dulla Bhatti*, echoing the local talent-scouting tactics of Pancholi.[35] Described as the 'tragedy of a beggar girl and the comedy of her romance', *Mangti* launched Mumtaz Shanti as an actress who would then be hired immediately by the studio Bombay Talkies. The next film *Shalimar* was started at the Shorey studio in Lahore and completed at the Rajkamal Kalamandir studios in Bombay. The three lead actors, Al-Nasir, Begum Para and Chandramohan, were taken from Bombay to Lahore for the film. Presented as the 'dilemma of jealousy' between two sisters who love the same man, the highlight of *Shalimar* was the humane sense of justice of Empress Nurjahan, which according to the the *Sunday Tribune* prevented it from becoming a tragedy.[36] A self-consciously trite dilemma, the synopsis of *Shalimar* suggests Lahore films' ironic relationship with the high-budget historical romances of Bombay, such as *Shahjehan* (1946) or *Pukar* (The Call, 1939), where the judicial system of an emperor briefly threatened by a crisis is restored at the end. *Shalimar's* tangential and most likely parodic rendition of a historical romance invests in an empress (and not an emperor) and positions romance as a source of crisis and not the resolution. Similarly, *Mangti* was not the only film of 1942 dealing with a penurious girl's romance. *Chowranghee* (1942), an adaptation of George Bernard Shaw's *Pygmalion* (1912), from the new toasts of Bombay, the Fazli Brothers, was the other one and could have been a possible reference or thematic competitor. And like the Pancholis, the Shoreys too regularly publicised their studio activities in the local dailies, at times emphasizing technical innovations – for instance, the underwater cinematography in *Shalimar* – and at others their social commitment – for instance, the desirous vision of widow-remarriage-informing *Khamosh Nigahein* (Silent Eyes).[37]

In 1946, the Shorey studio received its first major setback when a fire broke out on its premises on 24 August, reportedly due to a faulty electric fuse. The loss of equipment and buildings was estimated at several lakh rupees. Additionally, two films under production were lost to the fire. These were *Khamosh Nigahein*, directed by I. S. Johar, and *Rut Rangili* (A Colourful Season), actress Meena Shorey's first film with producer-director Roop K. Shorey.[38] While the Shorey studios made a 'phoenix-like recovery', the incident led to concerned debates in the local press over the location of film studios. Public resentment was reported at the reconstruction of the studio at its old location, McLeod Road, which was a residential locality close to the walled city.[39] The dangers of a film studio with its inflammable nitrates were acutely felt, and the city corporation authorities were urged to disallow the building of studios within the city limits. Following this incident, the Lahore Municipality laid down the regulation that all city studios were to be located outside the limits of old Lahore.[40]

It is remarkable, if not slightly suspect, how quickly the new Shorey studios 'emerged in greater glory' in September 1946 on Multan Road, part of greater Lahore at that time.[41] This is the area where later studios of Pakistan like Evernew and Bari came to be built. If the Shoreys had any plans to rebuild on the old site, the resistance of the local inhabitants and the new municipal laws would have made it a challenging task. Spread over an area of 150 *kanal*[42] of land, the amenities at the new Shorey studios were reportedly the largest in the East. Around this time, Roop Shorey had also made a trip to the United States, procuring the latest equipment for his ambitious studio. The Shoreys announced not just technical self-sufficiency but also the simultaneous shooting of six films in the autumn of 1946. By November these included *Humari Galiyan* (Our Alleys), to be directed by Majnu, and *Neela Parbat* (Blue Mountain), by the senior Shorey. It was reported that the new equipment would also make possible the parallel reshooting of the films stalled due to the fire. The famed imported equipment, as Meena Shorey recounts in her memoir, was in its sale packaging,[43] some of it unopened, when the new Shorey studio was attacked as 'Hindu property' in the partition riots in the summer of 1947 and set on fire, forcing the Shoreys out of Lahore.

The loss of Lahore's brief revival to partition needs to be highlighted, not only to dovetail with the challenging origins of the film industry in Pakistan but to consider the possibilities the city was poised for in terms of film style and production investment. Based on extant films and traces of plots, arguably a low-on-capital Lahore was privileging a parodic relationship with Bombay products, while innovating in terms of narrative and technique, often using facilities situated in Bombay. The Shoreys in particular infused the jocular spirit of the city in their films. The itinerant freelancer made possible by a weakened studio system allowed Lahore to briefly enter the all-India circuit largely dominated by Bombay and to meet capital with reflexive irony.

An All-India Film from Lahore

During the war years, the term 'all-India film' was frequently used to signal a national taxonomy for films produced in colonial India. This category was made coherent through the cartographic representations of undivided India, claiming connection between the on-screen and off-screen demography and linking film themes, often tenuously, to matters of 'national importance'. Produced just before the strict film licensing of the war years came into effect, *Khandaan* (Lineage, Urdu, 1942) was the second 'all-India film' of the Punjab-based Pancholi Art Pictures.[44] For a cinephilic South Asian film history, *Khandaan* is notable for several reasons. One of the rare films from pre-partition Lahore to have survived, it was one of singing star Noorjahan's earliest successes, starred arch-villain Pran in a rare role as the romantic lead and was among the earliest surviving Muslim social. Yet what if, faced with the absence of other revelatory material on the relationship between the film cities of Bombay and Lahore, *Khandaan* might also provide Lahore's cinematic comment on Bombay and its privileged position in the business of cinema? The opening sequence of the film, featuring 'royal personages' in an ornamental garden, strongly invites such a reading. Both the studio film and its publicity gesture towards the relationship between film cities and film genres, revealing the 'national' pressures on film enterprise in the 1940s. Through a reading of the interplay between the on- and off-screen images and stories that underlie the film,[45] including the vision and visuals of nation, I argue that a historically contextualised approach to the film draws attention to the problem introduced by partition to national film categorisation.

Khandaan opens with the song 'Ud Ja Panchi, Ud Ja' (Fly Away Bird, Fly Away) in which actress Noorjahan in royal finery enjoins a dove to fly free (Figure 1.1a). The leading man Pran materialises out of an overgrown shrubbery (Figure 1.1b) and asks 'Kya Noorjahan ga rahin hain'? (Is that Noorjahan singing?), in a double allusion to the historical character and the singing star.

He then joins in the love duet confirming that the emerging singing sensation of the 1940s was indeed playing her Mughal namesake, Empress Nurjahan. Gazing longingly at each other, the two sing not sweet nothings but lofty ideals.

> *Main pyar ka Kaba[46] banu, main husn ka mandir*
> *Phir Hind ko hum prem ka paigham sunaein*
> *Roothi hui praja ko hum phir se manaywein*
> *Inasan ko insan se azaad karayein*

> I become the Mecca of love, I the temple of beauty
> To free humans from the clutches of their fellow humans
> Then we narrate the message of love to India
> Let us persuade our piqued subjects once again

Here, in a moment of direct address within the song (Figure 1.1c), the actors are framed together articulating the nationalist vision, one that has routinely imagined India as the (golden) bird in imperial captivity. However, what is available on the screen is not a bird in cage but a free bird perched on Noorjahan's hands, unable to flutter until it is literally thrown upwards out of the frame. Thinking along with the film, one could argue that to fly, the bird needs the wings of oneness as evident in the stress on 'Hindu–Muslim unity', evoked through 'Kaba' and *mandir*. The song ends, and the royal couple take a leisurely stroll through the garden, when a sonorous off-screen voice intrudes. A hoary commoner appears to walk towards the lovers, singing at them in response (Figure 1.1d). In a sudden character switch from benevolent rulers to affronted royalty, the queen draws a pistol from her gown and shoots at the passer-by. Musically intoned, the mood switches from a 'historical romance' to the mildly comic, and the passer-by stands transfixed instead of collapsing on the ground. The royal act is over, and the hoary intruder turns out to be a young girl with a shrill voice who shouts at her co-players, refusing to collapse at the round of a fake pistol (Figure 1.1e). The 'king' and the 'queen' laugh, accepting the abrupt end of their Mughal performance. When the young girl calls it an unfair game, where the young lovers reserve royal roles for themselves while she is reduced to a passer-by with a 'billy goat beard', the 'queen' placates her by pointing out that 'they are after all just playing' (Figure 1.1f).

Figure 1.1a Queen Nurjahan enjoining the dove to fly free
Source: Screenshot from *Khandaan* (1942, VCD, Eagle).

Figure 1.1b King Jahangir making an appearance
Source: Screenshot from *Khandaan* (1942, VCD, Eagle).

Figure 1.1c The King and the Queen directly addressing the camera
Source: Screenshot from *Khandaan* (1942, VCD, Eagle).

Figure 1.1d The sudden appearance of the commoner in the 'royal' garden
Source: Screenshot from *Khandaan* (1942, VCD, Eagle).

Figure 1.1e The revelation of the commoner as a young girl who throws off her wig and fake beard
Source: Screenshot from *Khandaan* (1942, VCD, Eagle).

Figure 1.1f The elder sister, playing the queen, placating her younger sister
Source: Screenshot from *Khandaan* (1942, VCD, Eagle).

I propose that *Khandaan*'s opening is not only self-reflexive but also a parodic reference to a Bombay film, *Pukar* (The Call, 1939, dir. Sohrab Modi), released three years before *Khandaan*, and signals a crucial shift in film genres. Set in the Mughal past of the region, the 'historical romance' *Pukar* imagined a world more just than the colonial present.[47] Here, the self-righteous justice of the Mughal emperor Jahangir is put to severe test when his beloved wife, Nurjahan, accidently kills a washerman. Spoofing in particular the murdering queen of *Pukar*, *Khandaan*'s Noorjahan wears a crown similar to the one donned by the *pari chehera* (fairy faced) Bombay star Naseem. By foregrounding its small-scale production facilities, limited to a four-minute recreation of the historical romance and its material constraints implicit in imitative crowns, fake firearms and billy-goat-beard wigs, *Khandaan*, through its material poverty, lays bare the subterfuge of an extravagant film genre. More suggestive is the parallel drawn with play-activities, with an experimental playfulness inherent in film-making in Lahore at this time. At the heart of the sequence is also the vexing matter of film reception during these years. The institutions of film criticism and film policy in late colonial India were busy constructing the Indian viewer as a gullible commoner in whom the grand acts and on-screen gestures could produce tangible effects. The girl-posing-as-the-poor-commoner thus underscored the artifice of this imagined spectator. After a send-up of the historical romance within this sequence, *Khandaan* reveals the other genre it draws on, the Muslim social investing it with realism as well as political maturity, as opposed to the childlike playfulness of the opening sequence.

It has been argued in the instance of another early-1940s studio film from Bombay – *Kismet* – that 'pleasure and meaning in the cinematic experience is strongly self-referential rather than merely referring to the extra cinematic.'[48] *Khandaan*'s self-referentiality is not limited to its ironic distance from Bombay but also elaborates the off-centre film entrepreneurship of Lahore, of which it was a product. While *Khandaan* was independent director Shaukat Hussain Rizvi's directorial debut, its Lahore provenance was strongly emphasised by visual references to Pancholi Art Pictures' previous film. *Khazanchi*, also an 'all-India' success. The plotline of *Khazanchi* follows a family's ignominy and social ostracism after the father gets falsely implicated in the murder of a woman performer. The accusation is abrogated only when his innocence is established in the court of law. *Khandaan*, on the other hand, follows the continuing shadow on a family lineage, when the patriarch murders his mistress and is sentenced to life for the crime. Thus, as part of the studio oeuvre, *Khandaan* revisits the dilemmas of *Khazanchi* through a morally relativised subjectivity. It carries the cinematic echoes of the earlier Pancholi film in scenes at the doorstep of the lawyer-friend's house, where an aged and unkempt Akbar arrives, recalling the return of the accused father in *Khazanchi*, as well as in the spatial exposition of the hotel as the site of moral ambiguity, a place away from the home. The hotel in both *Khandaan* and *Khazanchi* is the urban site of ruse, blackmail, dalliances and murders.

There were a number of ways in which both films referenced – and implicitly commented on – the real-life world of the Lahore film business. The negative associations of a lodging space that was crucial not only for itinerant film personnel of pre-partition India but also for a film centre like Lahore that contracted freelancing actors from Bombay and Calcutta for individual films is striking. Arriving in Lahore from Calcutta to direct *Khandaan* at Pancholi Art Pictures, Shaukat Hussain Rizvi first moved into Hotel Elphinstone and then Hotel Mansarover.[49] Arriving in Bombay from Calcutta in the late 1930s, scriptwriter Agha Jani Kashmiri moved into an expensive hotel pretending to be a 'film hero' hired by the Ranjit film company and decamped when he could not pay the bills.[50] However, in what can be read as yet another reference in *Khandaan* to film-making in Lahore, the main source of anxiety at the hotel are not men but public women, namely the figure of the 'visiting actress'. Referencing a performative institution closely related to cinema, where many women had received training as courtesans or as singing women, the film communicates popular anxieties of the time around performing women. *Khandaan*'s lead actress, Noorjahan, too hailed from a family of *mughaniyas* (singers), and the group 'Baby Noorjahan and party' had gained fame for their travelling stage performances.[51]

In *Khandaan*, Miss Nargis (Manorama) is a stage actress who arrives in the city on a theatre tour but receives money to ensnare the young Anwar (Pran). Her arrival is a matter of public knowledge and anticipation, evident in Anwar's immediate and enthusiastic recognition. In the off-screen world, this public knowledge was created through publicity in Lahore newspapers and magazines in the 1940s, which often featured 'visiting stars' from another city, especially Bombay. For instance, the city newspaper *The Tribune* enthusiastically reported on actress Shanta Apte's arrival in early 1942 for *Zamindar*, the Pancholis' next film after *Khandaan*, and highlighted the attractive remuneration for the actress. Even for *Khazanchi*, the Pancholis engaged actress Ramola from the Calcutta film company, Film Corporation of India. A comment on the film actress' ability to swing profitable transactions with the studio can in turn be read into *Khandaan* in the bargain that Anwar's father wishes to strike by paying off Miss Nargis. The two conduct an extended negotiation between what he can offer and what she demands, which eventually falls through. To underscore the bittersweet dependence of the Lahore studio on 'visiting actresses', I am tempted to seize on another news nugget on Apte, who in mid-1942 was taken to court by the Pancholis claiming damages for a breach of contract for *Zamindar*. In the case of Apte, the Pancholis reached an agreement with the 'visiting actress', whereas in *Khandaan* Miss Nargis is killed off in a violent scuffle like her forerunner in *Khazanchi*.

Despite these distractions of the local, *Khandaan*'s ambitions were 'all-Indian' as is amply evident in its publicity (Figure 1.2). It is possible to read this as the anxiety of a Lahore studio regarding its circulation in the face of the technical and material superiority of Bombay. However, as the Pancholis also commanded an extensive

Figure 1.2   The cartographic representation of Pancholi Studio's all-India ambitions
Source: Filmindia, January 1942, 22.

distribution and exhibition network, such claims to the 'national market', which was
in essence the colonial subcontinent, may equally be read as evidence of the Lahore
studio's entrepreneurial muscle, joining in the 'contest for power' in the 1940s.[52]
The film's Punjab provenance became a crucial highlight of the campaign, where
in one instance the Pancholi lens literally magnified the regional into the national
(Figure 1.3). This unfurling of the local onto a nationwide scale is also evident in
the common practice of synchronising film publicity with the war propaganda of
the colonial state. In the instance of *Zamindar*, the film advertisement asked the
readers to do their bit to help win the war by travelling only when they must, giving
the journey undertaken by the hero of the film an exceptional spin. Underlining its
ambivalent relationship with colonial propaganda, undoubtedly motivated by the
allocation of restricted film stock, the advertisement of the Lahore film made the
'sweetie' by the hero's side into a cheeky case of 'must travel' (Figure 1.4).

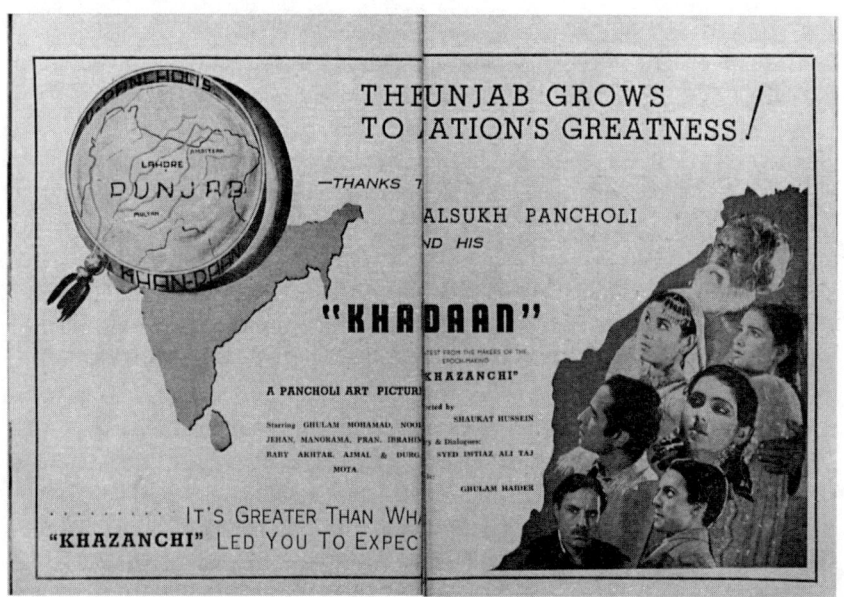

Figure 1.3   Advertisement reading 'The Punjab Grows to a Nation's Greatness! – thanks to Dalsukh Pancholi and his *Khandaan*'
Source: *Filmindia*, April 1942, 28–29.

Figure 1.4   Film publicity aligned with the colonial state's war propaganda
Source: *Filmindia*, August 1942, 14.

What is the significance of an all-India film made in Lahore? Arguably, the representational claim involved in an 'all-India film' was similar to the contest evolving in the political realm between the All-India Muslim League (hereafter, Muslim League) and the Congress. Punjab politics, however, was dominated by 'the cross-communal Unionist party' of landlords, which until 1947 championed the political vision of a 'United Punjab within a decentralized federal India', a tendency that underpins regional exceptionalism of *Khandaan*'s publicity.[53] This correspondence of cinematic imagination with the political realm thus imagines the film market as an electoral space and an arena onto which the exercise of universal franchise, albeit a mutated one, could be displaced until its realisation in the independent nation state.[54] As a film trade category, 'all-India film' signifies an attempt to map 'the national' onto the representational space of the film narratives, a claim which could be evidenced through revenues across a wide but limited territory. In the ongoing aspiration, hardly limited to film narratives and intensely evident in other performative arts, certain themes appear to have gained more 'all-Indian' traction than others. One of these was 'Hindu–Muslim unity', earning in many instances tax-free status and endorsement by public figures and the nationalist press. The theme appears as an important film-making resource in the late 1930s and 1940s, realised differently across different genres and already noted in *Khandaan*'s opening sequence. Suggesting that the masquerade of Mughal historicals was outworn in this regard, *Khandaan* offers within its Muslim social genre an innovative contemporary image of interfaith conviviality. Akbar, who had been serving a life term for murder, is amongst the prisoners pardoned on the occasion of the king's (George VI) coronation. He goes to his old friend and lawyer Ram's house to ask after his only son, who has left the city. Reunited after decades, Akbar and Ram, names pregnant with political significance, embrace spiritedly in a tableau containing a sacred Hindu image in the centre background. As a source of comfort for Ram, allaying anxieties of ritual pollution, and a reminder of Akbar's difference, the space of the communal embrace is sacred and not secular (Figure 1.5).[55] As someone outside the principal line of descent, which constitutes the core dilemma of the film, Ram expedites the damaged father–son relationship into a recuperative trajectory. It is a delicate balancing act between knowledge and its withholding, orchestrated by the family well-wisher, Ram, which reinforces the customary order through which matters of ancestry can come to terms with. The strong mediating role of a Hindu character in a genre that otherwise works out the aspirations of Muslim independence (see Chapter 2) is constituted in this film from the Muslim-majority province where the Unionist Party's 'United Punjab' held sway. Made at a time of increased yet uneasy collaboration between the Unionist Party and the Muslim League,[56] *Khandaan* remains singular in representing a convivial, multicultural social order where 'the Punjab grows to a nation's greatness', no less by offering federalism as a national template – one that combined the accommodation of an unmarked social film with the particularity of Muslim representation. Such a sensibility and ethos are missing from the Muslim social genre films produced in pre-partition Bombay, in post-partition India and in the Urdu films in Pakistan after independence. *Khandaan* proved to be a commercial success across film territories in undivided India, betokened by a surviving photograph of its silver jubilee celebrations (Figure 1.6).

Figure 1.5   Ram and Akbar embracing each other
Source: Screenshot from *Khandaan* (1942, VCD, Eagle).

Figure 1.6   'Silver Jubilee' celebrations of *Khandaan*, Lahore, 1942
Source: Hersh Pancholi, Mumbai.

I will conclude this examination of *Khandaan* by returning to its significance. With the strong presence of the nation within its trade and thematic horizons, *Khandaan* poses a delicious problem of categorisation. While it shares the concerns and motifs of Muslim socials of the 1940s, and therefore participates in the genre, its publicity as the 'all-India film' significantly denies any particularity. As a self-professed all-India film, it certainly cannot be termed 'prenational' unless we decidedly privilege nations that came to be over the ones that were imagined. Yet made in pre-partition Lahore, it is neither Indian nor Pakistani. The production team was also equally divided after partition: studio owner and producer Dalsukh Pancholi, actor Pran and actress Manorama moved to India, while director Shaukat Hussain Rizvi, actress Noorjahan, music director Ghulam Haider and writer Imtiaz Ali Taj opted for Pakistan. Paralleling the extra-cinematic experience, the film could offer a preliminary insight into the gains and losses of the division. The gains are the national cinemas of the subcontinent, while the loss is the all-India film enterprise as a territorial market and a provincially differentiated resource.[57] By resources here I mean the available templates of communal coexistence and entrepreneurial ease of the united Punjab province, one that was represented and secured by the ascendancy of the cross-communal Unionist Party until 1947. Beyond everything, as an all-India film of Lahore, Pancholi's *Khandaan* is a cultural testament to nation as both powerful and incomprehensible in a partition that was already in progress. In the following chapter, we move to the high noon of nationalisms in Bombay in the 1940s.

Notes

1   *Mahurat* is the auspicious ceremony that marks the commencement of a film's production, incorporating features from Hindu ritual worship.

2   *Roop Rekha* was most likely abandoned as a film project. Due to partition disturbances, it never got completed.

3   'Cinema Studios in Lahore', *The Tribune*, 31 January 1947, 8.

4   Ian Talbott, *Divided Cities* (Oxford: Oxford University Press, 2006), 6.

5   Explaining the expansion of the Bombay industry into a transregional context, Kaushik Bhaumik locates the high point of the Punjab film industry in 1931 and its collapse by 1933 as the film people in Punjab had been absorbed by Bombay. Kaushik Bhaumik, 'The Emergence of the Bombay Film Industry, 1913–1936' (PhD diss., University of Oxford, 2001), 125.

6   Erik Barnouw and S. Krishnaswamy, *Indian Film* (New York: Oxford University Press, 1980), 99.

7   Film Industry in Pakistan (Lahore: Board of Economic Enquiry, Punjab, 1957), 11.

8   Barnouw and Krishnaswamy discuss the instability of film production units, especially during the war years. Barnouw and Krishnaswamy, *Indian Film*, 128.

9   Contents of the letter are courtesy of Hersh Pancholi, Mumbai, India, August 2013.

10 Personal interview with Hersh Pancholi and family, Mumbai, India, August 2013.

11 Bunny Reuben, *And Pran: A Biography* (New Delhi: Harper Collins, 2005), 25.

12   Ibid.

13   Ibid., 37.

14   Pran Neville, *Lahore: A Sentimental Journey* (New Delhi: Penguin Books, 2006), 174.

15   Jankidas Mehra, *My Misadventures in Filmland* (New Delhi: Newman Group of Publishers, 1980), 36–40.

16   *Khazanchi* was publicised as starring the World Olympic Champion Cyclist. Advertisement reprinted in ibid., 40.

17   Ibid., 39.

18   Balraj Sahni, *An Autobiography*, trans. Ramesh Deshpande (New Delhi: Hind Pocket Books, 1979), 57.

19   Ibid., 58.

20   Ibid.

21   Advertisement, *Filmindia*, August 1941, 20.

22   Shaukat Hussain Rizvi, *Noorjahan aur Main* (Lahore: Atish Feshan Publications, 1984), 43.

23   The newspaper reports used the word 'Hindustani'. For instance, 'Shanta Apte Arrived in Lahore Last Week to Work on Pancholi's Next Hindustani Film "Zamindar"', *The Tribune*, January 21, 1942.

24   'India's Youngest Director Believes in Hard Work!' *Sunday Tribune*, January 13, 1946, 8.

25   'News from Indian Studios', *The Tribune*, 3 September 1942.

26   *The Tribune*, 21 January 1942.

27   Ibid.

28   'Shanta Apte and Dalsukh Pancholi', *Filmindia*, July 1942, 15.

29   'Shehr se Door: A Boring Hotchpotch from Punjab', *Filmindia*, March 1947, 60.

30   'Shehr se Dur: A Girl Meets Girl Story', *Motion Picture Magazine*, March 1947, 85.

31   *The Tribune*, March 23, 1947.

32   Rewashankar Pancholi passed away in 1942 and his sons joined Dalsukh in the business.

33   'Roshan Lal Shorey: He Set the Newsreel Rolling', *Filmfare*, 15 January 1971, 57.

34   This could be *Tarzan ki Beti* produced by Calcutta-based Aurora, which was distributed internationally across the Middle East and Southeast Asia. Ranita Chatterjee, 'Journeys in and beyond the City: Cinema in Calcutta 1897–1939' (PhD diss., University of Westminster, 2011).

35   'Ragini', in *Out of Date*, ed. Munir Ahmed (Lahore: Atish Feshan Publications, 1986), 35.

36   *Sunday Tribune*, 7 April 1946, 6.

37   'Sardar Vallabhbhai Patel and Nawab Liaquat Khan recently called upon the Indian Film Industry to turn its entertainment wheels from mere commercialism to promoting social welfare. The admonition has been heeded by I.S. Johar in his "Khamosh Nigahein", which is in full shooting blast in the Shorey Studios.' *Sunday Tribune*, 24 February 1946, 7.

38   'Shorey Pictures Premises Get Gutted', *The Tribune*, 25 August 1946, 3.

39   'Move to Reconstruct Film Studio on McLeod Road: Resentment among Public', *Sunday Tribune*, 15 December 1946.

40   'Cinema Studios in Lahore', *Sunday Tribune*, 24 November 1946.

41   The news of the new studio came within two weeks of the fire. 'Shorey Studios Arise Again', *Sunday Tribune*, 8 September 1946.

42   One *kanal* unit area is one-eighth of an acre.

43   'Meena Shorey' in *Out of Date*, ed. Munir Ahmed (Lahore: Atish Feshan Publications, 1986).

44   The industrial category of the 'all-India film' referred to films that could transcend regional markets and ensure widest possible revenue. The North Indian Hindi–Urdu speaking belts offered one such market, which along with the nationalist ascendancy of Hindi and Urdu meant that predominantly these films passed off as all-India films.

45   Rosie Thomas discusses the intertextual and complex processes of reading meaning derived from audiences' knowledge of other films, books and gossip. Rosie Thomas, 'Sanctity and Scandal: The Mythologization of Mother India', *Quarterly Review of Film and Video* 11, no. 3 (1989): 11–30.

46   Ka'ba is Islam's most sacred site, located in Mecca.

47   Priya Jaikumar. *Cinema at the End of Empire: A Politics of Transition in Britain and India* (Durham: Duke University Press, 2006), 211.

48   Ravi Vasudevan, 'The Cultural Space of a Film Narrative: Interpreting "Kismet" (Bombay Talkies)', *Indian Economic and Social History Review* 28, no. 2 (1991): 171–183.

49   Rizvi, *Noorjahan aur Main*, 44.

50   Agha Jani Kashmiri, *Saher Hone Tak* (Delhi: Imperial Press, 1965), 174.

51   The serialised biography of Noorjahan published in the *Nigar Weekly* in 1953 describes Noorjahan's family as *mughaniya* and states that many courtesans (*tawaif*) joined in her birth celebrations in Kasur. 'Noorjahan Ki Kahani', *Nigar Weekly*, October 1953.

52   Vasudevan, 'The Cultural Space of a Film Narrative', 173.

53   For a discussion of the way the Punjab Unionist Party limited the influence of the Muslim League separatism in Punjab, see Ian Talbot, *Khizr Tiwana: The Punjab Unionist Party and the Partition of India* (Routledge: Oxon, 2013), 1.

54   This may also be cyclically juxtaposed with Tejaswini Ganti's observation for the historical turn of neoliberalism, where middle-class citizenship is reinvented as an exercise in buying. See Tejaswini Ganti, *Producing Bollywood: Inside the Contemporary Hindi Film Industry* (Durham, NC: Duke University Press, 2012), 313–314.

55   One could also compare this to another image of conviviality in the opening sequence of Pune-based Prabhat Studio's *Shejari* (1940), where the mutual regard of communities is essential to the observance of personal religion, whereas in *Khandaan* a personal religious order is the *sine qua non* of mutual accommodation.

56   In October 1937, Sikandar Hayat Khan, the leader of the Unionist Party, signed a pact with Mohammad Ali Jinnah, according to which all members of the Unionist Party would become members of the Muslim League. For a detailed discussion of this pact and its implications, see Nevil Osman, 'Dancing with the Enemy: Sikandar Hayat Khan, Jinnah and the Vexed Question of Pakistan in a Punjabi Unionist Context', in *Muslims against the Muslim League*, ed. Ali Usman Qasmi and Megan Robb, 311–337 (Delhi: Cambridge University Press, 2017).

57   The loss of a territorial market may not be absolute with the on–off circulation of Indian films in Pakistan and an occasional circulation of Pakistani films in India since 2006.

PART 1

THE SECULAR STANCE
OF BOMBAY

2 'Hindu Camera, Muslim Microphone'

A Periodical and Two Memoirs

A British Quaker and partition relief worker in India during the late 1940s, Richard Symonds would often find himself in the company of Congress leaders and other political dignitaries. Once he had the occasion to meet someone from a different profession at the house of R. K. Nehru during the end-months of 1947.[1]

> In their [Nehrus'] house I met a Bombay film director who said that all Muslims had been squeezed out of the industry. This was easily done, as they were dependent on Hindu capitalists.[2]

Others too have referred to this 'squeezing out' – for example, short story writer Saadat Hasan Manto in his account of the Bombay Talkies where the studio owners received threatening letters against the retention of Muslim personnel.[3] The expulsive aspect of partition palpable in film-making processes suggests that political polarisation also marked cultural production at this time. The vexing question of 'how Muslims fared' in the Bombay film enterprise is one that arises repeatedly and is normally settled by citing the 'secular stance' of the film industry,[4] which was a heterogeneous space and where Muslims thrived as compared to other areas. The political fissures within the mainstream Mumbai film industry evident in the last six years, with many artistes and producers publicly issuing statements and making appearances that serve the Hindu nationalist ideology of the government,[5] allow us to historically better understand the polarisation that accompanied partition. More than ever before, there is a need to examine the time when many above-the-line Muslim film personnel left Bombay (that is, between 1947 and 1957).[6] This chapter analyses the emergence of this 'secular stance' and its relationship with film migration at the time of partition. In other words, how was a consensus around secularism built (if it was), given that the film industry did not have a sovereign government before partition and even afterwards, and when it was not a nationalised entity? Inferring from Priya Jaikumar's observation that 'conflicts internal to nationalism were part of the Indian film industry's formative reality',[7] this chapter attempts to map out the Bombay film industry as a terrain of competing interests and conflicts.

The challenge for a project that seeks to ascertain whether the Bombay film conglomerate became Muslim-wary at the time of partition lies in locating exactly how prejudice acquires functionality and force. Do partisan tendencies bear upon interpersonal interactions of professionals involving structures of capital, as Symonds suggests, or at the level of film representation? Which political interests were accommodated in the name of audience interests through the regulatory mechanisms of subsidies and censorship? What motivated film publicity and journalism in managing competing ideas of national interest at the time of impending nations? If pursued doggedly, the query risks becoming an exercise in essentialist characterisations; on the other hand, if not discussed, a crucial history of the Bombay film enterprise is repressed. The challenge is doubled as we visit this past at a time when even the secular stance has been done away with,[8] making the historian nostalgic even for an imperfect religious syncretism. For what it is worth, one can say that the Bombay film enterprise, like other spaces in India at that time,[9] did alienate many prominent Muslim film personnel, especially those who were public in declaring their support for the political abstraction of Pakistan. However, it must be said at the very outset of this chapter that not all Muslims were alienated from the industry, some never left Bombay and quite a few returned to the industry after a brief period spent in Pakistan. What I am pursuing here is not a simplistic claim of an 'anti-Muslim prejudice', for Bombay film industry's secular image could not have and certainly did not emerge by being 'anti-Muslim'. However, the secular image was constituted through an 'anti-Pakistan' discourse, and within this schema, the Muslim personnel could be engaged, patronised and celebrated as long as they remained distant from Muslim nationalism or Pakistan.

Therefore, instead of asking 'how Muslims fared', this part pursues how Muslim nationalism fared and thematically figured in the all-India film enterprise. Through a juxtaposition of partisan predilections in the Bombay film enterprise, communicating with other production centres such as Lahore and Calcutta in the 1940s, I examine political interests from three different vantage points. First among these is *Filmindia*, the leading film magazine in English of the 1940s, founded and edited by Baburao Patel. The life narratives of two Muslim film-makers, Shaukat Hussain Rizvi and M. Luqman, recorded four decades after they migrated from Bombay to Lahore, constitute the second vantage point. Finally, Prithvi Theatre, founded in 1944 by Prithviraj Kapoor, a leading actor of the Bombay film industry, and its performances reveal the ascendancy of secular nationalism in India

(Chapter 3). The creative interventions of these men stand at the cusp between their individual personalities and public consumption. While these can be seen as fuelled by three competitive nationalisms – Hindu nationalism, Muslim nationalism and secular nationalism, respectively – they in turn reinterpret and provide tangible shape to three sets of convictions.

The secular stance of the Bombay film industry is a product of the cultural ascendency in the 1940s of secular nationalism, also referred to as 'Indian nationalism' or 'the Indian ideology',[10] which stood in opposition to both communalism and colonialism. As a colonial term that presumes 'irreconcilable antagonism between homogenous Hindu and Muslim communities',[11] communalism 'calls for government by a modern, rational, third party'.[12] Secular nationalism, as represented by the Indian National Congress, however preferred to see 'communalism' as a story of colonial manipulation, popularly known as the policy of 'divide and rule', and sought to counter this challenge by inculcating the crucial ideal of secularism within rationality. Muslim nationalism, as represented by the Muslim League demanding either a decentralised state or a confession-based partition, was then seen as one face of communalism. The other was Hindu nationalism, best represented by the Hindu Mahasabha and the Rashtriya Swayamsevak Sangh (RSS), which operated on the 'morally overriding claim of nativism',[13] where India was held as the 'land of Hindus alone and Muslims were enemies, anti-national and traitors'.[14] The secular nationalists saw all forms of communalism as doomed from the start, including the idea of Pakistan, propelled as it was by Muslim nationalism. Not only was communalism ill-fated, but also, as Devji argues, it could not be treated as a political question because it was viewed as an unnatural departure from a universal or European ideal.[15] Signifying a deep political insecurity of a numerically smaller community, Muslim nationalism was seen by Indian nationalism as a social problem, namely that of Hindu–Muslim relations. Cast in narrow communal terms, the quest for the protection of Muslim rights was identified as 'illnesses, which have to be excised: difficulties not amenable to discussion because they are not rational in the first place'.[16]

Of the sources referred to, *Filmindia* and the performances of the Prithvi Theatre (Chapter 3) are preoccupied with 'communalism'. The memoirs of two migrant, above-the-line film personnel from Bombay, which in the schema of the other two qualify as communal voices, use the Urdu equivalents of the word 'prejudice' to denote majoritarian procedures. The chronic fixation with 'communalism' in *Filmindia* and Prithvi Theatre's praxis must be attended to, not to reify it as a conceptual category but to understand the struggle of cultural hierarchy and control of production. The memoirs of Pakistani film-makers provide us with the narratives of exclusions and contestation, and retrospectively defend a separate nation for British-Indian Muslims.

The Periodical *Filmindia*, 1940–1952

By the 1930s, Bombay cinema had inspired a growth in film journalism, and film critics came to mediate closer relations between the industry and its audiences,[17] thus emerging as the authoritative voice in setting forth the terms of engagement with cinema. *Filmindia* was an English-language film periodical – started in 1935 in Bombay – that became increasingly popular in the 1940s. To a large extent *Filmindia* owed its success and comparative longevity to its responsiveness to representational politics and providing an ideological reading of films. One of the earliest successes of the monthly magazine was a forceful campaign against the so-called empire films, which continues to exert tonal pressures on more recent deliberations on empire cinema.[18]

A film compendium published from Lahore in 1946 attributed *Filmindia*'s success to 'his relentless but sometimes malicious propaganda'.[19] The 'his' referred to the founding editor of the publication, Baburao Patel, who controlled the content, tone and agenda of the journal.[20] While *Filmindia* has been used as an archival source for film cultures of this period, it has not received an unqualified endorsement by film historians. Patel's all-pervasive 'poisonous pen' has made film historians wary, especially since the publication has the dubious distinction of an anti-Muslim prose, which ideologically shares ground with modern Hindu nationalism.[21] However, as Bhaskar Sarkar aptly argues, to reject *Filmindia* as an organ of Patel's 'politically partisan views'[22] – in favour of, for instance, *Filmfare*, which concurred with the hegemonic nationalist project – ends up making rabid sentiments 'the troubling subterranean unthought of the society'.[23] Yet despite his urgent call for the need to chart the 'evolution of factional rhetoric', Sarkar's own work focuses on a short span in *Filmindia* between 1947 and 1952 and ignores the evolution of *Filmindia* itself. Even though founded in 1935, the periodical enjoyed immense popularity through the 1940s and the 1950s, with the curtains finally falling in 1961.

A study of *Filmindia* over a decade reveals not only the changing tonality of the periodical but also the profitable marketability of vituperative prose. Arguably, the value of *Filmindia* lies in its troubling bias and incendiary prose. Even if it were to merely mirror the editor's partisan views, which were certainly not restricted to or emanated from him but had a wider ideological resonance, it offers a discourse espousing a supremacist nativism, which could appropriate secular nationalism as and when the situation demanded. The visual aesthetic and rhetoric of the magazine are characteristic of its diatribe, marked by humour, anger and loquacity. The appearance of cartoons in the periodical from the 1950s onwards made the rabid words more palatable. Many of these were drawn by none other than Bal Thackeray, who would later on become the leader of the Shiv Sena, the militant Maharashtrian chauvinist movement. In its attempts to make cinema relevant to Indians, *Filmindia* was ingenious in making cinema and those involved in its production relevant to the most pressing question of the decade: the independence of the subcontinent. In this regard, the film periodical is a crucial indicator of the insecurities that fed film culture and film migration of the partition decade. The journal by the mid-1940s had acquired an anti-Muslim image. Film-maker and writer Khwaja Ahmad Abbas, once a contributor to *Filmindia* and later a regular target of Patel's barbs in the magazine, remembers how he was invited over to a Muslim producers' tête-à-tête sometime in late 1939 or early 1940. There Abbas was asked to start a paper to rival *Filmindia*, which was allegedly pursuing a pro-Hindu policy. A committed communist, Abbas not only declined the Muslim lobby's offers but went on to 'expose the communal game in the (very) pages of *Filmindia*'.[24] Kaushik Bhaumik's study of the emergence of the Bombay film industry acknowledges 'indications that Muslims were *actively marginalized* in the years leading up to Partition'.[25] In particular, Bhaumik insists on the possible role that Patel played in the *betrayal* and *ousting* of many a Muslim film artiste. The following analysis will examine the discursive shape of *active marginalisation*, *betrayal* and *ousting*. Indeed, *Filmindia* could pursue extreme vendettas in its pages, but the periodical was a complex cultural product that strongly mediated a collective consensus, as gleaned in its profitable circulation, readers' mail, advertisements targeted at both consumers and the industry, endorsements from public figures and auxiliary ventures. The last included two Patel-directed films *Draupadi* (1944) and *Gvalan* (1946), starring his wife and *Filmindia* journalist Sushila Rani, along with film compendiums like *Stars of the Indian Screen* (1952); 'a bible of wit and humour', *Grey Dust* (1949); and 'a critical history of nine years of Nehru's rule', *Burning Words* (1957).

The key to *Filmindia*'s popularity was its self-stated objective 'to make the reading more interesting', thereby becoming a crucial medium of film publicity.[26] In a tone that was sarcastic, tongue-in-cheek and often confrontational, Patel goaded his readers to join in public ridicule of famous personalities. Little constrained by ethics, the editor saw himself as an insouciant pioneer, leaving the formulation of film-journalism ethics to future journalists.[27] The magazine gave favourable reviews to producers who doled out for advertisements, thus confirming Patel's bargaining power and the power of the periodical within the all-India film enterprise. *Filmindia* was also an extremely self-conscious magazine, largely due to the editor's penchant for responding, putting people in their place and having the last word. For instance, the accusations levied at Patel over paid reviews are something that the publication registers and responds to. Instead of maintaining silence, it retaliates and preserves the whispered allegations of the time, which otherwise would have no records.[28]

There is a considerable amount of unattributed writing in the magazine, which makes for a persuasive case to consider Patel and his wife Rani as sole authors.[29] However, *Filmindia* would also feature articles where prominent insiders and outsiders acknowledged Patel's 'unceasing efforts to improve the film industry on all fronts'.[30] Patel's specialities were the 'Editor's Mail' and 'You'll Hardly Believe', which were the most popular features of the publication, revealing inside information, which was 'always provocative and only sometimes vulgar'.[31] Columns like 'Editor's Mail' along with 'Woes and Echoes' offer the possibility of reader ethnography, though undoubtedly these were selective and modified. As the title suggests, 'Woes and Echoes' consisted of complaints and comments from the readers on films, which were based on the recognition of the mediatory role of *Filmindia*. The letters to the editor usually featured light-hearted enquiries by readers that ranged from details about their favourite stars and film enterprise to courtship, fashion and politics. These reveal an ongoing dialogue between the maverick editor and his readers, who above all were interested in his responses and repartee. Noticing the prejudicial tinge of *Filmindia*, several letters 'appear' in the late 1940s seeking Patel's opinion of the Muslim community and Pakistan. The responses were unpredictable and often contradictory, ranging from the editor declaring that 90 per cent of his friends were Muslims[32] to insidiously blaming the community for the partition violence.[33]

In its authoritative role, the periodical regarded the social domain as its own business, whatever others may have thought. The response to a reader's letter reveals how the magazine sought to locate itself as the appropriate platform even for concerns other than films. Yet the justification for inclusion remained a tangential connection with cinema itself.

> So far I thought that 'filmindia' was meant only for films. Was that thesis on marriage in the September issue necessary in 'filmindia'?

> It was. Don't we show these social problems in our films?... I think, with the vast *nationwide circulation of 'filmindia'*, a social problem gets a better platform in this magazine than in *other sectional or class magazines with tiny circulations*.[34]

Certainly, *Filmindia* sought to position itself as a national magazine not only in terms of its reach but also for sharing the concerns of the 'nation'. However, considering its lingua franca, *Filmindia* could only have a sectional or class appeal and can at best be 'a useful barometer of the opinions of the educated class'.[35] The language politics of the press in India has conventionally seen communalism and rabid hate-politics as the preserve of the vernacular media, and specific class dimensions are often associated with it. When located within this matrix, *Filmindia* demonstrates an increasing vacillation between secular and Hindu nationalism in the years leading to partition, thereby bringing into the domain of an English-language publication the unrestrained umbrage of the vernacular, more specifically of the Hindu right. Additionally, being a film publication, it clearly escaped the censorship that other newspapers were subjected to. Thus, the periodical treated rumours and facts with equanimity, privileged a provocative approach and inflamed sensitivities. As a result, *Filmindia* was anything but silent on the question of partition and filled its pages with discussions on communalism, loyalty, treason, rape, murder, migration, evacuee property and ultimately Hindus and Muslims – all forming the semantic field of the historical splitting.

Thus, in the 1940s the periodical became obsessed with the communal question, not in terms of performing scrupulous journalism but more as profitable vigilantism. Combining studio news with sectarian politics, it appears to have had its finger on the pulse of its readers. As film stars became 'a new symbol of glamour and affluence' replacing the old-world Maharajas,[36] the Bombay film industry held an increasing sway over people's imagination. Simultaneously, the transition from a colonial state to an independent nation was fuelled by competing nationalisms, charging the sociopolitical realm with sectarian politics. A survey that I outline here of *Filmindia* over the decade of the 1940s reveals that the discussion of the communal question happened in three ways. It began in the early 1940s with the denunciation of 'communalism' in film production and an emphasis on 'unity'. Almost simultaneously, somewhat triggered by its preoccupation with 'communalism', the publication began to identify partisan networks of film production and to critique films on the basis of the religious identities of the personnel. From the mid-1940s until 1947, Pakistan began to appear frequently as an expression of 'Muslim treachery', economic subterfuge in film processes and criminality. Finally, after independence, as the publication became overwhelmingly preoccupied with partition, it belaboured 'Hindu suffering' in the violence and migration, and trenchantly criticised the Indian government's evacuee property ordinances and refugee rehabilitation efforts, making its breach from the hegemonic nationalist project complete. Through a long-term engagement with *Filmindia* spanning more than a decade, my analysis qualifies what Sarkar calls the 'troubling subterranean unthought'. It argues that such thought was relegated to a subterranean realm only at the end of the 1940s, troubling as it was, given its earlier intimacy with hegemonic nationalism.

The Virus of Communalism

Appearing in 1940, the 'expose' by Abbas in the pages of *Filmindia* is the first available acknowledgement of the 'menace of communalism raising its ugly head in Indian studios'.[37] While conceding that communalism was neither a rare nor a recent phenomenon in the life of the Indian subcontinent, he claimed that the film industry had been impervious to the 'disease' until then.

> In this Sahara of communalism the only oasis was the film industry. The studios suffered from many diseases but they were at least free from the virus of communalism.... Not only Art but Commerce, too, decreed that communalism should be kept out of the studios.[38]

In the article, Abbas cited the example of Dadasaheb Phalke, a Marathi-Hindu director who gave the roles of Hindu gods in his devotional films to a young Muslim actor. This for Abbas was emblematic of the relaxed and liberal outlook of the 'Indian film industry'. Recounting how the previous generation of artistes saw themselves as members of one community – 'the community of artistes' – Abbas saw their religious identities as being 'communal labels' rather than determinants of artistic choices and professional networks. Locating a shift in the two years before his article was written (that is, between 1938 and 1940), Abbas noticed 'little straws in the wind' in an article published a month prior to the Muslim League's Lahore Resolution of 1940.

> And now suddenly we seem to have become conscious of each other's denominational affiliations. Baburao Patel is a *Hindu* journalist; Abbas Ahmad is a *Muslim* journalist:... Kardar is a *Muslim* Director and Nitin Bose is a *Hindu* Director: Kumar is a *Muslim* actor; Prithviraj is a *Hindu* actor.... I won't be surprised if we reach the ridiculous stage where we would be telling one another 'This is a *Hindu camera*, that is a *Muslim microphone*'![39]

The article detected a growing 'fanaticism' in films, especially the historicals. Calling them 'communal pictures', Abbas placed the responsibility on film-makers to guard against catering to 'popular' tastes, calling cinema a 'double-edged weapon'.

Alongside this article, Patel's editorial for this issue drew attention to the 'communal menace' exacerbated by film journalism. Calling the Hindu and Muslim lobbies 'the blackmailing twins', the article described the money-extracting tactics of certain journalists who threatened producers with libellous agitation against a film if they did not pay up.[40] Identifying the 'blackmailers' as North Indian journalists, Patel suggested that the practice was more acute in, if not restricted to, the North. This curious identification of the 'blackmailers' could be a reference to Lahore, which had seen the efflorescence of several film magazines around this time. Additionally, the northern territories of the pre-partition film trade were also considered Muslim. With Patel being based in Bombay, such labelling also disassociated *Filmindia* from such a practice, despite the fact that this was something Patel himself was frequently accused of.[41]

Anxieties over slander were hardly limited to the discursive space of a film periodical and frequently took a legal course. The role of the colonial state as the arbitrator was evident in mechanisms of censorship, especially in cases of libel or a threat to law and order. Eric Barnouw and S. Krishnaswamy detail how religious sensitivities around films started as early as the 1920s, the case in point being *Razia Sultan* (1927, dir. Dhiren Ganguly), which was uncertified in various areas in 1927 after Muslim protests.[42] On the other hand, Ravi Vasudevan draws attention to the founding of a private body, the All-India League for Film Censorship (AILFC), in 1937 to tackle what it perceived as an anti-Hindu dimension of the film industry.[43] One cannot but notice that the designation of this private body is similar to the Muslim League, the political party formed to protect Muslim political interests. The League for Censorship claimed that 'Muslims' and 'Parsis' dominated the all-India film industry and were as a result motivated to show Hindus in a bad light.[44] It can be surmised that the Muslim challenge to the 'All-India film' was conceived in two ways, which was amply evident in the pages of *Filmindia*. At the spectatorial level, there were violent responses of the Muslim groups to the content of a film, whereas, at the authorial level, the intent to pander to Muslim sentiments or assert a Muslim particularity generated 'communal pictures'. While in *Filmindia*'s scheme it was mostly the Muslim film-makers who engaged in communal pictures and a distortion of history, the magazine would neither spare those Hindu film-makers who humoured 'Muslim sensitivities'. The situation would become more volatile when Muslim directors made films on Hindu historical or legendary characters, which were attacked in the periodical as ignorant, indifferent and insulting, if not politically motivated. While representing Muslim audiences as intolerant, *Filmindia* took on the mantle of articulating a Hindu-sensitive reading of certain films. But, as mentioned earlier, this was preceded by a short-lived vogue of unity in the magazine.

The anti-colonial nationalist consciousness of the twentieth century stressed, among other things, 'the idea of the "fundamental" unity' of the vast Indian subcontinent.[45] India's past was read in terms of the unity of religions, cultural syncretism and synthesis. Unity was opposed to division, just as secularism was to communalism. By this logic everything nationalistic was to demonstrate the existence of such unity, including film enterprise. It was this understanding of the film industry that got challenged when Abbas was approached by the Muslim lobbyists to start a rival magazine to 'Hindu' *Filmindia*.

> I was surprised, for the film business, *whatever else* may be said of it, *was* and *is essentially secular* and non-communal.[46]

Film enterprise was therefore to exist as the modern preserve of the traditional quality of unity. In an issue of *Filmindia* from the war years, an interview with the Muslim actor-director Mazhar Khan identified the noble national role of the film industry. Films were seen as throwing a beacon of light in the midst of the discouraging darkness of communalism.[47] 'Filmdom in India had done much more for Hindu-Muslim unity and the national language than the leaders themselves,' remarked Khan. There were also occasional articles in the publication from public figures and political leaders endorsing *Filmindia*. In an interview with the Sheriff of Bombay, M. R. A Baig, the magazine commended him on declaring the film *Bhakta Kabir* (Devotee Kabir, 1942) tax-free for its Hindu–Muslim unity theme. On his part Baig stressed on the need for 'idealistic and patriotic artists and technicians' who would bring out 'the inherent underlying unity of the living conditions of Hindus and Muslims in India'.[48] The unity trend had caught on by the early 1940s, with both films and production companies taking to such projections. A brief look at the advertisements reveals films preoccupied with brotherhood and production companies embodying the nationalist spirit. For example, *Bhaichara* (Brotherhood,

1943) was produced by none other than 'Unity' productions and had the strong symbolism of a mosque and temple standing next to each other, casting their long shadows (Figure 2.1). Claimed to be a story 'interweaving the lives of Hindus and Muslims and presenting a national pattern of life for the future', the film was the next offering by the makers of the tax-free unity film, *Bhakta Kabir*.

Film-maker Nazir, who migrated to Pakistan immediately after partition, produced *Bhalai* (Goodness, 1943) that had a tagline of 'Hindu maiden had a Muslim Brother! And in their holy friendship … was embodied a nation's sigh!' (Figure 2.2). The tightrope walk of forging cross-community alliances (Hindu–Muslim) while precluding affiliated sexual anxieties (through the desexualised trope of brother–sister relationship and an averted gaze focused on the hands) conveyed the primacy of loyalty to the country over the community.[49] The Turkish *fez* of the Muslim brother and the altruistic hands of the Hindu maiden together evoked another 'strange love' of the Khilafat and non-cooperation of the early 1920s. Since 'unity' seemed to be in vogue, not only as a projected virtue but also as an opportunity for tax relief, it could also be depicted as an intrinsic value of many a film trademark. An instance would be the publicity advertisement of Fazli Brothers' company (Figure 2.3), who also migrated to Pakistan, with the younger brother in 1947 and the elder one in 1955. In the two-page spread, the trademark of two hands meeting against the map of peninsular India symbolised 'Hindu–Muslim unity'.

It would seem that unity films, having contemporary relevance, tax-free status as well as inoculation against barbs reserved for communal films, ought to have enjoyed a lasting stability. Yet this emphasis on Hindu–Muslim unity ran out of steam rather quickly. By the mid-1940s *Filmindia* had actively started campaigning against such endeavours. The offer made by the Unionist government of Punjab in 1946 of prizes worth 'Rs. 5000/- and Rs. 2000/- for documentary films promoting Hindu-Muslim Unity' was prominently attacked in an editorial as the anxiety of leading politicians at their wits' end.[50] The Unionist Party's pact with the Muslim League at the all-India level can explain *Filmindia*'s hostility to this particular 'Hindu–Muslim unity' on offer. Pointing out the futility of such an effort, the editorial argued that any film that tried to preach unity between the two communities only ended up reviving the bitter memories of the past. Written in the rabble-rousing and contrarian spirit characteristic of Patel's writing, the editorial was nonetheless making an astute point regarding the difficulty of making a 'correct' film on Hindu–Muslim unity in the political context of the 1940s. The difficulty lay not only in the content of the film but also in its reception.

Figure 2.1 An instance of the unity and brotherhood trend in film themes and publicity
Source: *Filmindia*, July 1943.

Figure 2.2 Desexualised cross-community alliances highlighted in the advertisement for the film *Bhalai*
Source: *Filmindia*, February 1943.

Figure 2.3 Two-page spread of Fazli Brothers' trademark as symbolizing Hindu–Muslim unity
Source: *Filmindia*, June 1943.

is no longer .... -

That Madhubala recently explained in an American magazine the true reason that made her give Rs. 50,000|- to the Bengal Refugee Fund. According to her she was "fiercely hunted" by the Hindus and "accused of eating the meat of a cow". So she gave Rs. 50,000|- and saved herself. Even beautiful lips can utter such a shameless lie under the Crescent.

.. ' .. - ---- breakdown

Figure 2.4 *Filmindia* calling Madhubala's interview in *Theatre Arts* 'a shameless lie'
Source: *Filmindia*, November 1952, 17.

Muslim Masses and Pakistani Producers

Over several issues in 1946, *Filmindia* reported a couple of cinema attacks as illustrative of the 'intolerance of Muslims'. The first was provoked by the controversy around the film *40 Crores* (1946), where certain Muslim spectators 'kicked up a row' and attacked the theatre screening the film in Bombay.[51] The film, written by Pandit Indira and produced for Chandra Art Productions, had some 'burning dialogues on Hindu–Muslim unity' and included newsreel footage of the famous Gandhi–Jinnah meeting of 1944.[52] The article wondered 'along with the Censors and Hon. Home Member Morarji Desai' as to why the 'Muslims still object'. It went on to rhetorically ask as to how long the intolerance of some 'rowdy' Muslims would continue to dictate what 400 million Indians could watch and ended on a threatening note: 'the knife is not a sole monopoly of the Muslims. The Hindus can handle it equally well'.

A much larger deliberation on the issue appeared three months later in August 1946, ten months before the formal announcement of partition, and overlapped with the bloody riots in Calcutta, following the Direct Action Day.[53] The article reported the attack on cinema halls screening the film *Hamrahi* (Co-traveller, 1945) by 'Calcutta Muslims' and characterised it as the blackmail of a national industry.[54] A 'Muslim newspaper' of Calcutta had described *Hamrahi* as 'a well-laid, deep and subtle plot to blacken the name of the Muslims'.[55] Calling the allegation childish, *Filmindia* suspected that such an attack was premised more on the Hindu identity of the film-makers rather than the content of the film. It then proceeded to list films made by Muslim film-makers, which 'slander the Muslim community terrifically', and instead of presenting their community in good colours, the Muslim producers 'become thus its greatest traducers'. Finally, the article went on to point out the crisis besetting the industry due to a lack of enterprise and foreign competition and argued that it must not go through additional spasms of communal conflicts. It summed up the piece rather paradoxically: '*Filmindia* is essentially a film magazine and does not bother about politics'.

The word 'Pakistan' first appeared in the pages of *Filmindia* in connection with film-makers like Mehboob Khan and Sibtain Fazli as early as 1945, two years before its creation. The magazine exposed the partisan networks of the 'Pakistani producers' and typified these relations in the manner of Mughal courtly culture.

> Jealous people wrongly call Mehboob Productions a Pakistan concern, saying that he doesn't employ Hindus. This is all wrong as Mehboob's second in command is Babubhai Mehta, a good fast-dyed Hindu just like Todarmal who served Akbar the great.[56]

And in later issues:

> A new institution named 'Pakistani producers' is gradually taking shape in the Indian film world. It is to help Muslim producers who must engage Muslim artists, Muslim technicians, Muslim directors, Muslim Urdu and take Muslim subjects for the glorification of Islam.[57]

Producer Shiraz Ali Hakim's 'Moghul-i-Azam' will not be completed till the quarrel about Pakistan is settled.[58]

Muslim film producers of Bombay are all living in Karachi these days till rumours of retribution die out in Bombay and the city becomes a safe asylum for Muslim producers to agitate for *lebensraum* and produce new pictures of Moghul glory.[59]

The historical genre became extremely popular in the 1940s. Many of these films were Mughal historicals and have been read as an 'anti-colonial gesture',[60] as these represented the grandiosity and justice of Mughal courtly culture. This preoccupation with the past was also evident in the nationalist consciousness of the twentieth century, wherein the movements for unity, syncretism and religious tolerance were said to have reached their climax in the centuries of 'Muslim rule' in the careers and thought of people like Kabir and Akbar.[61] While the secular nationalist position rendered the Mughal past as a moment of syncretism, the Hindu nationalist view of the period has been that of the external threat, the Muslim dominance over a Hindu India before the Christian proselytisation under the British.[62] It was this understanding that informed critique in the pages of *Filmindia*, where there were long deliberations on how the historicals were actually a 'plea for Pakistan' and a return to Muslim rule.

Film-maker Mehboob Khan's *Humayun* (1945) came under severe attack and led to a greater vigilantism in the pages of *Filmindia* around the content of historicals. If the past was becoming a tricky territory, the present was not safe either. While the dispute over the historicals has been well recognised,[63] little attention has been paid to the resistance to the Muslim social genre in the pages of *Filmindia*. The first among these was Sibtain Fazli's *Ismat* (1944), which was called 'an useless waste of celluloid [*sic*]'.[64] The film's high-flown Urdu added to the film's woes, which was 'a Muslim social story, typical of the times we are passing through'. K. Asif's *Phool* (Flower, 1945), which drew 'huge crowds at Roxy', had the makings of an excellent picture but suffered because the 'story is treated with too much communal enthusiasm', making it a 'trifle dangerous in its contents'.[65] S. M. Yusuf's *Nek Parvin* (Virtuous Parveen, 1946) was a 'love and revolver Muslim romance' and another instance of 'the belief that Muslim stories pay better nowadays'.[66] The rise of a separate genre propelled by Muslim producers and celebrated a few years earlier as an instance of Hindu–Muslim unity was now deemed futile, since there was little to choose between Hindu and Muslim subjects in terms of their orthodox and reactionary approach to life:

> The story of 'Nek Parvin' could as well have been written by our Daves and Dwivedis rather than by our Hashars and Qureshis. The only difference between the two seems to be that while our Daves and Dwivedis, being

non-violent Gujaratis, are scared of revolvers, our Hashars and Qureshis, being meat eaters, use the revolvers to shoot the theme further every minute.[67]

Denying difference at first, it is then deemed to be harbouring at best a negative value. The sources of this negative difference are the religious identities and sociocultural background of the personnel. By the end of 1947, the year of partition, the magazine became involved in exposing those film-makers who had been 'shuttling between India and Pakistan',[68] calling them 'wolves' and 'self-evident fifth columnists'.[69] It imparted nefarious designs to their decision to leave India and fuelled fears as well as suspicions by printing threats and rumours.

> That there is no storm anywhere except in the conscience of those who fought for Pakistan and talked and acted wickedly. No one in India says that Muslims should migrate but the Muslims are scared out of their wits. They know that the Hindus have read the grim stories of Muslim behaviour in west Punjab and stories often repeat themselves with characters reversed.[70]

Emerging as a progression rather than a singular event, partition was the impending Pakistan and an ultimate betrayal of the Indian nationalist struggle. Maintaining a watchful eye over the activities of the Muslim film-makers and the content of their films, the magazine reviews reserved different standards of critique as far as films from the 'Pakistani producers' were concerned.

Dangerous Pictures

Reviews of three films, which were made by Muslim film-makers who migrated to Pakistan, published in the post-partition December issue of *Filmindia*, provide insights into how the film-makers and their films were actively purged from the trade circuit of India. The first film was *Abidah* (1947) by Nazir, who owned Hind Pictures in Bombay before migrating to Pakistan. *Abidah* was released in Bombay on 26 September 1947, and by the time its review was published, Nazir had moved to Pakistan. The film was seen as sowing seeds of communal trouble and having 'a surfeit of Allah and Islam throughout and unnecessarily'.[71] In a now well-established tradition of *Filmindia*, the review ended with a thinly veiled warning:

> This picture is a dangerous experiment in *essentially Hindu towns* and villages and exhibitors should be prepared for local communal outbursts wherever this picture is shown.[72]

The next review was even more outright in asking for a censorship intervention. It was W. Z. Ahmed's final release in India, *Meerabai* (1947). Provocatively titled as 'Muslim Meerabai Grossly Slanders Hinduism', the article proceeded to ask if the censors were sleeping when they approved the film!

This picture is produced by Mr. W.Z. Ahmed who has only recently left for
Pakistan lock, stock and barrel *leaving behind a cartload of creditors* howling
for money.... Either intentionally or through rank ignorance of Hindu
tradition, this man has indecently *insulted the Hindus* and Hinduism by giving
us Meerabai.[73]

There were several objections to W. Z. Ahmed's *Meerabai*, including 'a Pakistani
marriage', which according to the review is a 'shameful one' involving abduction
and force. The reference to the gendered violence of partition became a peculiarly
Pakistani attribute in the magazine, unique and specific to people of a particular
politico-religious persuasion: Muslims for Pakistan. The review ends pretty much
like *Abidah*'s, stating that the picture is not suitable for Hindu audiences as it is a
gross misrepresentation of 'our cultural and religious heritage'. In its subsequent
issue of January 1948, the review praised a 'Tamil *Meera*' for the delightful concert
of M. S. Subbulakshmi, even though the reviewer could not resist remarking that
'the little Tamilians of South look very poor Rajputs'.[74] It was clear that, less than
for its own merits, the 'Tamil Meera' was being promoted more as an alternative to
'Muslim Meerabai'.

The third film, *Nateeja* (Outcome, 1947), by Najam Naqvi, earned the tagline
of 'the Pakistani way', a metaphor commonly used by the magazine for depraved
attributes. The film was seen as encouraging criminality, and the issue carried a
news story of a real theft inspired by the reel to substantiate its contention. The film
was treated as a product of a few criminal minds, drawing not-so-subtle parallels
with Pakistan itself:

Looked at humorously, 'Nateeja' gives you a glimpse of the present Pakistan
and perhaps of its future shape. Fittingly enough, its story has been written by
a Muslim and the picture has been directed by a Muslim whose sympathies for
Pakistan are not exactly a family secret.

The concern in the review was for the impressionable young minds, the 'little ones'
of the country, who would grow up to be 'Indians all, without communal labels'.[75]
Referring to the censors as the spiritual parents of millions of children, the magazine
urged the censor board to reconsider its decision to pass the film. In the final analysis,
Nateeja, like the other two, was declared 'a dangerous picture for any decent nation'.

While virulence was not new to *Filmindia*, it became unequivocal in the year of
partition, demanding the excision of many Muslim film-makers and their films from
the Indian circuits of production and circulation. The continued campaign to ban
these films often paid off, like it did in the case of *Mun ki Jeet* (Victory of the Heart,
1944), which was made by Ahmad, who also made the 'Muslim *Meerabai*'. While in
the year of its initial release *Filmindia* had let it off with an unflattering review, in
1947 the magazine took up cudgels against offensive and vulgar portions of Hindi
films and demanded that a song from *Mun ki Jeet* should be censored. A year later, in

January 1948, the magazine ran a gleeful announcement, commending the Bombay censors for cancelling the certificate of exhibition for *Mun ki Jeet* as well as the United Provinces government for banning the film.[76] Another of *Filmindia*'s targets discussed earlier, Yusuf's *Nek Parvin*, was banned in the province of Madras in 1948.[77] The impact of *Filmindia*'s campaigns can be discerned from the list of films initially certified by the Censor Board but subsequently re-examined and modified in 1948. The appendix provided in *The Report of the Film Enquiry Committee* mentions *Nateeja, Abidah, Mun ki Jeet, Meerabai* and *Elan* (Clarion Call, 1947), among other films which were cut or had their certificates cancelled.[78] Amusingly, Patel's own film *Gvalan* is among the films re-censored in 1948, encapsulating *Filmindia*'s peculiar relationship with the new national order as well as its editor being at the receiving end in the contest for power at the close of the 1940s.

The magazine also tried hard to secure a ban on Shaukat Hussain Rizvi's *Jugnu* (Firefly, 1947) for casting a heavily pregnant Noorjahan as a college girl and thus 'slandering the collegians of India'.[79] Similarly, A. R. Kardar's *Dillagi* (Attachment, 1949) was characterised as 'a disgusting slander of Hindu virgins'.[80] The readers too responded on cue and drew attention to other films. One reader, objecting to the 'overwhelming atmosphere maintained by Islamic crescent flags' in Kardar's film *Dard* (Agony, 1947), asked if the censors were once again asleep in the face of communal propaganda in a secular state.[81] Acting together as vigilantes of the new nation that after the formation of Pakistan was projected as consisting of 'essentially Hindu towns and villages',[82] *Filmindia* and its readers became increasingly invested in stipulating afresh a new cinema for the new nation. This 'decent' cinema in the name of a secular ideology would be shorn of at least any Muslim excesses, as *Filmindia* had successfully managed to link any such enterprise to the painful memory of partition.

Among the film-makers who stayed on in India, *Filmindia* kept its interrogative spotlight on Kardar and Mehboob until the early 1950s. The two had briefly left Bombay in late 1947 but returned after setting up distribution offices in Pakistan. A statue of Ganesha and later of Mahatma Gandhi were placed outside the Kardar studio to save it from being a sectarian target.[83] True to its form, *Filmindia* ran the story for months, leaving little scope for any ambiguity that may have offered protection in this case.[84] Mehboob repeatedly appears in connection with his personal property being attached to the evacuee property ordinance. His purchase of the Liberty Cinema at a pittance was reported as a favour to a friend leaving for Pakistan and preventing it from becoming an evacuee property of the Government of India.[85] The magazine also kept a close watch on donations and charity performed by Muslim film personnel for national refugees in the two countries to ascertain their allegiance. Mehboob's donation of a day's collections of *Elan* in Karachi to the Pakistani Refugee Fund was noted pointedly.[86] Another issue claimed that all donations from the Bombay film industry to the Indian Refugee Relief Fund came from its Hindu personnel.[87] In early 1949 when the magazine and Mehboob had begun mending fences, *Filmindia* publicised the film-maker's donation of 5,000 rupees to the cyclone relief fund and expected Kardar to do likewise 'as he had made millions in India.'[88] In January 1950, a year after the 'donation', Mehboob's evacuee property troubles were reported as over, and he was declared a free man. Yet the most celebrated donation in the pages of *Filmindia* was when the 'daughter of India', Madhubala, gave away her 'life savings' of 50,000 rupees for the 'suffering sons of the soil', that is, the refugees from East Bengal.[89] Reportedly, she was accompanied by 'friend and mentor' Sushila Rani, Patel's wife and *Filmindia* journalist, in handing over the cheque to the authorities.[90] The October 1950 editorial was enraptured by 'Madhubala's martyrdom'. Two years later, an American magazine, *Theatre Arts*, ran a feature on Madhubala, introducing her to American audiences. The following is an excerpt from the article, which also mentioned the 'life-saving donation' by Madhubala:

> It is a measure of India's ability to grow in tolerance that it … chose to love a Moslem Madhubala. However, anti-Muslim prejudice must continue to be one of her chief problems. She is the victim of a whispering campaign that accuses her, for example, of eating the meat of the cow, which is sacred to Hindus. To offset such rumours she gave her life-savings of fifty thousand rupees to Bengal Refugee Fund last winter to help Hindu refugees from Moslem East Pakistan.[91]

Nothing ever quite escaped *Filmindia*, especially as far as its own reputation was concerned, and it pointedly took note of Madhubala's statement in the American magazine. It ran a small cartoon of the actress with a cow in November 1952 (Figure 2.4), three months after the *Theatre Arts* article, and called it the deceit of 'beautiful lips [which] can utter such a shameless lie under the crescent', linking its celebrated donors with its cause celebre that year. This was the editorial of 'Crescent over India', where rape, murder and fanaticism were identified as 'common Islamic ritual'. As the periodical cried hoarse about the dangers of the Islamic state of Pakistan looming large over India, it also finally earned a ban in Pakistan in March 1952.[92]

Two Memoirs: The Life-writings of Shaukat Hussain Rizvi and M. Luqman

Following the public mode of articulation represented by *Filmindia*, this section looks at the life narratives of two Muslim film-makers who migrated to Pakistan in 1947. In doing so, this critical analysis is not interested in, as Sidonie Smith and Julia Watson argue, the truth status of autobiographical disclosure[93] but treats them as creative interventions, encoding particular values that may have shaped history and culture. These separate yet interconnected life narratives belong to Rizvi and Luqman, whose association began in the mid-1940s in Bombay when

Luqman assisted Rizvi on the film *Zeenat* (Beauty, 1945). Later, both migrated to Pakistan immediately after independence in 1947. That these life-writings discuss the film world of the late 1930s and the early 1940s as a dynamic place of creative opportunities and ambitions but also sectarian insecurities makes for a compelling case for their inclusion in this chapter. Both Rizvi and Luqman mention professional rivalries and collaborations that could run along religious divides. Their description of the heated debates, assertive cultural chauvinisms and identity-based networks imparts texture and detail to the rancour of cultural struggles otherwise insipidly designated as 'communal' in *Filmindia* and Prithvi Theatre. While their 'struggle' in the Bombay industry and intense support for the Muslim League appear to be mutually reinforcing, neither independently nor together do these necessarily translate into an intention to forsake Bombay.

Narrated to a scribe four decades later in the 1980s, Rizvi's memoir, *Noorjahan aur Main* (Noorjahan and Me), is predominantly an account of his tumultuous relationship with his actress-singer wife Noorjahan, which has been a subject of heightened curiosity and scandal in Pakistan.[94] His life-writing contains fascinating details of starting out as a technical assistant at the Bharat Lakshmi studio in Calcutta. Mostly self-taught, though briefly under the tutelage of film-maker Ezra Mir at Madan Studios, Rizvi became a film editor on serial contracts with film studios in Calcutta. At the newly established Film Corporation he met the distributors and studio owners, the Pancholi brothers.[95] Dalsukh Pancholi then invited Rizvi to Lahore, first to edit their *Gul Bakavali* (The Flower of Bakavali, 1939) and later to direct *Khandaan* (Lineage, 1942). Rizvi's next four films in colonial India were made in Bombay. As Rizvi's life narrative progresses, enumerating film collaborations and experiments, it encapsulates the euphoric film traffic between these three cities. Between 1941 and 1947, Rizvi directed five films: *Khandaan* (1942), *Naukar* (Servant, 1943), *Dost* (Friend, 1944), *Zeenat* (1945) and *Jugnu* (1947).

In another long interview for the Urdu publication *Out of Date*, during the mid-1980s,[96] Luqman remembered his early years in the Bombay film industry. Running away from home in Delhi while still at school, Luqman reached Bombay in 1937 and started working for the Minerva Movietone as one of their set painters. He then went on to become a small-time actor with Minerva before joining Rizvi as an assistant. Luqman speaks less about his professional trajectory and career in Bombay, possibly because it is less remarkable at this time, especially when compared to a senior Rizvi. Instead, the changing fortunes of Minerva, its work environment and the Bombay film world at large constitute the preponderant theme. Although Luqman is taciturn about his only directorial venture in Bombay that flopped, *Humjoli* (Companion, 1946) appears in tangential connection to the efforts he made to expedite friend Dilip Kumar's acting career in Bombay. It is with his films in Pakistan – *Shahida* (1949), *Pattan* (1955), *Lakht-e-Jigar* (Piece of Heart, 1956) and *Ayaz* (1961) – that Luqman discusses the creative decisions and the process of direction.

Read intertextually, these life narratives present shared themes and complementary world views. Both were reminiscent about the key men and women of the film enterprise, like Sohrab Modi, Nitin Bose, Dilip Kumar, Shiraz Ali Hakim, Mehboob, Dalsukh Pancholi, Jaddan Bai and Naseem. Their discourse is mutually congruous where words like *taasub* (prejudice), *motasib* (zealous or bigoted) and *taawun* (cooperation) are often used to describe professional transactions and networks within the Bombay film industry in the years leading to partition. Tensions appear not only over networks of cooperation, patronage and opportunities to make films but also over studio ceremonies and the choice of cultural idiom within films. Crucially, Muslim nationalism as a declared conviction of these film-makers emerges as a modality of contestation. The difference between the two narratives appears in their self-image and justification for the life narrative. While Luqman's account of his Bombay years is selective and narrowly motivated, for every anecdote is his illustration of 'Hindu prejudice' and 'Muslim struggle', Rizvi's main emphasis is on personal achievements and calibre, especially his years in Calcutta and Lahore. It is also an occasion to tell his side of the story of the marriage gone awry with Noorjahan. As for Luqman, the recollections are a part of his critique of the current state of the 1980s Lahore film industry. The reception context in both cases is 1980s Pakistan, when the film industry had suffered its severest blow from the official Islamisation under general Zia-ul-Haq.

By engaging with the past, these self-referential activities also reflect on identities in the present and are grounded in the larger collective identity of Urdu-speaking immigrant Muslims of Pakistan. This identity is worked through the cultural capital of Urdu and struggles in the face of a majoritarian work culture often read as 'prejudice' and an assertion of a politicised religious belonging. Free from the onus of secularism and unity, these narratives nonetheless negotiate multiplicity, through contestation and heightening difference. And yet, as they recall their moment of migration as almost an inactive one, the life-writings reveal an imagination less resistant to difference being constitutive of nation.

Cultural Capital

Both accounts touch on the aspect of language and see Urdu as a crucial part of their cultural capital. The language becomes an important source of self-worth and pride, enabling professional advantage and specialisation. Luqman lands his first role in a film by accident, while rehearsing Urdu dialogues with the stage actor initially chosen for the role.

> *Pehle din shooting shuru hoti hai toh Nathankar ki Urdu ka talafuz theek nahin hota jo maratha tha. Shooting cancel hoti hai.*[97]

> The first day when the shoot began, it was found that Nathankar's Urdu diction was not correct since he was a Maratha. The shoot was cancelled.

As a young employee of Minerva, Luqman rehearses dialogues with Nathankar, correcting his diction on the second day. Sohrab Modi, the owner of Minerva and director of the film, overhears this rehearsal in the make-up room. He decides to replace Nathankar, a more seasoned stage actor, by the inexperienced Luqman for his fluency in Urdu, the language of the Hamlet adaptation, *Saed-e-Havas* (Hamlet, 1936).

Making his directorial debut with *Khandaan* in 1942, produced by Dalsukh Pancholi of Lahore, Rizvi too highlights the experience of making an Urdu film. Until then the Pancholi studio had mostly dabbled in Punjabi films, the undivided Punjab being their immediate context of production and circulation. As discussed previously, *Khandaan* was Pancholi studio's second foray into an all-India market, and this time with Rizvi at the helm of the affairs. The film employed an Urdu-intensive idiom within the contemporary milieu.

> *Khandaan mein khala ka lafz tha. Pancholi waaley kehne lagey ye khala kya hota hai. Humne kaha maasi. Kehne lagey phir maasi rakho. Humne kaha, bhai, Urdu film hai, ismein maasi nahi, khala hoga.*[98]

> *Khandaan* used the term *khala* [maternal aunt]. The Pancholi people started asking what *khala* meant. I explained that it was the same as *maasi* [Hindi for maternal aunt]. Then keep it *maasi*, they said. I declared that it is an Urdu film; it would have *khala* and not *maasi*.

The term *khala* has been dominantly, though not exclusively, associated with an Urdu-speaking Muslim familial set-up. Rizvi's recollection of this incident is intended to convey the Pancholi staff's rather improbable ignorance of the Urdu-speaking Muslim families of North India and his own uncompromising stand as a stickler, as far as the representational 'authenticity' of this culture was concerned. It also conveys that while the original screenplay written by Imtiaz Ali Taj contained the Urdu term, it took the presence of Rizvi on the production floor as a decision-maker and director to ensure cultural authenticity in the film. Putting this alongside *Filmindia*'s review of Yusuf's *Nek Parvin*, which panned Muslim stories for employing Muslim writers and directors, one can read how identity-based representation at all levels of film-making – narrative, personnel and capital – had become a fraught issue.

Procedures of Prejudice

Of the two, Luqman is quicker to read religious prejudice in the challenges faced by the Muslim film-makers and artistes. The instances usually involve the identification of bigoted (*motasib*) film personalities, their partisan blind spots and how they created career obstacles for a Muslim artiste. One of the earliest instances of prejudice in Luqman's account involves the actress Prabha. Prabha was the daughter of the Lahore-based publisher Rajpal, who was murdered by a Muslim man, Ilm-ud-Din, in the late 1920s in the *Rangila Rasool* blasphemy case. Luqman furnishes this background to convey the historical potency in communal prejudice – constituted from a cycle of injuries inflicted by each community on the other. Prabha reportedly maintained a policy of 'non-cooperation' with Muslim actors, thus compelling producers to cast only non-Muslims opposite her. Luqman's other two prime illustrations of 'Hindu prejudice' involve 'Muslim personnel' who achieved unparalleled success in independent India, the first being film director Mehboob Khan and the other Dilip Kumar. While Khan's and Kumar's successful careers in independent India ought to render Luqman's recounting of an unfair treatment as overblown, these are possibly motivated to heighten the strain of struggle, where no one was immune to procedures of prejudice.

Starting off as an 'extra' in Sagar Movietone and keen on becoming a director, Mehboob gathered in his conversations with studio owner Chamanlal Desai ('Hindu')[99] that he could direct a film as long as he raised 50,000 rupees for the production. Who else could Mehboob approach, according to Luqman, but a well-heeled Muslim friend, Seth Ibrahim? This way Mehboob secured his first film, 'Al-Hilal (The Judgement of Allah) based on the Ottoman and Roman conflict. While the problem of capital was taken care of by Mehboob's friend, things were not so smooth when it came to the selection of the actors and actresses. Mehboob contacted the leading artiste of those days, Sabita Devi, who along with other studio actors refused to work in a film directed by an 'extra'. This, according to Luqman, was not the real reason.

> 'Extra' ka toh ek bahana tha. Asal mein Hindu artiste kissi Mussalman ko director banta dekhna nahin chahte they. Aaj agar hum kursiyon par baithein hain, khushhali aur aanaavi ki zindagi guzaar rahein hain, toh yeh sab Pakistan ke tazeel hai!… Jab har Hindu artiste ne Mehboob sahab ke saath kaam karne se inkaar kar diya toh phir yeh Kumar sahab ke paas pahonche.[100]

> 'Extra' was a mere pretext. Actually, none of the Hindu artistes could accept a Muslim director. If today we are sitting in these [director's] chairs, are leading lives of prosperity and respectability, then it has all been realised in Pakistan!… When each and every Hindu artiste refused to work with Mehboob, then he went to actor Kumar.

Kumar, a Muslim actor whose real name was Mir Ali, agreed to act in Al-Hilal, and that is how the film started. Luqman's blanket identification of all artistes as Hindu, when Sabita Devi was Christian, suggests that a hierarchical disdain may have as much to do with Mehboob's attempts to climb the production pyramid. In talking about Mehboob's struggle, what emerges is Luqman's impression of the destiny of his own ilk: Muslim film-makers of the subcontinent who migrated to Pakistan. Alongside this emerges the logic of Pakistan – as a nation where Muslims were assured of above-the-line film work. And yet when it comes to film-making in Pakistan decades later, Luqman is similarly contemptuous of Pashtun (also Muslim) film personnel of Lahore and dismisses their work by referring to their modest beginnings as light technicians.[101]

In an extended section devoted to Dilip Kumar, Luqman professes deep friendship with the star, who was then a struggling actor. He describes in detail the process of casting for the film *Milan* (Union, 1946) being produced by Bombay Talkies. An adaptation of Tagore's Bengali novella *Naukadoobi* (Boat Wreck, 1906), the film was being made in two languages, Bengali and Hindi, with Nitin Bose (Hindu) directing both versions. By this time, Bombay Talkies had been bought over by Shiraz Ali Hakim (Muslim), while the general manager there was Hiten Chowdhary (Hindu). According to Luqman, although Dilip Kumar was on the payroll of Bombay Talkies, Nitin Bose and Hiten Chowdhary did not want him in the film. Instead, Bose wanted Kumar's younger brother, Nasir Khan, in the film. Rather disingenuously, Luqman reads this as an excuse to get rid of Kumar and yet another instance of the difficulties faced by a Muslim actor. Lobbying for Kumar, Luqman claims to have persuaded Shiraz Hakim to put pressure on the makers of *Milan*.

> *Shiraz Hakim ne issi waqt phone par Hiten chowdhary se baat ki ke Hindi version tab banega agar Yusuf iss mein hero hoga.... Ab toh mamla set ho gaya ke 'Milan' mein Dilip hi hoga.... 'Milan' ke liye Nitin Bose pehle Acharya ka shot leta tha. Second shot iska leta tha. Yeh usse behtar shot deta tha. Taasub ka yeh alam tha ke Nitin Bose isse theek se baat tak nahin karte they. Phir voh waqt bhi aaya ke issi Dilip ne issi Nitin Bose ko apni film 'Ganga Jamuna' ki direction di.[102]*

Shiraz Hakim immediately spoke to Hiten Chowdhury on the phone and told him that the Hindi version will be made only if Yusuf (Dilip) is in it.... Now it was confirmed that Dilip would act in 'Milan'.... During the shoot, Nitin Bose would first take a shot with Acharya [Abhi Bhattacharya, for the Bengali version]. The second shot would be with Dilip. He would give a better shot than Abhi Bhattacharya. Such was the extent of prejudice that Nitin Bose would not speak to him properly. Then came a time when Dilip gave Nitin the chance to direct his home production 'Ganga Jamuna'.

While Luqman uses the word *taasub* (prejudice) to describe the strained relationship between Bose and Kumar, he glosses over the fact that Bose's preference for Kumar's younger brother, also a Muslim, contradicts the accusation of religious partisanship in the selection of the lead actor. Within Luqman's world of negotiations and networks, where he went with a (Muslim) friend, Mukri, to a (Muslim) studio proprietor, Shiraz Ali Hakim, to save the career of an (Muslim) actor-friend, Dilip Kumar, co-religionists played an important role. That Kumar later chose Bose to direct his own film hangs as an unresolved piece of information in Luqman's account, making his categorical claims tenuous.

Shaukat Hussain makes a somewhat similar remark about Bose but qualifies Dilip Kumar's relationship with the director and instead sees the prejudice directed at his own film *Jugnu*:

> *Yeh Bombay Talkies mein mulazim tha. Vahan Nitin Bose director tha. Bangali tha,... Dilip iska bada kayal tha. Baharhal maine Nitin Bose se baat ki ke meri shooting adjust karo. Voh sala bada mutasib tha. Humse haan haan toh kar diya, lekin jab meri shooting ho toh voh apni rehearsal rakh de.*[103]

He [Dilip] was employed at the Bombay Talkies studio. Nitin Bose was the director there. He was a Bengali. Dilip was deeply impressed by him. Anyway, I spoke to Nitin Bose about adjusting my film shoot to agree not to clash with his. That rascal was extremely prejudiced. He agreed to it at first, but then he would purposefully coincide his rehearsals with my shoot.

While the life-autobiographies were narrated in the 1980s and are mostly talking the situation in Bombay studios in the mid-1940s, one cannot help notice that Abbas' exposé of the communal game mentions the same personalities as Luqman and Rizvi. This suggests that the formation of different factions in the film industry based on a politicised religious identity had started as early as 1940.

In the narratives of the two migrant film-makers, the acts of cooperation and accommodation becomes a yardstick for ascertaining communal prejudices within individuals. It is also intimately connected with the nature of film production in India at this time that saw the decline of what Barnouw and Krishnaswamy call the 'one-big-family studios', paralleled by the rise of the independent producer. The structure of the 'one-big-family studio' composed of extended family and relatives of the owner meant they rarely needed to turn to outsiders for services.[104] With family bias inherent in it, the nepotism of film studios could take on a nefarious hue, causing community and caste-based exclusions. Another incident recalled by Rizvi involves the lower-caste Hindu studio-cleaners, or *jamadars*, who, while celebrating the success of *Zeenat* at the Shree Sound Studio premises, abused the owners in drunken resentment. As a freelancing director, Rizvi claims distance and ignorance of the hierarchical – and in this case caste-based – dynamics of the studio. The new independent film-makers were outsiders, like Shaukat Hussain, who rented studios and had stars working for them on a freelance basis. The clash described here denotes the larger struggle for survival between the old established companies and the new independent producer.

These two life-narratives also provide instances of how political disagreement and prejudice could have very concrete manifestations. Shaukat Rizvi recounts getting into an argument over Jinnah with the Hindu management of the Shree Sound Studio where *Jugnu* was being shot. For his readers, he lays special emphasis on being the only Muslim in the midst of several Hindus during the heated discussion and suffuses the memory with heroic courage. Being a supporter of Jinnah and the

Muslim League, he retaliated by disparaging Gandhi and the Congress. Shaukat reveals that even though he held Gandhi in esteem, the attack on Jinnah made him assume a hostile position on the political figure. After this particular episode, which most probably happened in late 1946, Shaukat had to bear the consequences for sticking to his political guns.

> *Iss vakye ke baad se meri film ke dabbon mein ched hone lage. Phir yeh hua ki mere gaane ka ek set tha jo mujhe ek hi roz mein khatam karna tha. Par voh khatam na ho saka…. Lekin voh doosre din ke liye nahi maane. Unhone Hinduana taasub ki vajah se voh set tod diya.*[105]

After this incident [the heated exchange on Jinnah and Gandhi], holes began to appear mysteriously on the cans of my films… Then there was a set for a song shoot, which I planned to finish in a day.… But I was unable to complete it and they [the studio management] didn't agree for a second day. Acting out their Hindu prejudice, they pulled down the set.

Holes in an exposed film-can could damage the shot stock, increase the financial burden and hinder the film in general. Reading active sabotage on the part of the studio owners, Rizvi moved his film to Modi's Minerva Movietone and completed his film. The sabotage narrative continues even after the film-makers move to Lahore after partition. Luqman recounts the experience of making his first film in Pakistan, *Shahida* (1949), which got delayed because of the botched quality of the film negative.

> *Hindu taasub ka yeh alam tha ki Kodak ka head office Bombay mein tha, Lahore mein branch thi. Hinduon ne saazish kar ke humein jo negative bheja voh dhundhla tha.… Humne 'Shahida' ke darmiyan shooting rok kar ke negative London se direct import kiya.*[106]

The extent of Hindu prejudice made itself evident in the advantageous location of the Kodak head office in Bombay, with only a branch office in Lahore. The Hindus schemed and exported us a negative that was foggy. We had to stop the shoot of 'Shahida' in between and import the negative directly from London.

Thus, the account of pre-independence prejudice feeds seamlessly into the post-partition national antagonism between the two film-producing centres.

Articulating Politicised Difference

Among the individuals discussed by Luqman and Shaukat, studio owner and film-maker Sohrab Modi is an important presence. As a non-Hindu and non-Muslim, the Parsi Modi mediates the articulation of politicised religious identities by both of them. Yet the Modi of Luqman's account is different in Rizvi's experience. Luqman recounts the strong opposition to Hindu religious practices by Muslim workers in Minerva Movietone, which was owned by Modi. According to him, such counterpoint or balance could happen only because of the principled neutrality of Modi.

Modi Sahab iss aqeede ke aadmi thay ke studios mein jo Hindus thay unhone ijazat maangi ki voh Shri Satyanarayan ki puja karana chahte hain. Modi sahab ne kaha 'theek hai, karein'. Hum logon mein jo Mussalman thay, kaha hum milaad sharif karenge. Fauran ijazat mil gayi. Humne kaha kyunki milad hai, hum stage bhi lagayeinge. Kehne lage theek hai, jaisa chahein karein.... Bada khoobsoorat masjid numa stage banaya. Bhindi bazaar se padhne waalon ka intezaam kiya. Studio mein maujood har Mussalman ne bharpoor hissa liya, milad sharif hua. Modi Sahab rumal sar par baandh kar dua tak baithe rahe.[107]

Modi was a man of such principles that when the Hindus of the studio wished to conduct a ritual worship for deity Shri Satyanarayan, he said 'Fine, do it'. We Muslims said we wished to organize Milad Shareef [birthday celebration of the Prophet]. We immediately got the permission. Since it was Milad, we said we would also put up a stage. Modi said, 'Fine, do as you wish'. It was such a beautiful mosque-themed stage. We arranged for trained recitals from Bhindi Bazaar. Every Muslim worker of the studio participated enthusiastically. The Milad started, and Modi Sahab sat with his head respectfully covered with a handkerchief right till the end of the prayer.

On the other hand, Rizvi cancelled a film contract with Modi within days of clinching it. According to Rizvi, Modi had a habit of interfering with the final shape and edit of any film made in his studio, and the question of creative control led to a professional breakdown between the two.

Modi sahab kehne lage, Shaukat sahab, maine dekha hai ki aap mein salahatein hain, aap se kaam liya ja sakta hai. Mera toh para chad gaya. 'Modi sahab, aap humse kya kaam lenge ... aap mujhse picture banwayeinge toh agreement mein yeh khaas clause hogi ke meri picture mein se na aap kuch kaat sakenge na aap koi izaafa kar sakenge. Paise ki koi baat nahin. Dekhiye, aap studio ke maalik hain, Shantaram bhi studio ke maalik hain. Aap aur Shantaram Jyoti studio chalein ek picture main banaoon, ek picture aap banayein, ek picture Shantaram banayein. Sab ko ek jaisi sahooliyatein haasil hon. Phir dekhtein hain aap log kya gul khilatein hain!' Maine kaha, 'Modi sahab aapne khaki kapda pehna hua hai. Jo aadmi khaki kapda pehanta hai main usse sakht nafrat karta hun.' [108]

Mr Modi remarked, 'Mr Shaukat, I have noticed that you have the capabilities and could be made to work'. I began to lose my cool. 'Mr Modi, I don't work for you. If I make a film with your studio, then the agreement must have this crucial clause that in my film you shall neither delete nor add any portions. Money is of little concern here. People like you and Shantaram have your own studios. Why not come to Jyoti studio and let us all make a film each with identical facilities? Then we shall see your filmmaking capabilities!' I said, 'Modi *sahab*, you are dressed in *khaki*. And I truly detest a man who has such sympathies'.

The reference here to *khaki* is largely proverbial, signifying political leanings towards the Hindu right.[109] After cancelling his contract with Modi, Rizvi signed a two-film contract with producer-financier Shiraz Ali Hakim. Even with Hakim, Rizvi had a deadlock over the ending for *Zeenat*, and eventually Hakim succumbed. Yet Rizvi does not read these differences as ideologically motivated, as he saw in the case of Modi. It is interesting to note that the consistency with Luqman's worldview is finally restored, as the indictment of Modi in Rizvi's account is rather short-lived. When forced to find a studio for his film during the making of *Jugnu*, due to growing tension with the Shree Sound Studio owners, Shaukat is chastened to find Modi cooperative and ready to forgive and forget. His final verdict on Modi in his memoirs is that 'he was a great man'.[110]

Luqman's account also reveals the close links of some producers and financiers in the Bombay film industry to the Muslim League. Shiraz Ali Hakim, who acquired controlling shares in Bombay Talkies in 1946, was the son-in-law of the treasurer of the Bombay Muslim League, Aziz Gafoor Qazi. If Hakim produced Rizvi's *Zeenat*, then Qazi was the producer of Luqman's sole directorial venture in Bombay, *Humjoli*. These links were marked by mutuality as Luqman occasionally joined another zealous Muslim League worker in Qazi's jeep to perform 'rescue' operations for Muslims during religious clashes in Bombay. As for supporting the Pakistan movement, Luqman categorically declares that all Muslim personnel of the Bombay film industry were supporters of the Muslim League resolution, with the exception of K. A. Abbas.

> *Agar ek K.A. Abbas Pakistan ke khilaf they kyunki voh Communist Party se taaluk rakhte the, toh voh kissi shumar katar mein nahin they. Mehboob sahab, Shaukat sahab, Sibtain Fazli sahab, Nazir sahab. Nazir sahab ne jab apna studio banaya toh voh Hindu artist ke muqable mein Mussalman ko tarjiye dete the.*[111]

> If a certain K. A. Abbas was opposed to the idea of Pakistan, it was due to his links with the Communist Party and so his views [as a Muslim] did not count. Mehboob, Shaukat Hussain Rizvi, Sibtain Fazli, Nazir [were all supporters of the Muslim League]. When Nazir made his studio [in Bombay], then he gave precedence to Muslim artistes over Hindus.

Nazir's studio hiring rule echoes *Filmindia*'s insinuations against the new institution of 'Pakistan producers' who would only employ Muslim personnel, confirming that there was indeed the formation of a Muslim network in Bombay. There is little discussion of women film artistes and their affiliation here. There is an equal silence on the Muslim personnel across crew hierarchies who did not migrate, as the names cited earlier are of those who migrated to Pakistan. Despite devoting considerable attention to Mehboob in his account, Luqman never deliberates on why Mehboob and Kardar returned to India. Nevertheless, support for the Muslim League also meant joining the celebrations of the formation of Pakistan on 14 August 1947. Both Luqman and Rizvi were present in Karachi for the festivities, and the latter wished to film the proceedings.

> *Ekam Agast 1947 ko apne technicians le karke main Karachi pahoncha taki 14 Agast ka jashan-i-azaadi expose kar sakun. 14 Agast ka jashn-i-azadi dekh kar ke 15 ko main Bambai fly kar gaya. Jahaz se Bambai chamakta hua dikhayi de raha tha.*[112]

On 1 August 1947, I reached Karachi along with my technicians to film the celebration of independence of Pakistan on 14 August. After watching the festivities, I flew back to Bombay on 15 August. From the plane, Bombay appeared to be glittering.

It is striking that Rizvi's memory of the festivities in Karachi consists of clear dates and the logistics of filming, while the visual imprint is a glittering Bombay seen from above.[113] Despite proclamations of support for the Pakistan movement in both life-narratives, the decision to migrate is revealed as a hasty one, involving little introspection, and is externalised. While for Rizvi it was the worsening communal situation and an advice by a well-wisher, Luqman sees himself as merely following the example of others.

> *Kuch dinn ke baad phir vahaan fasadaat shuru ho gaye. Jiss tarah Dehli mein Mussalmanon ke gharon ko nishanat lagaye gaye they, yahan bhi aisa ho raha tha. Vahi Jagmer Singh producer jisse humari mulaqat Jaddan bai ke yahaan hui thi, kehne laga Shaukat sahab mahine do mahine ke liye aap Bambai chorh kar kahin aur chaley jayiye. Isne isharan kaha, yahan gadbad hogi. Isne yeh nahin kaha ke aap permanent chorh dein.*

Some days after independence, riots started there [in Bombay]. Just like Delhi, Muslim houses were being marked out and targeted here. Producer Jagmer Singh, who we had met at Jaddan Bai's place, said, 'Shaukat *sahab*, you must leave Bombay for a month or two and go elsewhere.' He hinted about the impending trouble. *He never said that you leave forever.*[114]

Luqman moved quickly between Bombay, Karachi and Lahore in August 1947 and, seeing most of his associates leave, decided to join them in Karachi in October.

> *Phir Shiraz seth Pakistan aa rahe the. Shaukat sahab bhi aa rahey they. Kardar sahab bhi aa gaye, Mehboob bhi.... Mujhe kuch ajeeb sa lag raha tha, issliye main bhi aa gaya.*[115]

Then Shiraz Seth was coming to Pakistan. Shaukat *sahab* too was on his way. Kardar *sahab* also arrived, so did Mehboob. I was feeling a bit uneasy, so I came here as well [Pakistan].

This lack of agency in moving to Karachi in terms of active intent or desire is striking as, for both Rizvi and Luqman, Pakistan turned out to be a land of no return.[116] Rizvi started on an ambitious project of building a studio in post-partition Lahore. He was allotted the evacuee studio property of producer Roop K. Shorey, who had been forced by the riots to leave the city. The Shorey studio had been attacked by an arsonist, and Shaukat got involved in its reconstruction. The studio was to be called 'Shahnoor', a testimonial to Shaukat and Noorjahan's association in their new home country. In Rizvi's account one detects that returning to Bombay was more an option closed rather than not desired. The exclusions of the dominant anti-colonial nationalism ensured that the 'traitors' were in place before national independence. Those who returned from 'Pakistan' to 'India' had to prove their allegiances even more persuasively. Rizvi remembers that on being probed in Bombay about their trip to Karachi, returning film-makers Mehboob and Kardar held Rizvi responsible for influencing them to go to Pakistan and thus foreclosed any possibility of his return.[117] Rizvi pointedly chooses the lyrical refrain of a song from his film *Jugnu* – 'Yahan badla wafa ka bewafai ke siwa kya hai' (Here loyalty is requited by little else but betrayal) – to encapsulate his experience of the Bombay film industry. It was the set of this song that Rizvi recollects getting destroyed by the Shree Sound Studio management.

While emphasising that a return to Bombay was out of the question, even as old colleagues asked him to reconsider during a visit to the city in 1952, Luqman cannot but help a nostalgic reference to his Bombay years while critiquing the present state of the Pakistani film industry.

> *Uss mahaul jo humnein Bambai mein dekha aur aaj film industry ka jo yahaan mahaul hai, issmein zameen aasmaan jitna farq hai.... Humnein kaam unse seekha hai jo studio ke gate ko teen salaam karte they ki yeh rozi ki jagah hai.*[118]

> Comparing the work ambience of what we saw in Bombay [in the 1940s] with what exists here [Pakistan] today, is like comparing the high skies with the base level.... We have learnt our craft from those who would respectfully salute the studio gates thrice before entering, as that was the place of cherished livelihood.

From Muslim nationalism being a modality of contest, the narratives progressively transform it into a two-threaded strain of Pakistani nationalism, one sacrificial and the other aspirational.[119] While Rizvi's creatively pallid career in Pakistan makes his seven-year success in Bombay shine only brighter, it is also an intense signifier of a votive nationalism. Luqman's unhindered and more prolific career as a film director in Pakistan, on the other hand, reaffirms the exertions of a struggling assistant director in Bombay, which included some dilettante Muslim League activism. The despair at the later turn of events makes aspiration twine only closer to sacrifice.

Figure 2.5   Dilip Kumar Chilli Pickle sold by business interests represented by *Filmindia*
Source: *Filmindia*, February 1957, 12.

The juxtaposition of these two archives of polarisation and partisanship, *Filmindia* and the memoirs, is not to suggest their equivalence. Instead, I intend to draw attention to the cacophony around the partition, which was vociferously resisted and opposed as an impending Pakistan during the 1940s. Three aspects of film production in Bombay emerge through these oppositional narratives. First, the Pakistan movement for many Muslim personnel in Bombay became a way to carve a production solidarity within the film business in the 1940s. Muslim nationalism emerged, albeit for a short time, as a modality of controlling film production, especially above-the-line work and profits. Second, these sources are also united in conveying a key attitude of this time among those who supported the Pakistan movement: they never thought their political cause would mean giving up on film-making in economically and technologically advanced Bombay. Finally, political interests were closely tied to professional and commercial interests. Thus, donations, advertisements and endorsements must not be read merely as profit-seeking exercises but motivated at this time to seek national rehabilitation. That Muslim film artistes who stayed in Bombay needed to assuage the exploitative vigilantism of Hindu nationalism as that of *Filmindia* suggests the limitations of secular nationalism of this time. I seek these answers in the next chapter through the theatrics of Prithvi Theatre, representative of secular nationalism. The uncertainty and contestations of the 1940s paved the way for hegemonic clarity and categorical stances in the new nations in the next decade. Secular nationalism imbued professional postures and national film biographies in India. Baburao Patel changed the name of his popular publication to *Mother India* in 1961, its twenty-fifth year. Mnemonic of his ideological investment in Mehboob's magnum opus, *Mother India* (1957), 'in continuous circulation for over three decades',[120] it has persuaded a film historian to see Patel as one 'who championed Mehboob's films'.[121] This claim is unconvincing in the face of *Filmindia*'s distrustful reportage on Mehboob. In fact, Patel's association with the brand name 'Mother India' preceded the release of the film. Between 1955 and 1957, the magazine regularly advertised pickles with the bodiless head of Dilip Kumar manufactured by 'Mother India products', a firm that had the same business address as *Filmindia*, and presumably that is where the profits went as well (Figure 2.5). 'Dilip Kumar Table Tasties' was not a star endorsement nor an actor expanding his commercial ventures through his bodiless head. It was instead a matter of national appropriation,[122] much like Madhubala's donation episode. These ancillary ventures and acts are ultimately representative of the pickle that *many but not all* Muslim film personnel found themselves in – in the immediate aftermath of partition in Bombay.

Notes

1   R. K. Nehru was an Indian civil servant and a cousin of the first prime minister of India, Jawaharlal Nehru.

2   Richard Symonds, *In the Margins of Independence: A Relief Worker in India and Pakistan (1942–49)* (Oxford: Oxford University Press, 2001), 63.

3   Saadat Hassan Manto, 'Ashok Kumar: The Evergreen Hero', in *Bitter Fruit: The Very Best of Saadat Hasan Manto*, trans. and ed. Khaled Hassan, 447–460 (New Delhi: Penguin Books, 2008). The same Manto after reaching Pakistan would write in a tongue-in-cheek manner that the nation's only drawback was too many Muslims.

4   This is a very widely held position. For a record of this view, see Rachel Dwyer, *Yash Chopra: Fifty Years in Cinema* (New Delhi: Roli Books, 2002), 21.

5   These include actors such as Amitabh Bachchan, Anupam Kher, Akshay Kumar, Ajay Devgn, Priyanka Chopra, Kangana Ranaut and Anushka Sharma, and singers such as Sonu Nigam and Abhijeet. Lyricist Prasoon Joshi has penned several campaign songs for the BJP since 2014.

6   'Above-the-line' crew refers to roles in film-making, which have more creative clout and better terms of remuneration. These include directors, producers, writers, main actors and, in Bombay production, music directors and singers as well. The terminology refers to the hierarchies in a production unit and budgeting, with 'below-the-line' workers often considered replaceable and on contractual wages.

7   Priya Jaikumar, *Cinema at the End of Empire: A Politics of Transition in Britain and India* (Durham, NC: Duke University Press, 2006), 235.

8   In the past six years, since the Hindu nationalist political party's resounding electoral success, the film industry based in Mumbai has been more vocal in its support of the Hindu nationalist government and extremely guarded in their criticism. While highest-paid actors and directors have flocked around the prime minister of India in a selfie embrace, others ideologically committed to Hindu nationalism have used their social media presence to defend the regime against its critics.

9   For instance, see Amber Abbas' work on Aligarh Muslim University. Amber Abbas, 'Disruption and Belonging: Aligarh, Its University, and the Changing Meaning of Place since Partition', *Oral History Review* 44, no. 2 (2017): 301–321.

10   Perry Anderson, *The Indian Ideology* (London: Verso, 2013).

11   Pradeep Kumar Dutta, *Carving Blocs* (Oxford: Oxford University Press, 1999), 7.

12   Faisal Devji, 'Hindu/Muslim/Indian', *Public Culture* 5, no. 1 (Fall 1992): 1–18, 4.

13   Ibid., 4.

14   Aditya Mukherjee, Mridula Mukherjee, and Sucheta Mahajan, *RSS, School Texts and the Murder of Mahatma Gandhi: The Hindu Communal Project* (New Delhi: SAGE Publications, 2008), 79.

15   Faisal Devji, 'Hindu/Muslim/Indian', 2.

16   Ibid.

17   Kaushik Bhaumik, 'The Emergence of the Bombay Film Industry 1913–1936' (PhD diss., University of Oxford, 2001), 150.

18   An instance of this is Prem Chowdhry, *The Colonial India and the Making of Empire Cinema: Image Ideology and Identity* (Manchester: Manchester University Press, 2000).

19   R. A. Shaikh (ed.), *Filmdom: Who's Who in the Indian Film Industry* (Lahore: Globial Linkers, 1946).

20   Saadat Hassan Manto too devotes a section to Baburao Patel in his collection of portraits on the Bombay film world, and the inclusion underscores the importance of the editor-proprietor of the popular magazine. Saadat Hassan Manto, 'Babu Rao Patel: Soft-hearted Iconoclast', in *Bitter Fruit: The Very Best of Saadat Hasan Manto*, trans. and ed. Khaled Hassan, 552–561 (New Delhi: Penguin Books, 2008).

21   As referred to in the popular blog on old Hindi films, Memsahab Story, http:// memsaabstory.com/category/hindi-movies/baburao-patels-poisonous-pen/ (accessed on 10 November 2011).

22   Sumita Chakravarty, *National Identity in Indian Popular Cinema 1947–1987* (Austin: University of Texas Press, 1993), 69.

23   Bhaskar Sarkar, *Mourning the Nation: Indian Cinema in the Wake of Partition* (Durham, NC: Duke University Press, 2009), 100.

24   Khwaja Ahmad Abbas, *I Am Not an Island* (New Delhi: Vikas, 1977), 209.

25   Bhaumik, 'The Emergence of the Bombay Film Industry', 190 (emphasis mine).

26   In response to a reader's question on the magazine's tendency to change the language of the questions sent to the editor. 'Editor's Mail', *Filmindia*, January 1942, 21.

27   In response to a reader's question on ethics of film criticism. 'Editor's Mail', *Filmindia*, May 1944.

28   'When you don't see advertisements of your favourite producers in "filmindia", it means that the "milk" has been taken away from the "snake", because the "snake" has refused to dance to the tunes of the "snake-charmers".' *Filmindia*, February 1943, 37.

29 Debashree Mukherjee, 'Creating Cinema's Reading Publics', in *No Limits: Media Studies from India*, ed. Ravi Sundaram, 165–198 (New Delhi: Oxford University Press, 2013), 177.

30 'M.R.A Baig Wants Pictures on Hindu-Muslim Unity', *Filmindia*, February 1942, 45.

31 Abbas, *I Am Not an Island*, 200.

32 'Editor's Mail', *Filmindia*, March 1947.

33 Ibid.

34 'Editor's Mail', *Filmindia*, January 1942, 17 (emphasis mine).

35 Bhaumik, 'The Emergence of the Bombay Film Industry', 151.

36 Eric Barnouw and S. Krishnaswamy, *Indian Film* (New York: Oxford University Press, 1980), 130.

37 Khwaja Ahmad Abbas, 'Communalists, Keep Out!' *Filmindia*, February 1940, 31.

38 Ibid.

39 Ibid. (emphasis mine).

40 'The Blackmailing Twins', *Filmindia*, February 1940, 3.

41 In 1950, the magazine ran a special column where all leading film producers were asked to respond to the question posed by Baburao Patel: 'Am I a blackmailer?' They all denied it. 'Am I a blackmailer?' *Filmindia*, August 1950, 47.

42 Barnouw and Krishnaswamy, *Indian Film*, 48.

43 Ravi Vasudevan, 'The Politics of Cultural Address in a "Transitional" Cinema: A Case Study of Indian Popular Cinema', in *Reinventing Film Studies*, ed. Christine Gledhill and Linda Williams, 130–164 (London: Arnold Publishers, 2000), 156.

44 Vasudevan points out that the League for Censorship also hoped that the Congress government of Bombay would be responsive to their demand and ban certain films for their anti-Hindu features. Assigning itself a watchdog role and asking for stringent measures, the League was however dismissed by the Home Minister, K. M. Munshi, as bigoted. Ibid., 10.

45 Gyanendra Pandey, *The Construction of Communalism in North India* (New Delhi: Oxford University Press, 2006), 246.

46 Abbas, *I Am Not an Island*, 208 (emphasis mine).

47 'Mazhar Khan Hits Our National Leaders', *Filmindia*, May 1942, 59.

48 'M.R.A Baig Wants Pictures on Hindu-Muslim Unity', 45.

49 Pandey, *Construction of Communalism*, 246.

50 'Promoting or Provoking', *Filmindia*, November 1946, 3.

51 '40 Crores and 400 Millions', *Filmindia*, May 1946, 11.

52 Jinnah met Gandhi at his Malabar Hill residence in September 1944, a meeting seen as a last-ditch effort to seek a compromise between the Muslim League and the Congress.

53 In order to press for its demand for Pakistan and oppose the Cabinet Mission Plan, the Muslim League called for the observance of Direct Action Day on 14 August 1946. Communal violence broke, out and the first wave saw the 'Great Calcutta Killings' between 14 and 18 August 1946.

54 'Blackmailing a National Industry', *Filmindia*, August 1946, 3–7.

55 Ibid., 7.

56 'Bombay Calling', *Filmindia*, January 1945, 9.

57 'You'll Hardly Believe', *Filmindia*, September 1945.

58   'You'll Hardly Believe', *Filmindia*, September 1946, 23.
59   'You'll Hardly Believe', *Filmindia*, October 1947, 13.
60   Ira Bhaskar and Richard Allen, *Islamicate Cultures of Bombay Cinema* (New Delhi: Tulika Books, 2009), 6.
61   Pandey, *Construction of Communalism*, 247.
62   Christophe Jaffrelot, *The Hindu Nationalist Movement and Indian Politics, 1925 to the 1990s* (London: Hurst & Co., 1996), 6.
63   Urvi Mukhopadhaya, *The Medieval in Film* (New Delhi: Orient Blackswan, 2013), 145–195.
64   '*Ismat* Presents Common Uninteresting Plot!' *Filmindia*, April 1945, 37.
65   'K Asif Hits the Headlines in Phool', *Filmindia*, June 1945, 41.
66   '*Nek Parvin*: Love-and-Revolver Muslim Romance', *Filmindia*, June 1946, 41.
67   Ibid.
68   'Shuttling between India and Pakistan', *Filmindia* 1950, 11–13.
69   'Living with Wolves?', *Filmindia*, November 1947, 9–11.
70   'You'll Hardly Believe', *Filmindia*, November 1947, 22.
71   'Abidah, Good Picture Made Unpleasant!', *Filmindia*, December 1947, 65.
72   Ibid. (emphasis mine).
73   'Muslim "Meerabai" Grossly Slanders Hinduism', *Filmindia*, December 1947, 53–57 (emphasis mine).
74   'Tamil "Meera" Becomes a Hindi Musical', *Filmindia*, January 1948, 44.
75   'Nateeja: A Regular School for Crime!' *Filmindia*, December 1947, 58.
76   'At Home and Abroad', *Filmindia*, January 1948, 53.
77   'At Home and Abroad', *Filmindia*, April 1948, 59.
78   *Report of the Film Enquiry Committee*, Appendix IX (New Delhi: Ministry of Information of Information and Broadcasting, Government of India Press, 1951), 307.
79   'Bombay Calling', *Filmindia*, January 1949, 9.
80   'Dillagi, a Disgusting Slander of Hindu Virgins!' *Filmindia*, November 1949, 49.
81   'Woes and Echoes', *Filmindia*, January 1949, 68.
82   'Abidah, Good Picture Made Unpleasant', *Filmindia*, December 1947, 65.
83   While Mahatma Gandhi's statue stood as a symbol of Indian nationalism, the Ganesh statue would have associated the place with the Hindu denomination and thus inoculated the Kardar studios, whose owner was a Muslim, from any religiously motivated attacks.
84   From *Filmindia*, May 1950 to *Filmindia*, November 1950.
85   'You'll Hardly Believe', *Filmindia*, August 1949, 13.
86   'Mehboob and Pakistan', *Filmindia*, January 1948, 59.
87   *Filmindia*, January 1951, 14.
88   *Filmindia*, January 1949, 63.
89   *Filmindia*, September 1950, 49.
90   Ibid.
91   'Biggest Star in the World', *Theatre Arts*, August 1952, 26.
92   'Woes and Echoes', *Filmindia*, May 1952, 77.
93   Sidonie Smith and Julia Watson, *Reading Autobiography: A Guide for Interpreting Life Narratives* (Minneapolis: University of Minnesota Press, 2001), 15.

94   Shaukat Hussain Rizvi, *Noorjahan aur Main* (Lahore: Atish Feshan Publications, 1984).
95   While the Pancholis were based in Lahore, they were shareholders of the Film Corporation at Calcutta.
96   'Luqman', in *Out of Date*, ed. Muneer Ahmed, 101–134 (Lahore: Atish Feshan Publications, 1986).
97   'Luqman', *Out of Date*, 104.
98   Rizvi, *Noorjahan aur Main*, 47.
99   Religion is mentioned against each name to make clear that names in the Indian subcontinent usually carry a distinct identity. One's name conveys a variety of information like religious, regional and caste identities. The mention of a religious category is not a confirmation of their personal beliefs. It is how these people appeared to Luqman.
100   'Luqman', *Out of Date*, 118–119.
101   Ibid., 129.
102   Ibid., 115.
103   Rizvi, *Noorjahan aur Main*, 67.
104   See the discussion on 'one-big-family studios' in Barnouw and Krishnaswamy, *Indian Film*, 113–115.
105   Rizvi, *Noorjahan aur Main*, 67–68.
106   'Luqman', *Out of Date*, 160.
107   Ibid., 110.
108   Rizvi, *Noorjahan aur Main*, 62.
109   Knee-length *khaki* shorts have been the uniform for the cadres of the RSS, a militant Hindu nationalist outfit, making them quite conspicuous.
110   Rizvi, *Noorjahan aur Main*, 68.
111   'Luqman', *Out of Date*, 133.
112   Rizvi, *Noorjahan aur Main*, 71.
113   On 15 August 1947, a 'glittering Bombay' must have been the celebration of Indian independence in the city.
114   Rizvi, *Noorjahan aur Main*, 71 (emphasis mine).
115   'Luqman', *Out of Date*, 119.
116   Being closer to Bombay and not torn by riots like the Punjab region where Lahore was located, Karachi provided safe passageway to many migrants.
117   Rizvi, *Noorjahan aur Main*, 72.
118   'Luqman', *Out of Date*, 128.
119   I partly draw on Naveeda Khan's argument. Naveeda Khan, *The Muslim Becoming: Aspiration and Scepticism in Pakistan* (Durham, NC: Duke University Press, 2012).
120   Gayatri Chatterjee, *Mother India* (London: BFI Film Classics, 2002), 18.
121   Ibid.
122   Dilip Kumar is a film star who is interestingly claimed by both India and Pakistan. Even though he lived and died as an Indian citizen and worked only in Indian cinema, in 2000 he was awarded with the highest civilian award of Pakistan, Nishan-i-Imtiaz. Dilip Kumar was asked by the right-wing political party Shiv Sena to return the award to prove his loyalty to the Indian state.

3

Stages of Partition

The Early Years of Prithvi Theatre

In the early 1950s, the Indian Motion Picture Producers' Association (IMPPA) noted the difficulties in fully 'exploiting' Pakistani territories, which constituted nearly 20 per cent of the Hindustani–Urdu film market before partition.[1] While the import duties and sales tax were commonly applicable to all Indian films, there was an additional handicap for movies starring Prithviraj Kapoor and his son Raj Kapoor. In April 1951, the Karachi Board of Film Censors had 'informed the Sind and Baluchistan Film Distributors' Syndicate that pictures in which Prithviraj and Raj Kapoor appear will not be passed in future.'[2] This decision was based on a 'certain amount of public resentment against Prithviraj', and, accordingly, the films *Barsaat* (Rain, 1949) and *Dahej* (Dowry, 1950) were banned in Pakistan for some time. What were the reasons behind the Government of Pakistan's disfavour of Prithviraj? The answer may lie, as we will see, not in these films but in performances ancillary to film-making that initiated a rather public disaffection between Prithviraj Kapoor and the proponents of Pakistan.

The Indian films of the post-partition period continued to avoid sensitive contemporary themes partly out of censorship concerns and partly for commercial reasons. Ravi Vasudevan suggests that 'the dearth of films directly confronting this event indicates that the film industry trod warily around the subject for fear of sectarian controversy.'[3] Ira Bhaskar reasons that the immediacy and performative power of cinema made it a potentially dangerous medium for the communication of violence and displacement.[4] 'Partition violence or a depiction of inter-community Hindu Muslim relations ... did not figure in Indian cinema for four decades', as such representation had the potential of reopening old wounds.[5] Bhaskar Sarkar locates a 'resonant silence' around partition in films and argues that what the films were unable to directly depict registered in implicit ways.[6] And yet to a large extent this vacuum was filled in by theatre. Prithvi Theatre, a group closely associated with the Bombay chapter of the Indian People's Theatre Association (IPTA) as well as with the Bombay film industry, played partition right through the mid-1940s into the 1950s. While Prithvi Theatre has received attention in the recent decade or so,[7] it awaits an appraisal of the thematic pivot of partition in the troupe's early performances.[8]

In the histories of Indian theatre, Prithvi Theatre's plays are summarily mentioned as 'enormously popular secular narratives'[9] and among the anti-imperialist, anti-fascist, radical 'people's theatre' of this decade.[10] A closer engagement with the group's partition performances reveals them to be less benign as have hitherto been understood. Bringing together newly identified historical sources on Prithvi Theatre such as memoirs, biographies, contemporary commentary and extant play-scripts, I critically revisit some of the received ideas around Prithvi Theatre and the representation of partition right at the time it unfolded. My first set of sources are the play-scripts of *Deewar* (The Wall, 1945) and *Ahooti* (The Sacrifice, 1949) published in Devanagari script by Prithvi publications. The next set of sources are the memoirs by co-travellers and associates of Prithviraj Kapoor such as Jai Dyal (*I Go South with Prithviraj and His Prithvi Theatres*), Yog Raj Tandon (*Theatre ke Sartaj Prithviraj*) and actress Zohra Sehgal (*Close-Up*). Finally, *Filmindia* and the *Journal of the Indian Film Industry* offer an opportunity to situate these theatrical performances within the public discourses of the Bombay film enterprise.

In January 1944, film actor Prithviraj Kapoor founded the Prithvi Theatre. One of the most prominent actors of Hindi–Urdu cinema at this time, Prithviraj hailed from Peshawar in the North-West Frontier Province (NWFP), which became a key constituent area of Pakistan after partition. According to his mentor Jai Dyal of Edwards College, Prithviraj developed a keen interest in theatre and achieved recognition on the amateur stage in Peshawar and Lyallpur in the early 1920s. He then transitioned from stage to film, and from Peshawar to Bombay, then Calcutta and finally Bombay again. Making his debut on screen in silent cinema during the early 1930s, Prithviraj acted in several technological and artistic milestones like the first talkie of the sub-continent *Alam Ara* (1931, dir. Ardheshir Irani), the historical *Sikander* (1941, dir. Sohrab Modi) and the enduring *Mughal-e-Azam* (1960, dir. K. Asif).

In the early 1940s, Prithviraj involved himself in theatre once again and financed the new endeavour through his film income. Prithvi Theatre was also associated with IPTA and the Progressive Writers' Association (PWA). The communist writer-journalist Sajjad Zaheer recalls Prithviraj among the film industry regulars at the PWA meetings.[11] Like IPTA, Prithvi Theatre reinvigorated the relationship between cinema and theatre, where Prithviraj's troupe was often wooed by the film industry and he 'acted as a supplier of film stars, his son Raj being one'.[12] But despite remaining close to IPTA, Prithvi Theatre retained its distinctiveness and ideological distance through the assertions of this outspoken and politicised artiste.[13] If IPTA built a 'people's theatre' under the political guidance of the Communist Party, then Prithviraj's proximity to the Congress is attested to by his biographers as well as by the attendance of the Congress top brass at these performances. As the financier, director, co-author, lead actor and master of ceremonies, Prithviraj forged Prithvi Theatre as 'art in the service of the nation'.[14]

Founding choices are important, even if they occupy a marginal place in the oeuvre or – as in the case of Prithvi Theatre's *Shakuntala* – are described as 'false starts'.[15] The first performance of Prithvi Theatre in March 1944 was a modern Hindi version of the Sanskrit classic, as written by Parsi theatre veteran Betab. Central to the nineteenth-century orientalist construction of 'Indian theatre' as exclusively Sanskrit was the fifth-century playwright Kalidasa's *Abhijnanashakuntalam* (Shakuntala).[16] This play has since been claimed by Indian cultural nationalists as legitimate classical heritage. *Shakuntala* fitted the anti-colonial, nationalist stance of Prithvi Theatre well, except that it had incurred a tremendous financial loss by the end of its first run. This posed questions for the future repertoire of Prithvi Theatre. Actress Zohra Sehgal, who along with her sister Uzra Mumtaz was a key artiste of the Prithvi troupe, recounts the deliberations over future plays in her memoirs. If *Shakuntala's* box-office performance conveyed the impracticality and obsolescence of Sanskrit plays, then the modern adaptations of Western classics by Agha Hashr Kashmiri were seen to be unsuited to a self-consciously nationalist theatre practice aimed at social reform.[17] It was only later on that scholarship on Hashr's oeuvre would complicate the forms that anti-colonial nationalism could take. In her research on Parsi theatre, Kathryn Hansen describes Hashr's adaptation process as the blending of Shakespearean tales with elements of miraculous spectacle unfolding in a pseudo Indo-Islamic milieu.[18] While Hansen reads Hashr's *Yahudi Ki Ladki* as beginning 'a larger project of the critique of the colonial' state,[19] the Indo-Islamic milieu of miraculous spectacles of Hashr's repertory may have seemed outmoded to the 'level headed … Congress' sensibilities of Prithviraj inclined towards social realism in the mid-1940s.[20]

It also seems likely that in getting Betab to write *Shakuntala*, the last play to be penned by the playwright, Prithviraj was invested in the project of reinvention of tradition and social reform that has been associated with Betab's brand of mythologicals. These reinvented mythologicals offered a better vision of a national society through their sympathetic and uplifting treatment of women and the oppressed castes. Indeed, the conservative *Filmindia's* only objection to Prithvi Theatre's *Shakuntala* was the 'crude and ungraceful language' that Shakuntala uses when Dushyanta does not recognise her, thus challenging the 'die-hard Hindu notion' of a wife as one who 'will never address her lord lightly and ungracefully'.[21] In her history of Betab's first mythological Mahabharata (1913), Hansen astutely notes that the playwright's work was 'not meant to propagate Hinduism or Hindutva, but rather to reinterpret the epic within a notion of Hinduism as an expression of nationalism'.[22]

This distinction between reinvented tradition and traditional revivalism is critical in order to understand Prithvi Theatre, which, I argue, was imbued by the former.

After the disappointment of *Shakuntala*, Prithviraj decided to have plays written especially for his theatre, which would 'be understood all over India and have essentially Indian themes'.[23] Evident here is the desire, as identified by Partha Chatterjee in a different context, to construct an aesthetic–thematic form that was modern and national yet recognisably different from Western forms.[24] After *Shakuntala*, which was in keeping with the popular mythic-historical combination of those years, the plays that followed were starkly contemporary and overtly underwritten by the project of anti-colonial nationalism. Writers such as Inder Raj Anand, Ramesh Sehgal and Lal Chandra Bismil are recalled as sitting around Prithviraj while he poured out his ideas, his plots and his experiences.[25] By 1949, the Prithvi repertory consisted of no less than four original plays written and performed all over India, starting with *Deewar* and followed by *Pathan* (The Frontier Man, 1947), *Ghaddar* (The Traitor, 1948) and finally *Ahooti*, all drawing upon either the constituents or the legacies of partition. I identify this body of performances, all unified by an artistic desire to make meaning of partition as it unfolded, as the Partition Repertoire. In the following sections, I provide a close reading of the plays' narratives with attention to their performative strategies and treatment of Hindu–Muslim relations to show how Prithvi Theatre could freely claim a representational space that the films avoided.

The Partition Repertoire

Given the reticence of the Bombay film industry to produce films on partition, the alacrity with which Prithvi Theatre staged topical partition plays right through the tumultuous decade of 1945–1955 stands out in sharp contrast. All the first four plays commissioned to be written for the theatre company were partition-themed. As 'vehicle(s) of Prithviraj's beliefs',[26] each play represented the India–Pakistan division through the vantage point of Indian nationalism. *Deewar* elucidated the 'divide-and-rule policy', *Pathan* exemplified 'Hindu–Muslim unity', *Ghaddar* painted Pakistan as 'Muslim League opportunism' and *Ahooti* grieved the tragic fate of refugees and 'rescued women'. Involving extreme sacrifices, tragic denouements and contrasts of class, attire and language, the Partition Repertoire of Prithvi Theatre performed partition as melodramatic works 'of human emotions, dyed in blood and bleached with tears'.[27] All these plays were reviewed by *Filmindia*, making an exception as far as non-film performances in Bombay were concerned. These reviews hold valuable descriptions of *Pathan* and *Ghaddar*, otherwise no longer available in complete script form. The published scripts of only the first and the last of the four plays (that is, *Deewar* and *Ahooti*) are available. The fact that the scripts of *Pathan* and *Ghaddar* are unpublished suggests the erasure of ideological affinities and social histories of national transition, which in turn suggests the ambivalences of Indian nationalism.

A survey of the themes, content, strategies of and reactions to the Partition Repertoire enables us to reconstruct the Prithvi Theatre as one of the crucial sites where Indian secularism was not just enunciated but also embodied as the partition unfolded.

Deewar was hailed variously as an 'epic poem' and the 'world's best play'[28] by contemporary litterateur Ramvriksha Benipuri and the popular *Filmindia*, respectively, for dramatising the partition of the Indian body politic two years before the actual vivisection.[29] Employing the allegorical motif of a family feud, the play revolved around a household of two landowning brothers, whose harmonious relationship is disrupted by a band of machinating foreigners (Figure 3.1).

Figure 3.1   Colonising woman in the household of Indian brothers in *Deewar*
Source: Prithvi Theatre, Mumbai.

On the pretext of refuge and trade, the foreigners establish an exploitative relationship with the resources of the hosts' land. They then incite the younger brother to demand his property share to end a hierarchical joint family system. A partition wall is raised in the household that wreaks havoc on the agrarian countryside now separated into two. Finally, a non-violent uprising by the peasants pulls the wall down and brings a celebratory end to *Deewar*. While the elder brother Suresh was implicitly the Congress and younger brother Ramesh the Muslim League, the band of foreigners led by a woman were the colonising Europeans with a monarchical Britain at the forefront. As a warning against partition, the play represented the separatist demand as a 'ploy', suggested the economic non-viability of Pakistan and pointed towards the lack of territorial coherence in the two separated territories of east and west. The dialogues for key characters consisted of translations of speeches of Gandhi, Jinnah and T. B. Macaulay, incorporating notable political debates within the play's fold.[30] Sajjan, the actor who played the younger brother, was made-up to resemble Jinnah on stage, and this, together with the dialogues,[31] reminded the audiences of the real political feud outside the theatre right from the time it was first performed on 9 August 1945, two years before Indian independence and partition.

A closer look at the published script reveals the manner in which the 'indigenous' and the 'foreigner' are fashioned in this allegorical mode. The play opens on the festivities of Diwali in the household and devotional hymns to mother goddess Jagdamba, marking the national self as innately Hindu.[32] But perhaps more suggestive is the way language is deployed in the play. While the junior members and servants of the household use a less formal register of rustic Hindustani suggesting gullibility and simplicity, the elder brother's serious monologues in officious Hindi are used to convey ethical clarity and parochial pride.[33] The band of foreigners, representing colonial Britain, is distinguished by its use of ornate, Persianised Urdu. This linguistic choice for the foreigners, as opposed to Hindi and its rustic inflections by the brothers, complicates the contours of foreignness, with Indian actors dressed and made-up as Europeans, speaking a language narrowly associated with Muslim domination.[34] No doubt *Deewar* demonstrates the linguistic fluidity of the 1940s Hindustani films, and its use of lofty Urdu would have provided a tangible aural pleasure,[35] yet the displacement of English authority onto Mughal courtly culture would surely not be inconspicuous in a play that depended on allegories and stand-ins. When considered against the backdrop of the Hindi–Urdu controversy of the late nineteenth century, having the hated colonialists speak Persianised Urdu would not only muddy the notion of the coloniser in India but reinforce the foreignness of Urdu to India.[36] In her study of the circulation of hate, Sara Ahmed identifies the mechanism of displacement 'as evoking a history not declared'.[37] Curiously enough for a partition play, *Deewar* had no declared Muslim presence – the feuding brothers belonged to one household and one religion. Suggesting local religious differences as immaterial or non-existent, the conflation of British colonial history (economic exploitation, control of knowledge production) with Mughal history (Persianised language) would have comfortably accommodated a fluid range of spectatorial positions, including that of Hindu nationalism, which viewed India's past through the 'myth of the Muslim invader and Hindu resistance'.[38]

The Prithvi plays that followed *Deewar* were all cast in the mould of tragedies. Key protagonists ended up dead and their families wrecked, through the process of preserving a moral order. First performed on 13 April 1947, *Pathan* was themed around an exemplary Hindu–Muslim friendship in the NWFP, welded by acts of extreme mutual sacrifice. As the impending partition was construed as a question of Hindu–Muslim accommodation, the play privileged the ethnic customs of Pathans as a blueprint for reconciliation. Prithviraj played the Muslim Sher Khan whose loyal Hindu friend and manager Dewan Tarachand sacrifices his life to save Khan in a tribal war (Figure 3.2). Years later when a similar crisis arises, Sher Khan honours the life-debt and hands over his son to the enemies to save the life of his Hindu friend's son. Motivated by a desire to cease communal tensions, paradoxically the play countenanced violence to maintain Hindu–Muslim friendship. Plotted on the code of an eye for an eye, *Pathan* was yet another instance of the Prithvi stage being 'a living bit of the world around'.[39] It made 'one feel like running out of India and living in the world of Pathans', gushed the *Filmindia* review, already suggesting that the play had stretched the territorial limits of India.[40]

Figure 3.2   Tarachand's sacrifice to save Khan's life in *Pathan*
Source: Prithvi Theatre, Mumbai.

According to his biographers, the Peshawar-born Punjabi Pathan Prithviraj considered himself 'a Pathan first and foremost'.[41] *Pathan* not only was apparently an attempt to dispel certain stereotypes against the Pathans living in the rest of British India but also drew attention to the close neighbourly bonds shared by Hindus and Muslims in the frontier region.[42] A decade earlier, the empire film *The Drum* (1938), set in the NWFP area, had already cast a shadow over the perceived loyalty of the Pathans. The significance of the NWFP region where the story of *Pathan* was set – and that later went to Pakistan despite being the only Muslim majority area in British India that gave political support to the Congress – was immense.[43] While its Congress candidate won the provincial elections in 1946, it was also a time of extreme challenge to the leadership of provincial Congress and its affiliate, the Khudai Khidmatgars, from the supporters of the Pakistan movement in the region.

In October 1946, when the Congress leader, Jawaharlal Nehru, toured the region, his car was pelted with stones, and thereafter, the colonial authorities noted a 'swing in sentiment in favour of the Muslim League'.[44] By the time *Pathan* was being performed in April 1947, demands were being raised in the NWFP for a free Pathan state.[45] The political friendship between the Pathans and the Congress was under strain and was duly attended to in the Prithvi play.

The third play in the series, *Ghaddar*, was a grim choice to premiere on the first anniversary of Indian independence on 15 August 1948 in Bombay. This time the Prithvi group took up the 'Muslim dilemma' during the anti-colonial struggle covering the period 1921–1947. It revolved around Ashraf, a Muslim-Congress worker who is imprisoned for his anti-colonial political activities. Driven to desperation in his absence, the young leader's wife is influenced into dissuading her husband from his political persuasions. Further disillusioned by the political compromises of the Congress and pressurised by Muslim League propaganda,[46] Ashraf joins the movement for Pakistan (Figure 3.3). The turn that the narrative takes after this links partition violence with the Muslim League. While the play does not survive, the plot summaries reveal that Ashraf rejects 'Pakistan' after witnessing the partition violence. As the Indian Muslim returns to his former Congress loyalties, a Muslim League compatriot kills him.

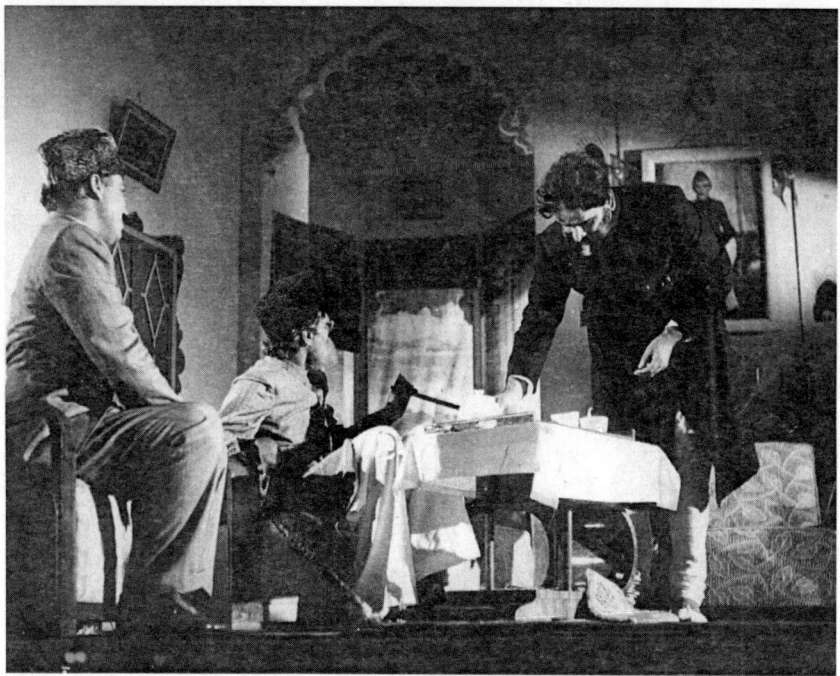

Figure 3.3   The 'Muslim dilemma' as explored in *Ghaddar*
Source: Prithvi Theatre, Mumbai.

While Prithviraj had received several threats during the first year of performances of *Deewar*, it was *Ghaddar* that reportedly provoked the further hostility of the 'Muslim press' towards him. The later hagiographic accounts of Prithvi plays describe *Ghaddar* as 'the story of the patriotic Muslims who stayed back in India after Partition and were branded as traitors', suggesting another purposeful intervention like *Deewar* and *Pathan*.[47] However, the details available in more contemporary commentary, that is *Filmindia* and Jai Dyal's account, present a more complex picture. According to Dyal, in *Ghaddar* 'the policy of Muslim League is discussed threadbare and Jinnah is held responsible for the holocaust that preceded and followed partition'.[48] Within the first three years of the Prithvi oeuvre, Jinnah had undergone a change from the misled younger brother in *Deewar* to the traitor in *Ghaddar*. Of the three Muslim protagonists and friends of the play, Ashraf, Maulana and Saleem, the first two undergo a change of heart and politics several times, outwardly expressed through the changing central portraits in Ashraf's living room from that of Gandhi to Jinnah,[49] and the changing caps and titles of his more outright 'chameleon' friend Maulana. Saleem 'sticks to national service', that is, remains a Congress supporter throughout, and is stabbed to death in partition violence.[50] Ashraf, the protagonist played by Prithviraj, finally opts for a 'truer nationalism', that is, one that is Indian and Congress-led, and brands Jinnah as a traitor. A Muslim League supporter, who is leaving for Pakistan and hence sees Ashraf as a traitor to the Muslim cause, shoots him. Before dropping dead, Ashraf has just enough time to take down Jinnah's portrait to convey the leader's erasure from the hearts of Indian Muslims. The opportunistic Maulana, who now wears a Gandhi cap as he intends to stay in India, marches out with the portrait cursing the devil. Could it be that instead of tackling the suspicion that Indian Muslims had to face, *Ghaddar* actually thrived on it? Or did the Prithvi play inevitably capture the flaws inherent in the post-colonial political options at hand for the Indian minorities? The script of *Ghaddar*, if ever found, would be a valuable archive of the ways in which Indian secular nationalism denied legitimacy to other political discourses.

The last in the Partition Repertoire, *Ahooti*, opened on 30 September 1949 and dealt with the ignominy faced by women abducted in the partition riots. The betrothed daughter of a blind but affluent Hindu resident of Rawalpindi is rescued and returned to her family after the violence of March 1947. Her extended community of refugees, who are otherwise united in their displacement and loss, is unable to overcome the stigmas of defilement and community dishonour associated with rescued women. Unable to bear any further humiliation, she ends her life, and her devoted fiancé too dies soon after. Touching on a particularly sensitive dimension of partition, that of sexual violence, *Ahooti*, along with two IPTA plays of this time, engaged with the gendered experience of the partition where the 'returned, refugee' woman finds herself unable to return either to the previous homeland or to society.[51]

In sharp contrast to the four previous plays, *Filmindia* was unenthusiastic about *Ahooti*. From its vantage point, the story 'of a Hindu maiden raped by Muslims but driven to suicide by the Hindus' was an appeal to the Hindus 'to lick their wounds and to forgive and forget',[52] something the magazine in the late 1940s was least inclined to endorse. In the three-act play, while the first act was set in the plush living rooms of prosperous residents of Rawalpindi (Figure 3.4), acts two and three take place in refugee camps and settler colonies. According to biographer Yograj, Prithviraj would visit refugee camps every day, meet victims and listen to their tales of trauma and loss.[53]

Figure 3.4   Betrothed couple before the outbreak of riots in *Ahooti*
Source: Prithvi Theatre, Mumbai.

Lal Chandra Bismil penned these tales accordingly into *Ahooti*. Yet an overarching inspiration behind *Ahooti*, which never finds a mention in any of the commentaries, is the epic Ramayana. Conspicuous through their names, the betrothed lead pair of Ram and Janaki is shown preparing for a neighbourhood Ramlila, in which they play their namesakes, on the night of Janaki's abduction.[54] Mohammad Shafi is the good Muslim who rescues Janaki from her Muslim abductors. Reunited with her father, Ram Krishna, and still cherished by her fiancé, Ram, Janaki is eventually pushed to commit suicide by the extended social circle. Invoking the epic narrative of abduction in a desire to socially and morally rehabilitate the Hindu refugees in India, the play celebrated Hindu transcendental values and shared the patriarchal idiom of the Indian state. Urvashi Butalia recounts the exhortations that Gandhi and Nehru issued to Hindu families to take back their women 'rescued' by the Indian state. Some pamphlets issued by the Indian ministry of relief and rehabilitation quoted the scriptural law-giver Manusmriti on restitution of female purity, while other stories reminded people that Sita remained pure despite her abduction.[55] With a strong social reformist impulse centred around survivors of gendered violence, which both communities visited upon each other in partition,[56] Prithvi Theatre appealed against the dogmas of chastity and pollution of caste Hinduism in order to save the 'recovered women'. Motivated as a reformatory appeal to one community (Indian-Hindu), the play once again effected a displacement whereby demonical acts could be relegated to the other (Pakistani-Muslim). This brings me to the core element of the Partition Repertoire and towards a potential explanation for the Prithvi Theatre's success in performing partition narratives, apart from Prithviraj's proximity to the politically ascendant Congress. Discernible in the partition dramaturgy of Prithvi Theatre is a seamless hybrid of Western melodramatic elements with narratives strongly anchored in the ethical relativism (*dharma*) characteristic of caste Hindu sensibility, where right and wrong are context sensitive and thereby never absolute. Addressing its spectators as spiritual Hindus, the Partition Repertoire recast a modern political problem into one involving a traditional moral order.

Melo*dharma* of the Colonised: *Deewar*

Of the Partition Repertoire of Prithvi Theatre, *Deewar*, which imagined the division of the Indian body politic two years before 1947, is an atypical and important archive of the colonial division. It was the most performed and adulated of the plays, existing as the master text around which Prithviraj Kapoor's image as a political crusader came to be built. Writing about Prithviraj's aspirations, Jai Dyal mentions two. The first was the setting up of a physical home for Prithvi Theatre, a permanent structure for the future generations of the Prithvi troupe. The other was the annulment of partition, as expressed in *Deewar*. In the foreword to the play-script, Prithviraj recounts the impulse behind the plot as follows:

> *Jab se mulk ke batwaare ki tahreek ne zor pakda tha, desh ke vatavaran mein kuch ajeeb sa kolahal mach gaya, jo zahira itna bhayanak nazar na aata tha, lekin jisne fizaon mein ek halchal paida kar di thi. Ussi halchal ne mere dil ke taaron mein ek ajeeb si jhankaar paida kar di. Unhi jhankaaron ne iss khel ko janam diya.*[57]

Ever since the demand for partition gained ground, it created an agitation in the country. While it was yet to take a frightening form, the air was tinged with restlessness. This restlessness struck a strange note on my heartstrings and led to the creation of this play!

Some regarded this 'self-imposed mission' of Prithviraj as a cultural moment in Indian history for using stage-art to conduct politics.[58] Parallels with political leaders were duly drawn 'for while India needed her Jawahars and Patels ... she needed no less her Prithvis'.[59] The allegorical restoration of 'Akhand Bharat' [Undivided India] within the play was a possibility that those closely associated with the Prithvi Theatre held dear and hoped that the ending of the play, the undoing of partition, would also be part of the clairvoyance. And so, the play with a purpose, *Deewar*, continued to be performed unchanged in the post-partition years.[60]

> *Bhagwan hi jaane bhavishya mein kya ho! Aisa bhi ho sakta hai ki bharat phir akhand ho jae, tab toh yeh natak iss vishay ka bhavishyavadi itihaas hi ban jaega!*[61]

> God alone knows what the future holds! It may transpire that a divided India may again become undivided. Then this play will become the prophetic history of this subject!

Melodrama as an aesthetic sensibility showcases emotional excess, marked by key constitutive features such as pathos, overwrought emotions, moral polarisation between good and evil, sensationalism and a non-classical narrative structure free of causation.[62] In the causation-independent narrative of melodrama, Peter Brooks locates the 'moral occult', the repository of fragmented and desacralised remnants of sacred myths.[63] While melodrama's imbrication with ethical dilemmas is well established, the 'random happenstance' in Prithvi Theatre worked with what psychoanalyst Sudhir Kakar discerns as the cultural preconscious of a Hindu worldview.[64] Kakar's explanation of this worldview is complex – involving *moksha* (self-realisation), *dharma* (moral duty) and *karma* (heritage of previous life) – one that is built through a combination of tragic human experience and romantic spiritual orientation. Here the question of right and wrong, melodrama's fecund terrain of moral polarisation, is negotiated as *dharma*, that is, moral action, to achieve the desired goal of *moksha* (release from the cycle of birth and rebirth). Where Hindu *dharma* diverges from ethical imperatives deriving from Semitic religions, according to Kakar, is in its relativistic and contextual approach to actions judged as wrong.[65] When right and wrong are relative, it not only lessens 'the burden of individual responsibility for action'[66] but also offers limitless possibilities for narrative directions and character development. Arguably, melo*dharma* was the secret ingredient of the Partition Repertoire of Prithvi Theatre, which sought to explain the colonial presence in Indian lives through domestic situations where individuals often found it hard to act in conformity with the truth of things simply because they did not know where truth lay. By integrating such a worldview, Prithvi Theatre to a large extent solved the representational dilemma of partition that lies in assigning culpability to the feuding factions. I will elucidate this briefly with instances from *Deewar*. In providing refuge to a band of foreigners whose machinations remain unknown to the close-knit and connected family, Suresh acts within the prescribed *dharma*: to treat guests as a divine presence. His largesse in sharing the plentiful resources and entering into a non-transactional relationship with the three guests is explained as gullibility by the villain- in-chief, the 'white woman':[67]

> *Inke dilon tak fareb ki gard nahin pahonchi? Ya yun kaho ki yeh log kitne ahmak hain, kitne jahil hain. Duniya ki chaalon se na-ashna, ghairon ki ravish se bekhabar. Maazi ke waqar mein khoye hue, haal se laparvah, dhokha aur fareb toh bilkul jaante hi nahin. Pehchante hain toh sirf apne farz ki raah, jo tabahi ke kuen mein ja kar khatam hoti hai. Kitne aasan hain yeh shikar, saapon ko kuchalte nahin, doodh pilate hain, doodh!*

> [You suggest] their hearts are free from the filth of deceit? Or one could say that these people are so ridiculous, so uncivilised. Unfamiliar with the ways of the world, ignorant of the foreign temperament. Lost in past glories, negligent by nature, little do they know of cunning and intrigue. They blindly follow the path of moral duty which can only lead the abyss of annihilation. Such easy prey, instead of trampling on poisonous snakes, they offer them milk!

The villainy of the colonial guests lies not only in their conscious designs and prejudice but also in their active exploitation of the moral imperatives that constrain their Indian hosts. As the 'white woman' confronts the divine idol and predicts the eventual humiliation of the mother goddess (Mother India), the first act comes to an end with thundering clouds and forbidding contortions of the deity's otherwise smiling contours. In true melodramatic fashion, psychic excess is made evident in the external environment – through lightening and a warning thunder, paving the way for a dramatic change. The narrative takes a sharp turn, as evident in a visibly colonial order in Suresh's household, conveyed through set design and the appearance of new trade commodities. According to the stage directions for the first scene of Act 2, the house is furnished in a 'Western style', with the old bamboo chair replaced by a couch and the two ends of the stage area occupied by the Indian *sitar* and the piano, encapsulating a split modernity.[68] The loyal servant is now dressed in pants and hums a ditty while at work:

> *Hum babu naye nirale hain, hum babu naye nirale hain / Ab rang naye, ab dhang naye, ab yeh sansar naya apna.*

> We are the nouveau gents, we are the nouveau gents / Now new hues and new ways, our cosmos is now new.

Communicating momentous changes through shifts in the inanimate and the divine, the play also takes responsibility away from the bellowing patriarch, who, for most part of Act 1, rejects the foreigners' ways and resists the white woman's overtures. Having initially lampooned the coloniser's language and musical preferences, he quickly turns into a caricatured brown *sahib* who recites Shakespearean sonnets and wistfully speaks of English 'home weather'. After temporarily dabbling in breeches and belts, the elder brother and the garrulous protagonist played by Prithviraj eventually realises his enslavement by colonial forces and returns to humble *khadi* and bamboo furniture. But the younger brother, Ramesh, is adamant over his share of the land. Citing instances of non-commensality and an unfair division of labour – a strong reference to ritual pollution and caste-based occupation in India – Ramesh strongly expresses his anguished state as a point of no return.

> *Maine apna haq manga hai aur voh main aapse leh kar rahoonga. Chahe iske liye mujhe apna khoon hi kyun na bahana pade.*
>
> I have asked for my rights and nothing can stop me. If it means blood bath, so be it.

The situation, a threat of violence, then dictates that Suresh must agree to the division. In such a scheme of events, partition becomes the right action, the ethical path. The scenes that follow the division, when Suresh shows a consciousness and insight superior to Ramesh's, is peppered with the former agonising over how best to deal with the latter. Here the 'Muslim problem' is expressed in what Faisal Devji identifies as the 'language of disease'.[69] The play reflects on the possible course of action in the present, one which would secure the future, and such knowledge could only be arrived at through a proleptic history:

> *Marz la-ilaaj hota ja raha hai, mareez ki zindagi bachaney ke liye kabhi uske jism ke hisse bhi kaat dene padte hain.*[70]
> *Kaash maine Ramesh ka gala ghont diya hota, ek jaan lene se lakhon jaane bach jaati.*[71]
>
> The affliction is getting beyond cure [and] to save a patient's life it is sometimes necessary to amputate body parts.
> Wish I had strangled Ramesh [younger brother]! Taking one life would have saved a million others.

Written over 1944–1945, the play could only dare imagine the division and saw it as cutting off of an infected body part. Guided by a notion of moral action, it asked for a strangulation of Muslim separatism. By anticipating the aftermath of partition and issuing *Deewar* as a warning, the play romantically pushes for dismantling the partition wall as the ultimate ethical action (Figure 3.5). This knowledge is arrived at through a proleptic vision, the only way to deal with a right and wrong made relative by incomplete human knowledge of the present and future. Ultimately, for those steeped in the Hindu cultural preconscious, Prithvi Theatre's dramatisation of the 'divide-and rule' principle as a family feud offered relief from the burden of responsibility.

Figure 3.5   A wall dividing the household and a map of colonial India in *Deewar*
Source: Prithvi Theatre, Mumbai.

Popularity and Power

Nearly three hours long, the plays, according to their witnesses, came alive
with powerful performances, exuberant songs and special effects of light and
sound. The songs of *Deewar* circulated independently of the performances
as gramophone records.[72] Most striking, however, was Prithviraj's booming
voice that could fill even an empty stage with magical presence and keep the
audiences spellbound.[73] Unlike the Parsi theatre, Prithvi plays adopted the new
trend of social realism that was dominant between 1942 and 1952, and consisted
of full-length, comparatively lowbrow vehicles that could be performed on a
proscenium stage. All the Prithvi plays opened their performances at the Royal
Opera House in Bombay and would later travel to other venues across different
cities in India. In many instances, cinema halls would be transformed into
makeshift stages for these performances.

These plays received high praise and admiration. *Filmindia* called *Deewar*
'the world's best play'[74] and *Pathan* 'a dynamic drama of elemental passions
which brings tears to the eyes of the audience'.[75] Veteran theatre artist Zohra
Sehgal remembers that the premier of *Deewar* filled her with enthusiasm, and

she begged Prithviraj to include her in his company.[76] According to biographer Yog Raj, the triple billing of Prithvi plays – *Shakuntala, Deewar* and *Pathan* – attracted full-house responses, and each evening crowds jostled hard to make their way into the hall. Many unable to afford the tickets surreptitiously made their way in. Jai Dyal recounts that wherever *Deewar* played, it drew big houses and deeply moved its audiences, completing its 450th performance in 1949.[77] According to Sehgal, every time in the climax of *Pathan*, when Sher Khan (Prithviraj) handed over his young son (played by his real sons Raj Kapoor and later Shammi Kapoor) to the enemies honouring the creed of an eye for an eye, there was not a dry eye in the house. Dyal describes a similar reaction to the Begum's (Uzra Mumtaz) plight in *Ghaddar* when, at the death of her husband, both men and women in the audience wept 'unashamedly'. *Ahooti* with its subject of abducted women was played out in the midst of the refugee crisis. The Hindu refugees displaced from West Punjab and East Bengal would also come to watch these performances and identify emotionally with the situation depicted in the play. Yog Raj recounts how once an old man broke down after watching *Ahooti* and went pleading to Prithviraj to help him find his abducted daughter. Prithviraj then requested the director general of the police of Bombay, also present for the performance, to help the old refugee and eventually managed to reunite father and daughter. Working for refugee rehabilitation and campaigning for communal peace, Prithviraj is widely remembered to have stood outside the theatre after each performance with his shawl spread out and eyes cast on the ground to collect the money for partition refugees.[78]

While the Partition Repertoire attracted extreme identification and popularity, there are also many accounts of opposition to the plays from the familiar protagonists, representing 'conservative' formations – the colonial state, the Muslim League, the Muslim press, Pathans – who are mostly portrayed as reacting to rumours. Often, these oppositional voices went to the extent of death threats to Prithviraj and his troupe. Prithviraj's strategy to deal with opposition could take two forms – the first being free invitations to illiberal opponents to watch the plays, which would reportedly end with their transformation into Prithvi fans. The other method was lambasting dissent and arguing forcefully, an approach reserved for a more hardened opposition. When *Deewar* and its subject matter became a topic of intense discussion in Bombay, it received censorship objections from the colonial state as well as from the Bombay Muslim League. According to one account, some Muslim League activists took Prithviraj and his close aide to their secret headquarters, where they pressurised him to abandon the play.[79] Prithviraj pleaded that Jinnah should see the rehearsals and decide, which the lower command reportedly refused, interpreted by Prithvi's biographers as protecting an 'emotional Jinnah' from the compelling message of *Deewar*. There are various versions of the obstacles Prithviraj supposedly overcame to perform *Deewar*. One version is that the colonial state added the caveat of a no-objection certificate from the president of the Bombay Provincial Muslim League, I. I. Chundrigar.[80] Since there was little chance of obtaining cooperation from the Muslim League, Prithviraj employed subterfuge to obtain the permission to stage the play.[81] Yet another version has it that Prithviraj went to the permission official, argued passionately for his play and thereby successfully got the clearance. Four months later, the leading Congress leader, Sardar Patel, declared *Deewar* tax-free after being visibly moved to tears by its performance in December 1945.[82]

After reportedly pacifying some irate Pathans from Bhindi Bazaar, a Muslim neighbourhood of Bombay, with an invitation to watch *Pathan*, Prithviraj's trouble with the censors returned with *Ghaddar*, even though this time around Congress was in power in independent India. The Bombay censors were wary of granting approval in view of the tense atmosphere of the country in 1948. Permission had to be sought at the highest office, and so Prithviraj met Jawaharlal Nehru, who directed him to Maulana Azad, a Muslim member of the Congress. At Azad's office, Prithviraj performed several extracts from the play far exceeding his allotted meeting time. Azad not only granted permission to stage *Ghaddar* but also got him a clearance for all future Prithvi Theatre performances and railway discounts for the troupe's tours. The significance of the ultimate arbitration lying with Azad, often disparagingly referred to by the Muslim League as the 'poster boy of Congress', cannot be missed. In the scheme of the dominant nationalism of the day, Azad signified the 'good Muslim', representing the compositeness and inclusivity of the Congress, as opposed to the 'bad Muslims' of the separatist Muslim League. The personal approval by Azad was the highest endorsement that *Ghaddar*, which indicted Jinnah – by then the worst Muslim in the Indian imagination – could ever hope to receive.

The Prithvi Theatre troupe would visit riot-affected areas to spread awareness and perform these plays to sensitise people against religious hatred. Many refugees also joined this group, which often led to serious altercations within the group. One was the induction of an anguished refugee, Shriram Shastri, into the group, who apparently threatened many Muslim actors of the group, including Uzra Mumtaz, the female lead of the Prithvi plays. On other occasions, Prithviraj received threats demanding the sacking of the Muslim artistes. While touring the riot-torn Punjab in the late 1940s, a Sikh group demanded the handing over of the Muslim artistes of the troupe. All memoirs and descriptions find Prithviraj weathering a variety of pressure and threats and are united in declaring Prithvi Theatre as having successfully manifested secular paternalism and being a mini-India in itself.

The other and more dogged opposition to Prithvi plays was recognised to have come from entities prefixed with 'Muslim' – the League, the press, goons, Pathans. Long speeches ran after the formal conclusion of the play, mostly by Prithviraj but in certain instances political dignitaries and special guests too. Sardar Vallabhbhai Patel was photographed while not only watching *Deewar* but also delivering a speech on the proscenium stage with his entourage and Prithviraj. The didactic impulse of Prithvi Theatre emerges strongly in the speech feature. Another photograph shows a towering Prithviraj, draped in *khadi*, standing between a microphone and a much larger tricoloured map of India (Figure 3.6). Consider this image in relation to the speech an angry Prithviraj made to the Muslim critics of *Ghaddar*, the play which had 'entirely shaken the outlook of Indian Muslims'.[83] It took place during the southern tour of the theatre company in June 1949 in Hyderabad, which Dyal calls 'another stronghold of the diehard kind':[84]

> Communalism is self-love of a despicable kind and will hang itself with its own rope. The rope given by Partition is long enough for the purpose. The Jinnah two-nation theory and its implications cannot hold water in a modern State and a modern world in which the only possible goal is Unity – *One-ness* – for all, not only for Muslims among themselves nor for Hindus in their exclusive fold. If they clung to the idea of a Theocratic State, they could not belong to the secular state of India. That Muslims might live happily in the Indian Union, a great Hindu was the victim of foul murder by a lesser Hindu. If they believe in Jinnah's two-nation theory they must, of their free-will, decamp to the land this 'beloved leader' created, nay grabbed for them. A Hindu *Padshahi*[85] stepping into the shoes of the old time Congress would send them packing on a forced march across the desert of Rajputana to the second nation of the deliberate choice of their beloved leader and idol – to Pakistan. How many would reach their destination who could say? *Prithvi dug into them hard and did not mince matters. This plain speaking did the Muslim pressman good – they changed their attitude of defiance, whether through policy or clear mindedness, who can say?*[86]

This paraphrased speech of the secular nationalist Prithviraj bellowing at the mischief mongers, the Muslim critics, succinctly outlined for the minority critics their limited political options. Prithvi Theatre had filtered in its public through narratives with a Hindu worldview and with meta speeches which remained explicitly anti-Pakistan. In a balancing act, consistent with the colonial and Congress paternalism, Prithviraj also managed to have a word with the RSS leader, M. S. Golwalkar, during the tour and asked him 'to control his followers and to give the right lead in these critical times'.[87]

Figure 3.6   Prithviraj Kapoor delivering a speech after a performance of *Deewar*
Source: Prithvi Theatre, Mumbai.

Golwalkar had been sent to prison after Gandhi's assassination by an RSS member, Nathuram Godse, and had been recently released at the time of this meeting. These reproduced speeches and conversations are significant not as a measure of Prithviraj's individual political influence but because these were in the service of constructing a secular Prithvi Theatre, which by that token became favourably placed to represent partition.

Starting its Partition Repertoire in 1945, the troupe performed nearly 1,800 shows of the four plays over fifteen years, with *Deewar* having the maximum number of performances at 712.[88] The Prithvi Theatre troupe travelled all over India performing to full houses in cities like Bombay, Nagpur, Delhi, Patna, Indore, Bangalore, Hyderabad, Mysore, Kolhapur and Cochin. The troupe consisting of nearly 150 people would go on regional tours, 'travelling in third class railway compartments to Maharashtra, Saurashtra [Gujarat], Punjab, Bengal, Bihar, United Provinces [Uttar Pradesh], Madhya Pradesh and Rajasthan'.[89] These performances depended a good deal on state patronage and support, be it subsidised travel, a tax-free status or basic logistics. For instance, in Mysore, the chief minister gave the state guesthouse for accommodation and the town hall for Prithvi performances.[90] These also included the several 'at-homes' and receptions for the troupe. Prithviraj's appointment to the Rajya Sabha (the Upper House in the Indian Parliament) by the Congress government in 1952, eight years after the first performance of Prithvi Theatre, is a testament to the cultural ascendancy of secular nationalism in independent India.

Prithvi Theatre travelled all over independent India and perhaps even to Ceylon, Java, Burma and Africa in the late 1940s and 1950s,[91] but they never went to Pakistan. As mentioned at the beginning of this chapter, by 1951 an unofficial ban on the films of Prithviraj Kapoor and his son Raj Kapoor existed as a feature of the film-trade deadlock between the two countries. While the institution of Prithvi Theatre was made intelligible by its open endorsement of Indian nationalism, the narrative lucidity of the plays depended on being imbued with a Hindu preconscious, as well as an investment in reformed Hinduism as an expression of patriotism. In the Partition Repertoire, Indian-Muslim political consciousness was represented as a colonial ploy, a disease and a treacherous project, while reserving the representation of partition suffering to the Indian-Hindu community. This narrative liberty was not an option available to Indian film-makers wishing to make profitable films on partition, because Pakistan was still a substantial market for films made in Bombay. The film publics were not yet nationally divided in the same way as the theatre-going public, and thus it was impossible to make a partition film which could be watched in both nations without courting opposition in either one.

While Prithviraj's proximity to the top brass of the Congress is emphasised by all biographers, my appraisal draws attention to the alignment of the Partition Repertoire with the pressing political challenges facing the Congress-led government.

This mutually beneficial relationship allows us to consider Prithvi Theatre as representative of the Congress-led Indian nationalism, which distinguished itself from both Muslim and Hindu nationalism on the grounds of secularism. How does the Prithvi Theatre's Partition Repertoire compare with *Filmindia*'s divisive prose? To return to Kathryn Hansen's argument around the reinvention of tradition as a way to summon a national community, it can be said that Prithvi Theatre's partition narratives anchored in a Hindu worldview of social reform alongside the didactic speeches targeting Muslim political formations and lobbies, consciously or unconsciously created common ground with *Filmindia*. I find these narratives not only coloured by a narrow idea of national community but, in the two plays after 1947, also permeated by Prithviraj's personal injury and resentment at the loss of his regional homeland to partition.

Owing his public stature and prominence to the Partition Repertoire, Prithviraj was in a creative position to impose his patriotic worldview on film-makers wishing to work with him. One such occasion is recounted by Yog Raj Tandon, who describes the actor being approached by K. Asif and Kamal Amrohi for the iconic role of Akbar in *Mughal-e-Azam*. The film had been shelved during partition, as its original financier, Shiraz Ali Hakim, migrated to Pakistan, and it took thirteen years to make. Prithviraj accepted the role on the condition that the screenwriters would excise any 'anti-national' tendencies that were present in Imtiaz Ali Taj's original play, *Anarkali*, written in 1922, on which *Mughal-e-Azam* was based.[92] Historicals had to stand up to the demands of contemporary India, and Imtiaz Ali Taj, the dramatist who was now a Pakistani, could not be trusted with India's past any longer. As Muslim film-makers who had stayed on in Bombay after partition, K. Asif and Kamal Amrohi assured Prithviraj that their film would stay clear of any 'mischief'. This censorial, watchful stance was less invested in the identity of the film personnel and more in the ideological content of the films. *Filmindia*, on the other hand, after 1947, was directing its publicity energies towards the financial and professional deterioration of prominent Muslim film-makers and actors, who may or may not have harboured sympathies for Pakistan. Years later, even the Muslim film-makers and actors who had supported the Pakistan movement would recall their migration as one necessitated by the worsening situation in Bombay.

The methodological interest of the section 'The Secular Stance of Bombay' in bringing these three different enunciations together is to insist on the discursive power of partition, which produces a cacophony ancillary to the film object. The weakening of the studio system in the early 1940s, as well as the wartime boom and its control, made film production in Bombay a fiercely competitive space where briefly Muslim nationalism emerged as a modality of contestation, especially for Muslim personnel aspiring to climb the creative hierarchies of film-making. At this time, the Bombay film industry's strong alignment with Indian nationalism served two purposes. First, it minimised its production losses and censorial intervention by isolating and managing 'Muslim intolerance' as the foremost threat to artistic expression in a free Indian nation. Second, in the contest for control, it selectively expunged the partisan networks of Muslim nationalism after identifying these as anti-national. Through a concerted belligerence to the idea of Pakistan, whose partisans posed a short-lived yet serious challenge to the existing pattern of financial and thematic control of the film production, the Bombay film industry reorganised itself primarily under the aegis of a 'secular stance'.

Notes

1   Anon, 'Indo-Pakistan Film Trade', *Journal of the Indian Film Industry* 12, no. 7 (March 1952), 13.

2   Anon, 'A Pakistan Hysteria', *Journal of the Indian Film Industry* 11, no. 2 (July 1951), 6.

3   Ravi Vasudevan, 'Dislocations: The Cinematic Imagining of a New Society in 1950s India', *Oxford Literary Review on India: Writing History Culture Post-coloniality* 16, nos. 1–2 (1994): 93–124, 109.

4   Ira Bhaskar, 'Trauma, Melodrama and the Production of Historical Affect: The Partition, Memory and the Contemporary Communal Riot in Indian Cinema', in *Film Melodrama Revisited*, ed. Dominique Nasta and Muriel Andrin, 339–356 (Brussels: PIE Peter Lang, 2014).

5   Ibid., 345.

6   Bhaskar Sarkar, *Mourning the Nation: Indian Cinema in the Wake of Partition* (Durham, NC: Duke University Press, 2009), 49.

7   Recent books include Deepa Gahlot, *Shashi Kapoor Presents the Prithviwallas* (Delhi: Roli Books, 2004) and Madhu Jain, *The Kapoors: The First Family of Indian Cinema* (New Delhi: Penguin Viking, 2005).

8   Jai Dyal mentions categorically in his memoirs that Prithviraj's convictions echoed those of the Congress. The published script of *Dewaar* is dedicated to Gandhi. Jai Dyal, *I Go South with Prithviraj and His Prithvi Theatres* (Bombay: Prithvi Publications, 1960), 36.

9   Anuradha Kapur, 'Reassembling the Modern: An Indian Theatre Map since Independence', in *Modern Indian Theatre*, ed. Nandi Bhatia, 41–55 (Delhi: Oxford University Press, 2009), 45.

10   Aparna Bhargava Dharwadkar, *Theatres of Independence: Drama, Theory and Urban Performance in India since 1947* (Iowa City: University of Iowa Press, 2005), 31.

11   Sajjad Zaheer, *The Light: A History for the Movement of Progressive Literature in the Indo-Pakistan Subcontinent*, trans. Amina Zafar (Karachi: Oxford University Press, 2006), 190.

12   Dyal, *I Go South with Prithviraj*, 48. One of the biggest film clans spanning four generations in the Hindi film industry started with Prithviraj, whose sons, Raj Kapoor, Shammi Kapoor and Shashi Kapoor, became stars of Hindi cinema in the post-independence decades, and currently the fourth generation of the Kapoor clan are prominent actors and actresses in 'Bollywood'.

13   Zohra Sehgal, who worked closely with Prithviraj Kapoor, brings up his temperament with respect to working in Calcutta. 'Perhaps he was too outspoken for directors

in Bengal,' says Sehgal. Zohra Sehgal, 'Theatre and Activism in the 1940s', *India International Centre Quarterly* 24, nos. 2–3 (1997): 31–39.

14   The cover page of the published script of *Ahooti* proclaims Prithvi Theatres as 'art in the service of the nation'. Lal Chandra Bismil, *Ahooti* (Bombay: Prithvi Theatre Prakashan, 1950).

15   Jain, *The Kapoors*, 31.

16   Dharwadkar, *Theatres of Independence*, 226.

17   Zohra Sehgal, *Close-Up: Memoirs of a Life on Stage and Screen* (New Delhi: Women Unlimited, 2010), 118–119.

18   Agha Hashr Kashmiri (1879–1935) was a prolific Urdu playwright and wrote for numerous Parsi theatre companies. Kathryn Hansen, 'Staging Composite Culture', *South Asia Research* 29, no. 2 (2009): 151–168, DOI: 10.1177/026272800902900203 (accessed 3 February 2013), 161.

19   Ibid.

20   Dyal, *I Go South with Prithviraj*, 36.

21   'Prithvi Theatres Present an Excellent Production', *Filmindia*, April 1945, 39.

22   Kathryn Hansen, 'Ritual Enactments in a Hindi "Mythological": Betab's "Mahabharat" in Parsi Theatre', *Economic and Political Weekly* 41, no. 48 (2 December 2006): 4985–4991, https://www.epw.in/journal/2006/48/special-articles/ritual-enactments-hindi-mythological.html (accessed on 10 August 2020), 4986.

23   Sehgal, *Close-Up*, 119.

24   Partha Chatterjee, 'Nation and Its Fragments', in *The Partha Chatterjee Omnibus*, 3–275 (New Delhi: Oxford University Press, 1999), 8.

25   Sehgal, *Close-Up*, 119.

26   Jain, *The Kapoors*, 34.

27   'Prithviraj Excels Himself in Pathan', *Filmindia*, September 1947, 34.

28   'Prithviraj Gives the World's Best Play', *Filmindia*, May 1946, 53.

29   In the introductory note to the published script, Ramvriksh Benipuri calls it a *mahakavya*, or epic poem. Prithviraj Kapoor, Inder Raj Anand and Ramesh Sehgal, *Deewar* (Bombay: Prithvi Publication, 1952), 10.

30   Sehgal, *Close-Up*, 120; Jain, *The Kapoors*, 32.

31   Yograj Tandon, *Theatre ke Sartaj Prithviraj* (Delhi: National School of Drama Publications, 2001), 90.

32   Such meaningful openings were already present in the films of the 1940s, as discussed by Ravi Vasudevan with regard to *Shejari* (1940). 'The film opens on a Hindu devotional space', and what is inaugurated is an incipient discourse of national origins. Ravi Vasudevan, 'The Politics of Cultural Address in a "Transitional" Cinema: A Case Study of Indian Popular Cinema', in *Reinventing Film Studies*, edited by Christine Gledhill and Linda Williams, 130–164 (London: Arnold Publishers, 2000), 155.

33   'Suresh: *Paani se aaye ho, toh bhai tumhare apne desh ke aadmi honge. Humare desh ke aadmi toh iss khaare paani mein paaon tak nahin rakhein. Jab bhi inki charcha suno bas lad rahey bas lad rahey.*' Kapoor et al., *Deewar*, 7.

34   Illustrative dialogue of the foreign woman/videshi Aurat: *Hum musafir hain, taajir hain, tijaarat ki garaz se hum apne mulk se nikle they magar raaste mein hi loot liye gaye*

humara zaade raah tak cheen liya gaya, ab hum ghar pahonchne ke liye bhi mohtaaj hain. Kapoor, Anand and Sehgal, *Deewar*, 7.

35   David Lunn, 'The Eloquent Language: Hindustani in 1940s Indian Cinema', *BioScope: South Asian Screen Studies* 6, no. 1 (2015): 1–26.

36   Ralph Russell delves into controversial relationship of Hindi to Urdu. 'There is no doubt that modern Hindi came into existence as the result of a widespread feeling amongst Hindus that Urdu was the product of centuries of Muslim domination and that Hindu self-respect demanded that "Muslim" words should be expelled from their khadi boli base and replaced by words of pure Indian origin.' See Ralph Russell, 'Some Notes on Hindi and Urdu', *Annual of Urdu Studies* (1996): 203–208.

37   Sara Ahmed, *The Cultural Politics of Emotion* (Edinburgh: Edinburgh University Press, 2004), 47.

38   For a detailed discussion on Hindu nationalism's view of Indian history and Hindu–Muslim relations, see Tapan Basu, Pradip Datta, Sumit Sarkar, Tanika Sarkar and Sambuddha Sen, *Khaki Shorts Saffron Flags: A Critique of the Hindu Right* (New Delhi: Orient Longman, 1993), 3.

39   'Prithviraj Excels Himself in Pathan', 34.

40   Ibid.

41   Gahlot, *The Prithviwallahs*, 34.

42   Both Jai Dyal and Deepa Gahlot mention that Prithviraj made *Pathan* to dispel stereotypes against the ethnic community. Bombay had a Punjab Frontier Association, and the actor was its president. When at a meeting of the association, some Pathans reported facing ethnic prejudice and getting stereotyped in their daily interactions, Prithviraj came up with the theme of the play.

43   The non-violent anti-colonial struggle of Khudai Khidmatgars of the NWFP was led by Khan Abdul Ghaffar Khan, also known as Frontier Gandhi, and they became a close ally of the Congress in 1930, after their political advances were rebuffed by the Muslim League.

44   Mukulika Banerjee, *The Pathan Unarmed: Opposition and Memory in the North West Frontier* (Karachi and New Delhi: Oxford University Press, 2000), 185.

45   Sumit Sarkar, *Modern India: 1885–1947* (Delhi: Macmillan, 1983), 449.

46   For more on shared ground and differences between the Congress and the Mahasabha before a more pronounced gulf after 1938, see Richard Gordon, 'The Hindu Mahasabha and the Indian National Congress 1915–1926', *Modern Asian Studies* 9, no. 2 (1995): 145–203.

47   Gahlot, *The Prithviwallahs*, 39. Zohra Sehgal's account also encapsulates the plot as a defence of Muslims who stayed back being treated as traitors.

48   Dyal, *I Go South with Prithviraj*, 29.

49   Photographs in Dyal, *I Go South with Prithviraj*, appendix.

50   'Ghaddar: A Great National Play', *Filmindia*, October 1948, 45.

51   These two IPTA plays were Ismat Chugtai's *Dhani Bankain* (Green Bangles) and Krishan Chandar's *Darwaza Khol Do* (Open the Door).

52   '*Ahooti* Becomes a Boring Play', *Filmindia* December 1949, 45.

53   Tandon, *Theatre ke Sartaj Prithviraj*, 125.

54   Janaki is Sita's maiden name since she is the daughter of king Janak.

55   Urvashi Butalia, 'Community, State and Gender: On Women's Agency during Partition', *Economic and Political Weekly* 28, no. 17 (24 April 1993): 12–24.

56   The estimates vary on both sides, and many of these lives have gone undocumented on both sides. Scores of women were killed by their own families lest they fall into the hands of the enemy community. The official estimate of the number of abducted women was placed at 50,000 Muslim women in India and 33,000 non-Muslim women in Pakistan. See Ritu Menon and Kamla Bhasin, 'Recovery, Rupture and Resistance: Indian State and the Abduction of Women during Partition', *Economic and Political Weekly* 28, no. 17 (24 April 1993): WS2–WS11, https://www.jstor.org/stable/pdf/4399640 (accessed on 10 November 2020).

57   Director's note by Prithviraj Kapoor. Kapoor, Anand and Sehgal, *Deewar*, 5.

58   Introductory remarks by Ramvriksh Benipuri. Ibid., 10.

59   As an *abhineta*, or actor, Prithvi was more than a *neta*, or leader. Dyal, *I Go South with Prithviraj*, 27.

60   Ibid., 9.

61   Introductory remarks by Radhey Shyam Kathavachak. Kapoor, Anand and Sehgal, *Deewar*, 15.

62   Ben Singer, *Melodrama and Modernity: Early Sensational Cinema and Its Contexts* (New York: Columbia University Press, 2001), 38.

63   Peter Brooks, *The Melodramatic Imagination: Balzac, Henry James, Melodrama and the Mode of Excess* (New Haven: Yale University Press, 1995), 5.

64   Sudhir Kakar, 'Culture and Psychoanalysis: A Personal Journey', *Social Analysis: The International Journal of Anthropology* 50, no. 2 (Summer 2006): 25–44.

65   For right actions depend on a variety of factors such as the culture of one's country, on the historical age, on the effort required at a particular stage in life and on the heritage from previous life, making it difficult for an individual to know the exact configuration and thus the right action at a given moment. See Kakar, 'Culture and Psychoanalysis', 30.

66   Ibid.

67   The gendered implications of the white woman serving as the trouble in the text is an exciting and important area for future elucidation. It could be suggestive of Queen Victoria, the monarch who in 1857 became the empress of India when undivided South Asia came under direct British rule. It could also be a way to claim a more masculine position for Indian nationalism as opposed to its feminisation by colonial knowledge production.

68   Kapoor, Anand and Sehgal, *Deewar*, 45.

69   Faisal Devji, 'Hindu/Muslim/Indian', *Public Culture* 5, no. 1 (Fall 1992): 1–18, 2.

70   Ibid., 18.

71   Kapoor, Anand and Sehgal, *Deewar*, 85.

72   I am grateful to Debashree Mukherjee for sharing an advertisement of *Deewar*'s HMV (His Master's Voice) records. *Filmindia*, December 1945, 44.

73   Foreword by J. N. Kaushal in Tandon, *Theatre Ke Sartaj Prithviraj*, xvii.

74   'Prithviraj Gives the World's Best Play', *Filmindia*, May 1946, 53.

75   'Prithviraj Excels Himself in Pathan', 32.

76   Sehgal, *Close-Up*, 108.

77   Dyal, *I Go South with Prithviraj*, 9.

78   Ibid.

79   This account is narrated in Yog Raj's biography of Prithviraj. According to Yograj, he has a clear description of what transpired at the Muslim League meeting with Prithviraj as the author's father was the aide who accompanied Prithviraj to the place.

80   Ibrahim Ismail Chundrigar later went on to become the prime minister of Pakistan in 1957 and was in office for two months.

81   According to Yograj, Prithviraj managed to co-opt a low-rank clerk in the government office where his file was awaiting permission. He then tore off the page that contained the objections to the play, and when the file reached the top official, he signed the 'permission' right away.

82   Dyal, *I Go South with Prithviraj*, 29.

83   The line appears in a question posed in a letter to the editor. Baburao's response was 'Muslims have not seen it to be shaken. The play is a balm to the Hindu mind outraged by the Partition of India.' 'Editor's Mail', *Filmindia*, February 1949, 23.

84   Dyal, *I Go South with Prithviraj*, 30.

85   Hindu *padshahi* refers to the political claims made by the Hindu Mahasabha for a militant, religiously resurgent order that India needed after decolonisation. The speech refers to the political situation in India after Gandhi's assassination in 1948.

86   Dyal, *I Go South with Prithviraj*, 31 (emphasis mine).

87   Ibid., 74.

88   Gahlot, *Prithviwallahs*, 30.

89   Kapoor, Anand and Sehgal, *Deewar*, 6.

90   Dyal, *I Go South with Prithviraj*, 18.

91   Anuradha Kapur identifies this itinerary for *Deewar*, *Ghaddar* and *Pathan*. Kapur, 'Reassembling the Modern', 43.

92   Tandon, *Theatre Ke Sartaj Prithviraj*, 175.

PART 2

BETWEEN BOMBAY AND PAKISTAN

4

The Partition Wish

Fazli Brothers and the Muslim Social

In 2013, the Pakistani newspaper *Express Tribune* published a correspondence between Jinnah and a certain Mohammad Masud from Aligarh. Presumably responding to Masud's curiosity in ascertaining Jinnah's opinion of cinema and of film-maker Mehboob Khan, who was then making the historical *Humayun*, the Muslim League leader wrote that he wished 'more Musalmans would enter the film industry as there's plenty of scope for them'.[1] While Jinnah expressed a willingness to facilitate such an entry, his enthusiasm for a Muslim-made historical film under production appears to be wanting. This seemingly unremarkable, short letter is truly a signpost of the complexity and ethos of Muslim representation in colonial Indian cinema. On the one hand, it signals a discontent with the state of things such as the existing number of Muslims in the industry as well as the hegemonic genre of historical associated with Muslim film-making; on the other, it identifies a certain scope for the community in Bombay film-making, which coincidentally had links to the reformist, Islamic modernism of the Aligarh Muslim University (AMU) where Masud lived before partition.

This chapter seeks to examine the sudden spurt of the Muslim social film in the Hindustani film industry between the years 1940 and 1947. As this period also spans the unprecedented ascendancy of Muslim nationalism in the Indian subcontinent, bracketed by the Lahore Resolution at one end and the formation of a separate Muslim nation on the other, I examine if the film genre representing the religious and cultural distinctiveness of Indian Muslims was also imprinted with the larger problem of Muslim nationality at this time. Representing contemporary urban Muslim lives in India, the Muslim socials focus on the family and its offshoots and emphasise particularity through language, poetry, clothes and customary practices. I approach this genre by foregrounding the neglected oeuvre of the 'pioneers of Muslim social subjects in India',[2] the Fazli Brothers, who migrated to Pakistan after partition. Working exclusively within this category, they were the earliest self-conscious producers of the genre. As most of their films are no longer available, I use three available film transcripts in combination with the one surviving film, newspaper classifieds, film reviews and government records to contextualise the genre historically. Scrutinising other extant Muslim social films of this period for their generic coherence and continuum with the Fazli oeuvre, this chapter delineates a genealogy of the genre.

In part, this genealogy is in dialogue with the existing scholarship on the Muslim social film, most notably Ira Bhaskar and Richard Allen's *The Islamicate Cultures of Bombay Cinema*, which traces the emergence of this genre to the secular and hegemonic nationalist project of creating brotherhood on screen. Within this framework, the double motivation and double address are seen as characteristic of the genre, whereby 'reform' and 'celebration of tradition' are seen as neutralising the threat posed by modernity. But what if there is no duality in reform and tradition, and instead of a contest between tradition and modernity, the films narrativised oppositions between different modernities? Given that Bhaskar and Allen's work treats the post-partition Muslim social as the classical Muslim social, their working backwards history of the genre misses an important stage of the genre. This stage is the 1940s when the first cycle of the Muslim social genre appeared in the midst of the partition question. Instead of the unqualified and singular modernity referred to in these instances, my analysis locates thematic continuity between the Muslim social film and the Muslim modernity of the late nineteenth to early twentieth centuries and argues that this genre is best understood as really a desire for Muslim independence.

Employing the triangular master image of genre criticism constituted by film-makers, films and audience, this chapter investigates the larger relevance of the Fazli Brothers and their 1940s film cycle to the Muslim social genre.[3] It highlights the networks that the Fazli Brothers – and other film-makers of the genre – formed and were sustained by during these years. Despite its stress on the directors and their identity, the argument is not one of untrammelled auteurism but brings in the institutional contexts of film publicity and journalism as well. In doing so, the chapter aims to provide the early history of a genre whose academic understanding has largely been based on post-independence cycles of the Muslim social, somewhat clouding the overriding context of construction (film-makers and publicity) and reception (journalists and audiences) when the genre first appeared. The struggle to articulate a connection between Muslim national sentiment and the Muslim social of the 1940s marks earlier scholarship on the subject. Bhaskar and Allen avoid spelling out 'the direct reasons in those tumultuous times', whereas Rachel Dwyer's analysis of 'clear resonances with contemporary politics' in K. Asif's *Phool* (Flower, 1945) remains only suggestive of the pressures of the demand for Pakistan and the Quit India Movement.[4] The reluctance to link Muslim socials to Muslim nationality stems to a large extent from the politicisation of history writing in post-colonial India, which imposes a highly sensitised approach. I use the term 'Muslim independence' to accommodate tendencies that went beyond the demand for Pakistan (Muslim nationalism) and animated discussions across political divides. Here my analysis of the Muslim socials follows the prognosis of B. R. Ambedkar, who in 1945 identified partition as arising out of a colonial national frustration. Based on the speeches and addresses of the Muslim members of both the Congress and the Muslim League, Ambedkar concluded that Muslims 'really want independence' from the colonial rule as well as the prospects of a 'Hindu Raj'.[5] It is this desire for independence which sometimes took the form of a self-enclosed world inhabited only by Muslims, while at others it accommodated Hindu characters in a world driven by Muslim freedom, such as the Caliphate cause identified by Dwyer in her analysis of *Phool*. The desire for independence can also be detected in the complaints directed at films, which represented Muslims in a less flattering light and suggested the need for each community to control the production of its moving image.

Filling a Lacuna in Representation

Two petitions reveal the fraught linkages made between religious collectivities and film production, representation and reception in India during the mid-1930s. In 1933, Sheikh Sadiq Hassan, a Muslim member of the Delhi Legislative Assembly, recorded a multidimensional grievance in the first petition:

> Will the Government be pleased to state if they are aware
>
> a. that nearly *all Directors* of the film making companies *are non-Muslim*
>
> b. that the directors are *ignorant of sentiments* of Muslim public
>
> c. that there is *great resentment among Muslim* public when scenes of harem life are depicted in films and especially when historic Muslim queens and princesses are shown making love?
>
> d. Are government prepared to *order stricter censorship* in the case of type of film mentioned above? [*sic*][6]

The record of the proceedings reveals that the trigger for Hassan had been the 'great deal of trouble in Amritsar over a film *Hur-i-Haram*'.[7] It also referenced a previous objection raised by Seth Haji Abdoola Haroon over the exhibition of the film *Noor Jahan* (1931, dir. Ezra Mir) as one of the 'false films relating to Mughal emperors and the descendants of Mohammad'.

In 1937, the AILFC, a private vigilante body, submitted the second set of petitions to the Home Department, Government of Bombay. Alleging that these 'antisocial pictures' vilified Hindu culture and religion, the League demanded stringent censorship action:

> Almost all the films in India relate to the Hindus and their religious, social and cultural ideas. Some of the Parsi and Muslim film companies produced films that tended to lower the estimate of the Hindus in the eyes of the public from one point of view or the other. Unfortunately there are no definite principles laid down for the guidance of Film Censors and so long as the film has nothing objectionable from the political point of view it is generally passed without having any regard to the feelings and ideas of the Hindus.[8]

Despite emanating from seemingly rival causes, these petitions shared considerable common ground. First, both made direct connections between the religious identity of the film personnel and the content of the films, making it a case of the 'other' controlling the representation of 'self'. This incriminating difference was at the root of offensive pictures. Additionally, both acknowledged the power of films to hurt and arouse sentiments, therefore necessitating stricter censorship. The difference lay, crucially, in the category of films the two petitions were concerned about. While Sheikh Sadiq Hassan and his colleagues were worried about the 'historicals', the AILFC was for the most part anxious about the 'social film' (any film set in a contemporary milieu), which rose in importance, especially through the 1920s (and the 1930s).[9] These socials often carried stories critical of the canons of Hindu society, and thus it was hardly surprising that a conservative AILFC referred to these as 'antisocial' films in their objective. As counterintuitive as it may seem, both these petitions, separated by an interval of four years, ultimately draw attention to a conspicuous gap in representation until the late 1930s – that of contemporary Muslim lives.

While it is difficult to make exhaustive claims, yet even by conservative estimates, at least twenty Muslim social films were made and released between 1940 and 1947. As all the directors of the listed films were Muslims, it must be asked, as Ravi Vasudevan does, whether 'the question of who could tell stories about contemporary Muslim life had anything to do with the representation of Muslims at the political level' during these years.[10] Table 4.1 lists the directors and the Muslim socials they made.

Functioning within an informal economy, the Indian film industry's history of production financing is a hazy territory. However, an interesting link between the Muslim League and film finance in the 1940s existed via a certain Aziz Ghafoor Qazi and his extended family, as referred to in the earlier chapter. A prominent member of the Bombay Muslim League, Qazi served as Justice of Peace in the Provincial Legislative Council. By 1946, together with his producer son-in-law, Shiraz Ali Hakim, Qazi had become a stakeholder and director in the studio company

Table 4.1 Muslim socials produced between 1940 and 1947

S. F. Hasnain Fazli	*Quaidi* (Prisoner, 1940), *Masoom* (Innocent, 1941), *Fashion* (1943), *Dil* (Heart, 1946)
Sibtain Fazli	*Chowranghee* (1942), *Ismat* (Purity, 1944), *Shama* (Flame, 1946),[11] *Mehandi* (Henna, 1947)
Shaukat Hussain Rizvi	*Khandaan* (Lineage, 1942), *Naukar* (Servant, 1944), *Zeenat* (Beauty, 1945)
Nazir	*Salma* (1943), *Abidah* (1947)
S. Khalil	*Bhai Jaan* (Elder Brother, 1945)
S. M. Yusuf	*Nek Parvin* (Virtuous Parvin, 1946)
Najam Naqvi	*Nateeja* (Outcome, 1947)
Mazhar Khan	*Yaad* (Memory, 1942), *Pehli Nazar* (First Sight, 1945)
K. Asif	*Phool* (Flower, 1945)
Mehboob Khan	*Najma* (1943), *Elan* (Clarion Call, 1947)
A. R. Kardar	*Dard* (Agony, 1947)

Source: Compiled by the author.

Bombay Talkies, which produced Najam Naqvi's *Nateeja* (Outcome, 1947).[12] Qazi's son K. Abdullah produced K. Asif's *Phool*, while Shiraz Ali Hakim was the producer of Shaukat Hussain's *Zeenat* (Beauty, 1945). Qazi's company, 'Indian Film Circuit', was also involved in film distribution and distributed S. M. Yusuf's *Nek Parvin* (Virtuous Parvin, 1946) and all Kardar films. The Fazlis' connection to the Muslim League seems to be limited to ideological subscription, however, as later stated by Sibtain and reinforced by the family relationship with Meerut's *nawab*, Ismail Khan, the long-serving president of the Muslim League in the United Provinces. Film-maker Nazir too supported the Muslim League and had daringly hoisted the party flag at his Hind Pictures office in Bombay, which earned the ire of arsonists during the partition disturbance.[13] While some of these film-makers migrated to Pakistan immediately in 1947 (Sibtain Fazli, Shaukat Hussain Rizvi, Nazir), many others followed later on (S. F. Hasnain, S. M. Yusuf, Najam Naqvi). The rest stayed in India (Mazhar Khan, K. Asif, Mehboob Khan and A. R. Kardar), though in some cases after temporarily considering Pakistan as a production base (Mehboob and Kardar). Often sharing family ties, as brothers (Fazlis) or brothers-in-law (Kardar–Mehboob and Nazir–K. Asif), there were also instances of friendship and long-lasting collaboration between these men, a case in point being Nazir and Kardar who had left Lahore together to work in Calcutta and then relocated to Bombay in the late 1930s.

A New Production Field in Colonial India

The brothers of the Fazli team were S. F. Hasnain and Sibtain Fazli. Hailing from Allahabad, Uttar Pradesh, the Fazlis were a family of government servants and modernised elites. Their father was a district magistrate, and Karim Fazli, the eldest brother, was an Indian Civil Service (ICS) officer who later made a few films in Pakistan. The family intended Hasnain to follow suit after graduating from Allahabad University. He, however, had other plans. Along with younger brother Sibtain, Hasnain arrived in Bombay in 1933 and a year later directed a social for the company Shakti Movietone. In 1935, he started *Triya Charitra* (Artfulness of Women) for Dean Films, but the film could not be completed due to insufficient funds. By 1937, the brothers had moved to film studios in Calcutta. Sibtain Fazli joined the well-known New Theatres the same year and assisted director Debki Kumar Bose on *Vidyapati* (1937). But, what brought recognition to the brothers was the film *Quaidi* (Prisoner, 1940), produced by the Film Corporation of India. Directed by elder brother Hasnain and scripted by the younger Sibtain, *Quaidi* appears in the classifieds as 'a saga of a youth in chains'.[14] In a gushing *Filmindia* article, *Quaidi* was treated as a courageous venture of Hasnain's, though hardly for any subversive anti-colonial pitch.

> In choosing 'Quaidi' he had taken *a grave risk according to the then existing code of production*, Indian producers never fancied Muslim subjects – least of all a social story of Muslim life, because certain sections of Muslim masses had made themselves notorious in making such pictures a holy cause for unholy riots.[15]

While the article makes much of *Quaidi*, as proving all fears unfounded and making a success of representing contemporary Muslim life in the subcontinent, there is evidence of other Muslim socials being produced simultaneously, if not earlier. Writing about his film days in Calcutta, scriptwriter Agha Jani Kashmiri mentions a 'Muslim film' *Aaminah* in which he acted opposite singer Begum Akhtar in the late 1930s.[16] A lesser-known yet quite successful film at the time was *Khan Bahadur* (1937) by Sohrab Modi, which migrant film-maker M. Luqman identifies as the 'first Muslim social' in the subcontinent. I will return to *Khan Bahadur* later, but here it will suffice to say that the importance of Fazli Brothers therefore does not lie in their being the pioneering practitioners of this genre but in the fact that they were conscious producers of the genre, with their pre-partition oeuvre exclusively Muslim social. *Quaidi* reportedly began with an *azaan*, the auditory motif, which became quite common in the opening sequences of Muslim socials that followed.[17] Useful in setting up the cultural milieu of these films, it could also serve as a signal to audiences to realign their expectations. The *Filmindia* article had only high praise for Hasnain for negotiating the infamous 'Muslim rage' of late colonial India.[18]

> By daring the wrath of the Muslim masses, Hasnain has opened *a new field of production for our producers.*

Quaidi's success saw the setting up of the production company Fazli Brothers in Calcutta in 1941, with the firm name in all likelihood inspired by the popular Warner Brothers of Hollywood and the Wadia Brothers of Bombay. The first film produced by the company was *Masoom* (Innocent, 1941). Characterised as the perfect portrayal of Muslim social life, Hasnain created a further buzz in the 'all-India market'. First released in Lahore, followed by Calcutta and Delhi, *Masoom*'s publicity in Bombay drew on endorsements by prominent members of the public and the press. One such letter reproduced in the publicity was by the mayor of Calcutta, Phanindra Nath Brahma, who found 'the graveyard scene' in the film quite powerful.[19] The news magazine *Karamvir*, published from Lahore, urged the public to see *Masoom*.

> Through films Muslims have known enough of Hindu life but Hindus are still in dark about their neighbours' life. For mutual understanding, it is essential that both the communities should know each other well.[20]

Actor-turned-producer Mazhar Khan, who had acted in *Masoom* and went on to make *Yaad* (Memory, 1942) a year later, similarly linked the 'present rift in the Hindu-Muslim relations to the lack of Muslim subjects on the Indian screen'.[21] Linking the Muslim social film with the project of Hindu–Muslim understanding during this time remained independent of the subject matter of the film but took the form of spectatorial accommodation and Samaritanism, as 'to see it [was] to foster Hindu–Muslim unity'. However, Hasnain's views on choosing Muslim subjects for his films were more to do with the emulative potential of Muslim life, with the principal imagined audience being Muslims themselves.

> Muslim social and cultural life must be portrayed on the screen as it has numerous facets worthy of emulation by the masses in general and unless the Mahomedans see them as presented through the artistic emotions of a motion picture producer, *how will they ever come to love their way of living*? I am a Mahomedan and if I don't risk it, who would?[22]

Hasnain imparts a degree of functionality to his films, and so do the reviews. The Fazli films were being discussed as useful, as 'involved more with functionality than with beauty', borrowing from Haidee Wasson and Charles Acland's premise of useful cinema.[23] In Wasson and Acland's work, useful cinema has been 'conceptualized as a body of films and technologies that perform tasks and serve as instruments in an ongoing struggle for aesthetic, social and political capital'.[24] For Hasnain, these films were instruments for Muslim self-fashioning and self-love. For the reviewers and other endorsing members of the public, these were a medium of insights into a community, whose religious beliefs and way of life were being cited as a critical factor in determining the kind of freedom that India were to have. Against the backdrop of the looming question of Muslim nationality and a quest for representation, the emergence of a network of Muslim personnel in Bombay around the Muslim social genre would undeniably be read in institutional terms – as producing propaganda for Pakistan.

By the end of 1942, Lahore too had produced a Muslim social, *Khandaan* (Lineage), directed by Shaukat Hussain Rizvi, though the film was never marketed as such.[25] The year 1942 also marked Sibtain Fazli's debut as a director, and he made the film *Chowranghee* under the Fazli Brothers banner. *Chowranghee* reportedly took root in Calcutta, where Sibtain Fazli regularly came across a beggar woman in the Chowranghee area and decided to adapt Bernard Shaw's *Pygmalion* for his directorial debut. It seems that the new-found enthusiasm for representation of contemporary 'Muslim lives' was not restricted to the fictional format but made inroads into documentary as well. The Fazli Brothers followed *Chowranghee* with two short documentaries – *Mushaira* (Poetry Reading) and *Yaadgaar Mushaira* (Memorable Poetry Reading),[26] which featured Urdu poets like Mir Taqi Mir, Mirza Ghalib, Bahadur Shah Zafar, Daag Dehalvi, Altaf Hussain Hali, Mohammad Iqbal and Jigar Moradabadi. Another notable documentary of this year was Khwaja Ahmad Abbas's biopic of Sir Sayyid Ahmad Khan, the founder of his alma mater, the AMU.[27] Established as the Mohammedan Anglo-Oriental College in the 1870s, the rationale for the British-styled yet Islamic educational institution was to promote the advancement of education in the colonial Muslim community. As David Lelyveld puts it, 'immersed in a whole new ideology about the history and present status of Indian Muslims, Aligarh was not only a school, it was a political symbol'.[28]

As the Second World War began affecting film production in Calcutta, the Fazli Brothers moved to Bombay by the end of 1942. While the company name remained the same, it acquired the striking new logo of two hands in a firm clasp across the map of India accompanied by the tagline 'Fazli Brothers Limited Bombay: The Symbol of Hindu–Muslim Unity'. Within months of their move, the brothers announced several films together, like *College, Humayun, Fashion* and *Bhai–Behan* (Brother–Sister). Out of these it seems only *Fashion* was completed and released in 1943. The review of the film reveals the theme of the corrupting influence of 'Western civilisation', common to all Fazli films.

> Very politely Hasnain points out that it is not right for all Indians to be misled by the superficial glamour of the gaiety goods the West brings along in its train for civilising the East.[29]

According to the *Filmindia* review, the story focuses on life after marriage for Razia and Yusuf. After moving to a city in search of a job, Yusuf is seduced by the big bad city life, lined with clubs and inhabited by modern women. Razia, on the other hand, remains true to her traditional convictions and silently accepts a subordinate position in the household, more so when Yusuf marries a Westernised and glamorous Farida. The film ends with Yusuf realising his mistake and reuniting with Razia.

Sibtain's *Ismat* (1944) followed, which was one of the earliest films of actress Nargis, who received the same remuneration as the established star Mehtab, ostensibly on the grounds of their equal share of screen time, but being Jaddan Bai's daughter would have certainly helped Nargis. Jaddan Bai, the famous courtesan-turned-Bombay-actress and producer of the 1930s, had by the mid-1940s commanded an influential position. The regular gatherings at her place also served as a networking space for established and upcoming film artistes of the Bombay film industry[30] and earned the epithet 'mini-Pakistan' in *Filmindia*.[31] *Ismat* was a box-office success, earning the tag of a silver jubilee grosser, that is, completion of twenty-five weeks at the box office. After *Ismat*, it was Hasnain's turn to make *Dil* (Heart, 1946), with Noorjahan in the lead. By this time several Muslim socials had been produced in Bombay. Mehboob Khan made *Najma* (1943), K. Asif made *Phool* (Flower, 1945), Shaukat Hussain Rizvi made *Naukar* (Servant, 1943), and Mazhar Khan made *Yaad* (Memory, 1942) and *Pehli Nazar* (First Sight, 1945). After the release of *Ismat*, Sibtain decided to co-direct the film *Shama* with a friend K. H. Qazi, with Minerva Movietone producing the venture. The Second World War had created a scarcity of film stock, and the mid-1940s were a time of carefully monitored licensing. Given the shortage, Sibtain purchased the film licence from Minerva's owner, Sohrab Modi, and commenced the film shoot in the Minerva studio. According to Fazli's memoirs, the collaboration between K. H. Qazi and Sohrab Modi could not last, and Sibtain withdrew from the project even though the film was nearly complete. Many decades later, he recalled in the Pakistani magazine *Musawar* that the idea for *Shama* had emerged from his discussions with Shaukat Hussain Rizvi, who in turn had heard it from K. Asif.

> I took the plot of the story of *Shama* from Shaukat Hussain Rizvi. Shaukat narrated two stories to me in a meeting and asked which one was better suited to a film.... being in favour of different stories, it was decided that I'll make a film on my favourite story and Shaukat will make one on his choice. He used this story for *Zeenat*. Shaukat Hussain Rizvi had originally heard these ideas from K. Asif.[32]

After the debacle of *Shama*, Sibtain made *Mehandi* (Henna, 1947), which turned out to be his last film in Bombay. *Mehandi* was about two female friends in love with the same man. Fazli's elder son, who also had a small role in the film, remembered the plotline as follows:

> You can say the idea was a bit like 'Saheli'.[33] There are two friends, Nargis and Begum Para. Nargis is married to the hero. The hero is quite religious, shown as keeping a full beard in those days. He is sent to England for higher education. In one shot it is shown that when he returns from England, he is absolutely modern, clean-shaven! He socialises actively, whereby he meets Begum Para and starts liking her. Nargis on the other hand is very simple and prays five times a day. So he asks Nargis what would she say if he were to marry a second time. She replies 'go ahead, what difference does it make'? She says 'Go ahead' in a lighter vein. Technically the religion allows for it, but those

are not her reasons to say 'go ahead'. However, he seriously interprets it as a
valid consent and proposes to Begum Para. Begum Para doesn't know he is
married and accepts. At Begum Para's henna ceremony – I am putting it in a
nutshell, my father must have handled it very well to ensure that little objection
comes from any quarter – Nargis gets to know that her best friend is getting
married to none other than her husband. What can she say, poor girl, she is
very obedient. So, when she is applying henna on her friend's hand, a tear falls
from Nargis' eye on Begum Para's hand. This is the special touch that my father
gave! Nargis conceals her tears in the henna, but Begum Para later learns of
the entire situation and calls off the wedding.... It was a very nice film, with a
happy ending.[34]

Mehandi was released in the partition months, and Sibtain was touring the country
to promote it and oversee its release:

> Our film *Mehandi* was released on 14 August 1947, the independence day
> of the subcontinent.[35] I had gone to Meerut to prepare for the release of the
> film. From Meerut, I went to Delhi.... After finishing my work, I returned to
> Bombay. On reaching there, I got to know that the film print, which had been
> sent to Karachi, did not contain the cuts I wanted in the final version.[36]

Sibtain Fazli decided to go to Karachi himself and on reaching there found an
immediate return to Bombay difficult. Due to large-scale evacuation by non-Muslim
Sindhis, flights from Karachi to Bombay were fully booked. Fazli then decided to
go to Delhi and continue his journey to Bombay from there. By this time, Delhi
was ravaged by riots, and Fazli spent several fraught days in the city, waiting for the
first opportunity to return safely to Bombay. Finally, he befriended a Sikh family
who helped him get a plane ticket for Bombay, and Fazli travelled under the alias
'Shantilal'. Published in a Pakistani film magazine two decades after partition, Fazli's
reminiscences were consistent with the official Pakistani rhetoric that mixed a sense
of entitlement to power with the certitude of disenfranchised doom.

> When the plane flew over Humayun's tomb, I could not miss the irony of my
> situation. Here was a Muslim leaving the place disguised as a Hindu, where
> 'Muslims' ruled for hundreds of years and where *their* cultural and religious
> buildings stand. Then I meditated on my name 'Shantilal' and realized that
> now the multitudes of Muslims here will have to become 'Shantilal' to continue
> living. This was the thought that proved decisive in leaving India. On reaching
> Bombay, I got to know that many Muslims of our group were contemplating
> moving to Pakistan. This included Wajahat Mirza, Mazhar Khan, K. Asif,
> Mehboob, Kardar, Nazir, Shaukat Hussain Rizvi, Noorjahan, W.Z. Ahmad,
> Neena, S. Yusni, M. Sadiq, Shiraz Ali Hakim and Dilip Kumar. Dilip was busy
> in a shoot those days, so he sent his brothers Nasir Khan and Ayub Khan
> with us to survey the film situation here ... once they came here, they were

very disappointed with the situation. This abandoned and desolate scene disappointed everyone who arrived from Bombay and consequently Mehboob, Kardar, Mazhar Khan, S. Yusni, Wajahat Mirza, K. Asif and M. Sadiq went back. Now only W.Z. Ahmed, Shaukat Rizvi, Nazir and I remained here. We were zealous in our love for the nation and community. In Bombay, we had openly favoured Pakistan and opposed India to an extent that we were at a point of no return. During the freedom movement, I had been a staunch supporter of Muslim League. Many elders of our family had been friends and fellow travellers of Quaid-i-Azam. My maternal aunt's husband Nawab Mohammad Ismail Khan was among his close companions.[37]

While Sibtain mentions many of his film colleagues, this account is curiously silent about his brother Hasnain. This is because Hasnain stayed on in India until the early 1950s and made films like *Rasta* (Road, 1947), *Khoobsurat* (Beautiful, 1952) and *Duniya* (World, 1949). The reviews of the films *Khoobsurat* and *Duniya* do not spell out if these were Muslim socials, but the 'ills of Westernisation' and the two-women structure are evident in these as well. The only instance of Hasnain's public interjection in those years is evident in a clarificatory letter published in *Filmindia* on behalf of Fazli Brothers Limited. Following partition, the magazine was busy identifying 'disloyal' film-makers who had left for Pakistan.

> Our attention has been drawn to a report published in the latest issue of your esteemed journal where you have referred to our president Mr. S.F. Hasnain as 'Pakistan returned'. We may tell you that the above remark is not correct as Mr. Hasnain has never shifted nor intended to shift from this place.[38]

The magazine ran a curt afterword in fine print below the letter stating that Sibtain Fazli, the other brother of the Fazli Brothers' company, had migrated to Pakistan, suggesting that the status of the Fazli production company remained nationally compromised.

> We are informed that Mr. Hasnain's brother, S. Fazli is in Pakistan.

Hasnain finally migrated to Pakistan in 1955 and died two years later, without any film to his credit in Pakistan. Sibtain Fazli's first film in Pakistan was *Dopatta* (Scarf, 1952) starring Noorjahan and Sudhir. The film was released in India and was one of the earliest production successes of Pakistan. Unlike the previous Fazli films, it is unmarked by any religious regime and instead of a space of worship, the film opens in a hospital. Noorjahan played the gullible damsel from a mountain tribe who falls in love with an urbane army officer. The names of the protagonists were ambiguous, Bulbul and Roshan, and nearly all the characters in the film were anglicised and not caricatured, unlike the previous Fazli films. Thus, tellingly, Sibtain's first film in Pakistan was not a Muslim social in the sense of the category that I will now identify using the pre-partition Fazli oeuvre (Figure 4.1).

Figure 4.1   The cover page of *Masoom*'s transcript
Source: Fazli Family, Lahore.

The Muslim Modernity of Fazli Films

One of my key departures from Bhaskar and Allen's analysis of the classical Muslim social is the idea of a singular modernity, which animates their analysis. The dependence on extant films leads them to locate the narrative tension as one between feudal values and modernisation:

> [T]he need to modernize the community from within in order to adjust to rapid social changes…, but to do so in ways that ensured both that the community was not left behind and that it maintained its distinctive cultural and social identity.[39]

The modernity available in the three transcripts of the Fazli films works differently from the tensions arising out of feudal and modern value systems (see Appendix). In Fazli films the narrative tension is between multiple modernities, where one kind of modernity triumphs over another. In these plots, lack of piety, deceit and personal fulfilment are associated with agents of Euro-American modernity (such as the English-speaking Ishrat in *Ismat* or the anglicised suitor in *Dil* or the

Chicago-returned blackmailer Hashmat in *Shama*), who eventually lose out to female agents of Islamic modernity or the 'apologetic modernity' who are pious, truthful and socially committed.[40] Centred on life within the domestic space, these stories are characterised by the melodramatic mode, with its narrative mechanisms of coincidence and manipulation of knowledge.[41] Two aspects are predominant: an anti-West stance and a stress on personal conduct. The women protagonists in all films are constructed in similar ways. The virtuous qualities of patience, self-denial, kindness and the unwavering (Muslim) faith of these women help overcome all odds. This exemplary character of the female protagonist of the Muslim social in the 1940s can be traced to a key reformist text from nineteenth-century colonial India.

Completed in 1869, Nazir Ahmad's *Mirat-ul-Aras*, or *The Bride's Mirror*, became 'the first Urdu bestseller'[42] and was the first of a three-series tale. As C. M. Naim points out, *Mirat-ul Aras*'s main motif of two sisters, one good (Asghari) and the other bad (Akbari), has been used ever since in innumerable novels and stories aimed at the female audience.[43] Other prescriptive texts for women from this time, like Altaf Hussain Hali's *Majlis-un Nisan* (An Assembly of Women) and Ashraf Ali Thanawi's *Bihishti Zevar* (Jewels of the Paradise), were also part of the literary tradition the Muslim socials were drawing upon. These books contain advice on conjugal and familial relations, household management, discussion on religious law and biographies of good women. Given to daughters as part of dowry, these books also inspired many ladies' journals in the early twentieth century. I would argue that the Fazli Brothers in particular, but also the Muslim social in general, solved the problem of representing Muslim lives on screen by making use of narrative themes, literature and character types already popular and cogent within the literate section of the community. Thus, the 1944 Fazli Brothers' film *Ismat* is telling in its choice of title, which it shared with the most popular Urdu home journal of the early twentieth century. *Ismat* (Purity), founded in 1908 and still in publication from Karachi, was Nazir Ahmed's nephew Rashid ul Khairi's journal for women.[44] Focused strongly on women's plight and experience, the journal placed emphasis on the education and cultivation of women. A couplet that frequently appeared in the magazine was:

Islah-i-qawm aap ko manzoor hai agar
Bachon se pehle maa'on ko taaleem deejyey.[45]

If you desire the community's betterment
Educate mothers before educating children.

The term *qawm* referring to a 'Muslim collectivity' or nation-group appears frequently in the Muslim socials of this decade. The nation-group here is not plain 'Muslim' but more specifically led by the North Indian Shurafa. Faisal Devji identifies the emergence of the Shurafa as a distinct 'Islamic' or revivalist polity in the colonial nineteenth century, distinguishing itself against both aristocrat and pleb on the basis of 'true' or 'orthodox' Islam.[46] Dislocated by colonialism, the Shurafa abstracted from the idea of moral city areas such as the mosque, the school and the domestic realm,[47] which were also the spaces of the Muslim social. The Shurafa were at the centre of the movement for women's reform in the nineteenth century, and, in the twentieth, it was this polity organising around the symbol of Islam that lay at the heart of the movement for Pakistan, what Francis Robinson refers to as one of the most striking examples of nation formation the world has seen.[48] Crucially, it is the manners and morality of the Shurafa that constitute the regime of social and cultural verisimilitude of the Fazli films. As delineated by Steve Neale, the systems of plausibility, belief and motivation, whereby participants would recognise shared knowledge as part of culture, constitute the social and cultural verisimilitude of a genre.[49]

Coming back to *Mirat-ul-Aras* and its motif of two sisters, Akbari 'behaves in every unsuitable way, quarrels with her husband and in-laws and storms off to her mother's house refusing to do domestic chores'.[50] Illiterate and ill-tempered, she ends up making a mess of the independent home that she fought for. On the other hand, married in the same house as her elder sister, Asghari is literate, talented and sweet-tempered. Disciplined in daily activities and the observance of religious duties, she transforms the life and fortunes of her husband's household. Time sees Asghari on a high-octane path of achievement. She starts a school for carefully selected girls from the neighbourhood in her house, brings Akbari back into the family-fold and rescues her husband from evil company.

In the Fazli films, the motif of two sisters is modified to two women of contrasting dispositions in comparable situations. Mostly the duo is in competition for the affection of a man, with one taking the place of the other through marriage. In *Ismat*, Ishrat falls in love with Aaliya's husband; in *Dil*, Ladli wants to marry the husband of her childhood rival; and in *Shama*, Noor Bano struggles to regain her rightful place in the face of the beguiling memory and scandalous conduct of the *nawab*'s dead wife. Four other Fazli films, *Masoom*, *Chowranghee*, *Fashion* and *Mehandi*, whose narrative plot can be broadly reconstructed, also have a two-women structure.

> *Masoom*: Masoom is in love with Rehana, a playmate of his childhood, while Jamil loves Shahida, a modern educated girl.[51]

> *Chowranghee*: Engaged to marry a princess, the young man is revolted by her worldliness and finds his ideal in the tattered but high souled beggar maid.[52]

> *Fashion*: In the beginning Yusuf induces his wife to go with him, but Razia stoutly refuses to do so saying that she was a woman of the home.... Very soon Yusuf meets Farida, a social butterfly ... [and] soon accepts Farida as his second wife.[53]

> *Mehandi*: The plot of the story is childishly simple. Kulsum and Nadira are friends. Kulsum is poor and Nadira is rich and fashionable.[54]

In addition to the two-women structure, other influences of the literature and home journals inspired by Nazir Ahmed are evident in the Asghari-like qualities of the protagonists of Muslim socials at this time. A heady concoction of piety, self-righteousness and innate capability in varying degrees, these are all cinematic daughters and disciples of Asghari. Shahida of *Pehli Nazar* immerses herself further in religious observances when her prospective suitor falls in love with her cousin, Husna, instead. Taking succour in the Quran received in her dowry, Najma in *Najma* decides to leave behind memories of her love for Yusuf. The only instance of a breakdown of prescribed forbearance is in *Dil*, when the oppressive guardian forbids the little girl to pray. Having tolerated whipping in the midst of her prayers, this embargo is the final straw, and she blinds the man, striking him across his eye, making it more akin to divine retribution than a human-inflicted injury.

Like Asghari, the women of Muslim socials take it upon themselves to reform their wayward husbands. The path of home-study, which the Muslim reformers of the nineteenth century prescribed for women, had the potential to make them *alim*, or authoritative scholars, and they were expected to 'educate not just other girls but men of their families as well if it were needed'.[55] Finding themselves married to extravagant and unemployed *nawab*s, these 'home-educated' women invested themselves in improving their husbands. While at times they succeed with comparative ease, like in *Najma*, and at others after a long-suffering struggle, as in *Nek Parvin*, there is also an instance of tragic failure in Mehboob's *Elan* (Clarion Call), which I will discuss later.

Finally, perhaps the most preponderant and ubiquitous concern in these films is for the education of the community. The calling of a teacher, especially a woman teacher in a girls' school or the schooling of poor orphans, is a common theme in most Muslim socials of this period. Like *Ismat*, *Nek Parvin* too begins with a devotional hymn at a school assembly set against the painted background of crescent moon, star and minaret.[56] *Dard* (Agony) opens with a similar assembly at a boys' orphanage, and *Zeenat* begins with a humorous episode of a little boy receiving religious instruction at home. *Dil* has several heated exchanges between the heroine and one of her suitors on the merits of vernacular home-study versus English education. To be instilled through proper upbringing, moral conduct has been identified as 'a cornerstone of (Muslim) cultural continuity, particularly in periods of perceived social and political dislocation'.[57] In their stress on the feminine ideal and education, these films were self-consciously located within the Shurafa-led modernity.

Another striking aspect of these Muslim socials is their use of the twentieth-century poet and philosopher Muhammad Iqbal's verses and references to his work. Iqbal's 'political legacy' for the subcontinent has been much debated, given his association with the Muslim League on the one hand and his rejection of territorial nationalism on the other. Naveeda Khan locates in Muhammad Iqbal 'a possible genealogy of Muslim aspiration' and argues that Pakistan was not the actualisation of Iqbal's ideals but the creation of his words.[58]

Mohammad Iqbal's words and works are ritually invoked in the Muslim socials of the 1940s. *Ismat* begins and ends with the 'Child's Prayer' by Iqbal, a staple of morning assemblies in schools in Pakistan and of Muslim community-backed ones in India. In *Dil*, unaware that his protégé's bride is his lost daughter, Saeed gifts the girl *Bang-i-Dira*, or *The Call of the Caravan*, which contains the two most significant and defining pan-Islamic poems by Iqbal, 'Shikwa' (Complaint) and 'Jawab-i-Shikwa' (Answer of the Complaint). The following exchange between the father and daughter ensues when the book is presented as a gift.

> *Noorjahan/Bachchi: Behtareen cheez hai.*
> *Maulvi/Saeed: Mere khyaal mein Hindustan ki har ladki ko yeh kitaab padhni chahiye.*
> *Noorjahan/Bachchi: Maulvi Sahab, main yeh kitab padh chuki hun, magar yeh voh kitab hai jisko hazaar baar padha jae toh kam hai.*

> Noorjahan/Bachchi: An object par excellence.
> Maulvi/Saeed: In my opinion, every girl of Hindustan ought to read this book.
> Noorjahan/Bachchi: Maulvi Sahab, I have read this book, yet even if read it a thousand times over, it will not quite suffice.

'Shikwa' and 'Jawab-i-Shikwa', in which Iqbal 'expresses the great longing of Muslims for new confidence and self-consciousness',[59] also make an appearance in Mehboob's *Najma* and *Elan* and in A. R. Kardar's *Dard*. The two films by Mehboob begin with verses from the poems:

> Ek hi saf mein khade ho gaye Mehmood-o-Ayaaz / Na koi banda raha, na koi banda nawaaz. (Second verse, strophe 11, 'Shikwa')

> Mahmud [General] and Ayaz [Soldier] were standing in a row / None was servant, nor was there his Lord.[60]

This couplet is not merely an aural accompaniment but supervises the visual arrangement and montage of the opening sequence of *Najma*. It is here that the two patriarchs of the narrative, the *nawab* and his family doctor, are introduced: praying together and established as equal. What later ensues in the film is in contrast to this egalitarianism, where despite their close friendship the two men marry their much-in-love son and daughter to other persons. By keeping apart the perfectly matched lovers for no justifiable reason, *Najma* tantalises by imagining a beautiful life foregone. Mehboob's other Muslim social, *Elan*, also opens with a couplet from 'Jawab-i-Shikwa', which will be discussed in detail in the final section of this chapter.

The reference to the philosopher-poet in Kardar's *Dard* is evident in the aspirational name of the orphan Iqbal. Quite like his namesake, the boy wishes to become a doctor, albeit a medical one. He fervently recites the following verse to convey his potential, which moves a rich patron to adopt this Iqbal.

Aaj bhi ho jo Baraheem ka imaan paida / Aag kar sakti hai andaz-e-gulistan paida. (Third verse, strophe 28, 'Jawab-i-Shikwa')

If also Ibrahim's faith existed today / The fire could create a rose-shaped garden.[61]

How do we understand the odes to Iqbal present in the pre-partition Muslim socials, which were all made within a decade of his demise in 1938? Faisal Devji describes the immediate as well as long-lasting significance of Iqbal thus:

> The greatest critic of nationalism in India was also the man known as the spiritual father of Pakistan. By the time he died in 1938, nearly ten years before that country's founding, Mohammad Iqbal had been recognized as India's most important Muslim thinker. Hugely popular in all classes of people, his poetry was declaimed in the streets of cities like Lahore, and his apparent support for Muslim nationalism gave the League an intellectual credibility it would otherwise have lacked.[62]

Arguably, the Muslim social made similar use of Iqbal. In transposing his words and works within a discursive space that drew on reformist literature of the nineteenth century and the popular journals of the twentieth, the Muslim socials produced a seamless diegetic space of Muslim aspiration for independence, unparalleled by and unavailable in any other cultural intervention.

Selling the Muslim Social

The 'common cultural consensus' as to what constituted a Muslim social can be gathered in the strategies of distribution, marketing and critical reviews that negotiated audience expectations and knowledge.[63] As noted by Barbara Klinger, the institutional contexts of film publicity and journalism are not external to the text and viewer but actively intersect the viewer–text relationship.[64] This is not to fix the experience of viewing these films but to interrogate axes along which the film trade imagined the audiences of the Muslim socials. The endeavour to appeal to large numbers was hardly easy given that not only was this 'a new production field' but it had a particularist label in a decade when the hegemonic Indian nationalism was suspicious of any community-based consciousness which could not be contained under the rubric of unity. What emerges from an examination of classifieds in an English-language newspaper and a film magazine of the 1940s is a publicity campaign targeted along two axes of identity – Muslim and women. While stressing the *particularity* of the genre depending on audience identification and curiosity, attempts were also made at *universality* to counteract any alienation that may have translated into business loss. It is in the publicity of the Muslim social during the 1940s that the 'double address of the genre directed towards both Muslims and non-Muslims' becomes most evident.[65]

As is usual with genres, in the case of *Muslim socials* too, the institutional and analytic categories dovetail with one another. In 1942, Fazli Brothers' *Masoom* was claimed to be the 'first Muslim social' in much of its publicity (Figure 4.2). As we have seen, in terms of a thematic pattern – pertaining to contemporary Muslim domesticity and the challenge of colonial modernity to Muslim privilege – *Masoom* was not the first Muslim social, having been preceded by *Quaidi* and *Khan Bahadur*. While none of the available advertisements of *Quaidi* mentions the term, the 1942 article of *Filmindia* called *Quaidi* the first Muslim social, and the pre-release publicity of *Khan Bahadur* refers to it as 'Muslim Society drama', acknowledging the particularity inherent in the film.[66]

While the publicity for *Masoom* saw a generous use of the label, it did not quite congeal into being the only nomenclatural possibility. The genre demonstrated remarkable flexibility as far as terminology was concerned and often depended more on visual signification than an explicit label. The exhaustively discussed iconography of the genre, typified by veiled women, bearded men, Turkish *fez*s, minarets and arches, and crescent and star, was present in the publicity design often rendering any labelling superfluous (Figures 4.2–4.4). Mazhar Khan's 1945 film, *Pehli Nazar*, was advertised in colour on the cover pages of *Filmindia* as a 'Muslim Costume' film (Figure 4.3).

The association of Muslim socials with decorative mise en scène, elaborate sets, traditional dresses and lofty dialogues was in place by the mid-1940s. The publicity for these films evoked these features, and the film-watching experience was likened to a 'privilege' and a 'cine treat'.

> It is Bombay's privilege to see first Muslim Social Fazli Bros.' 'Masoom'.[67]
> 'Naukar': a cine-treat on a grand Mohamedan social scale.[68]
> United Films' Great Muslim Social 'Bhaijan'[69]
> A Clarion Call for New Culture: Mehboob Productions purposeful social! Elan[70]

As if recalling the lost glory of a culture once associated with the ruling establishment, the premium attached to watching Muslim family life could have soothed the frayed nerves of the community, which had been outraged by previous representations. Both celebratory and respectful, such publicity could dispel any initial misapprehensions about the content and motives of the film as far as objection from within the community was concerned.

> GLIMPSES of MUSLIM family life and the DIGNITY of MANNERS and CUSTOMS: Fazli Brother's *Masoom* presenting intimate picture of domestic life.[71]
> She would rather die than say she was in love; the first Muslim social on the screen.[72]
> God's gift to the woman is the Altruistic instinct inherent in her, she lives for others, not herself! *Salma*![73]

Figure 4.2   *Masoom* advertised as the first Muslim social on Indian screen
Source: *Times of India*, 30 May 1942, 9. Image published with permission of ProQuest LLC.
Further reproduction is prohibited without permission. Image produced by ProQuest LLC as
part of ProQuest® Historical Newspapers. www.proquest.com.

Figure 4.3   Advertisement of *Pehli Nazar*
Source: *Filmindia*, April 1945, 44.

Figure 4.4   Advertisement of *Nek Parvin*
Source: *Filmindia*, October 1945, 6.

Figure 4.5   Actress Sitara in a Turkish *fez* on a cover-page advertisement of *Phool*
Source: *Filmindia*, May 1945.

Figure 4.6 *Ismat* publicised as a lesson for matrimony
Source: *Times of India*, 15 February 1945. Image published with permission of ProQuest LLC. Further reproduction is prohibited without permission. Image produced by ProQuest LLC as part of ProQuest® Historical Newspapers. www.proquest.com.

Figure 4.7 Muslim social films advertised as offering comparability across Indian homes
Source: *Times of India*, 10 March 1945. Image published with permission of ProQuest LLC. Further reproduction is prohibited without permission. Image produced by ProQuest LLC as part of ProQuest® Historical Newspapers. www.proquest.com.

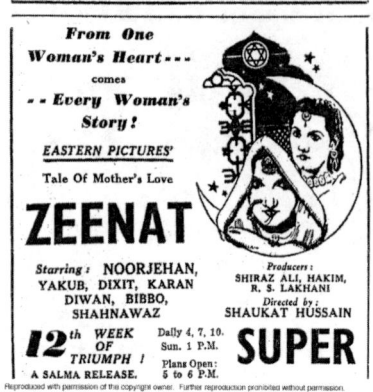

Figure 4.8   *Zeenat* as a tale of motherly love
Source: *Times of India*, 2 February 1946. Image published with permission of ProQuest LLC.
Further reproduction is prohibited without permission. Image produced by ProQuest LLC as
part of ProQuest® Historical Newspapers. www.proquest.com.

In their focus on female protagonists as well as female spectators, these films
had a gendered address. Casting the subject and spectator in a relationship of
transference, it interpellated the viewers within kinship and familial structures.
These selling strategies thus alleviated concerns around the breach of Muslim
female modesty, which the public cinema hall involved. Suggesting viewing
companions or chaperons in the cinema hall (mothers–daughters, girlfriends,
female relatives), the advertisements also presented the films as 'useful cinema' in
terms of its edification value.

> School of matrimony: Lesson 1 for Girls: Ismat! Fazli Bros.' *Ismat* is the one
> word for what every mother ought to tell her daughter on the eve of marriage.[74]
> (Figure 4.6)
> Mothers and Daughters acclaim it as best: Ismat: homely social.[75]
> From one Woman's heart comes Every Woman's story! Tale of Mother's love
> *Zeenat!*[76] (Figure 4.8)
> Modern Girls' Model Films; Fazli Films' *Mehandi* produced and directed by
> Sibtain Fazli, see it with your girlfriends.[77]
> From Friday a golden gift to the mothers of tomorrow, S.F. Hasnain's *Raasta*.[78]

While the Fazli Brothers may have started the trend of Muslim socials, in later
years (after 1943) the publicity for their films did not foreground the identity of the
genre in the same way as had been done before. In the publicity for *Najma*, while
the phrase was used initially, it was subsequently dropped.[79] As the genre became
more distinguishable and familiar, we can assume it would have dispensed with
the need to highlight the 'particularist' label. The film titles themselves often –
though not always – communicated this information. Thus, *Ismat, Najma, Abidah,
Bhai Jaan, Salma, Shama* and *Nek Parvin* left the viewers in little doubt about their

generic identity. While Hasnain's film *Fashion* largely steered clear of making any connections with a community in the publicity, *Ismat* was marketed as relevant to both Hindus and Muslims. In other 'Muslim socials', the reference to faith was kept hazy, allowing for inclusivity.

Glorifying the God-fearing man: *Phool*[80]
Every husband should bring his wife to see: *Fashion*[81]
Ismat: a film that no *modern* man should miss![82]
A moving story of memorable sacrifice: *Shama*[83]

These classifieds, which appeared in the newspaper dailies, also reveal how the industry read the consumption patterns of these films. While undoubtedly there was the exotic appeal for both Muslims and non-Muslims of watching the 'typical middle-class Muslim family' on screen, there were also risks in overemphasising the difference. An enlarged audience base could only translate into profit, and the Fazli Brothers employed a dual publicity design. It meant inclusion of different groups at least at the spectatorial base of the film, even if such an inclusion was not a part of the narrative of the films, which remained limited to an imagined universe of the North Indian Shurafa Muslim.

Engaged in a dialogue, the Muslim social increasingly constituted a contested ground between the publicity mechanism and film journalism. Reviews in the early 1940s found these films exceptional for bringing to the screen 'the intimate life' of Muslims, and their ethnographic potential was taken seriously right from the start.[84] As mentioned earlier, the usefulness of the Muslim social lay in what its makers wanted to convey not only of their community but to their community. Perhaps that is also why this category became a source of concern in later years. By the mid-1940s the Fazli films had a fair sprinkling of the word 'modern' in the classifieds. *Mehandi* was the 'Modern Girls' Model Film' and *Fashion* was an 'Ultra-Modern social'. These were the film-makers' attempts to counter an impression of Muslim stories being 'old-fashioned', 'traditional' and 'orthodox', an image that owed much to the press reviews.

A theme, which *by present standards* must be considered rather orthodox and reactionary ... if you are not a very progressive minded person, 'Bhai Jan' presents the usual sob stuff, this time from Muslim life. Quite a good picture to show to ladies *both old and veiled*.[85]

Over time, the enthusiasm for 'Muslim lives' on screen and 'the new production field' gave way to doubts regarding the necessity of a separate genre since 'there [was] little to choose between the Muslim and Hindu way of life'. Film criticism kept a close watch not just on the content of the film but also on its publicity. The song-plot booklets were a common medium of publicity, available and sold outside the cinema hall. A review article of the film *Kaneez* (Maid, 1949) takes exception to the didactic tone and content of the publicity booklet. It produces the publicity blurb verbatim, which contained phrases like 'national character', 'Muslim social' and 'Justice of God delayed but not waylaid' in an aversive combination. The angry

review in the *Times of India* tackled such claims of the film under the thematic
rubric of 'Justice Mislaid':

> We have in it the almost classical example of prodigality getting away with the
> fatted calf without one repentant pang of grave filial wickedness, not to say
> turpitude of the deepest dye, being rewarded in a manner highly subversive of
> every moral value enshrined in our impeccably virtuous Film Code.[86]

By 1947, an overarching anxiety emerged over the 'slant' of the Muslim socials
and whether these could be misunderstood in the political climate, given that the
genre traversed the distance of political signification from Hindu–Muslim unity
to filial betrayal. The two Muslim socials released immediately around partition,
Elan and *Dard*, were praised for the technical aspects, music and photography of
the films, but screenplays and stories were seen as 'disappointing', of 'poor worth'
and providing the 'wrong slant on Muslim life'.[87] Letters to the editor on *Elan*
and *Dard* questioned the legitimacy of 'communal propaganda in a secular state'.
Did Mehboob not know that in films 'one should not confine oneself to narrow
sectarian views?' wondered one A. P. Shukla.[88] But the most striking exchange was
between two 'Muslim readers' and was published in the pages of *Filmindia* within
six months of partition. V. K. Fazlur Rehman, who was a frequent letter-contributor
to the magazine, wrote about his experience of watching Mehboob's *Elan*, which he
believed was 'a welcome picture from the Muslim point of view'.

> The picture contains dialogues, which at certain places glorify Islam and its
> traditions without meaning any offence to others. But sad to say that two
> Hindu gentlemen sitting in front of me walked out of the theatre when
> they heard the name of 'Quran' being mentioned. May I ask whether the
> Hindus also have started believing in the two-nation theory? I have respect
> for every religion and have loved pictures like 'Tukaram', 'Dhyaneshwar' etc.
> Why not our Hindu brothers stick a bit of Muslim propaganda propagated
> by a Muslim for the betterment of his own community without meaning any
> offence to others?[89]

A response to this letter came from one Atib Usmani, titled as 'No Ram–Rehman':

> When a propaganda bears the label of a particular religion, it necessarily
> becomes isolationist because it ignores all the other religions; and this
> constitutes the offense of omission, which doesn't shed its character on
> account of that fact. The immediate history and the current events have
> demonstrated how disastrous this can be to the security of the individual....
> Have we not already paid for it in the form of India divided into Hindustan
> and Pakistan? [*sic*][90]

The letters converge in identifying *Elan* as propaganda, a fact that merits more
detailed attention at this point.

Muslim Social in Black-and-White

So far this chapter has examined the imprint of the historical context on the production of the Muslim socials of the 1940s, as typified by the Fazli films. With Mehboob's *Elan*, which arguably occupies a liminal position between the Muslim social of pre-independence and that of post-independence India, I propose to demonstrate the process by which a genre is transformed through its historical context. *Elan* reflects the pre-independence genre in its creation of a Sharif space through the thematic deployment of a Muslim modernity epitomised by the Aligarh movement, Nazir Ahmad's didactic literature and the popular appeal of Mohammad Iqbal's verses. The other side of *Elan* is more a function of censorial intervention, perhaps effected by the vigilante paranoia around 'communal propaganda in a secular state', having left its unmistakable traces on the film. *Elan* was among the sixteen films that had earlier been certified by the censor board but re-examined and instructed to 'delete portions' in 1948.[91] These censorial interventions excise the film of its political piquancy, in this case a speech or two, rendering the iconic manifestations in their most amenable form: exotic, hushed and at best ambivalent. The following analysis of *Elan* offers alternative motifs to consider, beyond those of *purdah*, *nawabi* architecture or *nautch* performances, all of which are present in *Elan*.

The opening credit sequence of *Elan* is strikingly distinctive. Instead of superimposed titles, names are arranged on a soil-base (Figure 4.9a), over which the camera pans across downwards in a long take without any cuts or transitions. The territorially embedded film credits are spatially contiguous with the opening shot of the film and not rendered as extra diegetic information: after grazing the soil's surface, the camera manages a bold upward tilt and brings into its purview the minaret of a mosque. *Elan*, like *Najma*, opens with the minaret image against the audio of *azaan* (Figure 4.9b). The opening auditory motif first noticed in Fazli Brothers' *Quaidi*, as well as *Dil*, carries over onto a painted view of a town's skyline dominated by a mosque (Figure 4.9c), thus establishing a Muslim locality and the cultural regime of the film.

The call for prayers continues over a montage of men, seemingly both rich and poor, fast asleep during the early morning hours. A lone man's unsuccessful attempts to awaken his sleeping friend for prayers (Figure 4.9d) is a visual enunciation of the first verse of strophe twelve in 'Jawab-i-Shikwa':

How hard is to you wakening in the morning,
When do you love us yea, Sleepiness is dear to you.[92]

An aerial view of a nearly empty mosque with three men prostrate in prayers follows, but this time the first half of the verse from 'Jawab-i-Shikwa' (in bold here) is recited in a low voice and left incomplete. The lofty and omniscient gaze evokes a divine presence, implicitly that with whom a dialogue is established in 'Shikwa' and 'Jawab-i-Shikwa' (Figure 4.9e).

Masjidain marsiya khawan hain ke namazi na rahe
Yaani woh sahib-e-ausaf-e-hijazi na rahe. (Third verse, strophe 19, 'Jawab-i-Shikwa')

The mosques are lamenting 'Devotees did not remain'
For men with the qualities of the Hijaz did not remain.[93]

The mosque's desolation is matched by the sparse attendance at the local *madrasa* in the next sequence where the students inside the classroom are far outnumbered by truants playing outside (Figures 4.9f and 4.9g). Before introducing its main protagonists, the film thus succinctly establishes its overarching concern: the need for the moral and intellectual regeneration of the *qawm*. The ineffectual and old-fashioned teacher of the *madrasa* comically croaks a couplet to this end. Associating the *maulvi* with the apathetic mores, the film establishes the context for its protagonists who are the conduits of reformation and modernity.

Figure 4.9a   The title sequence of *Elan*
Source: Screenshot from *Elan* (1947), DVD, Eros.

Figure 4.9b   *Elan*'s opening featuring a shot of a minaret against the audio of *azaan*
Source: Screenshot from *Elan* (1947), DVD, Eros.

Figure 4.9c   A town's skyline dominated by a mosque
Source: Screenshot from *Elan* (1947), DVD, Eros.

Figure 4.9d   A man trying to awaken another for morning prayers
Source: Screenshot from *Elan* (1947), DVD, Eros.

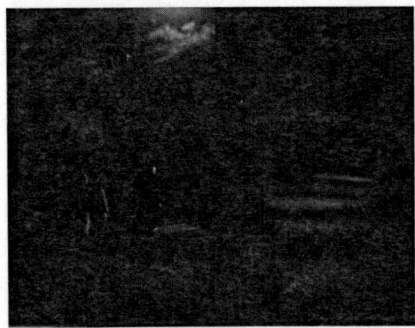

Figure 4.9e Sparse attendance at the mosque
Source: Screenshot from *Elan* (1947), DVD, Eros.

Figure 4.9f Students away from their school
Source: Screenshot from *Elan* (1947), DVD, Eros.

Figure 4.9g Students playing in local alleys
Source: Screenshot from *Elan* (1947), DVD, Eros.

Elan decentres the two-sister motif of the Nazir Ahmad–inspired literature by refashioning them as mothers of the hero and villain respectively. The austere upbringing by the virtuous and widowed elder sister makes her son Javed (Surendra) a conscientious and eminent lawyer, whereas the vile younger sister, married to a *nawab*, spoils her son, Sajjad (Himalayawala), who promises pure debauchery and villainy from a tender age (Figure 4.9h). The birthday celebration during the boys' childhood establishes the individual characters of the male protagonists; the good boy coded as such through his simple clothes and the Khilafat cap, while the bad boy wears a shining *sherwani* and a worthy scowl. But it is not just the Khilafat cap that anticipates the communitarian promise of the good boy. It is also the gift he intended for the spoilt cousin that reveals his aspirations and ideals. It is a brooch carved with the iconic image of Sir Sayyid Ahmad Khan (Figure 4.9i).

While the film may have begun with Iqbal's verses, the officiating deity of *Elan* is undoubtedly Sayyid Ahmad, which I read as a dedication that Mehboob once intended for the founder of the AMU but never made.[94] Javed's first appearance as a young man is that of a quintessential 'Aligarh College boy', who engages in impassioned oratory underneath the founder's portrait (Figure 4.9j). Content-wise Javed's speech is curiously tame, in sharp contrast to the ceremonious introduction before its commencement and the deafening applause at the end. Javed begins with his humble background and warms up to enlist debts to his alma mater when his speech is abruptly concluded. Here a mid-shot of Javed is cut to an extreme long shot of the gathering, introducing the visual expanse and the aural component of a drowning applause. The continuity jump of action in Javed's raised forefinger in the closing shot, unlike the hand position in the previous one, carries the traces of a censorial intervention in a film print certificated in India in 1952. Could Javed's original speech have consisted of more overt 'propaganda' as the two letter writers mentioned in early 1948?

The founding father of AMU resurfaces later, and rather uncharacteristically in the domestic quarters, indicating his paternal presence in fatherless Javed's life. Accidently contravening *purdah*, Javed spots his mother's young and charming instructor, Naaz (Munawar Sultana). Until then their mutual knowledge was confined to discreet letter correspondences, and the lovers see each other for the first time under the benevolent gaze of Sayyid Ahmed. While Naaz hides her face behind a hand fan, a yet-to-outgrow-his-Khilafat-cap Javed is dazzled by what he sees: the scenario exerts a double charge on him (Figure 4.9k). What stands between him and his inimitable favourite image is a new object of affection. Framed alongside Sayyid Ahmed's portrait, the educated yet modest Naaz is effectively associated with Shurafa values and endorsed as Javed's rightful companion (Figure 4.9l). Again, as in *Najma*, the possibility of a beautiful, bettered life is envisioned but suspended, and Naaz is married off to Javed's villainous cousin.

These marriages and the resulting denouements of the Muslim social have been bemoaned, as made plain in the following analysis of *Elan*'s ending. The film ends with the death of the villainous husband. Naaz, now a mother of a talkative toddler, decides to open a school for the neighbourhood children with Javed's support.

> Ironically, just at the moment of Sultana's (Naaz) liberation from an oppressive and violent marriage, when she could have set an example of liberation from feudal norms and the embracing of the ideal of modern companionate marriage, the genre refuses to be so daring on behalf of women. Instead Sultana embraces widowhood, reiterating, almost regressively, the need for a woman to be faithful to her husband however worthless he may be; and instead of seeking personal fulfilment, she finds fulfilment in service to the community.[95]

This reading, not only of the 'modern' but also of 'companionate marriages' and 'widowhood', is typical. First, *Elan* does consider the possibility of Naaz remarrying, as expressed by her father in his endorsement of Javed. Considering the particular regime of verisimilitude of a Muslim social, there is hardly anything daring about widow remarriage; there it is normative. Second, while she may embrace widowhood, what Naaz rejects in the process is the private role consigned to wives. By turning her feudal mansion into a *qawmi* school, she seeks personal fulfilment by assuming a public life as the head teacher of the school.[96] By the end of the film she is recast into a strong maternal figure through visual associations with her son.[97]

It is Naaz's disinterest in the personal or individual that qualifies her to lead a mixed gathering of deferential men and women, where she articulates her desire for the education and betterment of the entire *qawm* (Figure 4.9m). While the *nawabi haveli* turned into school is reminiscent of Asghari's homeschool, I argue that a more recent political memory imbues the last scene of *Elan* featuring the female protagonist's address behind the veil, surrounded by crescent and star flags (Figure 4.9n). It recalls an iconic congregation of 1917 when another prominent mother, Bi Amman, mother of Khilafatist leaders Shaukat Ali and Mohammad Ali, addressed a mixed gathering of the Khilafat Committee while wearing a *burqa*.[98] While the symbol of the crescent and star has had historically varied semantics – from the pan-Islamist Khilafat solidarity to the Muslim League–led separatism – in 1947 it would predominantly be associated with 'propaganda' for Pakistan. The reasons for such an association lie in the inadequacy of the film technology to register colour. 'The Caliphate flag looks identical to the Pakistan flag in black and white,' observes Rachel Dwyer in her analysis of *Phool*.[99] Certainly, the film-makers partook of the ambiguities inherent in filming a crescent and star flag in this era of black-and-white film-making.

Figure 4.9h Virtuous mother–son versus villainous mother–son
Source: Screenshot from *Elan* (1947), DVD, Eros.

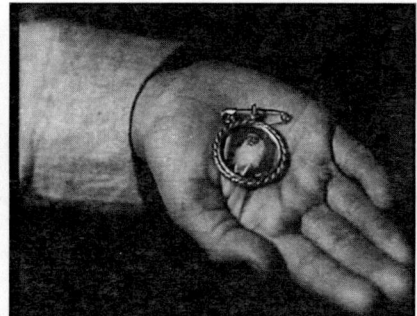

Figure 4.9i Brooch with the image of Syed Ahmed Khan
Source: Screenshot from *Elan* (1947), DVD, Eros.

Figure 4.9j Javed's impassioned oratory underneath Syed Ahmad Khan's portrait
Source: Screenshot from *Elan* (1947), DVD, Eros.

Figure 4.9k Javed dazzled by the sight of Naaz
Source: Screenshot from *Elan* (1947), DVD, Eros.

Figure 4.9l Naaz as the rightful Shurafa companion standing in front of Syed Ahmad Khan's portrait
Source: Screenshot from *Elan* (1947), DVD, Eros.

Figure 4.9m Naaz leading a gathering of deferential men and women
Source: Screenshot from *Elan* (1947), DVD, Eros.

Figure 4.9n Naaz invoking the memory of a key congregation of the Khilafat movement
Source: Screenshot from *Elan* (1947), DVD, Eros.

In the partition decade, therefore, the Muslim social not only imagines an all-Muslim ethnoscape but also privileges a particular form, that of a Shurafa morality and ensuing etiquette, whereby both ends of the community's spectrum, the rich and the poor, the *nawab* (princely landowner) and the *mazdoor* (labourer), can be reconciled and become members of a *qawm*, or national group. The spaces constitutive of the Muslim social genre – mosques, educational institutions and the domestic realm – are those that were appropriated by the reformers of the nineteenth century to create an abstract Muslim self. The conduits of the Shurafa modernity in the Muslim social, as in the Urdu home journals and reformist literature, are the exemplary women who as mothers, wives and daughters, both of struggling poor men and of indulgent rich *nawab*s, protect men from the amoral colonial city and create a national home. The heroes of the Muslim social, undoubtedly secondary to the heroines, are set apart from the villains through modern education often leading to urbane professions of doctors and lawyers (*Nek Parvin, Elan, Dard* and *Najma*). The union of the lead couple is desired not in terms of a universal romantic goal but so that they can become progenitors of a respectable lineage,[100] a possibility usually denied or delayed in the Muslim socials of this period. Poised at the cusp of power and powerlessness, the genre projected the community's strength and vulnerability at this time. After all, both strength and vulnerability were simultaneously important to the project of Muslim nationality, and strategically neither could be forsaken until a political solution was achieved.

The post-partition Muslim social cycle in India is markedly different: the reprimand of an imprudent aristocracy is replaced by a courteous nostalgia extended to the moribund elite. In the splitting of the woman figure between the *begum* and the *tawaif* noticed in the 1960s Muslim social is an evolution of the two-women structure that charts a complicated trajectory. The long-suffering women are not limited to exemplary characters but transform with equal ease into a *nawab*'s muse (lovers) or ignominy (illegitimate daughters) or a courtesan with agency who remains a sympathetic figure. Above all, the 1960s Muslim social revolves around courtship, whereas the 1940s cycle was about marital life, its challenges and the investment in the next generation, constituted by biological children from marriage as well as orphans of the community. After partition, the Muslim social became yet another register of romance, perhaps the romantic genre par excellence for Bombay cinema. That the first Fazli film in Pakistan, *Dopatta*, is not a Muslim social reveals the superfluity of the genre to post-partition Pakistan, as the genre was predicated on the community being a numerical minority.

Piecing together the Fazli archives with journalistic commentary and film publicity, the chapter has traced the emergence of the Muslim social genre parallel to the political demand of a separate nation, the raison d'être of partition. The Muslim social film of the 1940s is a self-critical look at the national group, or *qawm*, through the register of the self-assured and respectable (*sharif*), enumerating the challenges they must overcome for political self-realisation. Offering images of a perfect and beautiful life, the Muslim social became the genre to display the preparedness of the community to be independent and thus imagine the political solution to British India's inimitable minority, which was a majority in many regions. In the continuing ambiguity of the demand for Pakistan, arguably the best way to imagine Muslim independence was through the moral ideal of an abstract Muslim self. The Muslim social cycle of the 1940s then might be better identified as the Muslim political film, while an apposite Muslim social film emerges in the 1960s from the excisions and parings of the production context of an independent and partitioned India.

Notes

1   'Quaid Wanted Mussalmans to Enter Film Industry', *Express Tribune*, 20 January 2013, https://tribune.com.pk/story/496489/quaid-wanted-%E2%80%98mussalmans%E2% 80%99-to-enter-film-industry (accessed on 14 December 2020).

2   R. A. Shaikh, *Filmdom: Who's Who in the Indian Film Industry* (Lahore: Global Linkers, 1946), 78.

3   Steve Neale, *Genre and Hollywood* (London and New York: Routledge, 2000), 10.

4   Rachel Dwyer, *Filming the Gods: Religion and Indian Cinema* (Oxon: Routledge, 2006), 123.

5   Ambedkar furnishes a number of speeches from leaders of the Congress, the Muslim League, the Jamiat-ul-Ulema and the All-India Khilafat Conference to argue that 'Hindus really want Dominion Status, Muslims really want Independence'. For a more detailed exposition of this argument, please see B. R Ambedkar, 'Hindus Really Want Dominion Status, Muslims Really Want Independence', in *Pakistan, or the Partition of India*, 2nd edn. (Bombay: Thackers Publishers, 1945), http://www.columbia.edu/itc/ mealac/pritchett/00ambedkar/ambedkar_partition/412a.html#part_2 (accessed on 2 February 2021).

6   File No. 22/121, 1933, Home Department (Political), National Archives of India, New Delhi (emphasis mine).

7   *Hur-i-Haram* finds no mention in film encyclopaedias and compendiums, which suggests that perhaps it was not released after all or released under a changed name.

8   'Cinema Films', File no. 245, 1937–38, Home Department (Political) Maharashtra State Archives, Mumbai (emphasis mine).

9   Eric Barnouw and S. Krishnaswamy, *Indian Film* (New York: Oxford University Press, 1980), 61.

10   Ravi Vasudevan, 'Film Genres, the Muslim Social and Discourses of Identity, c. 1935–1945', *BioScope: South Asian Screen Studies* 6, no. 1 (2015): 27–43.

11   Sohrab Modi's Minerva Movietone produced *Shama*, and the final credits of the film do not carry Sibtain's name. Sibtain Fazli left at a time when the film was nearly complete, as attested by newspaper publicity and Fazli's own writings.

12   'Public Notice', *Times of India*, 17 September 1946.

13   Asif Nazir Khan, 'A Walk Down Memory Lane with Legendary Filmmaker Nazir Ahmed Khan', *Pakistan Today*, 25 August 2011, http://www.pakistantoday.com.pk/2011/08/25/ entertainment/a-walk-down-memory-lane-with-legendary-filmmaker-nazir-ahmed-khan/ (accessed on 10 January 2015).

14 Classified Advertisement, *Times of India*, 2 January 1941, 2.

15 'Silent and Smiling Hasnain Speaks', *Filmindia*, December 1942, 49 (emphasis mine).

16 Agha Jani Kashmiri, *Saher Hone Tak* (Delhi: Imperial Press, 1965), 162.

17 *Azaan* refers to the intoned call for prayers usually through a loud speaker. The beginning of *Quaidi* is recollected by Sibtain Fazli's elder son, Sohail Fazli. Interview with the author, Lahore, Pakistan, July 2012.

18 Julia Stephens, 'The Politics of Muslim Rage: Secular Law and Religious Sentiment in Late Colonial India', *History Workshop Journal* 77 (2014): 45–64, DOI: 10.1093/hwj/dbt032 (accessed on 25 April 2014).

19 'Masoom', Advertisement, *Filmindia*, March 1942, 13.

20 'The Press Pays Its Supreme Tribute to Masoom', Advertisement, *Filmindia*, February 1942, 30.

21 'Mazhar Khan Hits Out', *Filmindia*, November 1942, 61.

22 'Silent and Smiling Hasnain Speaks', 74 (emphasis mine).

23 Charles R. Acland and Haidee Wasson, 'Introduction: Utility and Cinema', in *Useful Cinema*, ed. Charles R. Acland and Haidee Wasson, 1–14 (Durham, NC: Duke University Press), 2.

24 Ibid.

25 *Khandaan* has been discussed in Chapter 1.

26 Information on the years in which the documentaries were released is not available.

27 'You'll Hardly Believe', *Filmindia*, December 1942, 11.

28 David Lelyveld, *Aligarh's First Generation: Muslim Solidarity in British India* (New Delhi: Oxford University Press, 1996), 103.

29 'Fashion, the Best Social Picture of 1943', *Filmindia*, May 1944, 47.

30 Different sources from this period refer to the regular meetings and get-togethers at Jaddan Bai's Marine Drive flat. Writer Agha Jani Kashmiri mentions it in his memoir, *Saher Hone Tak*, and Shaukat Hussain Rizvi also refers to it in *Noorjahan aur Main*. Kashmiri, *Saher Hone Tak*; Shaukat Hussain Rizvi, *Noorjahan aur Main* (Lahore: Atish Feshan Publications, 1984).

31 'You'll Hardly Believe', *Filmindia*, November 1947, 19.

32 Sibtain Fazli, 'Kal aur Aaj', *Musawar*, 29 May–4 June 1970.

33 S. M. Yusuf's *Saheli* (Friend) was first version made in undivided India in 1943 and then remade by the film-maker himself in Pakistan in 1960.

34 Sohail Fazli, interview, July 2012.

35 Referring to Pakistan's Independence Day.

36 Fazli, 'Kal aur Aaj'.

37 Ibid.

38 'Woes and Echoes', *Filmindia*, May 1949, 61.

39 Ira Bhaskar and Richard Allen, *Islamicate Cultures of Bombay Cinema* (New Delhi: Tulika Books, 2009), 69.

40 For an elaboration of the idea of apologetic modernity or the Muslim apologetics that emerged from the reformatory impulse of Sir Sayyid Ahmed Khan, see Faisal Devji, 'Apologetic Modernity', *Modern Intellectual History* 4, no. 1 (2007): 61–76, DOI: 10.1017/S1479244306001041 (accessed on 23 April 2014).

41 Ravi Vasudevan, 'The Melodramatic Mode and the Commercial Hindi Cinema', *Screen* 30, no. 3 (1989): 29–50.

42   Frances W. Pritchard, 'The First Urdu Bestseller', afterword to Nazir Ahmed, *The Bride's Mirror: A Tale of Life in Delhi a Hundred Years Ago*, trans. G. E. Ward, 204–223 (New Delhi: Permanent Black, 2001).

43   C. M. Naim, 'Five Prize Winning "Adab"', in *Moral Conduct and Authority: The Place of Adab in South Asian Islam*, ed. Barbara D. Metcalf, 290–314 (Berkeley: University of California Press, 1984).

44   Khairi's family migrated to Pakistan in 1947 and continued publishing *Ismat*, which recently completed 105 years. Peerzada Salman, 'Ismat Celebrates 105 Years', *Dawn*, 14 December 2013, http://www.dawn.com/news/1073704/ismats-105-years-celebrated (accessed on 12 February 2014).

45   Recalled by writer Intizar Hussain in Salman, 'Ismat Celebrates 105 Years'.

46   Faisal Devji, 'Gender and the Politics of Space', in *Forging Identities: Gender, Communities and the State*, ed. Zoya Hassan, 22–37 (New Delhi: Kali for Women, 1994), 24.

47   Ibid., 30.

48   Francis Robinson, *Islam and Muslim History in South Asia* (Oxford: Oxford University Press, 2003), 158.

49   Neale, *Genre and Hollywood*, 31–33.

50   Pritchard, afterword to Ahmed, *The Bride's Mirror*, 209.

51   'Masoom Portrays Muslim Life Excellently', *Filmindia*, July 1942, 55.

52   'On the Indian Screen', *Times of India*, 7 August 1943, 6.

53   'Fashion: The Best Social Picture of 1943', *Filmindia*, May 1944, 47.

54   'Mehndi Gives a Bad Headache', *Filmindia*, March 1948, 47.

55   Barbara D. Metcalf, 'Islamic Reform and Islamic Women: Maulana Thanawi's *Jewelry of Paradise*', in *Moral Conduct and Authority*, 184–195, 194.

56   'Teri zaat paak hai aye khuda teri shaan jallejala lahoo' (Your being is pure God, your authority the highest).

57   Barbara D. Metcalf, 'Introduction', in *Moral Conduct and Authority*, 1–21, 19.

58   Naveeda Khan, *Muslim Becoming* (Durham, NC: Duke University Press, 2012), 59.

59   Ernst Bannerth, 'Islam in Modern Urdu Poetry: A Translation of Muhammad Iqbal's "Shikwa wa Jawab-i-Shikwa" (The Complaint and the Reply to It)', in *Iqbal: New Dimensions*, ed. Iqram Chaghtai, 189–204 (Lahore: Sang-i-Mil, 2003), 191.

60   Ibid., 193.

61   Ibid., 201.

62   Faisal Devji, *Muslim Zion: Pakistan as a Political Idea* (Cambridge, MA: Harvard University Press, 2013), 110.

63   Neale, *Genre and Hollywood*, 18.

64   Barbara Klinger, *Melodrama and Meaning* (Bloomington: Indiana University Press, 1994), xii.

65   Bhaskar and Allen, *Islamicate Cultures of the Bombay Cinema*, 65.

66   'Sohrab Modi's Muslim Society Drama', *Times of India*, 28 May 1937, 5.

67   Classified Advertisement, *Times of India*, 3 June 1942, 3.

68   Advertisement, *Filmindia*, February 1943, 37.

69   Classified Advertisement, *Times of India*, 12 September 1945, 3.

70   Classified Advertisement, *Times of India*, 17 February 1948, 3.

71   Classified Advertisement, *Times of India*, 2 May 1942, 4.
72   Classified Advertisement, *Times of India*, 30 May 1942, 9.
73   Classified Advertisement, *Times of India*, 29 January 1944, 6.
74   Classified Advertisement, *Times of India*, 15 February 1945, 5.
75   Classified Advertisement, *Times of India*, 30 June 1945,8.
76   Classified Advertisement, *Times of India*, 2 February 1946, 9.
77   Classified Advertisement, *Times of India*, 27 December 1947, 15.
78   Classified Advertisement, *Times of India*, 4 November 1947, 3.
79   Bhaskar and Allen, *Islamicate Cultures of the Bombay Cinema*, 70.
80   Classified Advertisement, *Times of India*, 5 June 1945, 2.
81   Classified Advertisement, *Times of India*, 19 April 1944, 3.
82   Classified Advertisement, *Times of India*, 9 February 1943, 2.
83   Classified Advertisement, *Times of India*, 31 August 1946, 11.
84   'Masoom Portrays Muslim Life Excellently', *Filmindia*, July 1942, 55.
85   'Bhai Jan Exploits an Orthodox Theme', *Filmindia*, November 1945, 69 (emphasis mine).
86   'Review: Caravan Pictures' "Kaneez"', *Times of India*, 3 September 1949, 10.
87   'Mehboob's Elan Disappoints', *Times of India*, 28 February 1948, 11.
88   'Sleeping Censors', *Filmindia*, January 1949, 68.
89   'Woes and Echoes', *Filmindia*, January 1948, 69.
90   'Woes and Echoes', *Filmindia*, March 1948, 65.
91   'Appendix IX', *Report of the Film Enquiry Committee* (New Delhi: Ministry of Information of Information and Broadcasting, Government of India Press, 1951), 307.
92   Bannerth, *Iqbal: New Dimensions*, 198.
93   Ibid., 200.
94   'The National Studios intend to produce a short film depicting the biography of Sir Syed Ahmad, the illustrious founder of Aligarh Muslim University. Mehboob is in charge of direction.' *The Tribune*, 9 April 1942.
95   Bhaskar and Allen, *Islamicate Cultures of the Bombay Cinema*, 74.
96   Naaz even says it as much: 'Ab main apna ghar kissi aur tarah se basaoongi' (Now I shall set up my home in a different manner).
97   The maternal motif is available in an earlier Mehboob film *Aurat* (Woman, 1940) and later intensified in the mother of all films – *Mother India* (1957).
98   Gail Minault, *The Extended Family as Metaphor and the Expansion of Women's Realm* (Delhi: Chanakya Publications, 1981), 8.
99   Dwyer notes that the scenes featuring students in *sherwanis*, marching with the Caliphate flag, were asked to be deleted by the censors. See Dwyer, *Filming the Gods*, 124.
100   Also the thematic concern of Ahmed's *The Bride's Mirror*.

5 The Partition Romance

Meena and the Shorey Comedies

The Hindi screwball comedy was a short-lived and forgotten genre of the Bombay film enterprise in the late 1940s and the early 1950s. With debts not only to Hollywood but also to the pre-partition Lahore studios, these films comprised the post-partition oeuvre of a refugee film-maker, Roop Shorey, and were iconically linked with the lead actress, Meena. Privileging an unconventional female star with a flair for slapstick humour, the Shorey comedies emerge as a striking cultural negotiation of a historical experience, which was grim and gendered. Here the professional and conjugal relationship of a Muslim Meena and a Hindu Roop was remarkable for its disruption of communal boundaries during the partition decade when both communities were cast in positions of acute antagonism. While the Meena–Roop team was central to the Shorey comedies, these were also underwritten by a larger collaboration of film refugees driven out of Lahore into Bombay. Partition is critical to their collaborative work, not as a cataclysmic force that accidently brought them together, for their collaboration long preceded the partition induced migration, but for the evacuee experience that infused their collective film-making work.

Two aspects of partition come to fore in recovering the stardom and career of Meena Shorey. First, the concentrated and extended violence against women, recast as keepers of national honour and markers of boundaries, accentuated partition as a gendered experience. Ritu Menon and Kamala Bhasin's work draws attention to 'the figure of the abducted woman (who) became symbolic of crossing borders, and of

A shorter version of this chapter was originally published in *BioScope: South Asian Screen Studies* 6, no. 1. Copyright 2015 © Screen South Asia Trust. All rights reserved. Reproduced with the permission of the copyright holders and the publishers, SAGE Publications India Pvt Ltd, New Delhi.

violating social, cultural and political boundaries'.[1] This piteous partition figure is the historical underside of Meena who actively changed religious identities and national locations. The second aspect is detailed by Vazira Zamindar as 'the bureaucratic violence of drawing political boundaries and nationalising identities',[2] which impinged on the mobility and fluidity characteristic of the colonial empire. Born as colonial Indians who moved across the film centres of Bombay, Calcutta and Lahore, Roop and Meena died as circumscribed citizens of India and Pakistan, respectively. As against the stark identity logics of partition, a productive cosmopolitanism emerges in the Shorey comedies of post-partition Bombay. In Peter van der Veer's account, seen through the lens of colonial modernity, cosmopolitanism is defined as a 'form of improvisation, involving openness and mobility'.[3] Away from this intellectual and imperial cosmopolitanism, Mica Nava proposes a visceral one, based on the 'feelings of attraction for and identification with otherness'.[4] Exploring race relations and anti-Semitism in the twentieth century, Nava finds that conviviality and empathy have always coexisted with the most hostile manifestations of racialisation and identity formation, and mixed sexual–romantic relationships provide instances of a visceral cosmopolitanism that has allowed greater permeability of ethnic and social borders. Meena's star personality fashioned through the Shorey comedies displays both these modalities, enmeshing the intellectual with the emotional and producing a novel cosmopolitanism that could instinctively play with identities without being bounded by them. The film alliance between an itinerant actress and a refugee studio owner, who went their nationally separate ways to Lahore and Bombay after a decade-long collaboration, was also an adroit negotiation of what Neepa Majumdar has identified as 'the replacement of the studio system by the star system in the 1940s'.[5] Through a variety of archival sources on the Meena–Roop collaboration such as memoirs, film magazine reports, cartoons and the extant comedies themselves, I bring to fore a striking instance of historical trauma negotiated by humour.

An Actress Remembers

Meri kahaani sun kar koi shareef ladki film mein nahin aayegi, shareef toh kya buri bhi nahin aayegi.[6]

After hearing my life story, no respectable girl will join films. Let alone respectable, even the bad ones won't.

The life story that actress Meena Shorey considers a valuable lesson for aspiring actresses was one wrought by partition and its legacies. It was in 1986 that her abridged memoir appeared in a collection of life narratives published in Urdu by Atish Feshan, entitled *Out of Date*,[7] and it provides a fascinating account of the actress's life and career in India and later in Pakistan. Like most life writings, it raises the issues of authenticity, individual agency and identity. Autobiographical acts are 'anything but transparent' and are almost always 'symbolic interactions with the world'.[8] Yet, as Amelie Hastie argues, these constitute counter-histories motivated to set the record straight and correct institutionalised histories of their subjects who also happen to be the author-historian.[9] Particular to memoirs of film actresses where the narrative establishes a causal link between their real lives and their work on screen, Hastie proposes reading them in cinematic terms. Meena's memoir too takes on tropes prominent in her films – of candour, romantic muddles and risks. It points to the way her life was, as Hastie discerns of actress memoirs, 'literally influenced by work in fictional production and to the factuality of film production itself'.[10]

Meena's memoir proceeds chronologically, recounting a childhood of hardship combined with the instability of her parents' marriage. Born as Khurshid Jahan in the early 1920s in Raiwind, a village near Lahore, she was one of five children. Early in her memoir, she censures her father and elder brother,[11] and these accusations form a continuum with later troubled relationships with many men both professionally and personally. At the heart of this tension is the dichotomy inherent in 'the atypical figure' of an actress, as identified by Viv Gardner in her study of autobiographies of stage actresses, usurping the male right to a public persona without losing her subordinate and domestic role as a woman.[12] Emphasising the lack of formal education and options available to young women in her situation at that time, Khurshid deemed films a possible release from her family home, which signals her drive from childhood to be an actress.

> *Gyarhvein baras mein thi ke ghar walon ke saath film 'Achhut Kanya' dekhne ke ittefaq hua. Devika Rani ismein heroine aur Ashok Kumar hero thay. Iske baad Roop K. Shorey ki 'Dulla Bhatti' dekhi toh Ragini ka khoobsurat raag ka sa sarapa dekh kar mere napuqhta zehan mein bhi purdah screen par shokhiyan dikhane ki kasak paida hui. Yeh kaise hoga kuch samajh mein nahin aata tha.*[13]

At the age of eleven, I happened to watch the film *Acchut Kanya* [Untouchable Girl, 1936] with my family, Devika Rani was the heroine and Ashok Kumar the hero. After this, Ragini's exquisitely melodic personality in Roop K. Shorey's *Dulla Bhatti* [1940] created in my naïve mind a desire to dazzle on screen. How this was to transpire, was beyond my comprehension.

Made in Lahore, Roop Shorey's *Dulla Bhatti* may have inspired a young Khurshid, but she began her acting career in Bombay. Following her parent's estrangement, she had accompanied her mother to the city. There her brother-in-law took her to *Sikandar's mahurat* ceremony sometime in 1940 where film-maker Sohrab Modi spotted her. Describing her entry into Minerva studio in dramatic detail, Khurshid found herself the cynosure of all eyes. Hastie notes that a star's fascination with herself as a visual image reveals investment in her own stardom and her place in history (Figure 5.1).

> *Mehmanon ne galti se mujhe Sikandar ki heroine samajh liya tha agarche aisa galat fehmi ka nateeja tha lekin main khushi se phooli nahin sama rahi thi aur mujhe apni shakhsiyat ki fasoonsaazi par naaz hua.*[14]

The guests mistook me for *Sikandar*'s heroine. Even though it was the result of a misunderstanding, yet I was thrilled and proud of my charismatic personality.

Writing of film *mahurat*s, Tejaswini Ganti sees the auspicious commencement ceremony as a space of sociality, celebration and conviviality.[15] It is not difficult to imagine the excitement of such a gathering. A keen Sohrab reportedly lost no time in signing her for a studio contract at a monthly remuneration of 600 rupees as 'he was looking for someone to fill actress Naseem's shoes'. He also gave Khurshid her *nom-de-plume*, after chancing on the letter 'm' in the *Avesta*. An ambiguous and versatile 'Meena' replaced Khurshid, a name perhaps too quotidian, also one already taken by another actress at Ranjit Studios and of course strongly suggesting a Muslim background.[16] If Hindu majoritarian pressures have been understood as influencing name changes during this period,[17] then a Parsi studio proprietor consulting the Zoroastrian religious book to launch a Muslim actress reveals a complex matrix of multiple identities at play on and off the Indian screen. While name changes were a gesture aimed at the cinema public, the original identities resurfaced, especially once actors and actresses became relatively popular and subjects of fan curiosity. In her memoir, Meena does not discuss why a need was felt to change her name, and the ebullience of joining films makes name changing a mere procedural detail of being primed for an acting career.

Figure 5.1   Meena Shorey in her quintessential screen attire
Source: *Filmfare*, 16 May 1952. Image published with the permission of National Film Archives of India, Pune.

With *Sikandar* (Alexander the Great, 1941), Meena began an actress's career in films, playing the patriotic princess Sadhna who rebels against her brother and joins Indian king Porus to resist Alexander's offensive. Reading *Sikandar* as an analogy for India's struggle for independence, Priya Jaikumar refers to Meena's character as one whose 'obedience to an abstract higher authority disrupts her assimilation within an existing familial structure, while consolidating her allegiance to a future, utopian state'.[18] This 'admission of conflicting interests' within the space of the colonial historical romance, as Jaikumar notes, permitted female characters to make choices not solely determined by their domestic loyalties, which would change in post-independence films with the more effective realignment of the nation state and family. Enacting the transgressions made possible by the 'crisis of loyalties' in historical romances (*Sikandar* and *Prithvi Vallabh*, 1943), Meena's beginnings foreshadow her later persona and performances. A rebellious tone also marks the recollection of her start in films. Meena's family, especially her estranged father, did not approve of the decision. However, her regular film salary, by no means modest, quietened any further objections from a financially hard-up family. Though omitted from her memoir, Meena married her co-actor of *Sikandar*, Zahoor Raja, around this time. Appearing briefly in a publicity piece centred on Zahoor, Meena was reported to have been working on her last picture, *Phir Milenge* (We'll Meet Again, 1942), since her actor husband did not approve of married women working as actresses.[19] On hindsight, it certainly seems improbable that Meena would have stopped acting after her second film, but the views resistant to married women playing romantic leads in films were fairly commonplace.[20]

As a regular employee of the studio, Meena acted in several Minerva films during the early 1940s like *Phir Milenge*, *Prithvi Vallabh* (1943) and *Pattharon ka Saudagar* (The Stone Trader, 1944). In *Prithvi Vallabh*, she played the royal maiden Vilasvati betrothed to the crown prince but in love with Prithvi Vallabh's court poet. Something similar played out off-screen when she married her co-star in the film, Al-Nasir, after parting with Zahoor. It was around the making of *Pattharon ka Saudagar* that Meena made a decisive shift. Finding her options limited by a stifling studio contract with Minerva, she left Bombay for Lahore. While her memoir does not mention a precise date, it must have been around late 1944 or early 1945. This was preceded by a court case she filed against Sohrab Modi, entering into prolonged and bitter negotiations with the studio owner, who allegedly exploited her lack of education and did not make the terms of the contract explicit. Recalling a vulnerable phase, Meena claims to have lost out on films like Mehboob Khan's *Humayun* (1945) and K. B. Lal's *Laal Haveli* (Red Mansion, 1944). She decided to accompany her actor-husband, Al-Nasir, to Lahore, where he had been cast in Roop Shorey's *Shalimar* (1946). There Meena signed a contract with Pancholi Art Pictures at 7,000 rupees a month for *Shehar se Dur* (Far from the City, 1947).

It was Dalsukh Pancholi who helped Meena out of the Minerva studio tangle but not before Sohrab had slapped damages on Pancholi for recruiting her in Lahore. Meena went back to Bombay once more to finally settle the matter. Meanwhile, other projects in Lahore had materialised, and she returned to the city in no time. In pre-partition Lahore, Meena appeared in *Shehar se Dur*, and started work in *Arsi* (1947), *Patjhad* (Autumn, 1948) and *Rut Rangili* (A Colourful Season), which underwent several stops and starts during the process of partition.[21]

While Pancholi's *Patjhad* and Shorey's *Rut Rangili* were underway, the partition plan was announced. Meena had by then divorced a reportedly swinging Al-Nasir and, in her memoir, describes herself as heartbroken by his indiscretions while selectively omitting her own other two short-lived marriages, one to actor Zahoor Raja and another to her co-actor in *Shehar se Dur*, Raza Mir.[22] In mid-1947, when Meena left Lahore and moved to Bombay, it is most likely that she also parted ways with Mir. As a Muslim hailing from West Punjab, it is certainly striking that Meena did not choose to stay in Lahore, though the reasons are not hard to discern. The abandonment of the studios in the city did not leave artistes with much hope. Having seen her film associates Shorey and Pancholi leave Lahore, Bombay must have appeared to be a sound professional choice. Meena's decision also reveals that she did not unequivocally share the allegiances of her community; that these did not sit quite comfortably with her is evident from her later life in Pakistan.

On reaching Bombay with her younger siblings, she signed *Actress* (1948), *Dukhyari* (Unfortunate Woman, 1948) and *Kale Badal* (Dark Clouds, 1951). In Filmistan Studio's *Actress*, she played a stage actress, Ragini, who wishes to protect her sister from the pitfalls of a performer's life. When the two sisters fall in love with the same man, Ragini bows out of the love triangle by first feigning death and then laughing off such tragic dénouements. Around this time Meena heard about Roop's tremendous loss from their common friend Majnu who too had migrated to Bombay. Forced out of a volatile Punjab, Shorey had been living in a hotel in Bombay and was reportedly looking for collaborators to produce a film. A striking claim of initiative and agency emerges in Meena's narrative here. She claims to have paid Shorey's hotel bill of six months, brought him to her flat and offered astute advice.

> *Shorey sahab ko maine Punjabi film banane ka mashawra diya ke sasti bann jaegi. Main heroine hongi, koi sasta sa hero le lete hain. Unhein meri tajveez pasand aayi.*[23]

> I advised Shorey *sahab* to make a Punjabi film as it was economical. I would be the heroine and we could cast a low-priced hero. He liked my counsel.

The ensuing Punjabi film *Chaman* (1948) was film evacuees Roop and Meena's first collaboration in independent India. Even though the hero of the film was the title role of Chaman, in her memoir Meena insists on staking a more prominent space for herself, not merely as an actress but also one involved in controlling production decisions. This 'low-priced hero' was Karan Dewan and the producer was his brother, Jaimini Dewan, who a little later made the partition film *Lahore* (1949). Also set in Lahore, *Chaman* pivoted around electoral rivalries and turned out to be a profitable venture. Meena played the Punjabi girl Shanti who is out to avenge her father's humiliating defeat in local elections but ends up falling in love with the electoral rival. Encouraged by *Chaman*'s success, Meena and Roop made their most popular *Ek Thi Ladki* (There Was Once a Girl, 1949) followed by *Dholak* (Drumbeats, 1951), *Ek Do Teen* (One-Two-Three, 1953), *Aag ka Dariya* (River of Fire, 1953) and *Jalwa* (Lustre, 1955). These were all Shorey Art productions and were often referred to in the reviews as 'noisy stunt comedies', 'fast entertainers' and 'slapstick'. *Aag ka Dariya* was the only exception to the 'gay romance and rollicking comedy that filmgoers [had] come to expect in Roop Shorey's pictures'.[24] Apart from acting in husband Roop Shorey's productions, Meena also appeared in similar roles in *Shri Naqad Narayan* (Money Is God, 1955), *Shrimati 420* (Trickster Wife, 1956) and *Awara Shahzadi* (Vagabond Princess, 1956), as well as being the associate producer of films like *Ek Do Teen* and *Mukhda* (Face, 1951).

When *Ek Thi Ladki* released, Meena and Roop went to Calcutta for its publicity. After an evening at the nightclub, followed by a stroll in a park, an already married Roop proposed to Meena. This idyllic backdrop recalls the out-of-town trip undertaken by the boss and secretary in *Ek Thi Ladki*. However, in her memoir Meena pointedly denies harbouring any romantic affection for Shorey and peddles the marriage as her *qurbaani* (sacrifice) for a besotted and much-respected collaborator. Never inclined towards self-effacement, Meena the star claims to have told Shorey as much, professing herself to be 'emotional yet candid'. Retrospectively, and self-evidently motivated to soften her later decision to part with Roop, the account also carries traces of a screwball courtship devoid of sentimentality. However, in 1949, Roop and Meena decided to go ahead with the marriage in Calcutta itself, as Bombay laws against bigamy were stringent. While Roop suggested either a civil marriage or an Islamic ceremony, Meena surprised him by arranging an Arya Samaji ritual in a local temple. Ironically asking what good came from her 'Muslim family', one that remained ever-dependent on her while offering little in return, Meena characterises her decision as *poori qurbaani* (complete sacrifice). Underneath this sombre characterisation lurk her droll histrionics as the wedding ceremony, when recalled again in the narrative, appears in a much lighter vein.

After the marriage, Meena took on a new name yet again and became Kiran Shorey in her off-screen public life.[25] In the actress's narrative, her association with Roop came to be marked by what the man had lost during partition and her attempts to revive their careers in Bombay. Her claims resonate with the tongue-in-cheek gossip published in *Filmindia* in early 1950, which however may also hold a further clue to Meena's 'sacrifice'.

> Meena, the Pakistan-born Muslim actress, is reported to be doing better refugee-relief work than the Government of India. They say that she earns a lot of money doing hard work and with it helps a refugee producer to produce pictures and to relax when he is tired.[26]

While 'Pakistan-born' may have the markings of *Filmindia*'s deliberate anachronisms, it also signals the 'domicile' and 'birth' criteria of Indian citizenship introduced in late 1949. Vazira Zamindar's work reveals that by making 'domicile' a condition of citizenship, the Indian citizenship of women was subject to the location of their fathers and husbands.[27] With Meena's father and last husband now in Pakistan, her continued livelihood in Bombay was contingent on an Indian citizenship. Thus, her marriage to Roop would have also offered a way out of the problems generated by partition for a 'Pakistan-born' Meena wishing to work in Indian Bombay.

The actress locates a turning point in her career and national location with the 1954 '*Jaal* agitation' in Pakistan against the import of Indian film.[28] Until then Meena had arranged for a portion of the profits from her films exhibited in Pakistan to be sent to her family living in Lahore. Devised to overcome hurdles involved in monetary transactions between the two countries where artistes found it difficult to claim their dues and royalty, the ban on Indian films made the continuation of this arrangement difficult.[29] When J. C. Anand, the Karachi-based distributor of Shorey films in Pakistan, invited Roop and Meena to make a film, it offered a way out of the embargo dilemma and could solve her family's financial troubles. In 1956, Meena and Roop went together to Pakistan to make *Miss 56* (1956). Aligning a personal trajectory with a national industrial action led by the producers of 'Pakistani films', Meena signals in her narrative a reorientation of a national identity from that of an Indian to that of a Pakistani. She signed another film in Lahore, *Sarfarosh* (Defiant, 1956), which was released before *Miss 56*. Meena summed up her travels in 1956 when she was most sought after:

> *Lahore ke mehange tareen hotel Faletti mein teen char kamre le leti. 'Miss 56' ke muqmeel ke dauraan Karachi, Lahore aur Bambai teenon shehron mein mera aana jaana rehta.*[30]

> [In those days] I used to book three–four rooms in Lahore's most expensive Faletti's hotel.... During the making of *Miss 56*, I constantly moved back and forth between Lahore, Karachi and Bombay.

But 1956 was not 1946, a time only a decade ago when Meena had casually shuttled between different cities, settling legal matters with Minerva in Bombay and completing shoots at Pancholi and Shorey studios in Lahore. Bombay and

Lahore now lay in two different and mutually suspicious nations. During this trip, Meena decided to stay on in Pakistan. The reception Meena and her initial films got in Pakistan was a crucial reason for her to permanently leave India because lately her comedies there had not been performing well.[31] Alongside the fawning attentions of Pakistani producers, Meena provoked industrial competition as well and met with hostility reserved for itinerant Indian artistes working in Pakistan.

> *Shehariyat na milne tak toh yahan kayi logon ko ummeed thi ki main bharat wapas chali jaoongi.*[32]
>
> Till the time I got a [Pakistani] citizenship, most people here [the film industry of Lahore] hoped that I would return to India.

It was through the good offices of prime minister H. S. Suhrawardy, who in the same grateful breath Meena mischievously characterises as 'horny' (*tharki*), that she got her Pakistani citizenship by the end of 1957. Briefly, Roop too considered staying on in Lahore, which he had been forced to leave nearly a decade earlier. But faced with death threats in Pakistan and father Roshan Lal Shorey's summons from India, Roop returned to Bombay.[33] The threats had started when Roop announced his return and tried claiming his studio back. But the refugee film-maker's struggle for property compensation had started in Bombay, where Roop had petitioned against producer A. R. Kardar and made a bid for the Kardar studio, alleging him to be an 'intending evacuee'.[34] The Indian court rejected his petition in 1955, a year before Meena migrated to Pakistan.

When Meena decided to stay on in Pakistan, she reconverted to Islam and was renamed Khurshid Jahan. Her decision to work in the Pakistani film industry appeared alongside news of her separation from Shorey.[35] That Meena's religious and social transgressions could only be absolved by enacting a 'recovery' similar to what the paternalistic states of India and Pakistan had done in the case of abducted women required that her marriage with Roop be portrayed as short of consent. Thus, a Pakistani film magazine in 1956 reported it as a decision that did not sit comfortably with Meena and it was claimed that the actress had decided to terminate her relationship with Roop the day her mother passed away. While this is not corroborated by Meena's later memoir,[36] she does express her unease at remaining in India as a 'Hindu forever'. However, she is unequivocal about Roop's liberal cosmopolitanism and their overall indifference to their respective faiths. This insistence was not trifling as the readers the memoir addressed were Pakistanis living through General Zia ul-Haq's Islamisation years.

> *Shorey sahab bhi koi kattar qism ke Hindu na thay. Unn ke paas tamam mazahab ki muqqadas kitabein maujood thi. Humarey yahan Eidein, Shabbebarat, Holi aur Diwali sabhi tayohar manaye jaatey. Humara khansama*

Musalman tha, driver Sikh, baera Hindu aur aaya Isaayi thi. Beharhal na voh
kabhi mandir gaye, na maine kabhi masjid ka rukh kiya.[37]

Shorey *sahab* was hardly an orthodox Hindu. He kept the revered books of
all faiths. In our house we would celebrate all festivals like Eid, Shabbarat,
Holi and Diwali. We had a Muslim cook, a Sikh driver, a Hindu bearer
and a Christian nanny. However, neither did he ever visit a temple, nor I,
a mosque.

The dilly-dallying between the many film cities of the subcontinent, which had
continued for Meena even after 1947, materialises a response to an important
partition question: 'Do women have a country'?[38] By 1956, this movement was
no longer sustainable; belonging could no longer be adjourned nor escaped. The
so-called choice that Meena had could only be an exercise in exclusion – either India
or Pakistan, either Hindu or Muslim, thereby marking the claims of one nation and
community over another.

Highly Unfortunate but Highly Talented

Other than the Roop–Meena alliance, the Shorey brand of comedies in post-
partition Bombay was characterised by the collaboration of film evacuees
including both old Shorey collaborators as well as other film migrants from
Lahore. In different permutations across a body of films (Table 5.1), this
consortium of refugees provided continuity of personnel across the spatial and
political break caused by partition. Majnu, perhaps Roop's oldest collaborator
from his palmy Lahore days, played the comic sidekick, often with shades of grey
in the Bombay Shorey films. Writer-lyricist Aziz Kashmiri's collaboration with
Shorey had begun in the early 1940s with *Koyal* (Nightingale, 1944) and *Himmat*
(Courage, 1941). Vinod too had composed music for the Shorey productions in
pre-partition Lahore. The Shorey team also had other recent Lahore migrants like
Karan Dewan, Omprakash and Kuldeep Kaur. Kaur, who appeared in Shorey's
Chaman, *Ek Thi Ladki* and *Mukhda*, was charged with spying for Pakistan a few
years after independence.[39] I. S. Johar as, in two instances, the story-dialogue
writer and director of these comedies was an important collaborator. Starting
his career as a dramatist, Johar's satirical writing had a distinctive political edge
and his column 'Mumbo-Jumbo' was a regular in the *Sunday Tribune* of pre-
partition Lahore. In 1943, he had spent twenty days in jail during the individual
Satyagraha and, according to a magazine report, came out a disillusioned man.
One of his earliest essays, which lampooned the Congress, was published into
pamphlets and sold at the Muslim League sessions in Punjab.[40] After *Shalimar*,
Khamosh Nigahein (Silent Eyes, unreleased) and *Rut Rangili* in Lahore, *Ek Thi
Ladki* in Bombay was Johar's fourth film with the Shoreys (Figure 5.2).

Table 5.1 The Bombay collaboration of film refugees from Lahore

	Roop Shorey	Meena	I. S. Johar	Majnu	Motilal	Karan Dewan	Kuldeep Kaur	Aziz Kashmiri	Vinod	Omprakash
Aag ka Dariya	Director/Producer	Female lead				Male lead		Lyrics	Music	
Chaman	Director	Female lead				Male lead	Secondary character	Lyrics/Dialogue	Music	Secondary character
Dholak	Director/Producer	Female lead	Writer	Secondary character				Lyrics		
Ek Do Teen	Director/Producer	Female lead/Assistant producer			Male lead			Lyrics	Music	
Ek Thi Ladki	Director	Female lead	Writer/Secondary character	Secondary character	Male lead		Secondary character	Lyrics	Music	
Jalwa	Director/Producer	Female lead		Secondary character		Male lead		Lyrics	Music	
Miss56 (Pakistan)	Director	Female lead	Writer							
Mukhda	Director/Producer	Assistant producer	Writer	Secondary character			Female lead	Lyrics	Music	
Shrimatiji			Director/Writer	Secondary character						
Shrimati 420		Female lead								Secondary character
Shri Naqad Narayan		Female lead	Director/Writer	Secondary character	Male lead			Lyricist	Music	Secondary character

Source: Compiled by the author.

Figure 5.2   I. S. Johar and Meena Shorey in a publicity still
Source: *Filmfare*, 4 March 1955. Image published with the permission of National Film Archives of India, Pune.

Given that screwball comedy was a genre rare for Hindi cinema, what can explain the particular preference of a refugee team in post-partition India? There are several reasons. First, Roop Shorey showed a predilection for comedy from the start of his career. Second, his collaborators, Meena, Majnu and I. S. Johar, thrived in the genre, which in turn recalls pre-partition Lahore's ironic mode. The huge success of *Ek Thi Ladki* undoubtedly would have assured its makers that their film-making future in partitioned India lay in these comedies. However, here it is worth mentioning the road not taken in a letter published in *The Tribune* in late 1947, where film refugees from Lahore had expressed the desire to be rehabilitated as Information Film producers in India. Drawing attention to the 'Plight of Film Industry Refugees', the letter was of the opinion that the only hope for the film refugees was the revival of the Information Films of India.

Please permit me to draw the attention of the central and east Punjab Governments to the miserable plight of those poor and unfortunate workers of the Punjab film industry, who have been driven out of Lahore, which was the only centre of the industry in the Punjab.... Under the present circumstances the chances for the revival of film industry in the East Punjab are very few and the future of workers is dark.... The problem now is where to re-provide the field of these workers? There is no hope of their getting employed in the big centres of film production for the studios there are already lying idle. Therefore the only hope of relief and rescue for these workers lies in the early and immediate revival, expansion and reorganization of the Information Films of India Department, and the reservation of posts for these *highly unfortunate but highly talented* and intellectual refugees.[41]

A follow up column to this letter was written by I. S. Johar as the president of East Punjab Motion Picture Workers Union. Here he persuasively argued for utilising documentary as propaganda and the need for provincial governments in India to have a dedicated information films organisation. Among the various categories of information film outlined by Johar was the 'sugar pill documentary'.

It is a documentary with plot wherein information is imparted in story form. This type is useful for lengthier documentaries to avoid boring the audiences.[42]

While rehabilitation of film refugees would have been a pressing need, the turn to information films was not without precedent. Roop Shorey's father, Roshan Lal Shorey, had been involved in newsreels since the early 1920s, while Johar had served as the propaganda secretary of the Punjab Provincial Committee in the early 1940s. After partition he briefly joined the Films Division of India as a scriptwriter, writing many scripts that 'never got made'.[43] In the interview to *Filmfare*, Johar professed an aversion to fiction. As the writer and director of many feature films in Bombay, Johar's claim is certainly odd but consistent with his image as a maverick film-maker whose films often ran into censorship troubles. While Johar's censor troubles started with the song lyrics of the comedy *Shrimatiji* (My Wife, 1952), it was *Nastik* (Atheist, 1954), his third film as a director, which really rattled the Censor Board of India. It had taken several comedies and satirical articles before Johar could make a serious film about a man's loss of faith after living through partition. While *Nastik* has been recognised as one of the rare films on partition in the first decade of independence, I argue that the collective authorship of Shorey comedies by refugee film artistes makes these as much a partition film as any other. As witnesses and victims of a historic strain, the investment of these film refugees in two seemingly disparate film forms suggests a similitude of intentionality across a genre film and an information film.

The Cosmopolitics of Shorey Comedies

Signalling Shorey comedies' unconcealed and undoubtedly cosmopolitan embrace of a Hollywood form, the Indian film press identified a 'Shorey technique' akin to the

'Lubitsch touch' of Ernst Lubitsch's humorous classics. Apart from a recognisable cast which included secondary characters across a body of films, the other markers of the 'Shorey technique' were long climactic chase sequences, exaggerated stunts in incongruous locations and mind-boggling twists and turns to keep intact the humorous momentum of the story, making it akin to one big adventure. The characters in these films are always on the move, travelling to different cities, sometimes specified while at other times indicated. The songs are either frothy duets or ensemble performances – a gang of girls in a neighbourhood or colleagues in an office or students in college. A 'forceful dig in the ribs', 'bubbling with wit' and 'oodles of fun',[44] the films were reminiscent of the Hollywood comedies that regularly made their way into the colonial Indian market during the 1930s.[45] These shared similarities of mood, character types and eccentric misunderstandings of screwball comedies like *It Happened One Night* (1934), *The Awful Truth* (1937), *His Girl Friday* (1940) and *Mr. and Mrs. Smith* (1941). In particular, *Ek Thi Ladki*, which launched Meena into the comedienne star orbit, is an office romance between a boss and his new secretary organised around a world turned upside down bearing the lineaments of loss, dislocation and a heavy freedom. In true screwball comedy spirit, it maintains a precarious balance between total anarchy and stable resolution.

A debilitating and gendered partition was the historical context for the Shorey comedies. Arguably, these films were motivated by a progressive gender politics or at least a destabilisation of dominant gender regimes. Through their 'female dominated courtship' and action of screwball,[46] Shorey films worked out a comedic and cinematic transformation of the social. Innovating on the tropes of role reversal, unstable unions and the eccentric heroine, Shorey comedies featured the democratic couple and embodied the possibility of equality. A more companionate and quirky courtship was the highlight of these films. The publicity and reviews of films that followed the trend set by Shorey comedies appear conscious of this dimension, and often the plot of the films depended on the desire of women to achieve parity. The disapproving review of *Shrimati 420* calls the picture 'one long argument stretching 12,000 and odd feet and asserting that women have the right to do all that men do'.[47] The publicity page of *Shrimatiji* introduces the film as 'a social story produced by Filmistan Ltd. is a riot of girls – young and beautiful who decide to live like men a free and independent life in free India'.[48] The tagline for *Shri Naqad Narayan* acclaimed it 'a delightful satire on men and manners'.[49] Above all, this collective intention emerges in Meena's persona in these films, one not unlike her US counterparts with their 'chaotic force of the screwball heroine [that] defied convention and male prerogative'.[50]

With an upfront attitude and agency, in most of her films she played the working girl or one seeking employment. An office secretary in *Ek Thi Ladki*, a music teacher in *Dholak* and a shop attendant in *Shri Naqad Narayan*, Meena was rarely seen within the domestic space. The relationship between the lead couple was collegial, whether it be the household chores Meena and Ranjit perform as 'servants' in *Ek Thi Ladki* or winning cash in a singing competition in *Dholak* where Manohar composes and Mona sings. If in *Dholak* Mona is rescued by Manohar from a galloping horse gone berserk, then in *Ek Do Teen* she is, as Roma, equally adept at saving Ranjit from the gallows. In perhaps the most leisurely race against time on screen, Roma drives a bus, a tractor, a rail-trolley and finally a train in order to rescue Ranjit. As the train runs out of coal, Meena and her friends ingeniously proceed to chop the wooden carriages and feed the engine fire while crooning a song.

A liberating aspect of Meena's performance was her non-committal presence and wild gesticulations to aid comic comprehension. Her performative style would often attract qualified appraisals such as 'droll queen Meena Shorey who can make you laugh when she cries and cry when she laughs'[51] or the one published in *Pakistan Times* a year later: 'In the mobility of expression and freedom, Meena leaves everybody behind. She has interpreted the role fairly well but her performance lacks restraint. At moments the audience wishes there was someone to check her a bit.'[52] Meena's antics were regularly photographed and published in the film magazines – for instance, her proudly posing next to a vanquished wild boar in *Filmfare*.[53] If it was the 'big game' during *Aag ka Dariya* that included an incredible scene of her pulling out a thorn from a tiger's paw, then for *Ek Do Teen* she was reported to have learnt how to drive a tractor. 'The secret of her success is that she is utterly without fear and without nerves,' surmised a publicity insert in *Filmfare*.[54] The attributes of physical daring along with manic slapstick presence made Meena quite unconventional in terms of prevalent norms for leading female characters.

Meena's overweight body was eloquent with possibilities, where a potential impediment of the 'avoirdupois' was swivelled into pleasures both conventional and otherwise. An article in *Filmfare* on the star pair of Motilal–Meena attributed their comic success to being physically mismatched (Figure 5.3),[55] evoking the common humour around a fat woman and her frail spouse. The cartoons that appeared regularly in *Filmindia* also commented on her bulk and referred to her as the 'family balloon'[56] and 'bag of wheat from Punjab' (Figures 5.4 and 5.5).[57] These also carried publicity stories from the shoots of these comedies where her weight reportedly created medical emergencies for her co-actors and were aimed at amusing the reader. *Filmindia* reported how Meena knocked out Majnu with a single blow during a shoot, and in *Filmfare* a reader asked: 'Is it a fact that Majnu fainted on receiving a blow from Meena while acting in a scene in 'Ladaki'?[58] Similarly, Motilal was reported to have dislocated his shoulder after carrying her around for *Ek Do Teen*. The film carried a diegetic response to this news by having Meena carry Motilal in a scene. A recurring motif of film publicity, Meena's playful bodily combat was not limited to her male co-stars but included women too. One such instance was a suggestive cartoon of Meena wrestling with Begum Para, 'directed' by Shorey on the ringside (Figure 5.6).[59] The erotic polysemy of Meena's persona pre-dated the Shorey comedies, going back to Pancholi's *Shehar se Dur* (see Chapter 1) in parallel production with Shorey's *Shalimar* starring Begum Para in Lahore.

Figure 5.3 The comic success of Meena–Motilal
Source: Filmfare, 7 January 1955. Image published with the permission of National Film Archives of India, Pune.

Scaling walls, jumping off balconies and fighting her attackers, Meena's weight and size never interfered with her mobility. That her girl-with-gumption character was mostly thrown into such situations and was never quite in control became the source of humour. While these feats made Meena stand apart from the more conventional heroines of social melodramas at the time, like Kamini Kaushal, Suraiyya or Noorjahan, a lack of composure also distinguished her from stunt stars like Nadia.

That in his noble effort to reduce his family balloon, Producer Shorey makes his wife Meena drive a train, a trolley, a truck, a tractor and an aeroplane all in his new picture "Ek-do-teen". After six months of all that Meena is reported to have lost four ounces of weight.

Figure 5.4   Humour focused on Meena Shorey's physique
Source: *Filmindia*, August 1952, 22.

That film actress Meena, the big bag of wheat from the Punjab, knocked out Majnu, the comedian, with a single box while doing a shot for "Ladaki", the new Shorey picture. Majnu took a count of nine days in a hospital to come back to his own amazon in the home. Poor Majnu, he is always between the devil and the deep sea. Let us hope Roop Shorey's new picture doesn't knock out the audience as completely as in the case of "Aag-ka-Dariya".

Figure 5.5   Humour focused on Meena Shorey's physique
Source: *Filmindia*, June 1954, 17.

> That film actress Meena, our glamour balloon, is
> ~~st~~ developing into a champion wrestler the way she
> reported to have been throwing about men and things
> her new picture. Why not match her with Begum
> ~~ra~~ at the Vallabhbhai Stadium? There is more money
> this game than in cricket or films. And Morarji
> ~~esn't~~ mind girls rubbing each other off.

Figure 5.6   Meena Shorey and Begum Para sketched in bodily combat
Source: *Filmindia*, August 1954, 21.

Rosie Thomas in her study of the stunt star finds Nadia unambiguously in control whose significance stemmed from her body and what she could do.[60] Meena's body too was significant for her image as the 'droll queen', with humour evoked through a comic play on the limits and potential of such a body.

In part, the ancestral forerunner of Meena's persona lay in the 'modern girl' cinema icon of Indian cinema of the early 1930s. Priti Ramamurthy argues that this cosmopolitan icon had faded from the screens by the end of the decade for she was seen as 'being unfit for the all-important job of nurturing cultural nationalism'.[61] In 'modern girl' films, women lived in a metropolitan world, loved adventure and frequently transgressed religious boundaries. However, with the abducted and recovered women of partition becoming symbolic of crossing and re-inscribing religious boundaries, these transgressions also carried historical weight after 1947. Offering glimpses of what Kathleen Rowe identifies as the 'unruly woman' and Mary Russo as the 'female grotesque',[62] the nervously chaotic heroine of Shorey comedies threatened to upturn the world with her artful artlessness. Here the Shorey films offer an archive of feminine abandon and paternalistic rescue that radically repurpose a familiar and piteous partition figure into the chaotic screwball heroine and bring about a cinematic recovery.

As I have argued elsewhere, the uninhibited deployment of Meena's body was geared towards making a spectacle of the female body and stood in opposition to the deliberate erasures visited upon her historical underside – the abducted woman.[63] Characteristic of Meena's performance was her distinctive earthiness, located regionally as Punjabiyat through her parlance, bodily mannerisms and clothes. Dressed in a *salwar-kurta*, albeit with sneakers and hair braided in two, the Meena image traversed a narrative landscape that ranged from the traditional world of rural Punjab to the post-colonial metropolis. For instance, her sideways clap in 'Lara Lappa' and percussive hand tapping on office tables introduced a familiar cultural resonance and rhythm to the routinised protocols of the workplace that ordinary women in Shorey films had to negotiate. Such a negotiation speaks of the large number of women released into the workforce as a result of the mass destitution and displacement of partition.[64] Involving a resourceful improvisation on the conditions of her origins, her image expanded the possibilities of existence in a changing world.

The Partition Screwball: *Ek Thi Ladki* (1949)

Roop Shorey's first production in Hindi after partition was *Ek Thi Ladki* (There Was a Girl, 1949), a massive commercial success according to enthusiastic reviews of the film.[65] Termed slapstick, the film was an unusual genre as far as Hindi cinema was concerned. The reviewers did not miss the combination of humour with a refugee film-maker at that time.

> In 'Ek Thi Ladki', Roop Shorey refugee from the Punjab Partition Terror, with little cause for laughter and much for weeping were he the weeping kind, put down a new milestone for the industry by providing it with its first true slapstick farce.[66]

The central protagonist of *Ek Thi Ladki* is a young woman, Meena (Meena Shorey), in search of a job, who gets wrongly implicated by two conmen in a murder. Escaping the conmen as well as the police, Meena is accidently hired by Ranjit (Motilal) who is desperate for a personal secretary and tolerates Meena's quirky inadequacies (Figure 5.7). They travel to Delhi for work where Meena spots her pursuers at the hotel and cancels their reservation. Homeless and at their wits' end, Meena and Ranjit pose as married house servants to live with an elderly, rich couple. Their squabble over domestic chores undergoes a romantic transformation, and the two decide to marry in Srinagar, Ranjit's ancestral home. The conmen follow Meena here as well and decamp with the wedding jewellery. In a comic yet thrilling climax, Meena chases the crooks in a motorboat down Dal Lake and retrieves her wedding jewels. Playful and united, Meena and Ranjit sail in a *shikara* (wooden boats) against the scenic Kashmir valley.

Figure 5.7 A publicity insert for *Ek Thi Ladki*
Source: *Filmindia*, August 1949.

Ek Thi Ladki was a remake of Shorey's pre-partition film *Rut Rangili*. Made in Lahore over 1946–1947, *Rut Rangili* seemed jinxed as it was destroyed twice. First the film suffered in the Shorey studio fire in mid-1946. It was reshot when the new studio at Multan Road emerged but was left incomplete during the partition disturbance. *Ek Thi Ladki* was the third reincarnation of *Rut Rangili* and was released on 7 January 1950 in India and a little later in Pakistan. Along with Roop Shorey and Meena, I. S. Johar too had been part of the *Rut Rangili* project right from its inception. The review in the *Times of India* mentioned the context of production.

> Shorey deserves credit and congratulation on having made such a fine job of the film despite the difficulties and atmosphere in which he had to make it.[67]

Ek Thi Ladki is arguably a partition film. To be more precise, it is a partition screwball comedy – although it is not a direct or an allegorical representation of the terror of partition, it makes seemingly stray references, secondary to the plot, which constitute the emotional and experiential coordinates of the film. Here the partition imprint was registered through a cynical humour, the nostalgia for Lahore and the reorientations of national perspectives. Running contrary to the typification of early cinematic mediations of partition in terms of a 'ghostly pall [that] enveloped the cultural field',[68] *Ek Thi Ladki* sublimates partition anguish into a sparkling screwball comedy.

Gags abound in *Ek Thi Ladki*, from the slapstick lighting of matchsticks against baldheads to the swindling of unsuspecting targets by a play on words.[69] However, a distinctive edge emanates from the cynical humour around freedom, or *azaadi*, registered in the prison release of two con artistes Mohan (Majnu) and Sohan (I. S. Johar). Yet, made and released a little over two years from 1947, *azaadi* was also the independence that the subcontinent attained from its colonial rulers. Two minutes into the story, Mohan swells his chest, gleefully beating in the 'free air', which Sohan pointedly experiences to be 'colder' than that originating in the Himalayas. Trite references to the topographic coherence of the Indian nation are contiguous with gags on the language conundrum. Annoyingly repeating a statement twice over in closely related Hindi and Urdu languages, the two poke fun at the language politics that characterised the 1940s. The crooks also quote their old colonial masters, thus sparing none in their lampooning.

> Mohan: *Aur angrez bhi keh gaya hai, 'Honesty is the best policy'.*
> Sohan: *Arre bilkul aakhri dafa, yaani angrezi mein 'last but one'.*

> Mohan: And even the English claimed, 'Honesty is the best policy!'
> Sohan: This will be the last time, as they say in English 'last but one time'!

Often treated in a less than reverential manner and as a pretext for unhindered mischief making, freedom is as much an object of ridicule as anything else. The only time any serious thought is extended to *azaadi* is at the end when the crooks decide to surrender to the police authorities. Introspecting over the loss entailed in giving up one's liberty, the answer according to Sohan (I. S. Johar) lies in the kind of freedom.

> Sohan: *Yeh kahaan ki azaadi hai? Har awaaz par chaunkna, har khatre par bhag uthna. Na dinn ko chain, na raaton ko neend. Yeh jhooti azaadi hai, dost.*

> Sohan: What sort of a freedom is this? Getting startled at every sound, ready to escape from any threat, no peace during daytime and little sleep at night. It is a lie, this freedom, my friend.

The dialogue cited here echoes the sentiments of poet Faiz Ahmed Faiz in 'Subh-e-Azadi (August 1947)', written after the division of the subcontinent.[70] By implication the film points to the other side of freedom, where fear and displacement came to characterise the migrant experience of freedom. Meena as the fake royal, the princess of Champatpur (Abscond-ville), is a light-hearted reference to the uncertain times faced by the princely states with the attainment of freedom and yet another instance of political readings offered by the film.

The quips and humorous refrains of the characters in *Ek Thi Ladki* are specific to the partition experience. Jokes around homelessness, loss of property and missing servants as a result of demographic changes are all part of the partition landscape at different social levels. In her work on the bureaucratic negotiations between India and Pakistan, Pallavi Raghavan draws attention to the appointment of the 'custodian of evacuee property' in both countries in 1947 to arbitrate disputes and distribute allotments to refugees.[71] That these decisions were often controversial and based on a notion of presence–absence, is capitalised on by the film. The evacuee-property joke is premised on bureaucratic rules as a trick on unsuspecting people just like the one where Ranjit is swindled of his money by the con artists. While waiting in a Delhi office, Mohan challenges Ranjit to a bet that will 'prove' the latter's absence from the scene. Intrigued, Ranjit accepts the bet and this exchange involving Lahore and Bombay follows.

> *Mohan: Dekhiye, main abhi sabit karta hun ki aap yahan nahin hain. Batayiye sahab, aap iss waqt Bambai mein toh nahin hain?*
> *Ranjit: Ji nahin.*
> *Mohan: Aap iss waqt Lahore mein bhi toh nahin hain?*
> *Ranjit: Ji nahin.*
> *Mohan: Achcha toh aap iss waqt na Bambai mein hain na Lahore mein hain toh kahin aur hain.*
> *Ranjit: Ji haan, kahin aur hun.*
> *Mohan: Jab aap kahin aur hain, toh yahan nahin ho sakte! Aadab arz hai!*
> *Ranjit: Arre sahab yeh toh bilkul aapne jaadu kar diya. Mere paise bhi gayab kar diye aur mujhe bhi bilkul gayab kar diya.*
> *Mohan: Sahab, aise hi hoga, zamana hi aisa hai!*

Mohan: Look, I can prove it right away that you are not here.… Tell me, you are not in Bombay now, are you?
Ranjit: No.
Mohan: And you are not in Lahore either?
Ranjit: No.
Mohan: If you are neither in Lahore nor in Bombay, it means you are somewhere else.
Ranjit: Yes, I am somewhere else.
Mohan: If you are somewhere else, you cannot possibly be here! [*takes the ten rupee note from Ranjit*]
Ranjit: Indeed some magic here! You made my money vanish along with me!
Mohan: [*sheepishly and under his breath*] These things will happen. Such are the times we live in!

Ranjit's quip on dislocation and linked monetary loss was Shorey's own story as an evacuee from Lahore. The lack of belonging and risk of disappearing as a citizen of either state, caught 'somewhere else' between India and Pakistan, characterised the migrant experience. The dislocation and the refugee experience are also evident in the chronic homelessness in the film. Evicted by her landlady, Meena sleeps atop her boss's desk in the office on the first night of her getting a job. That all the hotels in Delhi are full may gesture to the influx of unforeseen visitors or refugees. As a result, Ranjit and Meena must spend their first night in Delhi crouching together underneath a bench in a public park. Both agree to live as servants in order to get a roof over their heads, and their employers are ready to put up with inept help, because servants of any sort are rare to come by. Threading its narratives around the demographic shifts and instability at that time, the film conveys the uncertain times that millions lived through in the aftermath of partition.

In terms of regional identity, Punjabiyat infiltrates this Bombay–Hindi film at many registers, from the heavily accented speech of its actors (Meena, Majnu, Johar, Kuldeep Kaur) to the use of colloquial Punjabi words and music in the film, including the song that made Meena famous: 'Lara lappa lara lappa lai rakh da.' Ranjit who is unfamiliar with the language, asks for a clarification in a scene preceding the song.

> Ranjit: Yeh laralappa aur addi tappa kya zabaan hai?
> Meena: Punjabi! Larelappe ka matlab hai talmatol aur additappe ka khamkhwaan jhagda karna.

> Ranjit: What sort of a language is lara lappa and addi tappa?
> Meena: Punjabi! Lara lappa means dilly-dallying, and addi tappa is unnecessary quibble.

The clothes and fashion within the film are customary of the region and Meena's dress leaves little doubt regarding her Punjabi origins. The policemen dressed in turrah pagris, or linen turbans with pleated fans, recall the significance of this item of clothing in Lahore, one that coded social class and identity. Nostalgia for that city is also evident in the variety programme presented at the hotel where Meena poses as royalty. The first is a ventriloquist's act featuring the puppet, Patay Khan, that carried a special resonance for old Lahoris. By the 1930s, the name Patay Khan in Lahore had become synonymous with power and influence.[72] Appropriately enough, Patay Khan's jokes about contemporary times were also in sync with the experience of many who had lived in Lahore once: 'Aajkal khuda mil jaata hai lekin makaan nahin milta' (Nowadays one can find God but not a house).

The other component of the variety programme is a short song performance, 'Dilli se Aaya Bhai Tingu' (Brother Tingu Arrives from Delhi), featuring Honey O'Brien, an actress of Anglo-Indian descent. While never made explicit, Lahore is the city where three intimate friends with nonsensical names, Tingu, Pingu and Shingu, from three disadvantaged caste-professions (washerman, tailor and blacksmith) arrive.

Teeno nikle Mall Road par matak matak chalte they
O Rama! Paaon patak kar chalte they
Haathon mein daale haath phirte they saath saath
Gaate they yeh baat
Hindoostan humara hai yeh sab duniya se nyara hai
Hindu, Muslim, Sikh, Isaayi, sab ki aakh ka taara hai.

The three set out on Mall Road, with a swinging gait
Oh dear, how they marched
Hand-in-hand, the three roamed together
Singing the refrain
'Our Hindustan is the best in the world
The apple of all eyes – Hindu, Muslim, Sikh, Christian'.

The Mall Road was a celebrated one in Lahore and held attractions for tourists and locals alike. As remembered by Pran Neville in his memoirs of the cosmopolitan, colonial city, the road had some magnificent views with prominent shops, restaurants and concrete presence of the colonial state in the buildings of High Court, Telegraph Office, the Reserve Bank of India and General Post Office.[73] The song and Tingu's story continue the geographic disorientation by referring to a city which was left behind and no longer part of Hindustan.[74] Its nostalgic past tense conveys the end of an era where one could stroll along with a sense of easy belonging in Lahore, now gently lampooned with an implicit awareness of being separated forever from that condition. Here, the film encapsulates Aamir Mufti's formulation of the post-colonial predicament where 'the past of the self is another country'.[75] The female protagonist Meena's past is composed of a memory flashback of land caving in, houses collapsing, trees falling and bodies under debris. This memory locates her origins in Quetta when she lost her parents and home in the earthquake, and which, after partition lay in Pakistan. A vivid recollection on screen revisits the massive earthquake that struck Quetta in 1935, and mobilises a pre-partition sensorium that would carry intimate meaning for the Quetta-born Roop Shorey.

Interestingly, Kashmir is the space of plot resolution where a motorboat chase unfolds. Srinagar, the capital, happens to be Ranjit's hometown, and he proudly claims to be as pure a Kashmiri as *pashmina*.[76] But it is Meena who chases the conmen on a boat crossing inlets and creeks under low and narrow bridges. Risking her life, she reaches the conmen's hideout and the room where she had relived her memories of the earthquake. I suggest that Meena's instinctive knowledge of the terrain and her ability to handle the enemy evoke a faculty to negotiate symbolically charged sites of competing claims. As the bone of contention between India and Pakistan right from 1947, Kashmir has been regarded as the unfinished business of partition. *Ek Thi Ladki* was one of the earliest films to be shot extensively in the valley, and this informed its publicity too. The sequences of surfing and *shikara* rides on the lake were combined with ethnographic shots of the locals dressed in traditional clothes. In bringing

Kashmir to the screen in a form akin to tourism documentary, this representation also involved a proprietary claim on behalf of India. The significance of the territorial claim is evident in the hypernationalist alarms raised in *Filmindia* over film shoots in the Kashmir valley. The magazine saw a serious security lapse in representing an 'important military objective' and 'the cockpit of national pride' on screen.

> Pictures like 'Barsaat', 'Ek Thi Ladki', 'Kashmir', 'Kashmir Humara Hai' have scenes and stories from Kashmir and some of these have been produced with the direct cooperation of the army authorities in Kashmir.... It is possible that quite unwittingly the profit-conscious film producer, while shooting on locations in Kashmir, may provide some clue to the war-hungry Pakistanis and contribute to their nefarious plans.... how can the government justify the present rush of the film producers to Kashmir, in the face of the cruel fact that the battlefield of Kashmir has today become the cockpit of our national pride and democratic ambitions...?[77]

In mid-1949, 'setting a fine example of patriotic responsibility', the Shorey team entertained the army men on active service in Kashmir. Despite torrential rains, Meena acquiesced to the soldiers' requests, and the stage show went on.[78] From a wistful nostalgia for a past homeland to aligning desires with the new nation, *Ek Thi Ladki* represented the old and new geographies that emerged in the wake of the partition of the subcontinent. While humour could well be the coping mechanism of the refugee film team achieving cathartic release, reviews declared the extreme popularity of the 'Shorey–Meena triumph' to have 'wiped the local eye'.[79]

The Hindu–Muslim Bug of Romance

The adversarial contest of screwball between male and female leads explored within marriage, breakup and remarriage exceeded the diegesis of Shorey comedies and escalated as star-curiosity around Meena's many husbands, Roop Shorey being the fourth. The discursive investment in the interfaith alliance between Meena and Roop, arguably the couple at the heart of Shorey films, signifies the historical underside of a communal division. Curious fan mails regularly enquired about the status of the relationship between the actress and the director.

> What will happen to Shorey when Meena dies?[80]
> I always see film actress Meena with Roop K Shorey. What is the relationship between them? Where is her husband if she has any?[81]

The 'seeing' refers to the strong visual presence of the couple in magazine cartoons and photographs, where more than her co-stars, Meena was photographed and sketched with Roop Shorey. As their utopian alliance had informed the circulation of these films, the romantic lead on screen was also 'seen' as a cipher for the Shorey couple.

'Somehow our artistes act more realistically with their directors than with their heroes,' noted *Filmindia* underneath a 'glimpse of human relationship' between Roop and Meena (Figure 5.8).[82]

Meena and Roop's inter-community alliance was not a rare one in the film industry at that time – in the 1940s, Nazir and Swarnlata, Durga Khote and Mohammed Rashid, provide other examples. However, risking a generalisation based on *Filmindia*'s more partisan prose after 1947, such marriages and the adjustments entailed in terms of conversions (mostly of women), were increasingly under attack. In 1951, the magazine reported a 'Hindu–Muslim bug' doing the rounds in the film industry.

> ... the Hindu–Muslim bug of romance is drawing blood and tears, the way a Pakistan conscious Muslim hero is reported to have induced a Hindu film girl to fall in love with him.[83]

In consecutive issues, the magazine warned of the 'Don Juans' that is young Muslim men who seduced Hindu women away from their communities. However, the magazine was not unequivocal in condemning all interfaith marriages and, in the case of Roop and Meena, noted with satisfaction that she had been converted during the wedding ceremony.[84] This was consistent with the imagination sustained by popular Hindi literature in the late nineteenth century, as pointed out by Charu Gupta, where 'the Muslim male was maligned for abducting and forcefully

Somehow our artistes seem to act more realistically with their directors than with their heroes. Here is a glimpse of human relationship between Director Roop K. Shorey and Actress Meena.

Figure 5.8 Roop Shorey and Meena Shorey featured together
Source: Filmindia, January 1951, 15.

converting Hindu women while stories of love and romance between a Hindu man and a Muslim woman provided titillation and a general sense of elation.[85] Seen as recovering Muslim women for something better, their conversion to Hinduism was encouraged within this discursive realm.

In Pakistan, many years later, Meena's conversion was reported as protection against the threat of a communal backlash in Bombay. And yet her insistence that she scripted and voluntarily underwent the rite of passage may point to the instrumental use of conversion 'as a mode of coping with, challenging and within limits transgressing an oppressive social order'.[86] Through the running critique of her family, and not holding Roop responsible for her conversion, Meena claims an arena of independent action through the crossing of religious boundaries. Yet consistent with her uncontainable persona, Meena did not take her transgressions too seriously either.

> *Jahan tak mere mazhab ka taaluk hai main toh apne aap ko Mussalman hi samajhti thi. Jab mahant humein aag ke pheray lagwa raha tha toh maine isse zehni taur par shooting ka ek hissa qarar de liya tha aur andar hi andar hans rahi thi.*[87]

> As far as faith was concerned, I considered myself a Muslim. When the priest was officiating our nuptial vows around the ritual fire, I had psychologically treated it like a film shoot. All this while I was laughing inside.

The coverage of Meena's decision to stay on in Pakistan after 1956, in the Pakistani-Urdu film magazine *Nigar Weekly* as well as the Indian-English *Filmindia*, reveals that the Meena–Roop split-up was an even more potent site for playing out communal and national tensions. A *Nigar* cartoon showed Roop willing to embrace Islam for Meena and vindictively called the producer a filmy *behroop*, or impersonator. Coded as Hindu with a *tilak* and *tikki*, the cartoon depicted Roop wielding 'a Muslim mask' complete with the Liaquat Khan cap while Meena sat far away (Figure 5.9).[88] The gap between the Roop represented in *Nigar* and the one that emerges in Meena's account could not be more striking. Back in Bombay, *Filmindia* cast Roop in the dubious light of a spy whose close links to Pakistan had to be monitored[89] and called Meena Pakistan's very own Panchali in a crass reference to her multiple marriages.[90] It lost no time in crudely recasting the marriage as one of the many ongoing contests between the countries, this time sexual.

> That what Nehru and his Cabinet colleagues could not do during the last nine years, Producer Roop Shorey and his wife Meena are reported to have done. With Meena deciding to become a citizen of Pakistan and Shorey of course, remaining the most loyal Indian citizen ever known, they have succeeded in putting India and Pakistan in the same bed. Indeed a unique feat. And India is still on the top, of course. Jai Hind![91]

Figure 5.9   'Inspired by Meena, director Shorey has decided to embrace Islam'
Source: *Nigar Weekly*, September 1956; courtesy of Aslam Ilyas, Karachi.

The irreverent ending in *Filmindia*, recalling the union at the end of many screwball films, also underlined that partition remained at the core of this coupling.

If Meena and Roop's Bombay years are marked by an intimate or *visceral cosmopolitanism*, then they also encompass 'the fragility of cosmopolitanism in deeply felt desires and conflicting attachments'.[92] This collaboration, which resisted parochial pressures of community and nation for nearly a decade, finally came to an end in 1956. With unconventional gender dynamics and Meena as the ultimate star of these comedies, the Shorey films were sublime renderings of partitioned social relations. Strikingly, what is available in Meena's image is a resourceful deployment of the figure of the abducted woman, though turned on her head through an active breach of communal and national boundaries by the actress. Making films closely modelled on the Hollywood screwball, a team of refugee film artistes in Bombay transformed dislocation into a volitional mobility of the characters, resisting containment and fashioning a cosmopolitan subjectivity. At the same time, their oeuvre carried traces of pre-partition Lahore's sardonic accent. A lot of things could be laughed at, including the new independence, as the world outside was no less topsy-turvy than the one inside Shorey comedies.

Notes

1   Ritu Menon and Kamla Bhasin, *Borders and Boundaries: Women in India's Partition* (New Delhi: Kali for Women, 1998), 20.

2   Vazira Zamindar, *The Long Partition and the Making of Modern South Asia: Refugees, Boundaries, Histories* (New York: Columbia University Press, 2007), 3.

3   Peter Van der Veer, 'Colonial Cosmopolitanism', in *Conceiving Cosmopolitanism*, ed. Steven Vertovec and Robin Cohen, 165–179 (Oxford: Oxford University Press, 2002), 165.

4   Mica Nava, *Visceral Cosmopolitanism: Gender, Culture and the Normalization of Difference* (New York: Berg, 2009), 8.

5   Neepa Majumdar, *Wanted Cultured Ladies Only!: Female Stardom and Cinema in India, 1930–1950* (Urbana: University of Illinois Press, 2009).

6   'Meena Shorey', in *Out of Date*, ed. Munir Ahmed (Lahore: Atish Feshan Publications, 1986), 6.

7   Meena's memoirs were narrated to a journalist, Munir Ahmad, who undertook to record experiences of pre-partition actors of cinema living in Pakistan.

8   Sidonie Smith and Julia Watson, *Reading Autobiography* (Minneapolis: University of Minnesota, 2001), 63.

9   Amelie Hastie, *Cupboards of Curiosity: Women, Recollection and Film History* (Durham, NC: Duke University Press, 2007), 72.

10 Ibid., 77.

11 The actress accuses her father of cruelty against her mother and of leaving the family to marry again. Her elder brother likewise turned out to be good-for-nothing and a vagabond (*awara*).

12 Vivien Gardner, 'By Herself: The Actress and the Autobiography 1755–1939', in *The Cambridge Companion to the Actress*, ed. Maggie B. Gale and John Stokes, 173–192 (Cambridge: Cambridge University Press, 2007), 174.

13 'Meena Shorey', *Out of Date*, 11.

14 Ibid., 12.

15 Tejaswini Ganti, *Producing Bollywood: Inside the Contemporary Hindi Film Industry* (Durham, NC: Duke University Press, 2012), 249.

16 Khursheed Bano was a singer-actress active in Lahore, Calcutta and Bombay in the 1930s and 1940s, achieving popularity for her films with K. L. Saigal at Ranjit Movietone in Bombay.

17 See Ravi Vasudevan, 'Dislocations: The Cinematic Imagining of a New Society in 1950s India', Oxford Literary Review on India: Writing History, Culture, Post-coloniality 16, nos. 1–2 (1994): 93–124, 109; Bhaskar Sarkar, *Mourning the Nation: Indian Cinema in the Wake of Partition* (Durham, NC: Duke University Press, 2009), 77; and Srijana Das 'Partition and Punjabiyat in Bombay Cinema: The Cinematic Perspectives of Yash Chopra and Others', *Contemporary South Asia* 15, no. 4 (December 2006): 453–471, 463.

18 Priya Jaikumar, *Cinema at the End of Empire: A Politics of Transition in Britain and India* (Durham, NC: Duke University Press, 2006), 215.

19 'Zahur Raja: A Rough Neck Guy', *Filmindia*, April 1942, 49.

20 These continued to hold ground for many decades afterwards, when marriages were seen as bad decisions for actresses wishing to continue work in the Bombay film industry.

21 While *Arsi* released in 1947, *Patjhad* was restarted by Pancholi and could get completed only in 1948 and *Rut Rangili* suffered twice – once by a studio fire and left uncompleted by the start of riots in Lahore. Though one history of Punjabi cinema claims that *Rut Rangili* was released briefly in Lahore's Nishat cinema, the rest of the accounts, including Meena's, claim it never saw the light of the day.

22 Raza Mir was Meena's third husband, who she most probably married in Lahore. 'Ek Thi Meena', *Nigar Weekly*, Golden Jubilee Edition, 2009, 140.

23 'Meena Shorey', *Out of Date*, 17.

24 'Aag ka Dariya: Powerful Romantic Drama', *Times of India*, 13 December 1953, 3.

25 'Star Profile Meena Shorey', *Filmfare*, 5 September 1952, 18.

26 'You'll Hardly Believe', *Filmindia*, March 1950, 23.

27 Zamindar, *The Long Partition*, 127.

28 '*Jaal* agitation' refers to the protests conducted by actors, producers and directors of the Lahore film industry in 1954, demanding the ban of Indian films in Pakistan. The agitation was so named because the protestors were seeking an immediate withdrawal of the Indian film *Jaal* (Trap, 1952) from local theatres.

29 The difficulty in monetary transactions is also mentioned in Ayesha Jalal's work on writer Saadat Hasan Manto. 'The imposition of the border was never more intrusive than in the difficulties it created for writers and artistes in the two countries who were due royalty and other payments', writes Jalal. Ayesha Jalal, *The Pity of Partition* (Oxford: Princeton University Press, 2013), 134.

30 'Meena Shorey', *Out of Date*, 19.

31 Mushtaq Gazdar refers to Meena's 'pampering' in Lahore and contrasts it 'with the treatment meted out to declining artistes by film-goers in Bombay'. Mushtaq Gazdar, *Pakistan Cinema 1947–1997* (Karachi: Oxford University Press, 1998), 53.

32 'Meena Shorey', *Out of Date*, 22.

33 According to Meena, the people who had been allotted the Shorey studios were behind the death threats. While she does not name them openly, Noorjahan and her husband, Shaukat Hussain Rizvi, were allotted the Shorey studio as compensation. By 1956, it had been renovated and resumed as the Shahnoor studio.

34 'Mr. Kardar Not an Evacuee', *Times of India*, 28 April 1955, 3. 'Intending evacuee' became a legislative category in 1950, created to take control of people's property before they became an evacuee.

35 'Roop K. Shorey Meena ka Ghar Chorh Kar Beech Luxury Hotel mein Muntaqil Ho Gaye', *Nigar Weekly*, 19 September 1956.

36 According to the memoir, Meena's mother passed away before she moved to Bombay in 1947 and therefore much before she married Roop Shorey.

37 'Meena Shorey', *Out of Date*, 20.

38 Menon and Bhasin, *Borders and Boundaries*, 251.

39 Saadat Hasan Manto, 'Kuldeep Kaur: Too Hot to Handle', in *Bitter Fruit: The Very Best of Saadat Hasan Manto*, trans. and ed. Khaled Hassan (New Delhi: Penguin Books, 2008), 508.

40 'Film Profile: I.S. Johar', *Filmfare*, 10 December 1954, 16.

41 'Plight of Film Industry Refugees', *The Tribune*, 1 January 1948, 4 (emphasis mine).

42 'It Is a Film Age', *The Tribune*, 10 February 1948, 4.

43   'Film Profile: I.S. Johar', 16.
44   Press quotes taken from *Filmindia*, 1953, 47; *Filmfare* 7 January 1955, 4; and *The Times of India*, 8 January 1950, 14.
45   Newspaper classified and reviews in the *Times of India* attest to the presence and popularity of Hollywood comedies of the 1930s like *It Happened One Night* (Indian release: 1935), *Bringing Up Baby* (Indian release: 1938) and *The Awful Truth* (Indian release: 1938). The releases seem to have lessened considerably by the early 1940s.
46   Wes D. Gehring, *Screwball Comedy: Defining a Film Genre*, Ball State Monograph Number Thirty-One (Muncie, IN: Ball State University, 1983), 1.
47   'Our Review: Shrimati 420', *Filmindia*, June 1956, 43.
48   'Glimpses from Shrimatiji', *Filmindia*, 1951.
49   'Filmfare Reviews', *Filmfare*, 2 September 1952, 38.
50   Kathrina Glitre, *Hollywood Romantic Comedy: States of the Union 1934–65* (Manchester: Manchester University Press, 2006), 1.
51   Advertisement, *Filmfare*, March 4, 1955.
52   'Miss 56', *Pakistan Times*, 22 June 1956, 6.
53   *Filmfare*, 29 May 1953, 4.
54   Ibid.
55   'Romantic Teams of the Indian Screen: Meena: Motilal', *Filmfare*, 7 January 1955, 4.
56   'You'll Hardly Believe', *Filmindia*, August 1952, 22.
57   'You'll Hardly Believe', *Filmindia*, June 1954, 17.
58   'Question Box', *Filmfare*, 28 May 1954, 30. It seems *Ladaki* (Combative Woman) was either renamed *Jalwa* or could not be completed.
59   'You'll Hardly Believe', *Filmindia*, August 1954, 21.
60   Rosie Thomas, *Bombay before Bollywood: Film City Fantasies* (New Delhi: Orient Blackswan, 2014), 111–112.
61   Priti Ramamurthy, 'All-Consuming Nationalism: The Indian Modern Girl in the 1920s and 1930s', in *The Modern Girl around the World: Consumption, Modernity and Globalization*, ed. Alys Eve Weinbaum, the Modern Girl around the World Research Group, Lynn M. Thomas, Priti Ramamurthy, Uta G. Poiger and Madeleine Yue Dong, 147–173 (Durham, NC: Duke University Press, 2008), 166.
62   Mary Russo, *The Female Grotesque: Risk, Excess and Modernity* (New York: Taylor and Francis, 1994); and Kathleen Rowe, *The Unruly Woman: Gender and the Genres of Laughter* (Austin: University of Texas Press, 1995).
63   Salma Siddique, 'Someone to Check Her a Bit!' *Feminist Media Histories* 3, no. 2 (Spring 2017): 36–56, https://doi.org/10.1525/fmh.2017.3.2.36 (accessed on 2 April 2020).
64   Menon and Bhasin, *Borders and Boundaries*, 20.
65   '*Ek Thi Ladki* Mobbed!' *Times of India*, 8 January 1950, 14.
66   'Shorey–Meena Triumph in Rollicking Slapstick Comedy "Ek Thi Ladki"', *Times of India*, 21 January 1950, 10.
67   Ibid.
68   Sarkar, *Mourning the Nation*, 114.
69   The review notes the 'brazenly borrowed gags from foreign films mostly Abbott and Costello'. 'Shorey–Meena Triumph in Rollicking Slapstick Comedy', 10.

70 'Ye dagh dagh ujala, ye shab gazida sahar, Vo intizar tha jiska, ye vo sahar to nahin.' (This leprous daybreak, dawn night's fangs have mangled; rhis is not that long-looked-for break of day.) V. G. Kiernan, ed. and trans. *Poems by Faiz* (London: George Allen and Unwin Ltd, 1971), 123.

71 Pallavi Raghavan, *Animosity at Bay* (New York: Oxford University Press, 2020), 182 (E-book edition).

72 Patay Khan in common parlance in Lahore refers to a local powerful person who is also boastful. The character is a familiar presence in traditional theatre and puppetry from the region. Additionally, the newspaper *Lahore Punch* was earlier published as *Patay Khan*, with the family who owned it later being associated with the name. Wahid-ud-din, *The Marching Bells: A Journey of a Life-time* (Lahore: Authorhouse, 2011), 3.

73 Pran Neville, *Lahore: A Sentimental Journey* (New Delhi: Penguin, 2006), 14–15.

74 Magazine columns in the early 1950s also mention a son adopted by Meena and Roop, nicknamed Tingu. Meena's memoir however makes no mention of her adopted sons in India, except for the reference to the 'Christian nanny'.

75 Aamir Mufti, *Enlightenment in the Colony: The Jewish Question and the Crisis of Postcolonial Culture* (Princeton, NJ: Princeton University Press, 2007), 218.

76 *Pashmina* is a fine variety of wool procured from a special breed of sheep found in the Himalayan region.

77 'Films on Kashmir!' *Filmindia*, May 1950, 15.

78 'Star Profile Meena Shorey', *Filmfare*, 5 September 1952, 21.

79 'Shorey–Meena Triumph in Rollicking Slapstick Comedy', 10.

80 'Editor's Mail' *Filmindia*, August 1957, 16.

81 'Editor's Mail', *Filmindia*, January 1950, 26.

82 Photograph published in *Filmindia*, September 1949, 69.

83 'You'll Hardly Believe', *Filmindia*, January 1951, 15.

84 'You'll Hardly Believe', *Filmindia*, May 1950, 18.

85 Charu Gupta, *Sexuality, Obscenity, Community: Women, Muslims and the Hindu Public in Colonial India* (New York: Palgrave 2001), 241.

86 Ibid., 327.

87 'Meena Shorey', *Out of Date*, 21.

88 Part of Hindu ceremonial observances, *tilak* refers to a ritual mark, mostly in vermillion in North India, while *tikki* is a careful hair extension at the back curve of the male head, connoting high-caste status and/or orthodoxy.

89 'You'll Hardly Believe', *Filmindia*, July 1956, 38.

90 *Panchali* refers to Draupadi of the Indian epic Mahabharata, who was married to the five heroic brothers, or Pandavas. 'Editor's Mail', *Filmindia*, August 1957, 11.

91 'You'll Hardly Believe', *Filmindia*, October 1956, 38.

92 Paloma Gay Blasco, 'The Fragility of Cosmopolitanism: A Biographical Approach', *Social Anthropology* 18, no. 4 (2010): 403–409, 403.

6 The Partition Doppelgänger

Rattan Kumar and the Pakistani *Charbas*

Let us drink.
To Pakistan, where you went,
To India, where you will return,
To the Siamese Twins.[1]

In cultural representation of partition, the divided nations of India and Pakistan are often anthropomorphised and likened to twins or two brothers. The desperate celebration of two inebriated friends in Attia Hosain's incomplete novel has its parallel of two feuding brothers in the Prithvi Theatre's play *Deewar* (Wall). The difference(s) and breakage of unity are recast in these as duality and replication. A common allegorical device in narrativising partition, the power of 'the double' also constitutes Lahore's industrial response to the territorial division and dislocation through *charba*s, or film remakes. I approach this category of film through the star biography of Rattan Kumar. Rattan, whose real name was Syed Nazir Ali, was a child star who started his film career in independent India in the late 1940s. After achieving popularity and recognition for his roles in Hindi films, Rattan migrated to Pakistan in 1956. Riding on this fame, his family started a film production company and produced several films featuring the adolescent. Like most child stars of Hollywood as well as popular Hindi cinema, Rattan's adult career was not a success. However, in his case the age divide between success and failure was also one highly charged with a split in national affiliation.

Rattan's migration has an ideological potency, evident in its marginality in Indian and centrality in Pakistani accounts. This potency is what Jane O'Connor refers to as the cultural significance of the child star as a 'complex figure with inherent powers to generate emotions and embody hope'.[2] A letter in a Pakistani film magazine published in 1963 – seven years after Rattan moved to Pakistan – diagnosed the actor's plummet in popularity after his move.

> Rattan had done well in *Jagriti* in India. No credit goes to him in *Bedari*. I know when he was a boy of 8 or 10 his acting was excellent and marvellous; I liked his childhood acting very much. I thought that when Rattan would be a young man of 25, he will become the best hero of Indo-Pak subcontinent and will even replace Dilip. But it was an unlucky career for Rattan for joining Pakistani screen. He had done a brilliant tragedy in film like *Baiju Bavra* but now he can't do such type of tragedy roles at all. What he can do is foolish swording [*sic*].[3]

The extract encapsulates the disappointment rife at Rattan's inability to successfully replicate his Indian stardom in Pakistan. By the age of twenty, when the letter was written, Rattan had already managed to shatter the hopes projected for him at age twenty-five. If 'no credit [went] to him in *Bedari*', it was deemed to be the case partly because the film was a Pakistani remake of the Indian film *Jagriti* (Awakening, 1954). Such remakes were locally and disparagingly known as *charba* (replica) and carried the taint of plagiarism. The other ignominy associated with Rattan in Pakistan was his appearance in the low-brow fantasy genre. Apart from being the generic constituencies of Rattan's star image in Pakistan, there is a considerable overlap between the categories of *charba* and fantasy. The fantasy films of the 1950s and the early 1960s of Pakistan often took their cue from their Indian counterparts in the 1950s, and together these *Arabian Nights* hybrids were a throwback to the era of the early talkies of colonial India, that is, the early 1930s. Therefore, I identify *charba* as a category of remake, which may vary in its degree of similarity to the referenced 'original'. In the course of this chapter, four remakes starring Rattan Kumar and their different stances towards the earlier version will be discussed. I re-evaluate these derided and 'minor' films through the concept of the doppelgänger to understand certain tropes of derided doubling, including preposterous double roles, poor copies, fantastic doubles revealing the copy as generative and constitutive of what is repressed by the original. My focus on Rattan uncovers some incoherence in the Dyerian star image, allowing us to think of the star not as a stable reconciliation of opposites but as a durational struggle to achieve coherence between self and other. As a methodological tool used to excavate the migrant, or *muhajir*, film experience, Rattan's star study throws up the fact of his double roles after arrival in Pakistan alongside the doubling effect of *charba*s. I seek to understand this twofold doubling and its relationship to a post-partition society through the psychological contemplations on the motif of doubles in literary and popular culture. Here the double has been understood variously as narcissistic absorption and a projection of the second self of unconsciousness.[4] However, an analysis that is attentive to creative energies as well as representational demands remains psychologist Otto Rank's concept of *der doppelgänger*, the double, as an immortal self, motivated by a mind's need for self-perpetuation as well as a threat of death.[5] It is this understanding of the double that I extend to the film remake or copy of 'Indian' or 'all-Indian' film in Pakistan.

Attentive to Rattan Kumar's star-image in both contexts, I first illustrate the global cinema influences that fashioned the peculiarly postcolonial Indian identity of Rattan in Bombay. Successfully commanding the image of the 'national orphan', Rattan's persona embodied futurity for a challenge-ridden newly independent India. The tensions between the star as person and his image became observably heightened with his migration, and Rattan's star persona stood at risk of being emptied of meaning. In Pakistan, Rattan's stardom was remade through *charba*s, with two identifiable impulses: competitive (retaliatory) and nostalgic. While the competitive *charba*s involve a disavowal of and distance from his Indian past, the *charba*s of hybrid fantasies selectively retrieve his image within the fantasy films in India and thereby convey loss.

In proposing a link between the social order and a star's appeal, Richard Dyer stresses on the need to consider 'specific instabilities, ambiguities and contradictions in the culture, which are reproduced in the actual practice of making films and film stars.'[6] Star charisma, according to Dyer, involves an effective reconciliation of contradictory elements. But contradictions, which in Rattan's case constituted the Rubicon of Indian nationalism, were difficult to condense into a single star image. Therefore, Rattan's move to Pakistan mobilises two distinct modalities of charisma – an Indian by truncation and a Pakistani by elaboration. Truncating his image to the childhood on screen, a silence is maintained in Indian sources such as *Filmindia* and *Filmfare* over his real-life migration and later career. In Pakistan, Rattan's migrant star image is elaborated through his double roles, the *charba*s and the swashbuckling acts in the fantasy hybrids. Neither a child nor an Indian anymore, his star image is set forth in a complicated orbit of disavowal and appropriation. Offering a broader perspective on film enterprise in post-partition Lahore, the doppelgänger becomes the privileged form of a reconstituted self, the ultimate embodiment of divided identities.

Bombay Beginnings and the 'Voice of an Orphan'

The earliest surviving film performance of Rattan is *Afsana* (Story, 1951). Produced in Bombay, the film was written by I. S. Johar and directed by B. R. Chopra, both film migrants from Lahore. Barely seven years old, Rattan made a brief but memorable appearance as a junior-school kid in a skit on Mughal imperial justice. During his school-play rehearsals, Rattan declaims a grandiose Urdu couplet while his peers engage in a spirited toy-sword duel. Treated in a lighter vein, the sequence is intended to evoke amusement at the child's oratorical talents. In the play-within-the film, Rattan appears at the end, riding a donkey and dressed in a shining 'Mughal' costume, complete with a flowing cape and a dome cap. Following the narrative-tradition of the extraordinary wit of ordinary men that supersedes imperial authority,[7]

Rattan counters the king's logic of who ought to be adjudged senior in a matter of, what else but, twins. Proving the 'younger' to be in fact older, Rattan settles not only the imperial dilemma but also the moral dilemma within the film where the twin brothers vie for the same woman. After evoking laughter, whistles and claps from the play's audience, Rattan directly addresses the camera before bowing out. This remains a perfect capsule for Rattan's later stardom and popularity, which pivoted around exceptionality and a performative capacity incongruous for his age.

Becoming the quintessential child of popular Hindi cinema, Rattan played nearly all key childhood roles on screen in the landmark Hindi films of the early 1950s. Before *Afsana*, Rattan had acted in progressive writer Krishen Chandar's *Dil ki Awaz* (Call of the Heart, 1948) and fantasy-stunt film-maker Homi Wadia's *Balam* (Beau, 1949). By 1956, Rattan had reportedly worked in close to fifty films. Notable among these were neorealist inspired Bombay films like *Do Bigha Zameen* (A Few Acres of Land, 1953, dir. Bimal Roy) and *Boot Polish* (1954, dir. Prakash Arora); fantasy, legend or costume films like *Baghdad* (1952, dir. Nanabhai Bhatt), *Laila Majnu* (1953, dir. K. Amarnath), *Baiju Bawra* (Crazy Baiju, 1952, dir. Vijay Bhatt) and *Bahot Dinn Hue* (Many Moons Ago, 1954, dir. S. S. Vasan); mythologicals like *Jai Mahalaxmi* (1951), *Radha Krishna* (1954, dir. Raja Nene) and *Ekadashi* (Auspicious Day, 1955, dir. Gunjal); and socials like *Afsana* (Tale, 1951, dir. B. R. Chopra), *Sargam* (Musical Notes, 1950, dir. P. L. Santoshi) and *Jagriti* (Awakening, 1954, dir. Satyen Bose). As genres and circuits of Hindi cinema go, this is quite a comprehensive inventory. While mostly Rattan played the childhood roles of leading heroes, in *Do Bigha Zamin*, *Boot Polish*, *Bahot Dinn Hue* and *Jagriti*, he occupied the key narrative space of a boy protagonist.

With a crisp and effective dialogue delivery, a round earnest face and somewhat tubby body, Rattan was regarded as excellent for tragic roles.[8] In most films, his parents were either dead and absentee (*Boot Polish*, *Baiju Bawra*) or extremely vulnerable themselves (*Do Bigha Zamin*, *Jagriti*, *Bahot Dinn Hue*), except perhaps in the mythological genre. Here, in at least two instances (*Radha Krishna* and *Ekadashi*), Rattan played the cherished and special divine child Krishna. Two films, *Do Bigha Zameen* and *Boot Polish*, crystallised his image as an exceptional child, struggling against the odds. Held as 'landmarks' of national cinema[9] and allegories of the newly independent 'infant' Indian nation,[10] both films won popular awards at home and received recognition in international film festivals.[11] Influenced by the neo-realism of post-war Italy, in particular Vittorio De Sica's oeuvre, these Bombay films were part of the realist image that Indian cinema was projecting abroad. Through a self-conscious and selective deployment of the neorealist aesthetics, these films 'sought to absorb it into the familiar tropes, narrative and performance resources and aesthetic ambitions of an Indian cinema, multiply conceived'.[12] Crucially, Rattan's stardom was a product of what Neepa Majumdar identifies as the neorealist realignment of Bombay cinema, one led by film journalism, involving a shift of interest from film directors to film stars.[13] While Rattan was neither an actual street child nor looked like one, he could well evoke the emotional reaction by being the idealised little citizen-boy, clear complexioned, healthy, clean, well-behaved and articulate, facing risks that were real: starvation, neglect and abuse. These two extremes coalesced in Rattan's star image, which was a product of the neorealist realignment of Bombay cinema.

Given that these films were more melodramatic than De Sica's neorealist films, Rattan's physical dexterity combined with emotive eloquence made him the perfect child star for Bombay films. Bimal Roy found his Bruno in Rattan, chubby-faced, pint-sized but also loquacious. In *Do Bigha Zameen*, he played the young son of poor farmers, idealised as responsible even if a little spoilt. Forced to mortgage their small plot of land, the farmer Shambhu (Balraj Shahni) leaves the village in search of better prospects in Calcutta. Stubborn in his insistence on accompanying his father to the big city, Kanhaiya (Rattan Kumar) sneaks into the same train. While initially a cause for concern and an additional burden on his father, the wide-eyed Kanhaiya melts many hearts in an otherwise unsparing city, and exceptions are made for the father–son duo. Proving himself able to better negotiate this urban world than his father, Kanhaiya's character recalls similar child figures in post-war European cinema, who elucidated male lack and stood on 'the ruins of masculinity'.[14] And yet, given the realignment of Bombay neorealism, the film had Kanhaiya's shoeshine friend hurrying to watch the new fantasy, *Baghdad*, also starring Rattan, at a nearby cinema, in a tiny ode to the child star's charisma. An intertextual but also a self-reflective comment on themes, circuits and stardom, it encapsulated the distance between *Do Bigha Zameen* (a realist rendition of rural–urban poverty circulating in A-circuits and international film festivals) and *Baghdad* (a fantastic *Arabian Nights* hybrid popular in subaltern circuits) – a distance that could be reconciled only by Rattan.

Made a year later, *Boot Polish* picked up the story of the urban street children Kanhaiya encountered in *Do Bigha Zameen*. It was also a more obvious imitation of the narrative premise of another De Sica film, *Shoeshine* (1946). Moving the narrative to life in the Bombay slums, *Boot Polish* was the story of two orphans, Bhola (Rattan) and the berry-loving Belu (Baby Naaz), and their quest to earn a dignified living in the city. It was set in the visible underside of Bombay with its underclass of prostitutes, liquor bootleggers, pickpockets, beggars, hawkers and shoeshine kids. That Bhola's father had been sent to serve 'Kala Pani'[15] would have underlined for contemporary post-colonial Indian audiences his respectable, nationalist roots and the irony of his destitution. The siblings' continuing alienation from the independent Indian state is evident not only in their penurious and abusive childhood but also in their deep dread of the train ticket inspector, the police and the municipal authorities who periodically 'clean' urban slums. While sharing the lot of millions in independent India, Bhola stands apart in his uncompromising honesty and his refusal to steal or beg. After several trials, both Bhola and Belu are adopted by a good-hearted and childless middle-class couple and sent to school, as befitting the future citizens of the then new nation.

Like the post-war European cinema, these films offered the male child as a possible solution to the problems posed by contemporaneous disappointments. But children have also been quite pivotal to post-colonial modes of representation where the trope of child development lends itself persuasively to narratives of nation-building and cultural transformation.[16] Examining the consolidation of state authority in Nehruvian India, Srirupa Roy points out that the ideal citizen was imagined as a masculine subject and iconically represented as a young boy. This frequently invoked figure of the 'infantile citizen' needed 'state tutelage and protection in order to realize the potential of citizenship'.[17] Courtesy of the neorealist films, the ideal yet infantile citizen became the overarching element of Rattan's persona. While himself embodying national futurity on screen, the guiding standard for Rattan's projected adult stardom was Dilip Kumar, 'Nehru's hero'[18] and the king of tragedy, whose monumental stardom exerted an inspirational hold on Rattan.[19]

Thus, carrying the Nehruvian hallmark, Rattan was a frequent presence in the film reviews and production reports of the 1950s. *Filmfare* included him in news stories, special columns and centrespreads: at least two dedicated star features on Rattan are available in *Filmfare*, together suggesting that he was both a star and not yet a star. The first one appeared in the February issue of 1954, where Rattan was anointed under 'Candidates for Stardom'.[20] The column had a full-page colour shot of Rattan dressed in a red coat and bow-tie (Figure 6.1). The description below revealed that Rattan was born in Ajmer and was one of nine children. Apart from acting, cricket and tennis were listed as his key interests. The second instance was a full feature called 'Star Profile' in a September issue of 1955.[21] The article carried three colour photographs of Rattan in different outfits and poses: as a rifle-wielding hunter with a sola *topi* and flamboyant red silken scarf against blurred, as a school-going boy next to his bicycle trees (Figure 6.2) and, lastly, in white cricket gear complete with a red cap and holding a bat. In his photographs, Rattan was almost always well-turned out, immaculately dressed, Westernised – dressed more like a colonial *sahib* than the poor orphan on the street.

Calling him and his *Boot Polish* co-star, Baby Naaz, accomplished 'veterans' and 'old hands', the article detailed Rattan's off-screen life. When not shooting, he attended the Anjuman-i-Islam (Islamic Association) school in Bombay and loved sports. Cricket clearly had a special place as he led the team of industry artistes and technicians for 'filmland cricket matches' for charity and fundraising. Rattan was even said to have been 'discovered' while playing cricket by writer Krishen Chandar. It was reported that Rattan was to put together a team of fifteen boys to play cricket in England in mid-1956.[22] None of Rattan's plans of working in Pakistan or contemplating a move to the country are ever mentioned in these articles; by the mid-1950s the hostility and suspicion towards Pakistan in the Bombay film industry was absolute.

These reports where Rattan was revealed to be different in real life than his on-screen role contributed to what Dyer identifies as the crucial marker of the 'authenticity of a star image'.[23] As a Muslim carrying a Hindu name, Rattan also signified a qualified national presence. Highlighting his Muslim identity through his real name and community school, the *Filmfare* article took care to effectively offset this 'fundamental anxiety of nationalism' by emphasising his birthplace, Ajmer,[24] an iconic place of Sufi devotion for both Hindus and Muslims. A further example of Rattan fitting neatly into the fraternal unity of post-independence India was his image crystallised in *Boot Polish* of an orphan of unknown ancestry and a caring brother. It was not only the dancing Travancore sisters, who 'treated Rattan like a brother'. Even for his fans, he held a similar appeal of a lost brother and a brother to the lost. An article on fan letters received by stars reproduced the contents of a letter written in 'human blood' to 'Brother Rattan Kumar'.

Figure 6.1   Rattan Kumar as a candidate for Indian stardom
Source: *Filmfare*, 5 February 1954, 31. Image published with the permission of National Film Archives of India, Pune.

Figure 6.2 A star-profile article on Rattan Kumar
Source: *Filmfare*, 16 September 1955, 12. Image published with the permission of National Film Archives of India, Pune.

Dear Brother Rattan Kumar, this is the voice of an orphan who is begging you again and again … to visit the fatherless and poor people in their affliction and to keep himself unspotted from the world.… I am a young man … I have no job and I want to be relieved from this sinful world … but I know suicide is cowardly.… I am well-educated and prepared to be your servant.… what kind of life is this? Is it not the duty of the fortunate ones to help the unfortunate? You are my younger brother … I promise to serve you well as long as I live.[25]

Yet another letter requested the child star's photograph as a keepsake in memory of a personal loss:

I wanted to write to you ever since I saw you in 'Boot Polish'. You resemble my younger and only brother whose death when he was just in his teens caused our family an irreparable loss.… please send us your photograph.… We have no photograph of our brother who is no more with us.[26]

Successfully incarnating the Indian national orphan for eight years, Rattan left for Pakistan in 1956. Once there, his film image became implicated in an impossible situation of disavowal and entanglement, characteristic of the long-winded partition.

Traces of Migration

A search for traces of Rattan's migration yields just one reference in *Filmfare* in early 1956. It appeared in a monthly column, 'Film Letter from Pakistan', where it was reported that the actress Rehana and Rattan were working in *Kafristan*, directed by Sibtain Fazli.[27] The magazine otherwise observed a studied silence on the topic, and Rattan's migration was subtly conveyed through placement of the news from regular (national) pages to 'news from other centres' within the periodical. Across the national border, the *Pakistan Times* also casually attributed his presence in Pakistan to a film assignment, *Masoom* (Innocent, 1957). However, the Urdu film magazine *Nigar Weekly* carried a full article on Rattan's arrival, and unlike the direct interfaces of the Indian profiles, the *Nigar Weekly* article was strongly mediated by his father, Abbas Ajmeri.[28] The article set out in detail Rattan's success: his excellent acting, the gifts he received and a deluge of fan mails – no less than that of Ashok Kumar or Dilip Kumar. At the peak of his stardom, when Indian producers were reportedly getting roles written especially for him, Rattan followed his father to Pakistan. Ajmeri's own reasons were to do with his close friendship with film-makers like S. M. Yusuf and Sibtain Fazli, who had apparently influenced him to bring Rattan to Pakistan.

The article, apart from highlighting Rattan Kumar's popularity in India as a child star, was designed to negate stereotypes that get attached to child artists. Originating in autobiographical disclosures of Hollywood child stars, such a discourse accepts child stardom as 'a kind of deviance which activates the worst characteristics of the children (precociousness and arrogance) and their parents (greed and ruthlessness)'.[29] Even P. G Wodehouse's humorous take on Hollywood and its child stars, *Laughing Gas*, published in 1936, confirms the vogue for such views around child stardom with its impertinent protagonist, Joey Cooley.

> And there's about six directors I'm going to poke in the snoot, and a whole raft of supervisors and production experts. And that press agent of mine. I'm going to poke him in the snoot, all right. Yessir! Matter of fact,' he said, summing up, 'you'd have a tough time finding somebody I'm not going to poke in the snoot, once I'm big enough. I've got all their names in a little notebook.[30]

Guarding against such impressions, the *Nigar Weekly* article highlighted the fact that his father always accompanied Rattan Kumar on shoots and took particular care of the child's health. Projected as a doting father, Abbas Ajmeri stayed up all night during night shoots and prepared fresh hand-squeezed juice for his son on the sets. Such good upbringing was evident in Rattan's demeanour, which was cordial, friendly and not at all arrogant, concluded the article. In contrast, the only time Ajmeri appears in the Indian sources is in *Filmindia*, probably around the time the family migrated.

> Does Rattan Kumar play cricket?
> His father does, and he wants all producers to play cricket with him. Our so-called child stars symbolise the frustrations of their parents and you can never say what they will do next.[31]

Increasingly under the aegis of his father, the news nuggets on Rattan in Pakistan seem incongruous for his age and experience. The key form of publicity for Rattan in the hiatus of nearly two years between his arrival in Pakistan and his first film release in the country was the production news from the sets of *Masoom*. Among other 'divulgences', one was about Rattan's breakdown as the scene of his father's death was being enacted.

> Even when the father, dead on the sets, came back to life off the sets, took off his bandages and assured Rattan that he was not really an orphan, *the little man* would not believe it.[32]

The dissonance between the old Rattan, whom the Indian film magazines called a 'veteran' and an accomplished 'old hand', and this new 'little man' of Pakistan, who was now a teenager, could not be greater. Hence, one of the earliest shifts in his persona was a weakening of the orphan image and turning the clock back by presenting him as a cherished, protected and naive child. While the idea of choice remains contentious and complicated when looking at partition migration, the case of Rattan Kumar as a young boy following his father underlines 'the complex phenomenon of the child star, in which the lines of distinction between childhood and adulthood, naivety and experience, and vulnerability and power are blurred'.[33] Having nurtured acting ambitions himself, in Pakistan Ajmeri claimed a greater role and cast a large paternal shadow on Rattan's orphan persona.

Producing Pakistani Cinema in Lahore

Rattan's film trail in Pakistan reveals the labyrinth of film enterprise in post-partition Lahore. The cul-de-sacs of local production, dead ends of infrastructure and finance, the multiple exits of realism and a one-way highway of Indian imports were seen as the key challenges to Lahore film being resurrected as Pakistan cinema. With production coming to a standstill in 1947, it was only in the mid-1950s that local output picked up. Table 6.1 shows the production figures for the first decade, against available figures for Indian imports.[34] The figures for Indian imports between 1948 and 1953 are unavailable, and by all accounts the number of Indian films in Pakistani cinema halls was much higher in the first five years of independence than in the years that followed.

Table 6.1   Local production and Indian imports in Pakistan

Year	Films produced in Lahore	Indian imports
1948	01	–
1949	07	–
1950	12	–
1951	10	–
1952	07	–
1953	10	–
1954	07	8
1955	19	3
1956	32	15
1957	27	13

Source: *Report of the Film Fact Finding Committee* (Karachi: Government of Pakistan Press, 1962).

The increase in 1955 was in part due to a restrictive import policy promulgated to reconcile exhibition demand with the protection of indigenous production. Under this restrictive policy, first introduced in 1952, though implemented more strongly after the 1954 *Jaal* agitation, licenses for import were allotted only to those who invested in production. This created an artificial boom as local finance was now being increasingly channelised into local production. The policy was further modified to allow only the import of 'B'- and 'C'-class films from India, whose screening it was believed 'would not have a drastic repercussion on the exploitation of Pakistan films in their own home market'.[35] Implicit in the concession to B- and C-circuits of India doubling up as B- and C-circuits of Pakistan were the calculations of a 'national industry': such imports, while meeting the exhibition demands of Pakistan, would simultaneously secure, if not catapult, the indigenous to produce their rightful and sovereign claim to the A-circuit.

Yet what appears to have followed was simply the opposite, where with comparatively poor production facilities, lack of technical expertise and a film tradition common to both, the Lahore produce became known as *charbas*, or pale copies – and the poor relation – of Bombay films. First, the popularity of B- and C-circuit imports, especially the *Arabian Nights* fantasies, in Pakistan seems to have encouraged similar low-cost productions in Lahore since import licensing became intertwined with production. Second, a comparatively lower ratio of Indian imports also led to the trend of *charbas* of the popular Indian films that had not been released in Pakistan. Thus, I suggest that the trajectories of fantasy and *charbas* in the late 1950s are entangled with, even bequeathed by the protectionist import policy of the mid-1950s. Both these production impulses came under continuing attack and criticism from official and elite commentaries, although the posture of protectionism was never quite questioned. Given that these were also the generic constituencies of Rattan's stardom in Pakistan, I now explore the previously unstudied territories of *charba*s and fantasy in Pakistan.

The 'primrose path of plagiarism',[36] signified by the fair sprinkling of *charba*s in Pakistan's film output, has remained a consistent concern in periodic evaluations of the industry. In elite and institutional commentaries, plagiarism was seen as antithetical to national aspirations and a source of national embarrassment. Symptomatic of an 'undue veneration of foreign films', the 1961 Fact Finding Committee saw the remakes as 'acts of piracy'.[37] Just a year before, in May 1960, the first meeting of the Pakistan Film Producers Association was disrupted by a heated exchange among members on the question of plagiarised films.[38] Particularly pointed was the absence of the president of the association, Attaullah Hashmi, himself a man of dubious production practices, who had recently remade I. S. Johar's *Nastik* (Atheist, 1956) as *Daata* (Almighty, 1957) in Pakistan.[39] And 'one of the most disgraceful instances of plagiarism', as the *Pakistan Times* unambiguously chose to call it, was *Bedari* (Awakening, 1957) starring Rattan Kumar in a double role. This was the year 1957, when remakes constituted nearly 20 per cent of local production, while together with official Indian imports these comprised almost 45 per cent of the total releases.[40] The overall threat of Indian imports for local production appeared exacerbated by local imitations. Any breach of copyright rules did not bother the bold *charba* producer, as the copied film was probably not shown outside Pakistan, most certainly not in India. Often frame-by-frame remakes of Indian films, with a different set of actors and poorer production values, these films were indeed meant only for the Pakistan markets. Such remaking could be seen as a precursor to the robust film pirate economy in Pakistan enabled by video and digital bootleg from the 1980s onwards.[41]

As the critical scholarship on film remakes as well as on copyright regimes has argued, duplicates not only are standard production and distribution strategies but also 'harbour a positive power, which denies the original and the copy'.[42] Shifting attention from 'what piracy is to what piracy does',[43] I am interested in the cultural logic of emulation and its permutations. In other words, my enquiry is invested in the relationship between 'original' and 'copy', which in turn depends on the relative economic and historical positions of the two (national) producers. While remakes of foreign films (largely French) by Hollywood have predominantly been associated with cultural piracy and ideological imperialism,[44] duplicates of Hollywood films made and distributed in India have been characterised as being 'rooted in the history of colonial mimesis'.[45] This section is interested in the particular cultural puzzle constituted by the twinning represented by the South–South copy: Pakistani *charba*s of Indian films, especially those starring Rattan Kumar.

In her fascinating study of the 'too many copies of *L'Arroseur arrose*', Jane Gaines brings forth the copying epidemic in early cinema, which made it 'an unfettered period of reproduction'.[46] Identifying it as much an industry practice as an industry problem, Gaines argues for a positive spin on the business practice, which provided 'a solution to the problem of too little product to meet the demand for moving pictures'.[47] Yet at the same time Gaines does not limit the 'enthusiasm' for copying to effortless profit; equally vital is the fun of subterfuge. She acutely observes in the duplicates the beauty of the business solution: speed, economy and, most strikingly, retaliation.

It is befitting that the 'free for all' and 'property-less' moment of early cinema should provide production parallels in early Pakistan where a combination of factors such as low output, exhibition demands and absent copyright controls created a similar situation. In juxtaposition with the Indian originals, the Pakistan remakes make their divergences and exceptions to Indian narratives evident. The pleasures of these remakes, I argue, lie in their continuing the oppositional conversation or retaliation, to follow Gaines, as mobilised by the bitter partition. That these were never released in India and therefore went 'unheard' on the other side does not diminish their significance. In their limited markets, these *charba*s were not a simple veneration of Indian films. Instead, they were complexly motivated with respect to Indian films still seducing Pakistani spectators and were as much about controlling images as controlling the market. Owing their existence and immunity to the segmented markets and separate sovereign authorities in the subcontinent put in place by partition, these *charba*s were a strategy to stand up to the domination of the Indian films. Through a matrix of star and genre study, the following sections unearth the ineradicable presence of Bombay in the film culture produced in Lahore after partition.

Charba as Competition

Rattan's arrival in Pakistan was announced through the simultaneous twin-release of the star-vehicles, *Bedari* (dir. Rafiq Rizvi) and *Masoom* (dir. Shareef Nayyar). Released on 6 December 1957, *Bedari* and *Masoom* were *charba*s of Hindi films *Jagriti* (1954, dir. Satyen Bose) and *Toofan aur Diya* (Storm and Lamp, 1956, dir. Prabhat Kumar) respectively. Careful not to affect each other's business prospects, *Masoom* was released in Karachi, inaugurated by the first 'first lady' of Pakistan, Begum Nahid Mirza, at the newly built Odeon Cinema, while *Bedari* promised a 'grand gala opening' at Regent Cinema, Lahore. The business figures of the two films are not available, but all film compendiums list *Bedari* as a 'superhit' film, and *Masoom* was among the nine films selected for export to Britain for the diaspora in 1960 suggesting its comparative success among early Pakistani films.[48]

Underlining the competitive impulse, Thomas Leitch points out that a film remake operates on the paradoxical premise that the remake is just like the original, only better.[49] Since these remakes are also star vehicles, the competitive exertions are evident in Rattan's performance as well. Most crucial in this regard were the first two films, released simultaneously, that bridged Rattan's Indian past with a Pakistani future. Imbued with disavowal, confrontation and opposition, the *retaliatory charba*s were the rite of passage that Rattan went through in order to remake his stardom in Pakistan. The first among these was *Bedari*, now inventoried as a patriotic film of Pakistan[50] but at the time of its release denounced as a 'national shame'.

> When one learns that this theme has not been conceived by any of our writers but the producer has lifted it – incidents, dialogues and music, all – from the Indian prestige picture *Jagriti*, the feeling of satisfaction is at once supplanted by shame.... Minor changes in scenes, substitution of Pakistan for Hindustan, *mulk* for *desh*, Quaid-i-Azam for Gandhiji, *Pakistan Zindabad* for *Bande Matram*, and *Aye Quaid-i-Azam* for *Raghupati Raghav Raja Ram*, do not in any sense give the theme a new treatment.... Already Bombay is jeering at the Pakistan film industry.[51]

'The bad name for Pakistan' had originally travelled over the air-waves of the subcontinent as the Hindi service station of Radio Ceylon made pointed references to Pakistan's copy. Caustically pointing out that 'even copying is difficult sometimes', the review called the Pakistan version 'a primitive film' and Rattan Kumar's performance was held as a repetition of his performance in *Jagriti*. Yet a close comparison of *Bedari* with *Jagriti* reveals significant departures, which are not 'minor', at least not when the remake mobilised the very political, religious and cultural differences that a decade earlier had made Pakistan possible.

Jagriti (1954, India, dir. Satyen Bose) and *Bedari* (1957, Pakistan, dir. Rafiq Rizvi)

Itself a remake of a Bengali film *Paribartan* (Transformation, 1949, dir. Subodh Mukherjee), *Jagriti* was a Filmistan production, a studio whose very name conjures for some 'a utopian, unified realm of belonging, away from the contentious sectarian invocations of *Hindustan* and *Pakistan*'.[52] No longer available, *Paribartan* was illustrative of 'Bombay's Bengali life made possible through Bengal's infiltration of Bombay cinema in the forties and fifties'.[53] *Jagriti* too evoked colonial Bengal, specifically the *bhadralok* (upper-caste and educated gentry) through character names, spatial features of the native village, attires and actors like Abhi Bhattacharya and Pronoti Ghosh, who were a 'feature of the

Bengali-Hindi combination of the 1950s Bombay film'.[54] Yet it was Rattan Kumar whose star appeal for the Hindi film audience was the greatest and who occupied the most prominent billing on the publicity poster. It depicted Rattan, Raj and Abhi Bhattacharya, with the close-up of Rattan's face contorted in a shriek as the disproportionately large centrepiece of the triad (Figure 6.3).

A quick look at *Jagriti* sufficiently unsteadies the claim that Filmistan was somehow invested in transcending national and sectarian boundaries. In its visual codes and narrative elements, *Jagriti* is intimately connected to the affect-laden popular print and calendar art of late colonial and post-colonial India and reproduces in film the popular cartographic imagination of Mother India. Sumathi Ramaswamy's examination of the patriotic association of India with the sensuous, sacred imagery of the Mother Goddess and her hallowed sons, or the 'pictorial big men', locates the primal tension of a nation striving to be plural, secular and modern yet resorting to the time-worn figure of a Hindu goddess for its form.[55] She concludes that the undertow of a modernised Hinduism propels the imagination of India as Mother India, irrespective of the medium of imagination.

Jagriti is set in a boys' residential school to which a mischievous village boy, Ajay Mukherjee (Raj Kumar Gupta), is sent as a disciplinary measure. There he meets the disabled Shakti Chowdhary (Rattan Kumar) who is subjected to derision for his humble background; his mother (Pronoti Ghosh) is a maidservant. Both boys of exceptional capabilities, they form a deep friendship. Soon enough, under Ajay's leadership, the students manage to oust the authoritarian warden of the school, who is replaced by an equanimous teacher (Abhi Bhattacharya) with new ideas. However, resistant to discipline and defiant of any authority, Ajay threatens to dismantle the enlightened regime. Ultimately, it takes Shakti's tragic death to transform a regretful Ajay.

Themed around the pedagogical preparation of 'young sons' of India as its future guardians, *Jagriti* emphasised a motivated vigilance regarding the nation's past and present to secure the freedom hard-earned by the 'pictorial big men' of India's national movement. Ubiquitous in popular calendar art, Mahatma Gandhi, Jawaharlal Nehru, Subhash Chandra Bose and Rabindranath Tagore are also plastered on the classroom walls in *Jagriti*. These images provide crucial close-ups and cut-ins during the film. An icon unacknowledged in the photos, yet strongly present, is Swami Vivekanand, the late nineteenth-century philosopher-patriot who, of all the 'neo-Hindu figures of Bengal ... acquired and retained, over time, a pan-India and pan-Hindu resonance'.[56] Abhi Bhattacharya's broad-shouldered, draped body, straightforward stare and cross-armed postures recall the popular representation of the 'indispensable Vivekanand'.[57]

Figure 6.3 Top billing for Rattan Kumar in an advertisement of *Jagriti*
Source: *Filmfare*, 4 February 1955. Image published with the permission of National Film Archives of India, Pune.

The influence, not limited to the teacher's physical appearance, is also evident in the pedagogical approach that the film upholds, with roots in the modernist (educational) initiatives of the Bengal region, which also recalled the Gurukula system at Tagore's Shantiniketan.[58]

The suffering and wronged 'Mother India', a favourite representation in the late colonial period, is embodied in Shakti's mother (Pronoti Ghosh). Pointing out the 'Bengal Beginnings' of the Mother India icon, Ramaswamy refers to the rare but extremely charged depictions of maternal acts, which work through the Mother's relationship with her sons of different religious communities.[59] In the song 'Chalo Chalein Maa' (Let Us Go then Mother), Pronoti Ghosh, with long hair and flowing sari, sits under a large tree with her incapacitated son, Shakti, leaning in her lap while Ajay lurks around. The song sequence evokes the painting 'Bande Matarang' (I Worship the Mother) that appeared in *Balak*, a Bengali children's magazine, where mother (India) 'appears seated in a densely planted grove with a naked infant in her lap and other babies at play around her.'[60] Mother India's inclusive yet equivocally imagined maternality is central to *Jagriti*. The divided territories (Indian and Pakistan) of the subcontinent are anthropomorphised and individualised as Ajay and Shakti respectively. Played by Rattan, Shakti's incapacitated existence references the famous words of Jinnah on a 'maimed, mutilated and moth-eaten' Pakistan and the accompanying doubts over its survival.[61] Thus, his handicap, accident and death, as a violent loss affecting transformation, could well signify the partition of the subcontinent – especially of Bengal in the east.

Enacting the imperfection and death of the nation to which Rattan eventually migrated required a disavowal performed in the same affective currency as the one cobbled together by *Jagriti*. While Rattan's performance in the mythologising *Jagriti* may have bolstered the patriotic credentials of his star image in India, in Pakistan it boded a political anathema. *Bedari* was therefore child star Rattan's declaration of allegiance to Pakistan, which could only be constituted through a blow-by-blow dismantling of all that he had done in *Jagriti* and what *Jagriti* had done to him. Retaliation was a way of managing the contradiction that was threatening to burst at the seams of Rattan's charisma. Thus came about *Bedari*, the first film produced by his family production company, Film Hayat. It was directed by Rafiq Rizvi, another recent film migrant from Bombay.

In a renegade fashion, *Bedari* transforms a patriotic Indian film into a 'gift to the [Pakistan] nation'.[62] In its corrections, *Bedari* reveals the excisions and selections of the original and appropriates the narrative of *Jagriti*, in order to get back at it. Grafted onto a new context and repurposed for a new political situation, the remake fulfilled particular needs. The new context of Pakistan where *Bedari* was set and meant to be disseminated required obvious changes in markers of identity like names, clothes and language. Ajay became Zafar and Shakti became Sabir. Instead of wearing a high-caste Bengali *dhoti* and eating on the low-rise wooden platform, the steadfast Anglo-Mohammaden paternal figure (played by Abbas Ajmeri) was dressed in a *sherwani* and ate on a dining table. While a recalcitrant Ajay scribbled his decision to go to school in Devanagari, Zafar did so in the Persian script. While *Bedari* covered nearly all of the action of a 180-minute-long *Jagriti*, it did so in an abridged form of 130 minutes and is faster paced. As a copy, it does away with formal niceties like establishing shots and smooth segues between sequences as a way to undermine the polite (yet problematic) 'stability' of the original. Nearly an hour shorter than the original, *Bedari* unfolds in an episodic manner, which is linked by inserts of the film title at regular intervals emphasising its Pakistan provenance.

However, the most significant changes of *Bedari* are evident in the pointed corrections of counteractive histories, song lyrics and the double roles of Rattan Kumar.

Bedari replaces the modern Indian national icons of *Jagriti*, namely Mahatma Gandhi, Jawaharlal Nehru, Subhash Chandra Bose and Rabindranath Tagore with Quaid-i-Azam Jinnah, Liaquat Ali and Mohammad Iqbal. The medieval heroes are duly replaced by Central Asian warriors like Bin-Qasim, Saladdin and Mahmud Ghazni. In the open-air history lessons, *Jagriti* rejects the Aryan invasion theory, whereas *Bedari* reinforces the iconoclasm of Mahmud Ghazni.[63] The play performed by students in *Jagriti* celebrates the (Hindu) militaristic figures, Maharana Pratap and Shivaji, known for their opposition to the Mughal state. In response, the play in *Bedari* features Akbar, Birbal, Jahangir and Anarkali – the part-legendary, part-historical but nonetheless charismatic Mughal quartet. Unclaimed by *Jagriti*, the Muslim figures associated with the subcontinent, medieval or modern, are at *Bedari*'s uncontested disposal as forerunners of the modern Muslim political state.

Jagriti features a total of four songs, while the remake, *Bedari*, has five. Retaining the tunes and overall lyrics of the original songs of *Jagriti*, *Bedari* repurposes them for the different context. The only addition introduced in the Pakistan version and thus 'bettering' the original is the 'food *qawwali*', sung enthusiastically by residential schoolboys tired of the repetitive menu of *daal*, or lentils. Poking fun at the obese and gluttonous warden, the boys revel in enumerating their favourite non-vegetarian delicacies associated with the Central Asian and Persian influence on subcontinental food like *kofte* (meatballs), *kebab* (meat cutlets) and *biryani* (meat rice). The petulant protests of students in *Jagriti* against the missing fish in the Bengali curry finds an accentuated counter in a somewhat ostentatious 'Muslim food' *qawwali* of *Bedari*.

The first song, 'Chalo Chalein Ma (Let Us Go then Mother), in *Bedari* transforms the forlorn yet calm, disabled son of Mother India in *Jagriti* into an anguished, embittered as well as disabled adolescent of *Bedari*, who lip-syncs the changed lines with a pointed grimace. The mother in *Bedari* is discernibly Punjabi in her attire and physical build, and is self-evidently actress Ragini, who debuted in pre-partition Lahore's Punjabi sensation, *Dulla Bhatti* (1938, dir. Roop Shorey). Changing the somewhat ambiguous and lyrical references of the original, the remake imposes one particular affect more strongly: that of indignation, severance and self-realisation. The change often comes at the expense of the metre, both poetic and melodic.

> *Chalo chalein Ma sapnon ke gaon mein*
> *Kaaton se dur kahin phoolon ki chhaon mein*
> *Ho rahe ishaare reshmi ghataon mein* (Jagriti)
> *Kaise koi jee sake dukh bhari fizaaon mein* (Bedari)

> Let us go then Mother to the idyllic dreamland
> Far from thorns, to the gentle shade of flowers
> The silken overcast clouds signal (*Jagriti*)
> How can one live in oppressive surroundings (*Bedari*)

Rehna mere sang Ma har dum
Aisa na ho ki bichad jaen hum
Ghoomna hai humko dur ki dishaon mein (Jagriti)
Mere sach ki duniya hai tumhare paon mein (Bedari)

Stay with me forever, Mother
Lest we get separated
Leisurely we will wander in directions afar (*Jagriti*)
My true world lies beneath your feet (*Bedari*)

The last replacement is a reference to a Hadith, making the mother of *Bedari* an Islamic one, with paradise at her feet.[64]

Appearing after the tragic death of Shakti, the last song in *Jagriti*, 'Hum Laye Hain Toofan Se' (We Have Ferried through a Storm), is a post-trauma articulation. It mobilises primordial obligations by linking past sacrifices to future compliance through a status quo. Endorsing a Nehruvian commitment to the non-aligned movement and anti-nuclear position in the international diplomatic realm, the stance of restraint and caution is unceremoniously dropped towards the end and raised instead is the teacher's fist calling forth the tricolour flag to be fixed on the peaks. Signalling a decisive shift in lyrics, crescendo and gestures, *Jagriti* ends on a rather thinly veiled reference to Kashmir. It is certainly interpreted as such by the corresponding song in *Bedari*, where going past the Quran and portraits of Muslim medieval warriors, suggested as inspirations for national foreign policy, the teacher reaches the map of Pakistan with ambiguous territorial limits. Not mincing any words, he reminds the students that Kashmir remains to be conquered and what must flutter on the peaks is the crescent moon and star banner.

Lena abhi Kashmir hai yeh baat na bhoolo
Kashmir pe lehrana hai jhanda uchhal ke (Bedari)

Kashmir remains to be conquered, do not forget
Throw the flag high to flutter there (*Bedari*)

However, the cherry on *Jagriti*'s patriotic cake was the most popular eulogy to Mahatma Gandhi, 'Sabarmati ke Sant' (Oh Saint of Sabarmati). Cast in the favourite song genre of Gandhi, the *bhajan*, or devotional song, it extolled the virtues of Mahatma's pacifist nationalist movement (Figures 6.4a and 6.4b).

De di humein azaadi bina khadag bina dhaal
Sabarmati ke sant tune kar diya kamaal (Jagriti)

You made us free without a sabre or a shield
Oh saint of Sabarmati you performed a miracle (*Jagriti*)

Visually, the scene consisted of a decorated hall in the school, filled with students facing the bust of a smiling Gandhi, on a raised platform surrounded by flowers, ceremonial lamps and garlands. Propped up by his crutches, Shakti (Rattan Kumar) lip-synced the ode sung by Asha Bhonsle, standing a little ahead of the rest and closer to Gandhi. The crowd of students behind Rattan stood with their heads lowered and hands folded and, as appropriate to their station, joined in the chorus refrain. A special relationship is established in the song by cutting predominantly between close-up shots of Rattan and panning-shots of Gandhi's statue, imbuing Rattan with a Gandhian charisma. The song irrevocably linked a teary-eyed Rattan with the Father of the Indian Nation, and nearly all songs in *Jagriti* were a staple for repeated TV telecast and radio transmission each year on 'national days', including Gandhi's birth and death anniversaries, Independence Day and Republic Day.

Figure 6.4a   A bust of Gandhi against the national tricolour
Source: Screenshot from *Jagriti* (1954), DVD, Ultra.

Figure 6.4b   Shakti (Rattan Kumar) 'singing' the ode to Gandhi
Source: Screenshot from *Jagriti* (1954), DVD, Ultra.

Figure 6.5a   Jinnah's portrait in the *Bedari* song
Source: Screenshot from *Bedari* (1957), VCD.

Figure 6.5b   Sabir (Rattan Kumar) 'singing' the ode to Jinnah
Source: Screenshot from *Bedari* (1957), VCD.

Figure 6.5c   The appearance of a footage of Gandhi–Jinnah negotiations in Bombay, 1944, in *Bedari*
Source: Screenshot from *Bedari* (1957), VCD.

The hold of the Gandhian charisma could only be countered, remade and in the process broken, by invoking the man with the most compelling charm in Pakistan: Mohammad Ali Jinnah. Logically enough, 'Ae Quaid-i-Aazam' (Oh Supreme Leader) replaced the Saint of Sabarmati in the *Bedari* eulogy.

> *Yun di humein azaadi ki duniya hui hairaan*
> *Ae Qaid-i-Azam tera ehsaan hai ehsaan* (Bedari)

> The world stood astonished at how you made us free
> Oh Supreme leader we are indeed indebted. (*Bedari*)

Marked by a *darsanic* mode, the paean in Jagriti is restricted to the indoor space of a prayer meeting, fixed on the beheld object and charged by the beholder's devotion. There are no diversions in this visually sealed space. In contrast, in *Bedari* there is a discomfort with the idolatrous aesthetics of the original eulogy (Figures 6.5a and 6.5b). A visually guarded adulation of Jinnah involved replacing the bust with a portrait and bleached-out stock-shots of his tomb, at the time still under construction in Karachi. It was no longer the relationship of the beholder–beheld, but a more distant and unfixed perspective. More striking is the generous use of newsreel stock footage in the song, breaking away from the indoor space and combining historic film footage of General Archibald Wavell recording a radio speech, a reference perhaps to the Shimla Conference of June 1945; Jinnah inspecting army formations; the celebrations of 14 August 1947, Pakistan's independence day; and military operations of the Pakistan army, suggesting perhaps the 1948 war with India over Kashmir. Significantly enough, *Bedari* challenged *Jagriti* (and India) where it truly hurt, that is, by making partition paramount. Insofar as *Jagriti* celebrated Gandhi's non-violent leadership of India's independence, this had been made possible only by a careful avoidance of any mention of partition. On the other hand, *Bedari* filled the visual space of its song with newsreel footage of refugee camps and the migrating populace, turning a representational constraint on its head by synchronising a colonial documentary form with an Islamic idiom in which willingly leaving one's homeland for the sake of faith has a strong resonance. While the eulogy to Gandhi identifies colonialism as the enemy and extols the virtues of non-violence, its counterpart in *Bedari* identifies Gandhi as the enemy by using the Indian News Parade film footage of the Gandhi–Jinnah Bombay negotiations of 1944 (Figure 6.5c) and unidentified military operations appearing *ad nauseam*, thus subverting the original ode across several registers.[65] *Bedari*'s eulogy ultimately posed the question of what was more exceptional: the independence of India or the attainment of Pakistan. While the partition footage besmirched any claims of a non-violent independence, *Bedari*'s celebration of the Quaid's miracle further dented *Jagriti*'s grandiose claim of exceptionality.

However, *Bedari*'s most outlandish departure was Rattan Kumar's double role: he played both his original role of the disabled boy Shakti/Sabir and that of the lead protagonist Zafar/Ajay. This fantastical premise of likeness, though acknowledged in the film, was hardly of any consequence to the plot. They were not twins separated at birth but friends who preposterously looked the same. Ironically, some elements of the films, like the instance of exchanging photographs between friends and coping with the tragic death, worked better with the identical friends premise of the Pakistan *charba*. With roots in magic and the occult, the ultimate power of the doppelgänger is expressive of both death and immortality. Otto Rank's psychoanalytical explanation of the double motif finds it posing a question of identity: 'the confrontation of man with himself [*sic*]'.

> The most prominent symptom of the forms which the double takes is a powerful consciousness of guilt which forces the hero no longer to accept the responsibility for certain actions of his ego, but to place it upon another ego, a double.[66]

The conundrum of Rattan's star image after migration to Pakistan, like the case of contrasting identities within a single mind, generates the double as a mechanism of self-preservation. Through the double role, *Bedari* simultaneously punishes 'Rattan' for his Indian act by killing off the homologous disabled character and reboots him as the able-bodied Pakistan. 'Intensifying star presence',[67] the double in *Bedari* offers the pleasure of a migrant star working through his changed nationality as well as offering a forthright denouement. In *Jagriti*, Shakti's death leaves the mother grief-stricken and nearly mad. While Ajay resolves to take responsibility for her, she continues to search for her dead son, suggestive of the haunting partition. After a brief interlude of reflection, the narrative moves to focus on Ajay's achievements, leaving the strand of the inconsolable mother unresolved. However, in *Bedari*, because of their identical looks, Zafar could convincingly dress up like Sabir and 'become' him to reassure the mother. The film ends with the duo walking into the horizon, with the surviving 'son' of *Bedari* at the side of the mother(land). Despite a much inferior technical quality, the fantastical premise of unrelated yet identical friends affords *Bedari* a more comforting finish and the projection of a more effective, 'bettered' nationalism.

One is tempted to pose a few 'what-ifs' regarding the circulatory context of the songs and the film. What if cinema-going Indians had seen the corrections of *Bedari*, especially the particular form of disavowal of a national hero by a child star? The replacement of Gandhi by Jinnah would have been considered incendiary in India and an added act of treason by a star wishing to rework his national stardom. What if the announcer on Radio Ceylon with audiences across the subcontinent who shamed Pakistan had also mentioned Rattan's transgression? What if the silence maintained was not merely for an already precarious image of the Muslim minority of India but more importantly to conceal the artifice that nationalism necessarily entailed? After all, *Jagriti*'s songs, including Rattan's ode to Gandhi, continued to be Indian patriotic songs par excellence until the liberal nineties introduced a more consumer-based and insouciant register of patriotism quite unlike the self-sacrificing and apprehensive tone of *Jagriti*. In Pakistan, there was a greater likelihood of familiarity with the Indian version, through illegal screenings of smuggled prints, maybe even a formal release, together with the movement of people across borders, Indian film magazines, song booklets and radio transmissions. *Bedari* was one of the eight commercial successes of the year. The pleasure of *Bedari* in Pakistan and its later status as a patriotic film, I suggest, lie in elaborating a severance and embodying an antithesis, the overriding cultural logic of *charba*s in Pakistan, making them doppelgängers materialised by partition

Toofan aur Diya (*1956, India, dir. Prabhat Kumar*) *and* **Masoom** (*1957, Pakistan, dir. Shareef Nayyar*)

Masoom was released first in Karachi, then the administrative capital of Pakistan and also where large numbers of Urdu-speaking migrants of North India referred to as *muhajir*s settled after partition. Rattan and his family were also *muhajir*s and set up their production company, Film Hayat, in the city.[68] If *Bedari* was a rite of passage for Rattan to become Pakistani, then *Masoom* was the psychoanalyst's couch customised for a *muhajir* star's performance.

The opening sequence in *Masoom* is a nod to Rattan's migration to Pakistan and his father Abbas Ajmeri's key role as a guardian. The title credit sequence in

Rajkamal's *Toofan aur Diya* introduces the motif of a temple lamp incandescent in a storm; *Masoom* replaces it with the image of a boat caught in a strong current of adversarial waters. Through an image match, the tiny boat on choppy waters dissolves into a stylised pattern of a high-mast sail on the doors of a house, one also highly reminiscent of the political symbol of Pakistan: the crescent and star. The shuddering windows and thunderbolt-lit panes of a writer's house separate the storm outside from one within. In the throes of dejection and desperation, the writer (Abbas Ajmeri) battles failure while his young son, Shaheen (Rattan), rushes to light a candle and pacify his father. The emotional exchange that follows between the two is marked by a loaded cut-in of philosopher-poet Iqbal's portrait on the wall. The name Shaheen itself recalls 'Iqbal's conception of the model youth'.[69]

Suddenly, on the street outside, a one-legged vagabond hopping on a crutch appears and smashes a windowpane of the house. Shaheen fearlessly chases him into the street outside, followed by his concerned father. As the storm bellows and shakes, Shaheen is nearly hit by a falling flowerpot. Reaching out just in time, the writer saves his son and regains his lost confidence. Akin to a nightmare, the sequence links disparate occurrences in the physical world (storm, burglar, falling flowerpot) with inner psychological turmoil, insecurities and reawakening.

The film review in the *Pakistan Times* also revisited the striking opening sequence. Producing a verbatim translation of the father's dialogue of vindication, the review found the speeches 'long and tedious' and remarked that 'such emotional outbursts hardly suit the occasion'.[70] Further, commenting on the verses of the credits song just before the opening sequence, the review found the jumbling together of a raging boat, a fatigued seafarer, a flag of hope and a rock of strength, meaningless. This melange of images, symbols, verses, characters and occurrences is not linked by causality and has a tenuous connection to the overall plot. Yet, given that it was Rattan Kumar and his father who played the father–son duo, the sequence was alluding to the biographical dimensions of a star vehicle. The difficult migratory journey implied in evocations of a fraught boat and a fatigued mariner who finally arrives in a rock-like home where the flag of hope flutters, insisted on a political spin to Rattan's arrival. Having a literary precedent in the late nineteenth century, nautical imagery was commonly invoked in the quest for self-awareness and self-realisation by Muslim writers of undivided India.[71] The above sequence in *Masoom*, apart from introducing the key protagonists of the film, Shaheen, his father, his sister and the limping criminal beggar, conceived Rattan's migratory journey in the idiom of Muslim self-realisation.

Masoom was not a close remake of Rajkamal studio's *Toofan aur Diya*, which revolved around Sadanand (Satish Vyas), an exceptional son of a posthumously celebrated writer, who struggles to provide for a still penurious family. A series of setbacks – the demise of their mother, the hasty departure of the sister's suitor and a liquidated house – force Sadanand and his sister to seek refuge in a Shiv temple. Here the ascetic caretaker of the temple extends his support to the siblings. Through hard work, enterprise and divine blessings, Sadanand gets a medical cure for his sister, saves her suitor's life and facilitates their wedding. Respite is also in store for him at the end as the ascetic resolves to provide for the exceptional boy and send him to school.

There were instances of close parallels but a different narrative trajectory in the Pakistan remake. The pre-release publicity for *Masoom* ran sensational advertisements calling it a 'shocking' and 'daring' film.[72] In the 1950s it was common for Hollywood melodramas, many of which found their way into Pakistan as well, to be presented as 'slick' and 'sexually explicit' and therefore daring.[73] While none of this was true for *Masoom*, what was certainly unusual about the film was its incorporation of a Gothic sub-narrative within melodramatic realism. This included two instances of approaching death in *Masoom*, represented as the shadow of a large winged figure cast on the victim. Gruesome and tailing shadows as the inescapable past clinging onto a person have been part of the universe of the doppelgänger narratives.[74] The modus operandi of *Masoom*, to better itself against *Toofan aur Diya*, was firstly to heighten the exceptionality of the boy protagonist and secondly to replace the narrative space of the Shiv temple by an underworld of maimed beggars, pickpockets, pimps and prostitutes.

Making the boy protagonist traverse greater contrast of subjecthood heightens Rattan's exceptionality in *Masoom*, which retains the provider-father figure for the first third of the film, thus allowing Rattan to play the carefree and cherished child in that duration. This was unlike *Toofan aur Diya*, where a fatherless Sadanand works hard throughout to fill the void of the breadwinner of the family. Yet, being a star-vehicle much depended on Rattan coming into his own within the film. Therefore, when the father dies, the 'challenges' that Shaheen overcomes are extraordinary, more pronounced and exaggerated than the ones in *Toofan aur Diya*. *Masoom* emphasised Shaheen's exceptionality making him 'the ideal child, the superman, who is not yet a man'.[75] His transformation from a treasured child to an independent adolescent follows a trajectory that is the reverse of Sadanand's, as evident in the closing sequences. In *Toofan aur Diya*, after a modest temple wedding, Sadanand bids a tearful farewell to his sister who departs in a modest bullock cart. The sobbing orphan boy finally receives a guardian at the end when the temple ascetic pledges to provide for him. In *Masoom*, Shaheen marries off his sister in a visibly grander style and she goes off in a car. While sombre at this parting, Shaheen marches ahead, independent and confident. In a low angle close-up, Rattan's smiling face is juxtaposed with the small boat in choppy seas.

The other more significant departure of *Masoom* was the introduction of the Gothic element of a syndicate of criminal beggars. This world, while seemingly separate and distant, comes in close proximity with Shaheen's, as his sister's suitor, Amjad, gets falsely implicated in a murder. In exchange for his life, Amjad agrees to hand over his sweetheart to the criminal beggars. In its nightmarish quality, *Masoom* is the unconscious of *Toofan aur Diya*. Appearing as a sub-plot to the larger narrative, it inserts itself in significant ways into the line of causality of the film's narrative. It substitutes the straightforward, even simplistic, motives within *Toofan aur Diya* such as the beau's departure, the ascetic's lifestyle and the stage-dancer's compulsions, with nefarious and bizarre designs of complex characters. It again offers a more compelling narrative proposition despite verging on the fantastical. The limping intruder introduced in the opening sequence, played by another pre-partition Lahore actor, M. Ismail, is the chief of a syndicate of dangerous beggars who blackmail, trap and even kill ordinary men and women. He blackmails Amjad to dupe Shaheen's sister into prostitution. However, Amjad undergoes a change of heart and confronts the beggar chief with a refusal. In retaliation, the beggar and his army of armless, legless underclass capture Amjad and torture him in a cave-like den.[76] Reminiscent of the many such wondrous caves in *Arabian Nights* fantasies, Amjad is finally rescued by Shaheen, who adroitly navigates the den, avoiding its tricks and traps.

Noting 'feats bordering on the incredible', the review of *Masoom* was critical of the 'missing vital links' in the script, which left the audiences to 'conjure more than is normally allowed'.[77]

> For instance nobody knows how Shaheen knew of Amjad's presence in Lahore, how he reached his place of confinement, how he, a mere boy of 13 or 14, managed to lift up and out of the den an invalid as heavy as Habib [Amjad].

The key to these questions lay in invoking an alternate image of Rattan, as also a star of Oriental-adventure and miraculous, mythological films in India, like *Baghdad*, *Laila Majnu* and *Ekadashi*. One of his crucial successes in this genre was S. S. Vasan's *Bahot Dinn Hue*. A reworking of the Ramayana legend, the imprint of *Bahot Dinn Hue* would linger on in Rattan's appearance in the fantasy genre in Pakistan. Playing a young prince whose parents have been bewitched and trapped by the powerful wizard Bhadrachamund, Rattan performs equally incredible feats in a film more obviously located in the fantastic. Pleased with Rattan's work, S. S. Vasan had given him a car as a token of appreciation. In the course of the film, Rattan had also learnt swimming, riding and, most importantly, fencing. Long popularised by Douglas Fairbank's swashbuckling hero in *The Thief of Baghdad* (1925), 'the most popular film ever shown in India',[78] fencing would be a crucial star skill that Rattan would carry to Pakistan. Thus, familiarity with wondrous caves and their entrapments lay in Rattan's persona and was independent of the coordinates of verisimilitude of *Masoom*. With self-inflicted blows to his persona linked to social and neo- realism, Rattan's adolescent 'adulthood' from this point onwards moves into the realm of fantasy.

Charba as Loss

The recent histories of early Bombay cinema have emphasised the considerable presence of the 'Islamicate oriental' ethos of the early talkies of the Indian subcontinent.[79] These hybrid fantasies, often also referred to as costume dramas, drew on the *Arabian Nights* stories while further intensifying the eclecticism of this transcultural body of stories. Rosie Thomas points out that extravagant spectacles of romance, adventure and magic characterised these, with novelties like 'oriental' dances, fighting, wrestling, acrobatics and other low-brow entertainments. The popularity of the hybrid fantasies of course preceded the advent of cinema, as these were a staple fare of the Parsi theatre. Reproduced here is an extract from Sajjad Zaheer's recollection of watching Urdu – Parsi theatre in his childhood days.

> The theme of the play was taken from anywhere: Shakespeare's plays changed beyond recognition; old Indian legends and stories from the *Arabian Nights* (eg. Raja Harishchandra, Princess Bakaoli and the Magic Flower), Classical Persian romances (eg. Shirin Farhad) etc. One was transported to a world of kings, lovely princesses, heroes, and evil men and women, joined in mortal combats of Good and Evil – crude, simple and direct. The costumes were a fantastic mixture of medieval modes of Indian aristocracy and Elizabethan style. There was nothing of realism in these plays.[80]

While in the later silent era (1925–1934) the fantasy and costume films accounted for nearly 40 per cent of production,[81] the arrival of sound inundated the early talkies with the ethos – 'orientalism, action and magic' – and experience of Urdu–Parsi theatre.[82] Many playwrights of the Parsi theatre were active in the early talkie period, of which Agha Hashr Kashmiri, Munshi Dil and Hakim Ahmad Shuja are particularly relevant to cinema in later-day Pakistan.[83] While Kaushik Bhaumik brackets this 'cosmopolitan *bazaar* cinema' in the period between 1928 and 1935, coinciding with the advent of the talkies, Rosie Thomas charts the enduring popularity of the 'hybrid fantasies' all the way through to pre- and post-independence Bombay. What is beyond dispute is that these films embodied a more cosmopolitan global modernity drawing from Urdu–Parsi theatre and Indo-Persian literary tradition, providing an alternative to both a Hinduised refraction of modernity and a Westernised one.

In her history of Bombay film from below, Thomas challenges the received histories of the waning popularity of stunt and magic films and the ascendancy of the social as the monolithic form from 1940s onwards. She argues that this neglect of magic, or *jadoo*, films is linked to their subaltern status, manifest in their B- and C-circuit identity as well as a disparaging tag of Mohammedan films.[84] Placing it in a pre-partition demographic perspective, Thomas points out that while 'the Islamicate world of the film(s) was undoubtedly designed ... to appeal to India's large Muslim audiences of the day', ultimately the aim was to reach a larger crossover audience.[85] This is evident in the wide and continuing popularity of the 'hybrid fantasy' in India in the mid-1950s when fantasy and costume films together accounted for nearly a third of all production in Bombay. In particular, three *Arabian Nights* hybrids made by film-maker Homi Wadia – *Aladdin and the Wonderful Lamp* (1952), *Alibaba and 40 Thieves* (1954) and *Hatimtai* (1956) – became top box-office successes.

If the 'hybrid fantasies' remained popular in India in the 1950s, despite the demographic shift associated with partition, these also saw a resurgence in Pakistan. Through the late 1950s and early 1960s, there is a strong presence of hybrid fantasies in Lahore. Undoubtedly, a crucial factor in this was the performative and narrative traditions of the region, attested by the Parsi theatre's extreme popularity in pre-partition Lahore as well as the strong tradition of *qissa-dastan* storytelling in Punjab.[86] Popularity of the *qissa-dastan* was evident in the popularity of folklore films like *Sassi* (1954), *Heer* (1955) and *Dulla Bhatti* (1956). But a decisive role must also have been played by the continued presence of these Indian films in the Pakistan market and the restrictive film policy discussed before.

Therefore, the year Rattan arrived in Pakistan, that is 1956, which also had a near-double increase in production, the locally produced box-office blockbuster was *Sarfarosh* (1956). *Sarfarosh* was set in medieval Baghdad with the world of bandits, viziers, kings and henchmen. It had a bandit-hero who would dutifully offer prayers in the midst of loot and a heroine who died in a military combat wearing an Arab *keffiyeh*, a Rudoph Valentino inspired trend of the early talkies but also refashioned in the fifties as a symbol of Palestinian nationalism. Later in the year, Karachi producer J. C. Anand made *Hatim*, a story of the 'most generous man of the Arab world' taken from the *Arabian Nights*, just a few months after Homi Wadia's Bombay spectacular and first full-colour film, *Hatimtai* (1956). Both were, in turn, cinematic successors of, among others, Krishnatone's early talkie, *Hatimtai* (1934, dir. G. R. Sethi). In 1959, J. C. Anand would venture again into the territory of fantasy and remake, by making *Alam Ara* (Ornament of the World, 1959) in Pakistan, inspired by the first talkie of the subcontinent, *Alam Ara* (1931).

Nearly a year after *Sarfarosh*, in late 1957, the theatres in Lahore – while offering a mixed fare of Indian films and European, Hollywood and local production – were decidedly partial towards an *Arabian Nights* ethos. While migrant film-maker W. Z. Ahmad's *Wadah* (Promise, 1957, Pakistan) and Indian *Sangdil* (Hard-hearted, original Indian release: 1952) would have represented the more respectable fare, the *Pakistan Times* classifieds announced the opening of Homi Wadia's *Aladdin and the Wonderful Lamp* (1954, India), the twenty-first week of Munshi Dil's *Ishq-e-Laila* (Love of Laila, 1957, Pakistan) and the release of Yves Allegret's *Oasis* (1955, France and Germany), an adventure film set against the backdrop of desert, date trees and camels. Munshi Dil's *Ishq-e-Laila* was the more successful film adaptation of the Laila–Majnu legend released that year, the other being *Laila Majnu* (1957, Pakistan), Anwar Kamal's follow-up film after *Sarfarosh*. This was neither the first instance of Laila Majnu's cinematic adaptation nor even that of a competitive release of two *Laila Majnus*. In 1931, two rival film companies of colonial India – the Madan studios at Calcutta and Krishna Movietone at Bombay – produced two *Laila Majnus* simultaneously.[87] The legend had also been remade in post-partition Bombay as *Laila Majnu* (1952, India) directed by K. Amarnath. Apart from sharing the legend and cinematic traditions, the Indian–Pakistani remakes were additionally entangled through the Film Hayat family as Rattan had played the childhood role of Majnu in Amarnath's *Laila Majnu* (Indian), while four years later, his elder brother Wazir Ali was credited as a crewmember in Munshi Dil's *Ishq-i-Laila* (Pakistan).[88]

In a manner befitting an *Arabian Nights* hybrid, *Ishq-i-Laila*'s continued presence in the *Pakistan Times* classified advertisements at the time of the release of Rattan's first films in Pakistan in early December 1957 was prescient for his later career (Figure 6.4). Equally indicative, given the popularity of quasi-*Arabian Nights* settings, was the release of 'recently ban-lifted' *Raqqasa* (Dancer) on the same day as *Bedari* and *Masoom*. A 'cocktail of dances, songs, fun and frolics', this was a filmed performance of Samia Jamaal, the personal dancer of former king of Egypt, Farooq.[89] The novelty of beguiling dances would be a feature of Rattan's sword-fighting films in the years to come, featuring a sensuous Neelo.[90] The final image in the classified, which would also set up a thematic correspondence with Rattan's later films as well as shifts within the *Arabian Nights* hybrids, was *Noor-e-Islam* (Light of Islam, 1957, Pakistan). A story of the 'clash between Infidels and Faithfuls', *Noor-e-Islam* set into motion the cycle of pseudo-historical combat films featuring superhuman Muslim heroes.[91] These stories were closer to the great prose epics, which built in stories from the crusades and were extremely popular in medieval Egypt.[92] Not surprisingly, *Noore Islam* (1934, Bombay) was an early talkie too, listed as a costume film and produced by Trilok Cine.

Figure 6.6 *Bedari* and *Masoom* in newspaper classifieds
Source: *Pakistan Times*, 6 December 1957.

Thus, through the late 1950s and well into the early 1960s, cinema halls in Lahore continued to play Hollywood *Arabian Nights* fantasies and orientalist desert adventures set against contemporary geopolitics, Indian *Arabian Nights* hybrids and the homegrown *Arabian Nights* hybrids. The cinema-goers of Lahore in June 1961 were spoilt for choice as far as oriental fantasies were concerned. On offer were the Indian fantasy *Saqi* (Cup Bearer, 1952), the Rattan Kumar-starring Pakistani *Sher-e-Islam* (Lion of Islam, 1961), two films from Hollywood – *Wizard of Baghdad* (1960) in cinemascope and Columbia Pictures' *1001 Nights* (1945) in technicolour and translated in Urdu as 'Chiragh-e-Alladin'. In addition to these, Munshi Dil was following up on his *Ishq-e-Laila* success with 'an Urdu–Parsi theatre favourite', *Gul Bakavali* (Flower of Bakavali, 1961). The story of Taj-ul-Mulk's adventurous quest for the miracle flower Bakawali had its earliest known film version, *Gul Bakavali* (1924, Bombay), made by the Kohinoor Film Company. This was followed by its remake as a talkie in 1932 by Saroj Company. Remade in the subcontinent several times since and in several languages, Lahore got its Punjabi version by the city's cinema *seth*, Dalsukh Pancholi, in 1938. The *Gul Bakavali* of Pakistan was released in 1961 on the fourth anniversary of the 'Green Revolution', the first military coup of Pakistan in 1957, and was advertised as the latest 'revolution in Film Industry of Pakistan' for introducing colour technology into local films.[93] With its opening and closing sequences shot in colour, the film also introduced new narrative details that capitalised on a star voice, generic formula and contemporary audience. Among the 'new tricks', the review noted, was one cognisant of a changed demography that the remake was addressing.

> Munshi Dil has been in the game too long to forget that his *audience is all Muslim*. Bakauli will have her freedom but not before Noor Jehan's singing of a prayer has demolished the idols around.[94]

Munshi Dil had indeed been in the game too long. A Parsi theatre playwright whose film activities had clearly not been limited to early talkies in Bombay, Dil had once insisted on retaining the 'artificial lilt of theatrical betbaji [*sic*]' for dialogues in the film *Shikari* (The Hunter, 1934).[95] The centrality of Urdu–Parsi drama to early cinema in Pakistan is evident in the continued association of three men of Urdu drama with Islamicate Oriental film enterprise in Pakistan. These were Munshi Dil, Imtiaz Ali Taj and Hakim Ahmad Shuja. The playwright of *Anarkali* in 1922, Imtiaz Ali Taj also wrote the screenplay of its film version, *The Loves of a Mughal Prince* (1928), and adapted it once again as *Anarkali* (1958) in Pakistan. *Anarkali* had also been adapted in India by Nandlal Jaswantlal in 1954 and of course the most popular of all adaptations remains *Mughal-e-Azam* (1960, India). In Pakistan, Taj also wrote the script of *Chanway* (Moon, 1951), *Gulnar* (Pomegranate Flower, 1953) and an adaptation of the *masanawi*, *Zehr-e-Ishq* (The Poison of Love, 1958). *Zehr-e-Ishq* had also been adapted in 1933 during the early talkie period by Jayant Cinetone in Bombay. Taj's *Anarkali* (1958, Pakistan) was directed by Anwar Kamal Pasha, who Mushtaq Gazdar calls the 'first indigenous film-maker of Pakistan'.[96] Director of the hit *Sarfarosh* and the flop *Laila Majnu*, Anwar Kamal Pasha was the son of Urdu dramatist Hakim Ahmad Shuja. It was Shuja's novel *Baap ke Gunah* (The Sin of Father) that Pasha had adapted for his first film, *Do Ansoo* (Two Teardrops, 1950), one of the earliest surviving and most successful films of Pakistan.

Sharing a relationship of the remake with not merely the Indian hybrid fantasy cycle of 1950s but also referencing the magical heyday of the early talkies, the *Arabian Nights* hybrids had captured the imagination of local enterprise in Pakistan. This went beyond film and is conspicuous in the listings of Rustom Sohrab bicycles and Alladin Flashlight batteries. The busy newspaper classifieds reveal a penchant for fantasy films, in which tensile film narratives accommodate the marvellous with the mundane, and many modernist Urdu playwrights of erstwhile, undivided India came to be associated with film enterprise in Pakistan. Together these invoked the past world of the early talkies, synchronised with the contemporary produce of India and fabricating a familiar, if somewhat adrift, topos. To return to Sajjad Zaheer's memory of Urdu – Parsi theatre:

> There emerged out of this rough *melee* of legend, didactic prose, popular Indian songs, melodies and dances, burlesque, satire and melodrama something elemental, popular and, above all, extremely Indian.[97]

This description is equally pertinent to films in Pakistan in the late 1950s. Could this mongrel element hold the key to the Pakistan elite's unequivocal disdain for the 'fantasy' films, expressed in committee reports, journalistic writing and critical commentaries? Despite an evident appeal and a possible artistic strength, the top–down ordering of national culture enforced an 'inferior' status on fantasy and its many variants,

> Characters dressed in cow-boy costumes capering across the pathan landscape or heroines in skin-tight blouses and breeches playing *havoc with our social traditions in town and country alike.*[98]

While its classified ads were filled with fantasy films, the *Pakistan Times* rallied around realism and stressed on the need for films to engage with contemporary national experience. As one might expect, it was dismissive of 'fantasy', which was found wanting in all respects: the lack of technical expertise, the repetitive formulas and most acutely the lack of geographical or cultural understanding of the Arab world. In effect, the newspaper questioned the definitive fluidity and cultural borrowings of the *Arabian Nights* by pointing out the inauthentic Arabia these films were busy producing:

> Somebody put Baghdad on the bank of Nile (or brought Nile into Iraq).... bamboos have been grown in Palestine and desert chiefs have held court under *neem* trees flanked by Roman functionaries.... one cannot create authentic Arabian background just by shouting *Habibi Habibi* or *Marhaba Marhaba* or racing camels in the desert of Sind.[99]

This brand of facetious attitude from newspaper critics was commonplace across writing on Indian popular cinema too.[100] Instead of the 'liberating global cosmopolitan modernity' that the fantasy hybrids afforded in pre-partition India, demands were being made in Pakistan for an authentic portrayal and researched knowledge of the Muslim Middle East. Holding Hollywood responsible for such erroneous and Orientalist imaginings, the article felt that Pakistan's film-makers had outdone everyone in persisting with 'fallacious notions about the geography, people and culture of the Orient' in their films. Easily recognisable in these images of the mythic and historic Middle Eastern world were contemporary spaces of Pakistan.

> The director puts the girl in Gulistani-i-Fatima (Bagh-i-Jinnah), and starts shooting. Similarly the Bhawalpur palace becomes a palace in Ghazni, the Afghans fight with straight Roman swords (and they fight so badly that you wonder how the Sultan won so many victories) and the dancers appear to be coming out of a Hollywood fantasy.[101]

While in the fantasy films of Lahore, the temporal and spatial incongruity could well be symptomatic of a complicated trajectory of fantasy hybrids via the detours of Hollywood and Bombay, these geographical aberrations were not limited to films. Not far from Bhawalpur, there had come into being the new urban development, Baghdad-ul-Jadid, or the new Baghdad, in Pakistan.

Finally, the intangible 'Islamic culture', with its representational dilemmas and mantle of 'cultivating national pride', furthered the gulf between fantasy and social realism. Any comparison of fantasy remakes in Pakistan with prior instances of pre-partition *Arabian Nights* hybrids is severely compromised by the sparse availability of the latter. If the surviving script of the silent *Gul Bakavali* Flower of Bakavli, Bombay, 1924) reveals a 'secular' cultural ethos achieved by paring off its Islamic context, as pointed out by Thomas, Wadia Movietone's early talkies like *Lal-e-Yaman* (Prince of Yemen, Bombay, 1933) and *Noor-e-Yaman* (Light of Yemen, Bombay, 1935) celebrate Islam through a 'Sufi mystical philosophy'.[102] Swaying further along the spectrum of 'Islamic context' was the iconoclastic dance of Munshi Dil's *Gul Bakavali* in Pakistan that revealed the *carte blanche* of Muslim majoritarianism. Undoubtedly, the changed demographic-political situation afforded the fantasy hybrids of Pakistan an opportunity for platitudes and postures of religion alongside magic, adventure, song and romance. Occupying a populist register of religiosity, manifested mostly in high-flown dialogues and magical wonders subservient to divine will, these films were certainly an adroit negotiation of the censors' propensity to see red in religion, especially in more realist registers. For instance, the deletion of the song in a film adaptation of Agha Hashr Kashmiri's play, *Aankh ka Nasha* (Intoxication of Eyes, 1957, dir. Sibtain Fazli), on the grounds that 'it was likely to cause hatred among people and militated against the Islamic conception of humility towards the Almighty',[103] is illustrative of the larger struggles of realist melodramas in the country. Despite this, respectable 'national aspirations' and 'national behaviour' could not be 'entrusted to these [fantasy] excursions into the world of nonsense'.[104] Reacting to the trite evocation of 'Islamic culture', the puritan champions of social realism opined that such a culture of empty slogans (of fantasies) should better go unrepresented.[105] It must be added that not all fantasies were reductively or essentially Islamised, and it is here that one of Rattan's films reveals the versatility of the form in Pakistan.

The Magic of Past: *Nagin* and *Alladin Ka Beta*

The next distinctive phase in Rattan's career, which saw nearly seven films in three years, lasted until the early 1960s. These were the costume or fantasy or better still 'foolish swording' films, like *Nagin* (Mystic Serpent, 1959), *Aladdin ka Beta* (The Son of Aladdin, 1960), *Neelofar* (1960), *Taj aur Talwar* (Crown and Sword, 1961), *Ghazi Bin Abbas* (Warrior Bin Abbas, 1961), *Sher-i-Islam* (Lion of Islam, 1961) and *Husn-o-Ishq* (Beauty and Love, 1962). Produced by Rattan's brother Wazir Ali under the banner of Film Hayat, these films had a fixed team of performers like Neelo, Saqi and Nazar and directors like Rafiq Rizvi and Riaz Ahmed Raju. After *Bedari*, Rafiq Rizvi had also directed Rattan in other *charbas* like *Waah Re Zamane* (What a World!, 1958) and *Do Ustad* (Two Masters, 1960). Before migrating to Pakistan, one of Rizvi's last releases in India was the fantasy *Alladin ka Beta* (1955), starring Mahipal and Chitra, which received unenthusiastic reviews.[106] Five years later, *Alladin ka Beta* (1960), starring Rattan, was made in Pakistan and in all likelihood was a remake of Rizvi's Indian film, although Riaz Ahmed Raju directed it in Pakistan. Close on the heels of *Alladin ka Beta*, Film Hayat also made *Neelofar* (1960). P. N. Arora's costume film *Neelofar* (1957) with the same title had been produced in India a few years earlier.[107] Only the earliest two of these fantasy hybrids, *Nagin* and *Alladin ka Beta*, survive. *Sher-i-Islam* and *Taj aur Talwar*, although no longer available nor reviewed by the *Pakistan Times*, carry the iconography of the 'costume' film, with Rattan wielding a sword in the advertisements. *Neelofar* (1960) was most likely a star-vehicle for the dancing sensation Neelo, reported to be Rattan's sweetheart at the time, and the film was publicised rather unusually in the sports pages.[108] An image of dancing Neelo framed the two innings 'Test Score Card' of a Pakistan versus India cricket match fusing Neelo's nymphal dances with Rattan's boyish cricketing, thus associating the film strategically with a sport that has always elicited extreme jingoism and competition between the two countries. Finally, the film *Ghazi-bin-Abbas* was based on the Islamic martyr of Karbala, Abbas-Ibn-Ali, and, refraining from any iconography, stuck to a minimalist bold typesetting in its publicity. But it too most certainly would have provided enough instances of sword-fighting.

In contrast to the more Islamised fantasy hybrids of its times, Rattan-starrer *Nagin* (1959, dir. Khalil Kaiser) drew on the Hindu–Jataka tradition of divine, mythical serpents and their descendants. Five years earlier, another *Nagin* (1954), directed by Nandlal Jaswantlal, had been made in Bombay and even officially exhibited in Pakistan. And their pre-partition instance from the early talkie period was a *Nagan* (Mystic Serpent, 1934), produced by Radha Film Company and directed by Jyotish Banerjee. While the earliest *Nagan* does not survive, Lahore's *Nagin* in its relationship with Bombay's *Nagin* is an instance of a non-remake, where a 'film is promoted on the basis of its supposed similarity to an earlier film it only incidentally resembles'.[109] In the publicity columns, the film's heroine, Neelo, is made to strongly

resemble the heroine of the Indian *Nagin*, Vyjayanthimala. While consistent with
the lore of the mythical cobra, or Ichchadhari Nag, including its motifs of the snake's
ability to assume human form at will, its power to inflict instantaneous death, its
guardianship of untold wealth and the allure of the cobra-maiden, the Pakistani
Nagin simultaneously made the myth insipid. The film review noted as much:

> The bulk of the plot is so common that one feels the need for introducing the
> two characters as snakes and ending them as such.... the story-writer could
> have managed without relying on the myth.[110]

The Pakistani *Nagin* revolves around the legendary devotion of the cobra couple
whose love survives separation and the assumption of human form. Hunted by a
snake charmer, the serpent boy (Rattan) seeks refuge on a *nawab*'s (Abbas Ajmeri)
estate while the serpent girl (Neelo) becomes a street dancer. Switching places with
the Nawab's adopted son (Rattan), his lookalike and double, the serpent boy gets
entangled in the intrigues of the *nawab* family. In a classic case of mistaken identity,
separated lovers and multiple villains, several swordfights and snakebites later the
wanton nephew of the *nawab* and the greedy snake charmer are finally killed. Both
characters played by Rattan live on, one as the *nawab*'s successor and the other with
his serpent sweetheart as snakes of the jungle.

    Nagin is the first film that casts Rattan as the male grown-up lead. This is
categorically signalled through the cobra first transforming into a small boy who
in turn 'grows up', in a matter of the film dissolve, into a chubby, adolescent Rattan.
This is the second significant shift in Rattan's persona, the expeditious 'adulthood'
assumed within three years of his arrival in Pakistan. It was Rattan's second double
role in Pakistan, and his father, Abbas Ajmeri, played the role of the *nawab*, the
guardian of the human Rattan. While concretising and furthering the shifts in
his star image, *Nagin* was imbued by Rattan's Indian persona. Registered through
iconography and star performance, the first among many instances is the poolside
song sequence. As the cobra-boy enters the Nawab's palace grounds, he witnesses his
lookalike serenading a young girl bathing in an open pool. With an Afghani *rabab* in
his hand and dressed in puffed-sleeved ornate costume, the boy leans against huge
metallic and decorative cobra-hoods lining the pool. In the Muslim princely orient
thus, there lurks a reminder of lands more east than west of Pakistan. It is also a
reminder of Rattan's cinematic Indian past, especially *Bahot Dinn Hue* (1955), where
the divine cobra was the guardian of little Rattan's clan and wore a crown of the
five-hooded mythical cobra, or the Sheshnaga. In mythological lore, this mythical
serpent protected infant Krishna, a role played by Rattan in the mythological films
in India. The heroic aspects of Rattan's performance in *Nagin* are the sword-fighting
scenes that recall his training at Gemini Studios for *Bahot Dinn Hue*. And yet when
he eventually kills his opponent, it is not so much the ferocity of the attack or a
strategically delivered fatal cut but a poisoned blade licked with his 'serpent' tongue.

A superimposed shot of Rattan and the serpent passing their tongues together over the sword is a rare instance of illusion within the film.

Another Pakistani film that incorporated the allure of the snake-maiden was *Zehr-e-Ishq* (1958), adapted for screen by Imtiaz Ali Taj. Released a year before the Pakistani *Nagin*, the critically acclaimed film was an undeniable influence on the latter. Recalling the snake-worshipping tribes of the Indian *Nagin*, the maiden in *Zehr-e-Ishq* was wild, attractive and belonged to one such tribe. The film adapted *Zehr-e-Ishq*, the *masnavi* of unconventional romance, into a story of neurotic love between an upper-class Muslim man, Jameel, and a tribal woman of the mountains, Sanwali (meaning, the dark one). In her obsession with Jameel, Sanwali even-handedly gets rid of anyone who poses a hurdle in their romance, including a cat, a dog, a bridegroom, Jameel's mother and Jameel's wife. While Sanwali does not possess any outward magical powers, an ensnared Jameel is evidence of the enigmatic powers of snake worship. The pleasures of an incredible, nearly absurd 'Orient' – haunting strains of the snake charmer's flute, matchmaking by wriggling snakes on horoscopes, the inebriating snake-bite and prophesies by a toothless crone – are offered and 'othered' by the film. Consigned to a realm outside the modern, upper-class or princely Muslim, the serpent-tribes with their primordial worlds are arguably a cipher for the 'tribal people living in the mountains of Chittagong'.[111] Both *Nagin* and *Zehr-e-Ishq*'s creation of a weakly magical yet exotic realm, and Rattan's double act, reveals the constitution of the religious 'other' in the fantasy hybrids in Pakistan.

As mentioned earlier, it is likely that the other one of Rattan's surviving fantasy films, *Aladdin ka Beta* (1960), was a copy of Rafiq Rizvi's Indian version of 1955. In India, it was among the next generation of *Arabian Nights* sequels like *Aladdin ki Beti* (Daughter of Aladdin, 1949, India), *Alibaba ka Beta* (Son of Alibaba, 1955, India) and *Hatimtai ki Beti* (Daughter of Hatimtai, 1955, India). Made in 1960, the Pakistani version was about a magician plotting to steal Aladdin's lamp. He sends his two daughters to ensnare Aladdin's young son and bring the lamp. While one of them falls in love with the son, the other successfully steals the lamp. Aladdin's son then sets out with his sword to retrieve his lamp and lady-love from the wicked magician's quarters.

The imprint of Rattan's *Bahot Dinn Hue* was evident on *Aladdin ka Beta* as well. The wizard's cave is a scaled-down version of Bhadrachamund's cave in *Bahot Dinn Hue*. Rahukaleshwar, the occult talking head of *Bahot Dinn Hue*, is transformed into his derelict twin Khiski Khopdi (cuckoo cranium) in *Alladin ka Beta*. Even the genie of *Alladin ka Beta* resembles the demons of *Bahot Dinn Hue* more than any of the surviving images of the *Aladdin* genies. The homecoming of Aladdin's son recalls the final sequence of earlier Aladdin fantasies, including Homi Wadia's *The Wonderful Lamp*, except that this time the son, his lady-love and two other friends ride the flying carpet. As the cheering public looks up, an adolescent Rattan gyrates with Neelo on the carpet.

In her study of the subversive potential of fantasy (literature), Rosemary Jackson argues that 'desire for what is experienced as loss and absence' is central to fantasy.[112] The expression of this unconscious desire, according to Jackson, can operate in two ways, either by manifesting desire or by expelling desire. In the case of expulsion, the desire is for an element that threatens the cultural order and is therefore expelled by being expressed. A Hindu–Jataka fantasy hybrid and Rattan's Indian past are the loss and absence evoked in these *charba* fantasies. The striking lack of magical effects in either *Nagin* (1959, Pakistan) or *Aladdin ka Beta* (1960, Pakistan) suggests that desire is being expressed rather than manifested.

> The film combines fantasy with reality like happenings in no certain measure, the writer following the demands of the box-office formula faithfully. The director is also very accommodating; where even trick photography is not possible he just uses a blank strip leaving the audience to guess about the hero's dangerous exploits. The whole seems to be a most amateurish effort.[113]

Built around stories abounding in magic and adventure that involve physical transformations, sword-fighting, hidden treasures, genies, flying carpets and wizards, the two films remain rather conservative in the use of special effects and creating magic. Simpler – and rarely used – tricks of making humans and objects appear or disappear and rough aerial shots of a barely visible flying carpet are the only instances of magic. The technological and aesthetic impoverishment of fantasy films in Pakistan suggests that the appeal of these films had little to do with the visceral pleasures of extravagant spectacle, stunts and special-effects magic. Evoking a semblance of magic, the pleasure instead seems to lie in summoning a memory of spectacular films once seen.

To limit the understanding of the cultural order alluded to in Pakistani fantasies to their contemporaneous and national limits of circulation and production would be to ignore their otherwise anachronistic and transnational referents – that is, the early talkies of the undivided subcontinent and the Bombay hybrid fantasies of the 1950s. Thomas draws out the cultural significance of the latter under the canopy of the B-film.

> If B-films are the space within which the 'return of the repressed' of the A-film erupts, the Bombay B-films of the 1950s and 1960s were arguably the place where the idealised Nehruvian 'nation' became messy and porous and could not be neatly severed from global popular culture.[114]

In Pakistan, there was no separate subaltern circuit to which these hybrids could be relegated, despite elite disdain. Winning popular awards, sharing personnel with other genres, receiving reviews (albeit critical) in English-language dailies and screened in A-category Pakistani cinema halls, the Pakistani hybrids were not a separate rung. Further, the popularity of B-circuit Indian films in Pakistan suggests that film circuits are nationally relative and not nationally sealed categories. If we accept Zaheer's identification of 'the rough melee of the Urdu–Parsi theatre as something extremely Indian', then surely this 'Indian' cannot be contained within the post-1947 territorial expression of India. Likewise, the many possibilities of 'the return of the repressed' of the idealised Nehruvian nation, not quite exhausted by the Bombay B-film, erupted in the Pakistani fantasy hybrid.

Figure 6.7　A synopsis page from a publicity booklet of Rattan Kumar's film *Clerk* (1960, Pakistan)
Source: Guddu Film Archive, Karachi.

After the fantasy films, Rattan appeared as the romantic lead in a couple of social melodramas in Pakistan. His last film was a self-directed *Dastaan* (1969) where his character of a young and educated jobseeker is introduced as an orphan who lost his parents in 1947, thereby underlining the long-lasting hold of a partition-imbued severance on the Rattan persona. In a career spanning two decades, Rattan's star image straddled two nations, and through his double roles, an increased paternal presence and expeditious adulthood, his films in Pakistan were a fascinating elaboration of a *muhajir* star trajectory with respect to an Indian past of a 'national orphan' and 'idealised citizen'.

Rattan's 'intensified star presence' in the double roles was a proud showcase of the Lahore film industry's newly acquired trophy from India. Such a register of competition was consistent with the retaliatory and expulsive postures of his intertwined constituencies, *charba* and hybrid fantasies, themselves exercises in duplication. Characterising the larger production trends of post-partition Lahore, the popularity and resilience of fantasy and remakes were in part a result of a protectionist home market but also a business solution designed to overcome the problem of low production and high demand. Wresting control of shared narrative traditions and historical events, the remakes confronted the hegemony and historicity of Indian cinema. As technically poor copies of their Bombay counterparts, lacking magic, spectacle and technical sophistication, these films conducted a dialogue of national difference. As an extension of the qualities that the original lacks, the Pakistani doubles (roles and films) were ultimately confrontations with self-identity and its entanglements with the ineradicable past.

Notes

1   Attia Hosain, 'No New Lands, No New Sea', in *Distant Traveller*, ed. Aamer Hussein (New Delhi: Women Unlimited, 2013).

2   Jane O'Connor, *The Cultural Significance of the Child Star* (New York: Routledge, 2008), 3.

3   'Readers Write to the Editor', *Eastern Film Magazine*, June 1963, 41.

4   The basis of the double as rooted in narcissism is psychoanalyst Otto Rank's initial reading of the double motif, based on the film *The Student of Prague* (1913). The explanation of the double as more allegorical and an expression of the second self is the contribution of literary historian Ralph Tymms. For a detailed comparison of these works, see Harry Tucker Jr, 'Introduction', in Otto Rank, *The Double: A Psychoanalytical Study*, tr. and ed. Harry Tucker Jr (Chapel Hill, NC: University of North Carolina Press, 1971), xiv–xv.

5   Rank, *Double*.

6   Richard Dyer, 'Charisma', in *Stardom: The Industry of Desire*, ed. Christine Gledhill (London: Routledge,1991), 57–59.

7   Folk legends around Birbal–Akbar, Mullah Do Pyaza–Akbar and Tenalirama–Krishnadevarya are illustrative of the relationship between men of wit and imperial authority.

8   'Candidates for Stardom No. 37', *Filmfare*, 5 February 1954, 31.

9   Sumita Chakravarty, *National Identity in Indian Popular Cinema 1947–1987* (Austin: University of Texas Press, 1993), 96.

10 Ashish Rajyadhaksha and Paul Willemen, *Encyclopaedia of Indian Cinema* (New Delhi: British Film Institute–Oxford University Press, 1994), 314.

11   *Do Bigha Zameen* won the first Filmfare award for the Best Film and the Best Director
      (1954), won the first National Award for the Best Feature Film (1954), won the
      International Prize at the seventh Cannes Film Festival (1954) and the Prize for Social
      Progress at the Karlovy Vary Festival. *Boot Polish* won three awards at Filmfare Awards
      (1955), including the Best Film and a special mention for child actress Naaz at the
      eighth Cannes Film Festival (1955).

12   Ravi Vasudevan, 'Voice, Space and Form Roja: (Mani Ratnam,1992), Indian Film
      and National Identity', in *Not on Any Map: Essays on Post Coloniality and Cultural
      Nationalism*, ed. S. Murray, 153–168 (Exeter: University of Exeter Press, 1997), 154.

13   Neepa Majumdar, 'Importing Neorealism, Exporting Cinema', in *Global Neorealism:
      The Transnational History of a Film Style*, ed. S. Giovacchini and R. Skalr, 178–193
      (Jackson, MS: University Press of Mississippi, 2011).

14   Jaimey Fischer, 'On the Ruins of Masculinity: The Figure of the Child in Italian
      Neorealism and the German Rubble Film', in *Italian Neorealism and Global Cinema*,
      ed. Ruberto and Kristi M. Wilson, 25–53 (Michigan: Wayne State University Press,
      2007).

15   'Kala Pani' refers to incarceration on Andaman and Nicobar islands, away from the
      main body of the subcontinent, a punishment usually reserved for serious dissenters
      against the colonial state.

16   Clare Barker, *Postcolonial Fiction and Disability: Exceptional Children, Metaphor and
      Materiality* (Basingstoke: Palgrave Macmillan, 2011).

17   Srirupa Roy, *Beyond Belief: India and the Politics of Postcolonial Nationalism* (Durham,
      NC: Duke University Press, 2007), 7.

18   Meghnad Desai's book on his film idol refers to him as Nehru's hero. Meghnad Desai,
      Nehru's Hero Dilip Kumar in the Life of India (New Delhi: Roli Books, 2004)

19   Both in India and Pakistan, film magazines suggest comparisons with Dilip Kumar, as
      does the extract cited at the beginning of the piece.

20   'Candidates for Stardom No. 37', *Filmfare*, 5 February 1954, 31.

21   'Star Profile: Rattan Kumar', *Filmfare*, 16 September 1955, 12–13.

22   Ibid.

23   Richard Dyer, 'A Star is Born and the Construction of Authenticity', in *Stardom: The
      Industry of Desire*, ed. Christine Gledhill, 136–144 (London: Roufledge,1991), 136.

24   Faisal Devji, 'Hindu/Muslim/Indian'. *Public Culture* 5, no. 1 (Fall 1992): 1–18, 1.

25   *Filmfare*, 18 March 1955, 55.

26   Ibid.

27   'A Film Letter from Pakistan', *Filmfare*, 16 February 1956, 51.

28   'Inse Miliye Kamsin Adaakar: Rattan Kumar', *Nigar Weekly*, 14 October 1956.

29   O'Connor, *Cultural Significance of the Child Star*, 4.

30   Fictional Hollywood child star Joey Cooley's exasperated outburst in P. G. Wodehouse's
      Laughing Gas (London: Everyman, 2001), 61.

31   'Letters to the Editor', *Filmindia*, January 1956, 14.

32   *Pakistan Times*, 4 January 1957, 7 (emphasis mine).

33   O'Connor, *Cultural Significance of the Child Star*, 3.

34   Production breakdown in *Report of the Film Fact Finding Committee* (Karachi:
      Government of Pakistan Press, 1962), 48 & 121.

35   *Report of the Film Fact Finding Committee*, 105.

36   Ibid., 88.

37   Ibid.

38   'Around Lahore Studios', *Pakistan Times*, 10 May 1960.

39   I. S. Johar's *Nastik* is about a displaced man's passage from partition-induced scepticism to religious nationality. This is discussed briefly in Chapter 3.

40   Calculated for the year 1957 on the basis of production and import figures of vernacular language films (Hindi, Urdu, Bengali and Punjabi), available in *Report of the Film Fact Finding Committee* (1961) and the film compendium *Pakistan Filmdom* (1966).

41   Ziad Zafar, 'The Big Steal: Cover Story', *Newsline*, July 2005, 16–35.

42   Ravi Sundaram, *Pirate Modernity: Delhi's Media Urbanism* (New York: Routledge, 2009), 105.

43   Lawrence Liang, 'Beyond Representation: The Figure of the Pirate', in *Access to Knowledge: In the Age of Intellectual Property*, ed. Amy Kapcyznski and Gaëlle Krikorian, 353–376 (New York: Zone Books, 2010), 362.

44   J. Forest and K. Leonard, 'Introduction', in *Dead Ringers: The Remake in Theory and Practice*, ed. J. Forest and K. Leonard, 1–20 (Albany: State University of New York Press, 2002), 3.

45   Nitin Govil and Eric Hoyt, 'Thieves of Bombay: United Artistes, Colonial Copyright, and Film Piracy in 1920s', *BioScope: South Asian Screen Studies* 5, no. 1 (2014): 5–27, DOI: 10.1177/0974927614532878 (accessed on 29 October 2014).

46   Jane Gaines, 'Early Cinema's Heydey of Copying', *Cultural Studies* 20, nos. 2–3 (2006): 227–244, DOI: 10.1080/09502380600551485 (accessed on 3 November 2014).

47   Ibid., 228.

48   'Demand for Pakistan Films in Birmingham, Bradford and Glasgow', *Pakistan Times*, 25 March 1960.

49   Thomas Leitch, 'Twice-Told Tales: Disavowal and The Rhetoric of the Remake', in *Dead Ringers: The Remake in Theory and Practice*, ed. Jennifer Forest and Leonard R. Koos, 37–62 (Albany: State University of New York Press, 2002), 44.

50   A comprehensive and popular film website Mazhar.dk lists *Bedari* as one of twenty-four patriotic films of Pakistan till date. 'Patriotic Movies from Pakistan', Mazhar, http://mazhar.dk/film/db/Patriotic.php (accessed on 10 November 2014).

51   '*Bedari*: Another Plagiarised Version', *Pakistan Times*, 13 December 1957, 6.

52   Bhaskar Sarkar, *Mourning the Nation: Indian Cinema in the Wake of Partition* (Durham, NC: Duke University Press, 2009), 65.

53   Sharmishta Gooptu, *Bengali Cinema: An Other Nation* (London: Routledge, 2011), 97.

54   Ibid.

55   Sumathi Ramaswamy, *The Goddess and the Nation: Mapping Mother India* (Durham, NC: Duke University Press, 2010), 181.

56   Amiya P. Sen, *The Indispensable Vivekananda: An Anthology for Our Times* (Delhi: Permanent Black, 2006), 5.

57   Ibid.

58   Abhi Bhattacharya's new syllabus, which involved travelling the length and breadth of the country, encapsulated in the song 'Aao Bachon Tumhe Dikhaein Jhaanki Hindustan Ki', evoked the reformer of 'the pre-Gandhian era when few English educated Indians

had travelled so widely across the length and breadth of the country and mixed as freely with so wide-variety of peoples and cultures'. See Sen, *Indispensable Vivekanand*, 9–10. Additionally, it also recalled the 'Gurukula system' of Tagore's Shantiniketan based on the personal relationship between the teacher and the pupil and the importance of living close to nature. See Vivienne Baumfield, 'Science and Sanskrit: Vivekananda's Views on Education', in *Swami Vivekanand and the Modernization of Hinduism*, ed. William Radice, 194–212 (Delhi: Oxford University Press, 1998), 208. Like Shantiniketan, Ajay's school had daily meditation, and instead of religious festivals, the school celebrated the birthdays of great men. The popular eulogy to Gandhi in the film is sung on the occasion of the Mahatma's birth anniversary.

59   One such particular illustration that appeared in *Intiya* (1906) shows the deity suckling four infants, suggesting the four religious communities of India. See Ramaswamy, *The Goddess and the Nation*, 24.

60   Ibid.

61   Ayesha Jalal, *The Sole Spokesman* (Lahore: Sang-i-Meel Publications, 1999), 121.

62   'Once in a decade comes, a motion picture which is remembered forever: A gift to the nation: Film Exchange presents *Bedari*.' *Pakistan Screen Annual* (1957), 206.

63   The interpretation of Mahmud Gahzni's raid of the Somanth temple in 1026 has been projected as central to Hindu–Muslim relations. See Romila Thapar, *Somanatha the Many Voices of History* (Verso: London, 2005).

64   This particular Hadith, the Prophet's reported utterances, is attributed to Imam Ahmad an-Nasa'i. Virginia Gray Henry-Blackmore (ed.), *Voices of Islam, Vol. 3: Voices of Life: Family, Home and Society* (Westport: Praeger Publications, 2007), 93.

65   Indian News Parade short 'Gandhi and Jinnah Negotiate for Communal Unity (1944)', https://www.youtube.com/watch?v=e-Z--dSJE94 (accessed on 10 November 2014).

66   Rank, *Double*, 76.

67   Neepa Majumdar, *Wanted Cultured Ladies Only! Female Stardom and Cinema in India, 1930s–1950s* (Champaign, IL: University of Illinois Press, 2009), 136.

68   However, the shooting of *Bedari* happened largely in Lahore studios.

69   'The Lesson from Masoom', *Pakistan Times*, 20 December 1957, 7. Among other references is of course the famous couplet 'Tu shaheen hai, parwaz hai kaam tera / Tere saamne aasman aur bhi hain' (You are an eagle, flight is your vocation / You have other skies stretching out before you), from 'Gabriel's Wings', trans. Muntasir Mir, http://www.allamaiqbal.com/works/poetry/urdu/bal/translation/06gabriel.pdf (accessed on 2 April 2020).

70   'The Lesson from Masoom', *Pakistan Times*, 7.

71   In Hali's influential *Musaddas*, the boat and its difficult journey was invoked to refer to the loss of power, recovery and progress of Indian Muslims after 1857. Christopher Shackle and Javed Majeed (eds.), *Hali's Musaddas: The Flow and Ebb of Islam* (Delhi: Oxford University Press, 1997), 21.

72   Classified Advertisement, *Pakistan Times*, 1 December 1957.

73   Barbara Klinger, *Melodrama and Meaning* (Bloomington: Indiana University Press, 1994), xv.

74   Rank, *Double*, 6–10.

75   'The Lesson from Masoom', *Pakistan Times*, 7.

76   One may pause to ask about the ubiquity of disability in both these films. While *Bedari's* disabled boy was connected to Rattan's character in *Jagriti*, what about the figure of the limping beggar and his connection to Rattan's past life? Did it recall the limping but lovable bootlegger, John Chacha, the only guardian of Bhola and Belu in *Boot Polish*? Played by actor David who won the Filmfare Award for the Best Supporting actor for the film, John Chacha was an important character associated with the *Boot Polish* children.

77   'The Lesson from Masoom', *Pakistan Times*, 7.

78   'Observation of the Indian Cinematograph Committee (1927)', cited in Rosie Thomas, *Bombay before Bollywood Film City Fantasies* (New Delhi: Orient Blackswan, 2014), 39.

79   See Thomas, *Bombay before Bollywood*; Kaushik Bhaumik, 'The Emergence of the Bombay Film Industry 1913–1936', PhD diss., University of Oxford, 2001; and Virchand Dharamsey, 'The Advent of Sound in Indian Cinema: Theatre, Orientalism, Action and Magic', *Journal of Moving Image* 9 (2010): 22–51, http://www.jmionline. org/article/the_advent_of_sound_in_indian_cinema_theatre_orientalism_action_ magic_1 (accessed on 25 July 2014).

80   Sajjad Zaheer, 'Urdu Drama', *Indian Literature* 1, no. 2 (1958): 139–144, 142.

81   Thomas, *Bombay before Bollywood*, 9–10.

82   Dharamsey, 'The Advent of Sound in Indian Cinema', 22–24.

83   A longer list of the Parsi theatre playwrights who were active at the time of the talkies is available in Dharmsey, 'The Advent of Sound in Indian Cinema', 27.

84   The instance of associating the *Arabian Nights* fantasy with 'the Muslim Class' appears in the film magazine *Varieties Weekly* in 1934, cited by Bhaumik, 'The Emergence of the Bombay Film Industry', 169.

85   Thomas, *Bombay before Bollywood*, 84.

86   For the persistence of *qissa-dastaan* in Punjab, see Farina Mir, *The Social Space of Language: Vernacular Culture in British Colonial Punjab* (Berkley: University of California Press, 2010).

87   Dharamsey, 'The Advent of Sound in Indian Cinema', 26.

88   Credits for *Ishq-i-Laila* carry Wazir Ali's name rather prominently, though the role title is barely legible in the rather poor copy available of the film.

89   Classified Advertisement, *Pakistan Times*, 6 December 1957, 3.

90   Neelo's dancing became a moment of 'national reckoning' as Mushtaq Gazdar details in his book. 'During Ayub Khan regime, the emperor of Iran paid an official visit to Pakistan. For the entertainment of his Imperial Majesty, the organizers wanted Neelo to give a live dance performance. When she refused to comply with their wishes, they harassed and threatened her with dire consequences.' Mushtaq Gazdar, *Pakistan Cinema 1947–1997* (Karachi: Oxford University Press, 1998), 92.

91   Classified Advertisement, *Pakistan Times*, 19 November 1957, 3.

92   Robert Irwin, *The Arabian Nights: A Companion* (New York: Tauris Parke, 1994), 88–89.

93   Classified Advertisement, *Pakistan Times*, 27 October 1961, 3.

94   'Films: Gul Bakauli', *Pakistan Times*, 3 November 1961, 11 (emphasis mine).

95   Dharmsey, 'The Advent of Sound in Indian Cinema', 28.

96   Gazdar, *Pakistan Cinema*, 33.

97   Zaheer, 'Urdu Drama', 143.

98   *Report of the Film Fact Finding Committee*, 249 (emphasis mine).

99   'Arabian Fantasies in Hollywood Style', *Pakistan Times*, 29 April 1960, 6.

100   I am grateful to Rosie Thomas for pointing this out in our discussions.

101   'Ayaz: A Story of Love, Rivalry and Intrigue', *Pakistan Times*, 12 May 1961, 8.

102   Thomas, *Bombay before Bollywood*, 55.

103   'A Questionable Decision', *Pakistan Times*, 7 June 1957, 5.

104   *Report of the Film Fact Finding Committee*, 88.

105   'Sarfarosh', *Pakistan Times*, 22 June 1956, 6.

106   'Alladin ka Beta Deplorably Crude Production', *Times of India*, 4 December 1955, 3.

107   Firoze Rangoonwala, *Indian Filmography* (Bombay: J. Udeshi, 1970), 343.

108   Advertisement, *Pakistan Times*, 16 December 1960, 10.

109   Leitch, 'Twice-Told Tales', 43.

110   'Film Reviews', *Pakistan Times*, 27 June 1959, 3.

111   In a 1949 article, Hasan Askari outlined his expectations from 'Pakistani cinema' as one that would aid in nation-building by representing the lives and aspirations of communities on territorial fringes, especially in East Pakistan. Muhammad Hasan Askari, 'Building Pakistan and Filmmaking', trans. Ali Nobil Ahmad, *BioScope: South Asian Screen Studies* 5, no. 2 (July 2014): 175–181, http://bio.sagepub.com/content/5/2/175.full.pdf+html (accessed on 20 January 2015), 176. Also see the Conclusion in this book.

112   Rosemary Jackson, *Fantasy: The Literature of Subversion* (London: Metheun, 1981), 3.

113   'Around Lahore Studios', *Pakistan Times*, 3 June 1960, 8.

114   Thomas, *Bombay before Bollywood*, 16.

Conclusion

Evacuee Cinema

This study of cinema during British India's partition has actively drawn on existing paradigms of partition and histories of nationalisms in the subcontinent. In doing so it has consciously placed cinema in the field of impending and in-transition nations, even though the sites of production of film cultures are cities and the political context transcends nation states. However, instead of suggesting either the nation state as the exhaustive imaginative horizon of film culture on the one hand or, on the other, the cities' cinematic absorption in the localised urban, I have emphasised the parallax involved in sighting the national. Through different vantage points of cinema cities lying in different nations now, but also the cinematic lens, the territorial and national ambiguities at the heart of partition become starkly evident. And yet the organising power of this parallactic view cannot be underestimated, as is evident in the enduring 'secular stance' of the Bombay film industry, an idea whose hegemony was established in the partition years, that is, 1940–1960. Partition was central to the creation of this stance, achieved through a discursive management and, eventually, the excision of Muslim nationalism, as both a network of film production and a thematic ideology. While this discursive management was coded as belligerence to Pakistan, in both *Filmindia* and Prithvi Theatre's partition repertoire, the investment in the political also reveals the social processes of film-making in an industrial context polarising along a new national divide. Here, as I have argued in Chapter 2, Muslim nationalism temporarily emerged as a modality of contestation and competition within the Bombay film industry over control of film trade and narratives.

By juxtaposing the incendiary prose of a film magazine and resentful accusations of émigré memoirs, the power of vitriolic enunciations, which create categorical identities amidst turmoil and movement, emerges. These interventions that speak to each other despite being separated in time and space attest to the formation of competing interest groups within the Bombay film industry with critical stakes in the political wrangles of the 1940s. Amidst these feuding articulations, there is Prithvi Theatre with strong links to the Bombay film industry, represented by its star performer Prithviraj Kapoor and fuelled by his film earnings. The group rose to pre-eminence within a few years of its founding in 1944 by performing partition narratives on stage, which were anchored in caste Hindu worldview. Immune to considerations of creating sectarian controversy or risking business with painful reminders of a trauma, Prithvi Theatre played partition 'fearlessly through thick and thin'.[1] In a *Filmfare* article during the mid-1950s, Prithviraj delineated 'how [the] stage [could] serve the screen':

> A novel theme, a realistic tragedy and a hilarious comedy can be experimented with on the stage and then filmed on its merits. That to a great extent hedges the film producer's investment. Through experiments on the stage the particular emotions which appeal most are known and the film director has therefore little difficulty *in knowing what is needed*.[2]

Going by the timing of Prithvi plays, it seems that 'knowing what was needed' was the troupe's key forte. The overlap of *Pathan* (The Frontier Man, April 1947) with the North-West Frontier Province crisis, and Prithviraj's bellicose speech after *Ghaddar* (The Traitor) in Hyderabad (June 1949), nine months after the Indian state violently annexed the princely state, could hardly be coincidental. Successfully reconciling the film industry's capital and resources with the state's power to grant censorship approvals, tax exemptions and subsidies, Prithvi Theatre's 'experiments' are an important example of partition's productive force. Through its starkly contemporary and up-to-the-minute thematic renditions of the partition, Prithvi Theatre performances were repeated across different venues and cities, including makeshift stages in cinema halls for nearly a decade. Immensely powerful and popular by all accounts, these plays would have added to the real-life saturation around partition narratives at that time, alongside establishing the limits of its representation. In drawing attention to three diverse articulations on the partition experience via a film magazine, theatre repertoire and film memoirs, this book refutes a silence around partition and instead locates a cacophony.

The productive force of partition is evident in the three cinematic artefacts of this historical passage. The first is the Muslim social film, which, as I have demonstrated, is a genre that works out the aspirations of Muslim independence. The second are the satirical romantic comedies loosely modelled on a Hollywood genre that the Shorey team produced in post-partition Bombay, sublimating partition trauma into a sparkling screwball genre. Finally, the much-censured category of *charba*s, or duplicates, of Indian films is a genre of retaliation and correctives which brings out the competitive stance of Lahore film production with respect to Bombay, no less motivated by the antagonism between Pakistan and India. Meant only for the Pakistani markets, the *charbas* restate the unequal and unfavourable film-trade patterns between India and Pakistan. Serving both ritual and ideological needs of audiences and industries, including different interests, a network of independent Muslim film-makers in pre-partition Bombay, the studio-less refugee personnel from Lahore in post-partition Bombay and a fledgling Pakistani film production fighting for its home market, these three genres are intimately connected with partition.

The two collectivities of nations and genres are often described as intimately tied together, and in one instance it has been said that film genre theory might help us think about nations.[3] Yet this study has identified émigré personnel at the heart of these genres: the directors, producers and actors who shifted their location of film practice from one city to another, from one nation to another. Context-wise there is a larger shift involved here too: the dismantling of the all-India film enterprise through the national apportioning of film cities and publics. Therefore, a double dislocation orders the inflections in the practice of these previously unstudied film personnel. Film migrants Roop K. Shorey, Meena Shorey, Fazli Brothers and Rattan Kumar are the key figures of this research, along with Dalsukh Pancholi, Shaukat Hussain Rizvi and I. S. Johar. These different trajectories of displacement, offering a 'before' and 'after' to the curious historian, provide the texture, complexity and subjective mediations of the divide. These personnel are significant for their performative images and larger body of work, working out the dilemmas of identity, cultural authenticity and individual ambitions in wide public glare, the context for which cinema is made. Fazli Brothers solve the representational dilemma of Muslim lives by introducing a *shurafa* modernity in their films. Meena Shorey's return to the national fold in Pakistan is made possible by mobilising the figure of the abducted woman, even though her collaboration with Shorey in Bombay was characterised by a visceral cosmopolitanism. And the foremost manner in which Rattan Kumar can remake himself as a star in Pakistan is by foregrounding his *muhajir*, or immigrant image.

The contours of active migration merge with an enforced one, with partition becoming not only an uprooting but also paradoxically the cessation of professional mobility between and within film cities. In a succinctly crafted inner dialogue, writer Saadat Hassan Manto embraces the well-meaning advice given to actor Ashok Kumar while driving in a restive Muslim locality in Bombay sometime in the troubled months of 1947, as a migratory cue for himself.[4]

> *Manto bhai, aage rasta nahin milega, motor rok lo, udhar baaju ki gali se nikal jao. Aur main chup chap baju ki gali se Pakistan chala aaya.*[5]

> Brother Manto, you will not find a way ahead. Stop the motor, exit using the side lane. And quietly taking the side lane, I came to Pakistan.

The characterisation of migration as the side-lane, which offers escape and safety precisely because it does not draw attention to the act of exit, is revealing. The partition migrations from Bombay were mostly *discreet*, in the hope of safety but also to keep the option of return open. The treason and disloyalty that Pakistan represented in the scheme of Indian nationalism dictated such care and may explain the lack of reliable accounts regarding partition migration to Pakistan in contemporary sources from India. On the other hand, the foremost manner in which émigré personnel are constructed across Pakistani sources is through first-hand accounts of the Bombay film world along with interiorised narratives of migration.

How does the partition migration compare with other film migration in the world? Thomas Elsaesser in his examination of German film-makers in Hollywood examines the mixture of economics and politics in the decision to migrate. As far as the German migration of the 1920s was concerned, he states that these film-makers were 'neither poor immigrants fleeing their country of origin to escape hunger in search of the American dream, nor political exiles and refugees, but film artists and cinema professionals who were attracted because of the technology, resources and rewards that Hollywood could offer'.[6] In contrast, the 1930s migration from Germany had a fraught political dimension. Here Elsaesser reasons that 'although everyone who was in the public eye was affected by the changes in Germany after 1933, often it was actors, writers, composers and singers who experienced Fascism and anti-Semitism more directly as a threat to their lives as well as livelihood'.[7] The 1947 migration between Lahore and Bombay is closer to the German migration of the 1930s, whereas the later individual migrations from Bombay to Lahore are more comparable to the 1920s German–Hollywood migration.

After August 1947, threats, film bans and attacks on studios compelled many prominent Muslim personnel of Bombay – those who had professed support for the Muslim League but also someone like the *khadi*-donning Manto – to migrate or at least leave temporarily. While threat to life and property may have been considerations, the decision to migrate to Pakistan was strongly linked with livelihood. Through the memoirs of directors Shaukat Rizvi, Sibtain Fazli and M. Luqman, this study has identified the decision to migrate as a mutually reinforcing one. The momentum for this departure had less to do with Lahore offering economic rewards than the gradual realisation for many above-the-line workers, who had benefitted from the Muslim networks, that their film 'motor' in Bombay was moving towards a dead end in the immediate political climate. The only lure of Lahore, in the macabre logic of partition survival, was then of an abandoned film city up for grabs.

The Sindhi–Hindu–Sikh migration from Lahore was more unavoidable, and nearly all film families and personnel had left by the end of 1947. An exception to this exodus was the manager of the Pancholi studios, Dewan Sardari Lal, who stayed on, and his presence stalled the sealing off of the two Pancholi studios as evacuee property, thus making them the only working film facilities for film-makers in the early years of Pakistan. While we have no way of knowing how Pancholi and Sardari Lal reached this arrangement with the new administration in Lahore, it surely reveals partition to be also a time of brokering mutual self-interests and not only mindless destruction.

The studios under the aegis of Sardari Lal in fact produced two films in independent Pakistan, including the country's first film, *Teri Yaad* (Your Memory, 1948). The two Pancholis studios were finally declared evacuee property in the early 1950s and were temporarily allotted to film-maker Nazir and actor Himalayawala and then re-allotted to singer Mallika Pukhraj and film distributor and exhibitor Agha G. A. Gul respectively in 1954.[8] Pancholi Studio Number One was renamed Mallika, while Agha Gul renamed Pancholi Studio Number Two as Evernew. The burnt Shorey studio, as has been noted in earlier chapters, was allotted to Shaukat Hussain Rizvi and Noorjahan, and was renamed Shahnoor. The fourth studio premises of pre-partition Lahore was Leela Mandir, which was sealed immediately after partition and remained so until the mid-1950s until it was finally renamed Screen and Sound Studio.

The later migrations from Bombay to Lahore in the late 1950s of Rattan Kumar, Meena Shorey, S. M. Yusuf and Zia Sarhadi appear to have been more influenced by economic considerations, especially as the move in these cases offered a chance for reinvention. Thus, the stir Meena created through her trip to Pakistan, combined with the difficulties of repatriation between the countries, coalesced the Lahore–Meena relationship into permanent citizenship. While Rattan's migration could be a case of 'trophy hunting' by Pakistani film-makers, as suggested in the contemporary press accounts by his father, surely the unwritten rule of child stardom – the infamous obscurity of their mature lives – would have loomed large over a Rattan moving towards adolescence. These prominent migrations also attest to the optimistic mood around film production in Pakistan from the mid-1950s onwards, offering more scope for above-the-line film workers looking for alternatives to the highly competitive and high-stakes production in Bombay.

Having briefly outlined the political compulsions and economic considerations of film migration between Bombay and Lahore, I offer that the creative practices of these émigré personnel display characteristics of exilic cinema and, given the specificity of partition, may be called an *evacuee cinema*. The bureaucratic category of *evacuee property*, which refers to a concrete edifice emptied of its original occupants and replaced by evacuees from another context, was used by the post-partition nation states and can be extended to film as well. This observation draws on Hamid Naficy's contention that 'de-territorialized peoples and their films share certain features' and some of the features that Naficy locates in de-territorialised film practice are available in these films too.[9] The Shorey comedies ascribe importance to 'transitional and transnational places and spaces', such as hotels, the disputed Kashmir territory, a Lahore or Quetta now in Pakistan, and motifs of journeying such as 'trains, buses and suitcases', often in the climactic chase sequences.[10] Similarly, performing a changed identity through 'doppelgangers, doubling and duplicity' is the strategy available in Rattan Kumar's reworked stardom and his family-produced *charbas*.[11]

While Shorey comedies and Rattan's *charbas* fit more obviously into this category, even the Fazli Brothers' Muslim socials have an important role in the making of evacuee cinema identified here. The inclusion of the Fazlis is not governed by the retrospective fact of the film-makers' migration but because the 1940s cycle of the genre was underwritten by the claims of a 'people without a territory for its own "national home" in India'.[12] The pre-partition genre of Muslim independence thus became superfluous to Pakistan once it became a nation state and inimical to India since it was established as a secular polity. Partition thus produces a chasm in the colonial Muslim social genre to continue as post-independence Urdu films in Pakistan and the Islamicate Muslim social genre in independent India. In addition to this, what Elsaesser notes of German émigrés in Hollywood – the 'networks of ethnic bonding, trading on the common culture and cashing in on kinship contacts'[13] – parallels the networks created by the film-makers of the Muslim socials in the 1940s described in Chapter 4. These networks too were interrupted and purged with the division.

To return to *evacuee cinema*, it is foremost an exilic cinema in the sense that Naficy uses, given the centrality of film personnel as well as spectatorial displacement. Yet it does not share the artisanal mode of production or the total artistic control that Naficy highlights in the case of the post-1960s exilic and diasporic cinema the world over. A pre-existing production mode and structure mark this exilic film practice as *evacuee cinema*. Evacuee cinema is materially evident in the case of the sealing up of film studios and their reallocation, where the film evacuees' escape from danger and arrival to safety figuratively encapsulate cultural production in the nationalising decade of the subcontinent, characterised by inflammable religious sensitivities, political compulsions and arbitrating censorship mechanisms. Furthermore, in both post-partition Bombay and Lahore, the émigrés continue their film activities not through a total control over production and exhibition but by using the existing infrastructure and their previous experience of it: the 'immovable property' of the all-India film enterprise.

While evacuee cinema is neither limited to nor exhaustive of cinema in early Pakistan, early Pakistan had the spectatorial environment created by displacement that produces different demands and expectations, which are 'torqued not only by market forces but also by nationalist politics and by politics of ethnic representation'.[14] Thus, *charbas*, or duplicates, as discussed in Chapter 6, were a strategy of production to ensure speed, output and profits in a home market still under the spell of films from Bombay. Amidst these duplicates, there are also instances of migrant personnel remaking their Bombay successes in Pakistan with a difference. For instance, Nazir remade the Bombay film *Gaon ki Gori* (Village Girl, 1945), in which he played the male lead, as *Pheray* (Nuptial Vows, 1949) in Punjabi, while S. M. Yusuf remade his Bombay success *Saheli* (Friend, 1945) with a polygamous twist in Pakistan, also called *Saheli* (1960). Incorporating linguistic, political and cultural correctives, the film-makers attempted to realign Lahore's pre-partition turf of regional Punjabi cinema with the expectations of a demographically altered character of the national market, now a Muslim majority. On the other hand, the larger reflection of 'what should things be like in Pakistan' became a film question as well, adding an ideological burden to an infrastructural impasse.[15] As early as 1949, the cultural and literary commentator, Muhammad Hassan Askari, outlined his expectations for a 'Pakistani cinema':

> A nation's identity is not built in 1 or 2 years; it takes time.... Nor can this task be left to the masses—their imagination needs support to develop.... Our writers, artists, and finest filmmakers can provide this kind of support for the development of the national imagination.[16]

He further adds:

> The lives of tribal people living in the mountains of Chittagong [East Pakistan] should be as important to us as those of other Pakistanis; our films should provide space for their cultural life's expression so that the sense of being outsiders is extinguished from their hearts, allowing them to be useful citizens of Pakistan.[17]

Here, Askari's deliberations are only indicative of the multifarious pressures on early 'Pakistani Cinema'. Unlike the producers who were guided by the perceived changes as well as continuities in the spectatorial demography, Askari is interested in a nationally supportive imagination that makes citizens out of spectators. The reworked mode of address of early cinema in Pakistan, cognisant of the spectatorial environment as well as the national disciplining of spectatorship, will also require an engagement with the longer history of the all-India film publics.[18]

A little over a decade after *Khandaan*'s cinematic caution against the wandering actress, yet another visiting actress would become the centre of gossip and levity in Lahore – 'like a monsoon storm invading the stillness of times'.[19] This was the American actress Ava Gardner, who along with a sizeable Hollywood crew arrived in the post-partition city in the summer of 1955 to shoot an 'imperial romance',[20] the MGM studio's *Bhowani Junction* (1956, dir. George Cuckor). An adaptation of a British novel,[21] this film more than any other empire film 'represented Britain's hopes regarding its links with India and an attempt at the moral rehabilitation of imperialism'.[22] And yet the film was shot in Pakistan and not India with an accredited support of the Government of Pakistan,[23] who in this case demonstrated an attitude distinctly obverse to their dealings with the local producers. What were the reasons for filming a romance between an Anglo-Indian woman and a British officer posted in central India in 1947, in Pakistan instead? (Figure C.1) One explanation could be the cold-war dynamics of the 1950s. Hollywood producers would have found it easier to shoot a film pivoted on an exacerbated communist threat to the receding British Empire, in a country that had a military agreement with the US government and involved a sizeable appearance of armed forces on the screen. But Pakistan as the eventual location choice was also a result of the Indian state's objection to the script, which included an unflattering representation of the Indian nationalist movement in the film as fractured and predominantly a high-caste Hindu one.[24] *Bhowani Junction* constitutes an exciting milestone in an otherwise sombre film-making memory of

Lahore in the early 1950s and remains a revealing instance of the overall *evacuee cinema* culture that emerged in the wake of partition, one whose narrative expulsions and rehabilitations were completely cogent only within the cultural contestations and national rivalries between India and Pakistan.

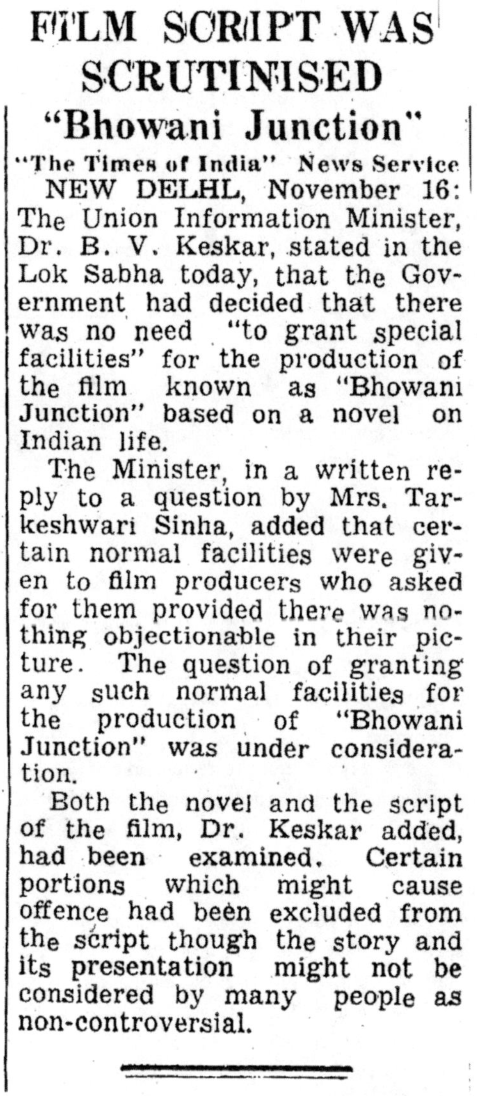

FILM SCRIPT WAS SCRUTINISED

"Bhowani Junction"

"The Times of India" News Service

NEW DELHI, November 16: The Union Information Minister, Dr. B. V. Keskar, stated in the Lok Sabha today, that the Government had decided that there was no need "to grant special facilities" for the production of the film known as "Bhowani Junction" based on a novel on Indian life.

The Minister, in a written reply to a question by Mrs. Tarkeshwari Sinha, added that certain normal facilities were given to film producers who asked for them provided there was nothing objectionable in their picture. The question of granting any such normal facilities for the production of "Bhowani Junction" was under consideration.

Both the novel and the script of the film, Dr. Keskar added, had been examined. Certain portions which might cause offence had been excluded from the script though the story and its presentation might not be considered by many people as non-controversial.

Figure C.1 India's Union Information Ministry scrutinised the script of *Bhowani Junction*

Source: *Times of India*, 17 November 1954, 11. Image published with permission of ProQuest LLC. Further reproduction is prohibited without permission. Image produced by ProQuest LLC as part of ProQuest® Historical Newspapers. www.proquest.com.

Notes

1   Jai Dyal, *I Go South with Prithviraj and His Prithvi Theatres* (Bombay: Prithvi Publications, 1960), 29.

2   Prithviraj Kapoor, 'How Stage Can Serve the Screen', *Filmfare*, 16 May 1952, 33....

3   Rick Altman, *Film/Genre* (London: British Film Institute, 1999), 206.

4   The famous short story writer of partition, Saadat Hasan Manto, worked as a script-writer in Bombay till early 1948, when he left for Pakistan.

5   Saadat Hasan Manto, *Ganje Farishte*, http://www.scribd.com/doc/101672143/Ganjay-Farishtay-by-Saadat-Hasan-Mantto#scribd (accessed on 15 April 2015).

6   Thomas Elsaesser, 'Ethnicity, Authenticity and Exile: A Counterfeit Trade?: German filmmakers and Hollywood', in *Exile, Home and Homeland*, ed. Hamid Naficy, 97–124 (New York: Routledge, 1998), 103.

7   Ibid., 104.

8   Details on studio allocation have been taken from *Pakistan Film Annual* (Karachi: Ameen Tareen, 1957).

9   Hamid Naficy, *An Accented Cinema: Exilic and Diasporic Filmmaking* (Princeton: Princeton University Press, 2001), 3.

10   Ibid., 5.

11   Ibid., 272.

12   Faisal Devji, *Muslim Zion: Pakistan as a Political Idea* (Cambridge, MA: Harvard University Press, 2013), 13.

13   Elsaesser, 'Ethnicity, Authenticity and Exile', 109.

14   Naficy, *An Accented Cinema*, 6.

15   Muhammad Hasan Askari, 'Building Pakistan and Filmmaking', tr. Ali Nobil Ahmad, *BioScope: South Asian Screen Studies* 5, no. 2 (July 2014), http://bio.sagepub.com/content/5/2/175.full.pdf+html (accessed on 20 January 2015).

16   Ibid.

17   Ibid., 178–179.

18   Iftikhar Dadi has proposed a preliminary *dastan* mode of cinema in Pakistan, based on the limited argument that Muslims do not share the devotional practices of *darsana*. While Dadi's intervention is a useful problematising of *darsana*, his thesis of *dastan* and *darsana* as analogous modes marking national difference has all the dangers of simplifying spectatorial subjectivities. It also has implications for locating a conscious authorial and production intent, based on either an ideological commitment (to Islam?) or commercial viability dictated by audience sensibility (Islamic?). This two-nation theory of filmic address in the subcontinent, while beyond the current scope of this research, is unconvincing in its current state of elaboration and requires historicisation of the spectatorial practices of the prenational past of 'Pakistan cinema' as well as in the demographic transmutation produced by partition. See Iftikhar Dadi, 'Registering Crisis: Ethnicity in Pakistani Cinema of the 1960s and 1970s', in *Beyond Crisis*, ed. Naveeda Khan, 145–176 (New Delhi: Routledge, 2010).

19   Minoo Bhandra, 'Ava Gardner and I: Post-Partition Lahore', in *City of Sin and Splendour: Writings on Lahore*, ed. Bapsi Sidhwa, 183–188 (New Delhi: Penguin, 2005).

20   Jaikumar identifies imperial romance films as part of the colonial film aesthetics, 'creating grand narratives of legitimation for an empire and its sustaining vision while confronted

with imminent dissolution'. Priya Jaikumar, *Cinema at the End of Empire: A Politics of Transition in Britain and India* (Durham, NC: Duke University Press, 2006), 135.

21   John Masters, *Bhowani Junction* (New York: Viking Press, 1954).

22   Prem Chowdhary, *Colonial India and the Making of Empire Cinema: Image, Ideology and Identity* (Manchester: Manchester University Press, 2001), 267.

23   Film credits of *Bhowani Junction* DVD.

24   One example of such a representation, changed slightly from the book. In a tense scene, the British officer, Colonel Savage, has to ensure that a goods train must leave the local station, Bhowani Junction, without any delay as the Indian communists have planned its sabotage. On the other hand, the Congress nationalists stage their peaceful protests by lying on the rail tracks in front of the train and refusing to move. Savage then arranges for sewage water to be thrown at peaceful protesters, who being 'high-caste Hindus' immediately get up at the threat and abandon the act of disobedience.

Appendix

Three Film Transcripts from the Fazli Family Collection

With the exception of *Shama*, none of the pre-partition Fazli films survive. Transcripts of two other films, *Ismat* and *Dil*, along with *Shama*, are available in the Fazli family collection. Using the details available in the surviving ephemera, this appendix will describe the narrative content of the Fazli oeuvre.

Ismat (Purity, 1944; Director: Sibtain Fazli; Cast: Nargis, Nandrekar, Mehtab)

Retailing at five *annas* as 'an Islamic, progressive achievement', the transcript of *Ismat* was published by a Lahori Gate press.[1] The opening scenario is of a girls' school assembly where Mohammad Iqbal's popular 'Child's Prayer' is being sung.[2] The teacher in charge proceeds to narrate a didactic story of two young women, Ishrat (Mehtab) and Aaliya (Nargis), who receive divergent upbringings. While Aaliya is noble, devoted to her husband and respectful of traditions, Ishrat is spoilt, estranged from her husband, Shafi, and depicted as too 'Westernised' for her own good. The lives of the two women cross when Aaliya's husband, Aslam, meets with a car accident with Ishrat behind the wheels and loses his memory. Ishrat brings him to her house to recuperate, and an arrangement of restitution transforms into a romantic attachment. Meanwhile, the noble and suffering Aaliya sets out to win back her husband. Finally, Aslam regains his mind and returns to his wife, whose prayers and good conduct have kept her in good stead. A chastened Ishrat becomes a teacher in a girls' school and is the narrator of this moral lesson for girls.

In the first half of the published script, these lives unfold in parallel, offering the pleasures of contrast, where considerations of modesty, marital and filial obligations, and class govern daily life. The primary opposition in the narrative is between Islamic and Western value systems, with the former vindicated and upheld. The story starts off with two weddings. In the first, the officiating minister solicits the bride's consent. Modestly unresponsive, the veiled bride, Aaliya, murmurs a faintly audible assent, or a *hunh*, on being coaxed by her spirited girlfriends. Meanwhile, at the other wedding, the minister refuses to proceed, as the bride does not observe *purdah*. Her comically insouciant family quickly fabricates a screen to hasten the ceremony. The minister is further outraged when the recalcitrant bride, Ishrat, utters an emphatic and English 'yes' and dismisses his request for a more modest consent.

> *Qazi: Zara maadari zabaan mein boliye.*
> *Ishrat: Keh diya na haan-hunh!*

> Minister: Please respond in our mother tongue.
> Ishrat: I said 'Yes'-whatever!

The importance of upbringing is emphasised through contrasting parental figures. On the one hand, Aaliya's mother writes occasional loving letters in Urdu, reiterating that the rightful place of a woman is her marital house. In sharp contrast, Ishrat's father is caricatured as the anglicised 'Daddy' who reminds the daughter that she is most welcome to return to the parental home if there is any trouble. The film portrays this assurance as instigation and implicates him in the breakdown of Ishrat's marriage.

> *Daddy: Shafi! Hum toh aapko phool samajhte they, lekin aap toh damn fool nikle.*

> Daddy: Shafi, I took you to be a pleasing blossom, but you turned out to be a damn fool.

As a product of 'corrupt' upbringing, Ishrat has little regard for Islamic modesty and freely mingles with her husband's friends. Lazy and self-indulgent, she relishes the material comforts hard earned by her husband. In contrast, Aaliya is the epitome of chastity and restraint. This is evidenced by her complete devotion and servitude for she insists on being her husband Aslam's *laundi* (servant-girl). But not even his entreaties can persuade her to come out of the religiously enjoined *purdah*. She refuses to meet his friends and instead sends out tantalising *gilori*, making them all wonder with envy:[3]

> *Jab gilori itni nazuk hai toh isko banane wali kalai kitni nazuk hogi.*

> How delicate the hands be that wrapped so delicate a *gilori*.

Aaliya's self-realisation is routed through self-abnegation. Winning her husband by her morally upright conduct, the sobriquet of *Ismat* (honour) is bestowed on her. She spends her day in household duties, in the company of her mother-in-law, whereas Ishrat's more diverse interests of dance and music keep her away from domesticity, often at intriguing rehearsals. The dialogues are peppered with references to 'true' Islamic faith and the 'hallmark' of true followers, making orthodox Islam the moral compass within the film. An instance of this is the discussion over a painting of a solitary female swan made by Aslam that portends the destiny of the couple within the film. The husband concludes with the following remark on the whereabouts of the missing male.

> Aslam: *Phande mein phasne waale Islaami nahin.*
>
> Aslam: The ensnared are not Islamic.

Therefore, when Aslam is unable to return to Aaliya even by the sighting of the Eid moon and instead starts living with Ishrat, it is caused by a loss of memory and not a 'false' faith. The quandary created by the memory loss forces Aaliya to go out in the outer world to bring back her husband who no longer recognises her. This requires a selective negotiation of the gaze, whereby Aaliya must engage Aslam's attention in a public space without exposing herself to any other man. While the transcript does not detail the 'meeting of eyes', Sibtain Fazli's elder son recalls the scene still vivid in his memory:

> The hero sits in a theatre box watching a play. Nargis (Aaliya) is taken there by her well-wishers and her face is veiled. When he glances sideways at the audiences, he spots Nargis sitting in the opposite box. For that brief duration, she removes her veil. Attracted and drawn by her face, he keeps gazing at her. Later on he regains his memory and the film has a happy end. It's not as if the other woman Mehtab (Ishrat), now disappointed in love, will commit suicide. No, she becomes a teacher in a school and sings *lab pe aati hai dua*.[4]

A servile attitude ironically proves valuable when Aaliya starts living with Ishrat and Aslam, posing as a maidservant. Staying by Aslam's side, she reminds him of their time together and successfully revokes the memory loss. While Aaliya's prayers are answered, Ishrat too is not beyond redemption in the world of the Muslim social, as is emphasised in the above extract. She finds a new lease of life by educating young girls about the correct path and is absolved of her past transgressions.

Dil (Heart, 1946; Director: S. F. Hasnain; Cast: Noorjahan, Baby Zubeida, Kamal Zamindar, Geeta Bose)

The dialogue-heavy transcript of *Dil* contains fewer screen details than *Ismat* and conveys a more episodic structure. *Dil* is the story of a poor widower, Saeed, who struggles to provide for his young daughter, Bachchi. While food and comfort may be hard to come by, he instils piety and religious obligations in his daughter at a tender age. Circumstances take a turn for the worse, and the girl is placed in the care of a crooked family friend, Karar. Tortured by her new guardians and their obnoxious daughter, Ladli, Bachchi runs away and finds a foster family. Several years pass with the father and daughter lost to each other, until Bachchi marries a rich young man, Kamaal, who has received religious instruction from Saeed. Bachchi chooses Kamal over an anglicised suitor, Sikandar, and moves to his house, though the couple decide to keep their marriage a secret. Ignorant of their past connections, Saeed, Bachchi and the crooked family's paths cross again. Once Bachchi's identity is revealed, Ladli's villainous father attempts to kill her and secure Kamaal as Ladli's husband. However, this time Saeed is able to protect his daughter, and both men die in a violent struggle. Bhachchi and her rich husband, Kamaal, live happily ever after, free from the shadow of the conniving family.

The narrative begins with the strain of *azaan* against clouded skies. A poor widower, Saeed, prays for his little motherless daughter. The young child, in what possibly could have been a montage demonstrating the passage of time, is offering prayers, reading the Quran and cooking meals! While Bachchi is taught to serve and take care of the poor, the rich Karar family exploit her father in their greed. They not only charge him exorbitantly for her monthly maintenance but also mistreat her. And while she endures much in silence, she stands up to cruel Karar when he whiplashes her in the midst of her daily prayers.

> Bachchi: *Chachajaan agar main badshah hoti toh jiss haath se tumne namaaz padhte mein koda maara hai, voh jhat se katwa deti.*

> Bachchi: Uncle, had I been the king of this land, I would have ordered your hands to be chopped off as punishment for whiplashing a praying person.

Blinding him in the eye, she escapes the family of tormentors. While Saeed and his daughter are mostly stoic and able to guard secrets despite personal desires, what creates momentum in an otherwise verbose and tedious story is religious apostasy. The challenge to the pious by the profane recurs again at the end of the film.

> Ladli: *Aapko namaz padhne ka bada shauq hai. Bhala isse kya fayda?*
> Noorjahan/Bachchi: *Jo khuda ko yaad rakhta hai voh insaniyat se nahin girta.*
> Ladli: *Toh aapka matlab hai ki jo log khuda ko yaad nahin karte vog sab janwar hote hain.*
> Noorjahan: *Janwar toh nahin, janwar se bhi badtar.*

> Ladli: You are quite fond of praying. What is the use of it?
> Bachchi: One who prays to God retains his humanity.[5]
> Ladli: So you are implying that people who do not pray are savages!
> Noorjahan/Bachchi: Not quite savages, worse than savages.

Unaware that Noorjahan is the grown-up version of Bachchi who Ladli has taken for being dead, the latter cites the instance of the pious Bachchi whose faith could not save her. As keeping her past hidden any longer would be tantamount to an aspersion on the higher powers that have protected her all along, Noorjahan/ Bachchi reveals her identity. This revelation causes Ladli to instigate her father to settle the matter of her enduring rival once and forever. Karar hurtles towards Noorjahan/Bachchi's room in rage, only to find his path blocked by her father. Serendipitously, if not surprisingly, Saeed is praying at that moment and is immediately alerted to Karar's intentions. The two men kill each other in a much-needed scuffle. While Karar's death is divine justice, Saeed's is a fulfilment of his own prayers at the beginning of the film where he had wished for a life dedicated to his daughter.

The dialogues of *Dil* are replete with homilies which configure the ideal relationship between parent and child, husband and wife, rich and poor, and finally God and his followers. These are mobilised in disparate contexts like father–daughter revelry, teacher–student lessons and woman–suitor wooing. Incongruity is hardly an issue here because in the orthodox scheme there is no separation of domains, and all of human life is analysed within a religious idiom.[6] Thus, Kamal unleashes a charm offensive of doctrines on Noorjahan/Bachchi, and in him she finds her true companion. Soon enough they are completing each other's homilies.

> *Kamaal: Khushnaseeb hai voh aurat jisko khidmat karne ka mauqa mile.*
> *Noorjahan/Bachchi: Bachpan mein aulad apne ma-baap ki khidmat karti hai.*
> *Kamaal: Aur badi ho kar apne shauhar ki khidmat karti hai aur ma bankar bachchon ki khidmat karti hai.*

> Kamaal: Fortunate is the woman who gets an opportunity to serve...
> Noorjahan/Bachchi: In childhood she serves her father and mother...
> Kamaal: And on growing up, her husband and then serves her children on becoming a mother.

Like *Ismat*, the anglicised suitor is comical, inadequate and therefore fails to win Noorjahan. The two heatedly debate the merits of home study, as against English education, and Noorjahan sermonises her other suitor Sikandar on proper conduct by giving examples from older times.

> *Sikandar: Kya main pooch sakta hun ki ghar ki chardiwari mein kya sikhaya jaata hai?*
> *Noorjahan/Bachchi: Toh sunein, bachpan se hi tamam ghar grihasti ke kaam sikhaye jaate thay. Uss zamane mein yeh nahin sikhaya jaata ki khana hotel se aayega kyunki memsahib toh khana pakana jaanti hi nahin.*
> *Sikandar: Subhanallah, aapne kitni achchi taleem payee hai!*
> *Noorjahan/Bachchi: Shukriya, khas taur par iss baat ka ki aap jaise angrezi padhe likhe ko ek jaahil ladki ke khayalat pasand aaye.*

> Sikandar: May I enquire what else has been taught within the confines of the home?
> Noorjahan/Bachchi: Sure, listen to this. Right from childhood every girl was taught to stitch and sew along with all household tasks. In these years it was

not encouraged that food will arrive from a hotel because the lady of the house does not know how to cook.

Sikandar: God be praised! You have been a beneficiary of such excellent education.

Noorjahan/Bachchi: Thank you, especially because an English-educated person finds an illiterate girl's worldview agreeable.

Ladli, competing with Noorjahan for Kamal's affection, loses out as her upbringing is marked by materialism, godlessness and greed. Indoctrination at a young age is presented as leaving a lasting impact, and though Bachchi is separated from the father at an early age, she lives by his adages in her adult life and manages to carve out a beautiful life for herself.

Shama (The Flame, 1946; Producer: Sohrab Modi; Disputed Director Credits, Cast: Mehtab, Wasti, Prakash)

Shama follows the upheavals in the life of Noor Bano who is married off to a bereaved *nawab*, still fiercely in love with his dead wife, Anjuman, whose portraits dominate the house. With her patience and meekness, Noor Bano wins over her husband. However, their happiness is short-lived when her noble attempts to settle the dead wife's murky past with a blackmailer make Noor Bano the object of the *nawab's* suspicion. Pregnant with the *nawab's* child, she is banished from the palatial house and finds shelter in a girls' orphanage. Her refusal to divulge her son's paternity costs her the orphanage job and she is back on the streets. She then entrusts the *nawab's* faithful servant with her son and finds work as a maid at an elderly woman's house. As it transpires, the blackmailer, Hashmat, happens to be the son of the elderly woman. Touched by Noor Bano's selfless service, Hashmat decides to reveal the truth to the *nawab*. A repentant and much wiser *nawab* smashes all the portraits of Anjuman and brings back Noor Bano into the house, where the entire family is reunited.

In making *Shama*, Sibtain Fazli was reportedly inspired by Hitchcock's *Rebecca* and its theme of the overwhelming presence of a dead wife whose secrets are unearthed by the new wife.[7] The opening sequence of *Shama* unfolds in the dimly lit grand hall of the Nawab's mansion, decorated with large portraits of Anjuman. The visual distinction between Noor Bano and Anjuman is explicit as Noor is attired in *gharara*s in keeping with upper- and middle-class North Indian Muslim conventions, with her head covered, and Anjuman is dressed in a *sari* in the photographs. Noor's attempts to woo her temperamental husband by wearing Anjuman's *sari*s and humming her songs are only met with a reprimand to return to modest clothes. Unable to ensnare the Nawab by lesser tricks, Noor Bano finally wins him over by contributing to his doleful poetry and adopting time-tested servitude. Even when the *nawab* quite rightly regrets his bad behaviour, Noor Bano encapsulates the lot of her ilk in these words:

Aap mujhe gunahgaar na kijiye. Aurat dukh na paye toh hai kis marz ki dawa.

Please do not condemn me by apologising. What is a woman's life worth if she does not suffer?

It is Noor Bano's alacrity to suffer and her uncompromising chastity that presumably made this excessive adaptation of *Rebecca* pleasurable, despite there being little mystery. The anxiety around women learning to read and write as involving a breach of modesty is present in Anjuman's love letters. Here too the villain is Westernised and caricatured: he is an ardent admirer of the 'freedom' of foreign lands and hopes to make money out of the scandalous letters penned by the first wife. Mistaking Noor Bano for Anjuman, the blackmailer, Hashmat, threatens her with making public the contents of the letters. Hashmat, we learn, has spent time in Chicago, and he boasts to his simple mother of the skills acquired abroad.

Isse kehtein hain blackmail, iss art ko vilayat waale khoob samajhte hain, Hindustan waale kya jaane.

This is called blackmail. While the foreigners patronize this art, the simpletons of Hindustan remain clueless!

Hashmat's redemption lies in behaving in congruity with traditional kinship patterns. As his mother instructs him to take care of his 'sister' Noor Bano, Hashmat must let go of his 'foreign tricks' and salvage the situation. The *nawab* too must smash his blind devotion and realise its impropriety. The beguiling seductiveness of Anjuman's memory eventually gives way to the genuine sacrifice of Noor Bano's existence.

Notes

1   '*Ismat*: Fazli Brothers ka Islami, islahi shahakar jisko Rai Jagdish ne purdah screen par dekh kar qalamband kiya.'

2   'Lab pe aati hai dua bann ke tamanna meri.' (Through the lips come forth my desire turned into a prayer.)

3   *Gilori* is a flavoured and stimulating preparation of betel leaf and tobacco.

4   Sohail Fazli, Interview, July 2012.

5   In passages of the protagonist girl's adult life, the transcript makes a switch from Bachchi to Noorjahan, referring to the character by the actress's name. So for exchanges in the lead character's adult life, 'Bachchi' and 'Noorjahan' are used together.

6   Barbara Metcalf, 'Islamic Reform and Islamic Women', in *Moral Conduct and Authority: The Place of Adab in South Asian Islam*, ed. Barbara Metcalf, 184–195 (Berkeley: University of California Press, 1984), 187.

7   Sohail Fazli, Interview, July 2012.

Filmography

Actress (1948), directed by Najam Naqvi, India.

Afsana (1951), directed by B. R. Chopra, India.

Aladdin ka Beta (1960), directed by Riaz Ahmed Raju, Pakistan.

Aladdin and the Wonderful Lamp (1952), directed by Homi Wadia, India.

Anarkali (1954), directed by Nandlal Jaswantlal, India.

Anarkali (1958), directed by Anwar Kamal Pasha, Pakistan.

Bahot Dinn Hue (1954), directed by S. S. Vasan, India.

Baiju Bawra (1952), directed by Vijay Bhatt, India.

Bedari (1957), directed by Rafiq Rizvi, Pakistan.

Behrupia (1960), directed by Aslam Irani, Pakistan.

Boot Polish (1954), directed by Prakash Arora, India.

Chaman (1948), directed by Roop K. Shorey, India.

Clerk (1960), directed by Khalil Qaiser, Pakistan.

Dard (1947), directed by A.R. Kardar, Bombay.

Dastaan (1969), directed by Rattan Kumar, Pakistan.

Dholak (1950), directed by Roop K. Shorey, India.

Do Aansoo (1950), directed by Anwar Kamal Pasha, Pakistan.

Do Bigha Zameen (1953), directed by Bimal Roy, India.

Dopatta (1952), directed by Sibtain Fazli, Pakistan.

Ek Do Teen (1953), directed by Roop K. Shorey, India.

Ek Thi Ladki (1949), directed by Roop K. Shorey, India.

Elan (1947), directed by Mehboob Khan, Bombay.

Gaon ki Gori (1945), directed by K. Amarnath, Bombay.

Hatim (1956), directed by Dawood Chand, Pakistan.

Humayun (1945), directed by Mehboob Khan, Bombay.

Ishq-e-Laila (1957), directed by Munshi Dil, Pakistan.

Jagriti (1954), directed by Satyen Bose, India.

Jugnu (1947), directed by Shaukat Hussain Rizvi, Bombay.

Kartar Singh (1959), directed by Saifuddin Saif, Pakistan.

Khandaan (1942), directed by Shaukat Hussain Rizvi, Lahore.

Khazanchi (1941), directed by Moti B. Gidwani, Lahore.

Lahore (1949), directed by M. L. Anand, Bombay.

Laila Majnu (1953), directed by K. Amarnath, India.

Lakhon mein Eik (1967), directed by Raza Mir, Pakistan.

Masoom (1957), directed by Shareef Nayyar, Pakistan.

Mother India (1957), directed by Mehboob Khan, India.

Mughal-e-Azam (1960), directed by K.Asif, India.

Nagin (1954), directed by Nandlal Jaswantlal, India.

Nagin (1959), directed by Khalil Qaiser, Pakistan.

Najma (1943), directed by Mehboob Khan, India.

Nastik (1954), directed by I. S. Johar, India.

Nek Parvin (1946), directed by S. M. Yusuf, Bombay.

Pehli Nazar (1945), directed by Mazhar Khan, Bombay.

Prithvi Vallabh (1943), directed by Sohrab Modi, Bombay.

Pukar (1939), directed by Sohrab Modi, Bombay.

Saheli (1960), directed by S. M. Yusuf, Pakistan.

Sarfarosh (1956), directed by Anwar Kamal, Pakistan.

Shahjahan (1946), directed by A. R. Kardar, Bombay.

Shama (1946), Minerva Movietone, Bombay.

Shrimatiji (1952), directed by I. S. Johar, India.

Sikandar (1941), directed by Sohrab Modi, Bombay.

Toofan aur Diya (1956), directed by Prabhat Kumar, India.

Zeenat (1945), directed by Shaukat Hussain Rizvi, Bombay.

Zehr-e-Ishq (1958), directed by Masood Pervez, Pakistan.

Bibliography

Official Reports

Film Industry in Pakistan, Publication no. 117. Lahore: Board of Economic Enquiry, Punjab, 1957.

Report of the Film Enquiry Committee. New Delhi: Ministry of Information of Information and Broadcasting, Government of India Press, 1951.

Report of the Film Fact Finding Committee. Karachi: Government of Pakistan Press, 1962.

Government Records

'Cinema Films'. File no. 245, 1937–1938, Home Department (Political), Maharashtra State Archives, Mumbai.

File No. 22/121, 1933, Home Department (Political), National Archives of India, New Delhi.

Newspapers

Pakistan Times (1950–1962), Microfilm, British Library, London, and Nehru Memorial Museum and Library, New Delhi.

The Tribune (1940–1947), Microfilm, Nehru Memorial Museum and Library, New Delhi.

Times of India, Proquest Historical Newspaper Database: 1838–2005, British Library, London.

Sunday Tribune (1940–1947), Microfilm, Nehru Memorial Museum and Library, New Delhi.

Film Journals and Magazines

Eastern Film Magazine (Select issues 1962–1965, English), Courtesy: Asif Noorani, Karachi.

Filmfare (1952–1957, English) National Film Archive of India, Pune.

Filmindia (1940–1957, English) National Film Archive of India, Pune, and Reuben Library–British Film Institute, London.

Journal of the Indian Film Industry (1952, English), Reuben Library–British Film Institute, London.

Musawar (1970, Urdu), Fazli Collection, Lahore.

Newline (2005, English), Courtesy Saeed Shiraz, Karachi.

Nigar Weekly (1952–1958, Golden Jubilee Edition, 2009, Urdu), Nigar Magazine Office, Karachi.

Pakistan Screen Annual (1957, English), Reuben Library–British Film Institute, London.

Motion Picture Magazine (1947, English), National Film Archive of India, Pune.

Theatre Arts (1952, English), The Internet Archive. https://archive.org/details/sim_theatre-arts_1952-08_36_8/mode/2up. Accessed on 24 May 2022.

Memoirs, Film Compendiums and Published Plays

Abbas, Khwaja Ahmad. *I Am Not an Island*. New Delhi: Vikas, 1977.

Ahmed, Muneer (ed.). *Out of Date*. Lahore: Atish Feshan Press, 1986.

Bismil, Lal Chandra. *Ahooti*. Bombay: Prithvi Theatre Prakashan, 1950.

Dyal, Jai. *I Go South with Prithviraj and His Prithvi Theatres*. Bombay: Prithvi Publications, 1960.

Hassan, Khaled (ed. and trans.). *Bitter Fruit: The Very Best of Saadat Hasan Manto*. New Delhi: Penguin Books, 2008.

Kapoor, Prithviraj, Inderraj Anand and Ramesh Sehgal. *Deewar*. Bombay: Prithvi Publication, 1952.

Kashmiri, Agha Jani. *Saher Hone Tak*. Delhi: Imperial Press, 1965.

Mehra, Jankidas. *My Misadventures in Filmland*. New Delhi: Newman Group of Publishers, 1980.

Rizvi, Shaukat Hussain. *Noorjahan aur Main*. Lahore: Atish Feshan Publications, 1984.

Sahni, Balraj. *An Autobiography*, translated by Ramesh Deshpande. New Delhi: Hind Pocket Books, 1979.

Sehgal, Zohra. *Close-Up: Memoirs of a Life on Stage and Screen*. New Delhi: Women Unlimited, 2010.

Shaikh, R. A. (ed.) *Filmdom: Who's Who in the Indian Film Industry*. Lahore: Globial Linkers, 1946.

Private Papers

Fazli Family collection.

Hersh Pancholi's collection.

Books and Articles

Anon. 'A Pakistan Hysteria'. *Journal of the Indian Film Industry* 11, no. 2 (July 1951), 6.

———. 'Indo-Pakistan Film Trade'. *Journal of the Indian Film Industry* 12, no. 7 (March 1952), 13.

Abbas, Amber. 'Disruption and Belonging: Aligarh, Its University, and the Changing Meaning of Place since Partition'. *Oral History Review* 44, no. 2 (2017): 301–321.

Ahmad, Ali Nobil. 'Introduction: Is There a Muslim World?' *Third Text: Cinema in Muslim Societies* 24, no. 1 (January 2010): 1–10.

Acland, Charles R., and Haidee Wasson. 'Introduction: Utility and Cinema'. In *Useful Cinema*, edited by Charles R. Acland and Haidee Wasson, 1–14. Durham, NC: Duke University Press.

Ahmad, Nazir. *The Bride's Mirror: A Tale of Life in Delhi a Hundred Years Ago*, translated by G. E. Ward. New Delhi: Permanent Black, 2001.

Ahmed, Sara. *The Cultural Politics of Emotion*. Edinburgh: Edinburgh University Press, 2004.

Altman, Rick. *Film/Genre*. London: British Film Institute, 1999.

Ambedkar, B. R. 'Hindus Really Want Dominion Status, Muslims Really Want Independence'. In *Pakistan, or the Partition of India*, 2nd edition. Bombay: Thackers Publishers, 1945. http://www.columbia.edu/itc/mealac/pritchett/00ambedkar/ambedkar_partition/412a.html#part_2. Accessed on 2 February 2021.

———. 'Pakistan or the Partition of India (online text)'. In *Dr. Babasaheb Ambedkar: Writings and Speeches*, vol. 8. Bombay: Education Department, Government of Maharashtra, 1990.

Anderson, Benedict. *Imagined Communities*. London: Verso, 2006.

Anderson, Perry. *The Indian Ideology*. London: Verso, 2013.

Ansari, Rehan. 'On Mushtaq Gazdar's History of Pakistani Cinema'. In *Sarai Reader: The Public Domain*, 69–70. New Delhi: Centre for the Study of Developing Societies, 2001.

Askari, Muhammad Hassan. 'Building Pakistan and Filmmaking', translated by Ali Nobil Ahmad. *BioScope: South Asian Screen Studies* 5, no. 2 (July 2014): 175–181. http://bio.sagepub.com/content/5/2/175.full.pdf+html. Accessed on 20 January 2015.

Aziz, K. K. *Rehmat Ali: A Biography*. Lahore: Vanguard Press, 1987.

Badiou, Alain. *Cinema*. Cambridge: Polity, 2013.

Banerjee, Mukulika. *The Pathan Unarmed: Opposition and Memory in the North West Frontier*. Karachi and New Delhi: Oxford University Press, 2000.

Bannerth, Ernst. 'Islam in Modern Urdu Poetry: A Translation of Muhammad Iqbal's "Shikwa wa Jawab-i-Shikwa" (The Complaint and the Reply to It)'. In *Iqbal: New Dimensions*, edited by Iqram Chaghtai, 189–204. Lahore: Sang-i-Mil, 2003.

Barker, Clare. *Postcolonial Fiction and Disability: Exceptional Children, Metaphor and Materiality*. Basingstoke: Palgrave Macmillan, 2011.

Barnouw, Eric, and S. Krishnaswamy. *Indian Film*. New York: Oxford University Press, 1980.

Basu, Tapan, Pradip Datta, Sumit Sarkar, Tanika Sarkar and Sambuddha Sen. *Khaki Shorts Saffron Flags: A Critique of the Hindu Right*. New Delhi: Orient Longman, 1993.

Baumfield, Vivienne. 'Science and Sanskrit: Vivekananda's Views on Education'. In *Swami Vivekanand and the Modernization of Hindusim*, edited by William Radice, 194–212. Delhi: Oxford University Press, 1998.

Bhabha, Homi K. *The Location of Culture*. London: Routledge, 1994.

Bhandra, Minoo. 'Ava Gardner and I: Post-Partition Lahore'. In *City of Sin and Splendour: Writings on Lahore*, edited by Bapsi Sidhwa, 183–188. New Delhi: Penguin, 2005.

Bharat, Meenakshi, and Nirmal Kumar (eds.). *Filming the Line of Control: The Indo-Pak Relationship through the Cinematic Lens*. New Delhi: Routledge, 2005.

Bhaskar, Ira. 'Trauma, Melodrama and the Production of Historical Affect: The Partition, Memory and the Contemporary Communal Riot in Indian Cinema'. In *Film Melodrama Revisited*, edited by Dominique Nasta and Muriel Andrin, 339–356. Brussels: PIE Peter Lang, 2014.

Bhaskar, Ira, and Richard Allen. *Islamicate Cultures of Bombay Cinema*. New Delhi: Tulika Books, 2009.

Bhaumik, Kaushik. 'The Emergence of the Bombay Film Industry 1913–1936'. PhD dissertation. University of Oxford, 2001.

Blasco, Paloma Gay. 'The Fragility of Cosmopolitanism: A Biographical Approach'. *Social Anthropology* 18, no. 4 (2010): 403–409.

Butalia, Urvashi. *The Other Side of Silence*. New Delhi: Penguin, 1998.

———. 'Community, State and Gender: On Women's Agency during Partition'. *Economic and Political Weekly* 28, no. 17 (24 April 1993): 12–24.

Brennan, Timothy. 'The National Longing for Form'. In *Nation and Narration*, edited by Homi Bhabha, 23–43. London: Routledge, 1990.

Brooks, Peter. *The Melodramatic Imagination: Balzac, Henry James, Melodrama and the Mode of Excess*. New Haven: Yale University Press, 1995.

Bruno, Giuliana. *Streetwalking on a Ruined Map: Cultural Theory and the City Films of Elvira Notari*. Princeton: Princeton University Press, 1993.

Chakrabarty, Dipesh. 'Modernity and Ethnicity in India: A History for the Present'. *Economic and Political Weekly* 30, no. 52, (December 1995): 3373–3380. http://www.jstor.org/stable/4403623. Accessed on 29 January 2013.

––––––. 'Postcoloniality and the Artifice of History: Who Speaks for "Indian" Pasts?' *Representations* 37 (Winter 1992): 1–26.

Chakravarty, Sumita. *National Identity in Indian Popular Cinema 1947–1987*. Austin: University of Texas Press, 1993.

Chatterjee, Gayatri. *Mother India*. London: BFI Film Classics, 2002.

Chatterjee, Partha. *The Partha Chatterjee Omnibus*. New Delhi: Oxford University Press, 1999.

Chatterjee, Ranita. 'Journeys in and beyond the City: Cinema in Calcutta 1897–1939'. PhD dissertation, University of Westminster, 2011.

Choudhari, Shohini. *Contemporary World Cinema*. Edinburgh: Edinburgh University Press, 2005.

Chowdhry, Prem. *Colonial India and the Making of Empire Cinema: Image, Ideology and Identity*. Manchester: Manchester University Press, 2001.

Crofts, Stephen. 'Reconceptualising National Cinema/s'. In *Film and Nationalism*, edited by Alan Williams, 25–51. New Jersey: Rutgers State University, 2002.

Dadi, Iftikhar. 'Bioscopic and Screen Studies of Pakistan'. *BioScope: South Asian Screen Studies* 1, no. 1 (January 2010a): 11–15. DOI:10.1177/097492760900100103. Accessed on 5 December 2010.

––––––. 'Registering Crisis: Ethnicity in Pakistani Cinema of the 1960s and 1970s'. In *Beyond Crisis: Revaluating Pakistan*, edited by Naveeda Khan, 145–176. New Delhi: Routledge, 2010.

Das, Srijana. 'Partition and Punjabiyat in Bombay Cinema: The Cinematic Perspectives of Yash Chopra and Others'. *Contemporary South Asia* 15, no. 4 (December 2006): 453–471.

Desai, Meghnad. *Nehru's Hero Dilip Kumar in the Life of India*. New Delhi: Roli Books, 2004.

Devji, Faisal. *Muslim Zion: Pakistan as a Political Idea*. Cambridge, MA: Harvard University Press, 2013.

––––––. 'Apologetic Modernity'. *Modern Intellectual History* 4, no. 1 (2007): 61–76. DOI: 10.1017/S1479244306001041. Accessed on 23 April 2014.

––––––. 'Gender and the Politics of Space'. In *Forging Identities: Gender, Communities and the State*, edited by Zoya Hassan, 22–37. New Delhi: Kali for Women, 1994.

––––––. 'Muslim Nationalism: Founding Identity in Colonial India'. PhD dissertation, University of Chicago, 1993.

––––––. 'Hindu/Muslim/Indian'. *Public Culture* 5, no. 1 (Fall 1992): 1–18.

Dharamsey, Virchand. 'The Advent of Sound in Indian Cinema: Theatre, Orientalism, Action and Magic'. *Journal of Moving Image* 9 (2010): 22–51. http://www.jmionline. org/article/the_advent_of_sound_in_indian_cinema_thea   tre_orientalism_ action_magic_1. Accessed on 25 July 2014.

Dharwadkar, Aparna. *Theatres of Independence: Drama, Theory and Urban Performance in India*. Iowa City: University of Iowa Press, 2005.

Dhulipala, Venkat. *Creating a New Medina*. New Delhi: Cambridge University Press, 2015.

Dutta, Pradeep Kumar. *Carving Blocs*. Oxford: Oxford University Press, 1999.

Dyal, Jai. *I Go South with Prithviraj and His Prithvi Theatres*. Bombay: Prithvi Publications, 1960.

Dwyer, Rachel. *Yash Chopra: Fifty Years in Cinema*. New Delhi: Roli Books, 2002.

———. *Filming the Gods: Religion and Indian Cinema*. Oxon: Routledge, 2006.

Dyer, Richard. *Stars*, 2nd edition. London: British Film Institute, 1998.

———. 'Charisma'. In *Stardom: The Industry of Desire*, edited by Christine Gledhill, 57–59. London: Routledge, 1991.

———. 'A Star is Born and the Construction of Authenticity'. In *Stardom: The Industry of Desire*, edited by Christine Gledhill, 136–144. London: Routledge, 1991.

Evans, Mary. *Missing Persons: The Impossibility of Auto/Biography*. London: Routledge, 1999.

Elsaesser, Thomas. 'Ethnicity, Authenticity and Exile: A Counterfeit Trade?': German Filmmakers and Hollywood'. In *Exile, Home and Homeland*, edited by Hamid Naficy, 97–124. New York: Routledge, 1998.

Fischer, Jaimey. 'On the Ruins of Masculinity: The Figure of the Child in Italian Neorealism and the German Rubble Film'. In *Italian Neorealism and Global Cinema*, edited by Laura E. Ruberto and Kristi M. Wilson, 25–53. Michigan: Wayne State University Press, 2007.

Forest J., and K. Leonard (eds.). *Dead Ringers: The Remake in Theory and Practice*. Albany: State University of New York Press, 2002.

Gahlot, Deepa. *Shashi Kapoor Presents the Prithviwallas*. New Delhi: Roli Books, 2004.

Gaines, Jane. 'Early Cinema's Heydey of Copying'. *Cultural Studies* 20, nos. 2–3 (2006): 227–244. DOI: 10.1080/09502380600551485. Accessed on 3 November 2014.

Ganti, Tejaswini. *Producing Bollywood: Inside the Contemporary Hindi Film Industry*. Durham, NC: Duke University Press, 2012.

Gardner, Vivien. 'By Herself'. In *The Cambridge Companion to the Actress*, edited by Maggie B. Gale and John Stokes, 173–192. Cambridge: Cambridge University Press, 2007.

Gazdar, Mushtaq. *Pakistan Cinema 1947–1997*. Karachi: Oxford University Press, 1998.

Gehring, Wes D. *Screwball Comedy: Defining a Film Genre*. Ball State Monograph Number Thirty-One. Muncie, IN: Ball State University, 1983.

Gellner, Ernest. *Nations and Nationalism*. Oxford: Blackwell, 1983.

Glitre, Kathrina. *Hollywood Romantic Comedy: States of the Union 1934–65*. Manchester: Manchester University Press, 2006.

Gopal, Priyamvada. *Literary Radicalism in India: Gender, Nation and the Transition to Independence*. London: Routledge, 2005.

Gordon, Richard. 'The Hindu Mahasabha and the Indian National Congress 1915–1926'. *Modern Asian Studies* 9, no. 2 (1975): 145–203.

Gooptu, Sharmishta. *Bengali Cinema: An Other Nation*. London: Routledge, 2011.

Govil, Nitin, and Eric Hoyt. 'Thieves of Bombay: United Artistes, Colonial Copyright, and Film Piracy in 1920s'. *BioScope: South Asian Screen Studies* 5, no. 1 (January 2014): 5–27. DOI: 10.1177/0974927614532878. Accessed on 29 October 2014.

Gul, Aijaz. *Noorjehan: The Melody Queen*. New Delhi: Vista, 2008.

―――. 'Pakistan'. In *Being and Becoming: The Cinemas of Asia*, edited by Aruna Vasudeva, Latika Padgaonkar and Rashmi Doraiswamy, 329–345. New Delhi: Macmillan, 2002.

Gupt, Somnath. *The Parsi Theatre: Its Origins and Development*, translated and edited by Kathryn Hansen. Calcutta: Seagull Books, 2005.

Gupta, Charu. *Sexuality, Obscenity, Community: Women, Muslims and the Hindu Public in Colonial India*. New York: Palgrave, 2001.

Hansen, Kathryn. *Stages of Life: Indian Theatre Autobiographies*. Ranikhet: Permanent Black, 2011.

―――. 'The Indar Sabha Phenomenon: Public Theatre and Consumption in Greater India (1853–1956)'. In *Pleasure and the Nation: The History, Politics and Consumption of Public Culture in India*, edited by Rachel Dwyer and Christopher Pinney, 76–114. New Delhi: Oxford University Press, 2001.

―――. 'Staging Composite Culture'. *South Asia Research* 29, no. 2 (2009): 151–168. DOI: 10.1177/026272800902900203. Accessed 3 February 2013.

―――. 'Ritual Enactments in a Hindi "Mythological": Betab's "Mahabharat" in Parsi Theatre'. *Economic and Political Weekly* 41, no. 48 (2 December 2006): 4985–4991. https://www.epw.in/journal/2006/48/special-articles/ritual-enactments-hindi-mythological.html. Accessed on 10 August 2020.

Hansen, Miriam Bratu. 'Fallen Women, Rising Stars, New Horizons: Shanghai Silent Film as Vernacular Modernism'. *Film Quarterly* 54, no. 1 (Autumn, 2000): 10– 22.

―――. 'The Mass Production of the Senses: Classical Cinema as Vernacular Modernism'. *Modernism/Modernity* 6, no. 2 (1999): 59–77.

Hastie, Amelie. *Cupboards of Curiosity: Women, Recollection and Film History*, Durham, NC: Duke University Press, 2007.

Henry-Blackmore, Virginia Gray. *Voices of Islam, Vol 3: Voices of Life: Family, Home and Society*. Westport: Praeger Publications, 2007.

Hjort, Mette, and Scott Mackenzie (eds.). *Cinema and Nation*. London: Routledge, 2000.

Hosain, Attia. *Distant Traveller*, edited by Aamer Hussein. New Delhi: Women Unlimited, 2013.

Hoek, Lotte, 'Cross-wing Filmmaking: East Pakistani Urdu Films and Their Traces in the Bangladesh Film Archive'. *BioScope: South Asian Screen Studies* 5, no. 2 (2014): 99–118.

Irwin, Robert. *The Arabian Nights: A Companion*. New York: Tauris Parke, 1994.

Jackson, Rosemary. *Fantasy: The Literature of Subversion*. London: Metheun, 1981.

Jaffrelot, Christophe. *The Hindu Nationalist Movement and Indian Politics, 1925 to the 1990s*. London: Hurst & Co., 1996.

Jaikumar, Priya. *Cinema at the End of Empire: A Politics of Transition in Britain and India*. Durham, NC: Duke University Press, 2006.

Jain, Madhu. *The Kapoors: The First Family of Indian Cinema*. New Delhi: Penguin Viking, 2005.

Jalal, Ayesha. *The Pity of Partition*. Oxford: Princeton University Press, 2013.

————. *The Sole Spokesman*. Lahore: Sang-i-Meel Publications, 1999.

Jameson, Fredric. 'Third-World Literature in the Era of Multinational Capitalism'. *Social Text* 15 (Autumn, 1986): 65–88.

Kabir, Alamgir. *The Cinema in Pakistan*. Dacca: Sandhani Publications, 1969.

————. *Film in Bangladesh*. Dacca: Bangla Academy, 1979.

Kakar, Sudhir. 'Culture and Psychoanalysis: A Personal Journey'. *Social Analysis: The International Journal of Anthropology* 50, no. 2 (Summer 2006): 25–44.

Kapila, Shruti. 'Armitage on Civil Wars'. *Global Intellectual History* 4, no. 3 (2019): 318–321.

Kamra, Sukeshi. *Bearing Witness: Partition, Independence, End of Raj*. Calgary: Calgary University Press, 2002.

Kamtekar, Indivar. 'The Fables of Nationalism'. *India International Quarterly* 26, no. 3 (Monsoon 1999): 44–54.

Kapur, Anuradha. 'Reassembling the Modern: An Indian Theatre Map since Independence'. In *Modern Indian Theatre*, edited by Nandi Bhatia, 41–55. Delhi: Oxford University Press, 2009.

Kesavan, Mukul. 'Urdu, Awadh and the Tawaif: The Islamicate Roots of the Hindi Cinema'. In *Forging Identities: Gender, Communities and the State*, edited by Zoya Hassan, 244–257. New Delhi: Kali for Women, 1994.

Khan, Ali, and Ali Nobil Ahmed. 'From Zinda Laash to Zibahkhana: Violence and Horror in Pakistani Cinema'. *Third Text* 24, no. 1, Special Issue: Cinema in Muslim Societies (January 2010): 149–162.

Khan, Ali, and Ali Nobil Ahmed (eds.). *Film and Social Change in Pakistan*. Karachi: Oxford University Press, 2016.

Khan, Naveeda. *A Muslim Becoming*. Durham, NC: Duke University Press, 2012.

Kiernan, V. G., ed. and trans. *Poems by Faiz*. London: George Allen and Unwin Ltd, 1971.

Klinger, Barbara. *Melodrama and Meaning: History, Culture and the Films of Douglas Sirk*. Bloomington: Indiana University Press, 1994.

Kumar, Krishna. *Battle for Peace*. New Delhi: Penguin. 2007.

———. 'Peace with the Past'. *Seminar: Rewriting History* (February 2003). http://www.indiaseminar.com/2003/522/522%20krishna%20kumar.htm. Accessed on 20 November 2012.

———. *Prejudice and Pride*. New Delhi: Penguin, 2001.

Kumar, Nirmal. 'Kaisi Sarhadein Kaisi Majbooriyan'. In *Filming the Line of Control: The Indo-Pak Relationship through the Cinematic Lens*, edited by Meenakshi Bharat and Nirmal Kumar, 128–139. New Delhi: Routledge, 2008.

Liang, Lawrence. 'Beyond Representation: The Figure of the Pirate'. In *Access to Knowledge: In the Age of Intellectual Property*, edited by Amy Kapcyznski and Gaëlle Krikorian, 353–376. New York: Zone Books, 2010.

Lelyveld, David. *Aligarh's First Generation: Muslim Solidarity in British India*. New Delhi: Oxford University Press, 1996.

Leitch, Thomas. 'Twice-Told Tales: Disavowal and The Rhetoric of the Remake'. In *Dead Ringers: The Remake in Theory and Practice*, edited by Jennifer Forest and Leonard R. Koos, 37–62. Albany: State University of New York Press, 2002.

Lunn, David. 'The Eloquent Language: Hindustani in 1940s Indian Cinema'. *BioScope: South Asian Screen Studies* 6, no. 1 (2015): 1–26.

Majumdar, Neepa. 'Importing Neorealism, Exporting Cinema'. In *Global Neorealism: The Transnational History of a Film Style*, edited by S. Giovacchini and R. Skalr, 178–193. Jackson, MS: University Press of Mississippi, 2011.

———. *Wanted Cultured Ladies Only!: Female Stardom and Cinema in India, 1930–1950*. Champaign, IL: University of Illinois Press, 2009.

Manto, Saadat Hasan. 'Pakistan Ke Film/Pakistani Film (1948)', translated by Ali Nobil Ahmad. *BioScope: South Asian Screen Studies* 5, no. 2 (July 2014): 163–166. DOI:10.1177/0974927614550752. Accessed 20 January 2015

———. *Ganje Farishte*. http://www.scribd.com/doc/101672143/Ganjay-Farishtay-by-Saadat-Hasan-Mantto#scribd. Accessed on 15 April 2015.

Masters, John. *Bhowani Junction*. New York: Viking Press, 1954.

Mazumdar, Ranjani. *Bombay Cinema: An Archive of the City*. Minneapolis: University of Minnesota Press, 2007.

Menon, Ritu, and Kamla Bhasin. *Borders and Boundaries: Women in India's Partition*. New Delhi: Kali for Women, 1998.

Menon, Ritu, and Kamla Bhasin. 'Recovery, Rupture and Resistance: Indian State and the Abduction of Women during Partition'. *Economic and Political Weekly* 28, no. 17 (1993): WS2–WS11.

Metcalf, Barbara D. (ed.). *Moral Conduct and Authority: The Place of Adab in South Asian Islam.* Berkeley: University of California Press, 1984.

Minault, Gail. *The Extended Family as Metaphor and the Expansion of Women's Realm.* Delhi: Chanakya Publications, 1981.

Mir, Farina. *The Social Space of Language: Vernacular Culture in British Colonial Punjab.* Berkley: University of California Press, 2010.

Mufti, Aamir. *Enlightenment in the Colony: The Jewish Question and the Crisis of Postcolonial Culture.* Princeton: Princeton University Press, 2007.

Mukherjee, Aditya, Mridula Mukherjee and Sucheta Mahajan. *RSS, School Texts and the Murder of Mahatma Gandhi: The Hindu Communal Project.* New Delhi: SAGE Publications, 2008.

Mukherjee, Debashree. *Bombay Hustle: Making Movies in a Colonial City.* New York: Columbia University Press, 2020.

———. 'Creating Cinema's Reading Publics'. In *No Limits: Media Studies from India,* edited by Ravi Sundaram, 165–198. New Delhi: Oxford University Press, 2013.

Mukhopadhaya, Urvi. *The Medieval in Film.* New Delhi: Orient Blackswan, 2013.

Naficy, Hamid. *An Accented Cinema: Exilic and Diasporic Filmmaking.* Princeton: Princeton University Press, 2001.

———. *Home Exile and Homeland.* New York: Routledge, 1999.

Nava, Mica. *Visceral Cosmopolitanism: Gender, Culture and the Normalization of Difference.* New York: Berg, 2009.

Neale, Steve. *Genre and Hollywood.* London and New York: Routledge, 2000.

Neville, Pran. 'Going to the Cinema'. In *Penguin: The Non-Fiction Collection 2.* New Delhi: Penguin, 2007.

———. *Lahore: A Sentimental Journey.* New Delhi: Penguin, 2006.

O'Connor, Jane. *The Cultural Significance of the Child Star.* New York: Routledge, 2008.

Pandey, Gyanendra. *The Gyanendra Pandey Omnibus.* New Delhi: Oxford University Press, 2008.

———. *The Construction of Communalism in North India.* New Delhi: Oxford University Press, 2006.

Pinny, Chris. *Photos of the Gods.* Chicago: University of Chicago Press, 2004.

Prasad, Madhava. *Ideology of the Hindi Film: A Historical Construction.* Delhi: Oxford University Press, 1998.

Qasmi, Ali Usman, and Megan (eds.). *Muslims Against the Muslim League: Critiques of the Idea of Pakistan.* Delhi: Cambridge University Press, 2017.

Raghavan, Pallavi. *Animosity at Bay* (New York: Oxford University Press, 2020).

Rajyadhaksha, Ashish, and Paul Willemen. *Encyclopaedia of Indian Cinema*. New Delhi: British Film Institute–Oxford University Press, 1994.

Ramamurthy, Priti. 'All-Consuming Nationalism: The Indian Modern Girl in the 1920s and 1930s'. In *The Modern Girl around the World: Consumption, Modernity and Globalization*, edited by Alys Eve Weinbaum, the Modern Girl around the World Research Group, Lynn M. Thomas, Priti Ramamurthy, Uta G. Poiger and Madeleine Yue Dong, 147–173. Durham, NC: Duke University Press, 2008.

Ramaswamy, Sumathi. *The Goddess and the Nation: Mapping Mother India*. Durham, NC: Duke University Press, 2010.

Rangoonwala, Firoze. *Seventy-Five Years of Indian Cinema*. New Delhi: Indian Book Co., 1975.

———. *Indian Filmography*. Bombay: J. Udeshi, 1970.

Rank, Otto. *The Double: A Psychoanalytic Study*. Translated and edited by Harry Tucker. Chapel Hill, NC: University of North Carolina Press, 1989.

Raychaudhuri, Souvik. *Partition Trauma, the Oedipal Rupture, Dreaming: The Cinematic Will of Ritwik Ghatak*. Calcutta: Papyrus, 2000.

Reuben, Bunny. *And Pran: A Biography*. New Delhi: Harper Collins, 2005.

———. *Dilip Kumar: Star Legend of Indian Cinema*. New Delhi: Harper Collins/India Today, 2004.

———. *Mehboob, India's DeMille: The First Biography*. New Delhi: Indus, 1994.

Robinson, Francis. *Islam and Muslim History in South Asia*. Oxford: Oxford University Press, 2003.

———. *Separatism among Indian Muslims: The Politics of the United Provinces' Muslims 1860–1923*. Cambridge: Cambridge University Press, 1974.

Rowe, Kathleen. *The Unruly Woman: Gender and the Genres of Laughter*. Austin: University of Texas Press, 1995.

Roy, Srirupa. *Beyond Belief: India and the Politics of Postcolonial Nationalism*. Durham, NC: Duke University Press, 2007.

Russell, Ralph. 'Some Notes on Hindi and Urdu'. *Annual of Urdu Studies* (1996): 203–208.

Russo, Mary. *The Female Grotesque: Risk, Excess and Modernity*. New York: Taylor & Francis, 1994.

Saeed, Humaira. 'Ramchand Pakistani, Khamosh Pani and the Traumatic Evocation of Partition'. *Social Semiotics* 19, no. 4 (December 2009): 483–498.

Saeed, Yousuf. *Muslim Devotional Art*. New Delhi: Routledge, 2012.

———. 'Muslim Exotica of Hindi Filmdom'. *Book Review South Asia Special* August–September 14 (2009): 23–24.

Sarkar, Bhaskar. *Mourning the Nation: Indian Cinema in the Wake of Partition*. Durham, NC: Duke University Press, 2009.

Sarkar, Sumit. 'The Limits of Nationalism'. *Seminar: Rewriting History* 522 (February 2003). http://www.india- seminar.com/2003/522/522%20sumit%20sarkar.htm. Accessed on 20 November 2012.

———. *Modern India: 1885–1947*. Delhi: Macmillan, 1983.

Schechtman, Joseph B. 'Evacuee Property in India and Pakistan'. *Pacific Affairs* 24, no. 4 (December 1951): 406–413.

Sehgal, Zohra. 'Theatre and Activism in the 1940s', *India International Centre Quarterly* 24, nos. 2–3 (1997): 31–39.

Sen, Amiya P. *The Indispensable Vivekanand: An Anthology for Our Times*. Delhi: Permanent Black, 2006.

Shackle, Christopher, and Javed Majeed. *Hali's Musaddas: The Flow and Ebb of Islam*. Delhi: Oxford University Press, 1997.

Shaikh, Farzana. *Community and Consensus in Islam*. Cambridge: Cambridge University Press, 1989.

Shohat, Ella, and Robert Stam (eds.). *Multiculturalism, Postcoloniality and Transnational Media*. New Jersey: Rutgers State University Press, 2003.

Siddique, Salma. 'Someone to Check Her a Bit!' *Feminist Media Histories* 3, no. 2 (Spring 2017): 36–56. https://doi.org/10.1525/fmh.2017.3.2.36. Accessed on 2 April 2020.

Singer, Ben. *Melodrama and Modernity: Early Sensational Cinema and Its Contexts*. New York: Columbia University Press, 2001.

Smith, Sidonie, and Julia Watson. *Reading Autobiography*. Minneapolis: University of Minnesota, 2001.

Symonds, Richard. *In the Margins of Independence: A Relief Worker in India and Pakistan (1942–49)*. Oxford: Oxford University Press, 2001.

Stam, Robert. *Film Theory: An Introduction*. Malden: Blackwell, 1999.

Steedman, Carolyn. *Dust*. Manchester: Manchester University Press, 2001.

Stephens, Julia. 'The Politics of Muslim Rage: Secular Law and Religious Sentiment in Late Colonial India'. *History Workshop Journal* 77 (2014): 45–64. DOI: 10.1093/hwj/dbt032. Accessed on 25 April 2014.

Suleiman, Susan Rubin (ed.). 'Introduction' In *Exile and Creativity: Signposts, Travelers, Outsiders, Backward Glances*, 1–8. Durham, NC, and London: Duke University Press, 1998.

Sundaram, Ravi. *Pirate Modernity: Delhi's Media Urbanism*. New York: Routledge, 2009.

Symonds, Richard. *In the Margins of Independence: A Relief Worker in India and Pakistan (1942–49)*. Oxford: Oxford University Press, 2001.

Tandon, Yograj. *Theatre ke Sartaj Prithviraj*. Delhi: National School of Drama Publications, 2001.

Taneja, Anand Vivek. 'Stereoptying the Muslim in Bombay Cinema'. *Economic and Political Weekly* 45, no. 4 (January 2010): 30–32.

Talbott, Ian. *Divided Cities*. Oxford: Oxford University Press, 2006.

———. *Khizr Tiwana: The Punjab Unionist Party and the Partition of India*. Routledge: Oxon, 2013.

Thapar, Romila. *Somanatha: The Many Voices of History*. Verso: London, 2005.

Thomas, Rosie. *Bombay before Bollywood: Film City Fantasies*. New Delhi: Orient Blackswan, 2014.

———. 'Melodrama and the Negotiation of Morality in Mainstream Hindi film'. In *Consuming Modernity: Public Culture in a South Asian World*, edited by Carol Breckenridge, 157–182. Minnesota: University of Minnesota Press, 1995.

———. 'Sanctity and Scandal: The Mythologization of Mother India'. *Quarterly Review of Film and Video* 11, no. 3 (1989): 11–30.

———. 'Indian Cinema: Pleasures and Popularity'. *Screen* 26, no. 3 (1985): 116–131.

Toor, Sadia. 'Containing East Bengal: Language, Nation and State Formation in Pakistan, 1947–1952'. *Cultural Dynamics* 21, no. 2 (2009): 185–210.

Tymms, Ralph. *Doubles in Literary Psychology*. Oxford: Alden Press, 1949.

Van der Veer, Peter. 'Colonial Cosmopolitanism'. In *Conceiving Cosmopolitanism*, edited by Steven Vertovec and Robin Cohen, 165–179. Oxford: Oxford University Press, 2002.

Vasudevan, Ravi. *The Melodramatic Public: Film form and spectatorship in Indian Cinema*. Basingstoke: Palgrave Macmillan, 2011.

———. 'Film Genres, the Muslim Social and Discourses of Identity, c. 1935–1945'. *BioScope: South Asian Screen Studies* 6, no. 1 (2015): 27–43.

———. 'Geographies of the Cinematic Public: Notes on Regional, National and Global Histories of Indian Cinema'. *Journal of the Moving Image* 9 (2010): 94–117. http://www.jmionline.org/article/geographies_of_the_cinematic_public_notes_on_regional_national_and_global. Accessed on 10 July 2011.

———. 'The Politics of Cultural Address in a "Transitional" Cinema: A Case Study of Indian Popular Cinema'. In *Reinventing Film Studies*, edited by Christine Gledhill and Linda Williams, 130–164. London: Arnold Publishers, 2000.

———. 'Addressing the Spectator of a "Third World" National Cinema: The Bombay "Social" Film of the 1940s and 1950s'. *Screen* 36, no. 4 (1995): 305–324.

———. 'Voice, Space and Form Roja: (Mani Ratnam, 1992), Indian Film and National Identity'. In *Not on Any Map: Essays on Post Coloniality and Cultural Nationalism*, edited by S. Murray, 153–168. Exeter: University of Exeter Press, 1997.

———. 'Dislocations: The Cinematic Imagining of a New Society in 1950s India'. *Oxford Literary Review on India: Writing History, Culture, Post-coloniality* 16, nos. 1–2 (1994): 93–124.

Vasudevan, Ravi. 'Shifting Codes, Dissolving Identities: The Hindi Social Film of the 1950s as Popular Culture'. *Journal of Arts and Ideas* 23–24 (January 1994): 51–79.

Vasudevan, Ravi. 'The Cultural Space of a Film Narrative: Interpreting "Kismet" (Bombay Talkies)'. *Indian Economic and Social History Review* 28, no. 2 (1991): 171–183.

———. 'The Melodramatic Mode and the Commercial Hindi Cinema'. *Screen* 30, no.3 (1989): 29–50.

Virdi, Jyotika. *The Cinematic ImagiNation: Indian Popular Films as Social History*. New Delhi: Permanent Black, 2003.

Vishwanath, Geeta, and Salma Malik. 'Revisting 1947 through Popular Cinema: A Comparative Study of India and Pakistan'. *Economic and Political Weekly* 44, no. 36 (September 2009): 61–69.

Vitali, Valentina, and Paul Willemen. *Theorising National Cinema*. London: British Film Institute, 2006.

Wahid-ud-din. *The Marching Bells: A Journey of a Life-Time*. Lahore: Authorhouse, 2011.

Williams, Alan (ed.). *Film and Nationalism*. New Jersey: Rutgers University Press, 2002.

Wodehouse, P. G. *Laughing Gas*. London: Everyman, 2001.

Zaheer, Sajjad. *The Light: A History for the Movement of Progressive Literature in the Indo-Pakistan Subcontinent*, translated by Amina Zafar. Oxford: Oxford University Press, 2006.

———. 'Urdu Drama'. *Indian Literature* 1, no. 2 (1958): 139–144.

Zamindar, Vazira. 'The Rite of Passage: The Partition of History and the Dawn of Pakistan'. In *Partition and Post-colonial South Asia*, edited by Gyanesh Kudaisya and Tai Yong Tan, 137–154. London: Routledge, 2008.

———. *The Long Partition and the Making of Modern South Asia: Refugees, Boundaries, Histories*. New York: Columbia University Press, 2007.

Zamindar, Vazira, and Asad Ali. *Love, Longing and War: Essays on Cinema in Pakistan*. Karachi: Oxford University Press, 2020.

Zhang, Zhen. *An Amorous History of the Silver Screen: Shanghai Cinema, 1896–1937*. Chicago: University of Chicago Press, 2005.

Web Resources

1947 Partition Archive. https://www.1947partitionarchive.org/mission. Accessed on 11 June 2021.

Ambedkar, B. R. 'Pakistan or the Partition of India', with a foreword by Francis Pritchett. http://www.columbia.edu/itc/mealac/pritchett/00ambedkar/ambedkar_partition/index.html. Accessed on 11 June 2021.

Express Tribune. 'Quaid Wanted Mussalmans to Enter Film Industry'. 20 January 2013. https://tribune.com.pk/story/496489/quaid-wanted-%E2%80%98mussalm ans%E2%80%99-to-enter-film-industry. Accessed on 14 December 2020.

Indian News Parade. 'Gandhi and Jinnah Negotiate for Communal Unity (1944)'. YouTube video. https://www.youtube.com/watch?v=e-Z--dSJE94. Accessed on 10 November 2014.

Iqbal, Allama. http://www.allamaiqbal.com/works/poetry/urdu/bal/translation/06gabri el.pdf. Accessed on 20 June 2022.

Khan, Asif Nazir. 'A Walk Down Memory Lane with Legendary Filmmaker Nazir Ahmed Khan', *Pakistan Today,* 25 August 2011. http://www.pakistantoday.com. pk/2011/08/25/entertainment/a-walk-down-memory-lane-with-legendary-filmmaker-nazir-ahmed-khan/. Accessed on 10 January 2015.

Nasar, Hammad. 'Lines of Control: Partition as a Productive Space'. *Tanqeed* (e-magazine), December 2015. http://www.tanqeed.org/2015/12/lines-of-control-partition-as-a-productive-space. Accessed on 18 June 2021.

Pakistan Film Magazine. '1948: Pakistan Film History in Details'. https://pakmag.net/ film/db/history.php?gid=1948%20reg=1948. Accessed on 20 June 2022.

Salman, Peerzada. 'Ismat Celebrates 105 Years', *Dawn,* 14 December 2013. http://www. dawn.com/news/1073704/ismats-105-years-celebrated. Accessed on 12 February 2014.

Index